MORTUARY PRACTICES AND SOCIAL IDENTITIES

IN THE MIDDLE AGES

This book sets a new agenda for mortuary archaeology. Applying explicit theoretical perspectives to case studies based on a range of European sites (from Scandinavia to Britain, Southern France to the Black Sea), *Mortuary Practices and Social Identities in the Middle Ages* fulfils the need for a volume that provides accessible material to students and engages with current debates in mortuary archaeology's methods and theories.

Duncan Sayer lectures at the Centre for Death and Society at the University of Bath. His principal area of interest lies in medieval and post-medieval burial grounds, and he has recently contributed to the *Handbook of British Archaeology* (2008), revising the medieval and early medieval chapters.

Howard Williams is a senior lecturer in Archaeology at the University of Chester. He has published widely on medieval and mortuary archaeology. He is author of *Death & Memory in Early Medieval Britain* (2006), and co-editor of *Early Medieval Mortuary Practices: Anglo-Saxon Studies in Archaeology and History* 14 (2007).

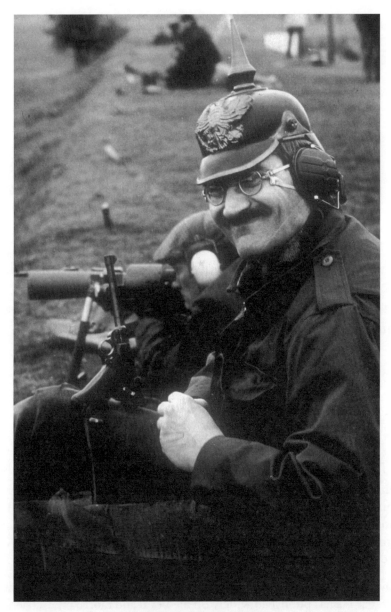

Photograph of Heinrich Härke
enjoying his sport of target-shooting with suitably historic head gear.

Mortuary practices and social identities in the Middle Ages

Essays in burial archaeology in honour of Heinrich Härke

edited by
Duncan Sayer and Howard Williams

UNIVERSITY
of
EXETER
PRESS

First published in 2009 by
University of Exeter Press
Reed Hall, Streatham Drive
Exeter EX4 4QR
UK
www.exeterpress.co.uk

British Library Cataloguing in Publication Data
A catalogue record for this book is available from the British Library.

ISBN 978 0 85989 831 7

Typeset in Stempel Garamond, 10.5 on 13 by
Carnegie Book Production, Lancaster
Printed in Great Britain by
Short Run Press Ltd, Exeter

FSC
Mixed Sources
Product group from well-managed
forests and other controlled sources

Cert no. SA-COC-002112
www.fsc.org
© 1996 Forest Stewardship Council

Contents

Figures

Preface

IN THE SPRING OF 2007, we first discussed the idea of editing a *Festschrift* in honour of Heinrich Härke to mark the occasion of his retirement. Both of us owe Heinrich a debt of gratitude for his academic support over the years, having completed PhDs under his supervision. Heinrich has remained in contact with us following our graduation and has continued to comment happily (and critically) on our work. He was also kind enough to attend and contribute to the proceedings of a conference Howard organised.

In November 2007, while work on the book was ongoing, we organised a day-conference with the invaluable help of Heinrich's colleagues and hosted by the Department of Archaeology at the University of Reading. The conference was an extremely positive and good-humoured event with a diverse range of papers presented to an audience of friends and colleagues from Reading, the UK and beyond, including archaeologists, historians and sociologists. All of the papers presented have found their way into this book and we are now pleased to see the volume through to completion as an up-to-date and landmark collection of essays addressing medieval mortuary archaeology.

However, from an early stage in our discussions, we agreed that a traditional German *Festschrift* was not wholly appropriate to mark Heinrich's retirement. Heinrich remains an Honorary Fellow in the Department of Archaeology at Reading. The volume neither marks his sixtieth birthday nor his retirement from research-active archaeology. Instead, the book simply marks Heinrich's departure from Reading for residence in Germany and to pursue his research in Russia and elsewhere. For this reason, we decided to produce a collection of essays that aimed to address one principal theme of Heinrich's past work: the relationship between mortuary practices and social identities in the Middle Ages. Therefore, the contributors represent only a sample of those who may have wished to honour Heinrich by contributing to a traditional *Festschrift*. Given this context, the book does not aspire to cover all aspects of Heinrich's career and deliberately avoids attempting to summarise or comment in detail upon his ongoing research. Indeed, Heinrich himself is best left to discuss this in future publications.

The book may be in Heinrich's honour but it is far from being an act of funerary commemoration itself. If Heinrich is in any way an 'ancestor' deserving a memorial, he is one who is certainly still alive, kicking, biking, target-shooting, star-gazing – and digging! He is an individual who still has a lot of life and ideas left in him and therefore this volume is as much written in anticipation of his future research as to celebrate his past achievements.

The distinctive project needed a title to reflect its focus and character. It is here necessary to mention that, inspired by the German racial stereotype as depicted in the *Biggles* comics, Heinrich was often fondly called 'the Hun' at Reading. He embraced and promoted the nickname with due irony (see frontispiece) and has employed this stereotypical view of Germans by the British in a publication discussing perceptions of German archaeologists and archaeology (Härke 1995b). It was inevitable that the project's working title reflected this persona and the book became affectionately dubbed the *Hunschrift* by Heinrich's Reading colleagues. However, in fairness, the final and more sober title of *Mortuary Practices and Social Identities in the Middle Ages* serves to describe much more clearly the nature and scope of the volume for the contributors themselves, our publisher and (most importantly) the readers. Each paper addresses this theme in a distinctive way and together they provide testimony to the scope of Heinrich's own work and its interaction with many debates in medieval archaeology and related fields.

We acknowledge the support for this project provided by University of Exeter Press. The guidance and financial assistance of the Historical Archaeology Research Group, the Prehistoric Archaeology Reserch Group and the Archaeological Science Research Group at the Department of Archaeology at the University of Reading are gratefully appreciated as well as the support of all Heinrich's Reading colleagues. We are very grateful for the numerous anonymous referees who read through drafts of the papers (you know who you are!) as well as to Roberta Gilchrist and Sonja Marzinzik for commenting upon the Introduction and overall scope and character of the book. Special thanks go to Eva Thäte for reading and commenting upon the entire book in manuscript form; a monumental task for which we are both extremely grateful.

Duncan would like to add his personal thanks to Howard for his ceaseless energy and enthusiasm and for taking on the nuts and bolts of the editorial responsibility of the manuscript. Like Heinrich, whose good-humoured correction has always been invaluable, Howard has an eye for language, and it is deeply encouraging to know that two such dedicated and meticulous academics are able to find the time for such tasks. He would also like to thank his wife Meredith Carroll for her patience and for her support and advice throughout the editorial process. Without the input of these people this project would never have happened.

Howard also has people to thank, beginning with Duncan, for the original idea for this book and for all the work, dialogue and humour that he put into this long collaboration. He is extremely grateful for the support and assistance of Philip, Sue and Ralph Williams, Keith and Margaret Wilson, and Gwen, Iain and Suzanne Raw. Howard also thanks his wife Libby and their daughter Jemimah for so much support and for somehow giving him the time to work on this book.

Together with all the contributors to this volume, we would like to wish Heinrich a very happy retirement from British academia and all the very best for the future. We hope he enjoys reading (and no doubt disagreeing with) the papers presented here in his honour. Our only hope is that Heinrich is pleased enough with this book to let us send him some of our essay-marking and proof-reading once in a while!

Duncan Sayer and Howard Williams,
February 2009

Chapter 1

'Halls of mirrors': death and identity in medieval archaeology

Howard Williams and Duncan Sayer

Abstract

This book is a collection of studies in celebration of Heinrich Härke's significant contribution to medieval mortuary archaeology. It marks the occasion of his retirement as Reader in Archaeology at the University of Reading. The chapters reflect the diverse contributions of Härke's research interests while simultaneously each engages with a particularly important theme in Härke's work.

The introduction points to ongoing research that is developing new understandings of mortuary evidence in the investigation of early medieval social identities. It evaluates the implications of both Härke's work and the papers presented in this volume for the direction of future studies in this field. The starting point must be to regard mortuary practice as neither a mirror nor mirage of past social identities and social structures. Instead, graves need to be viewed as 'halls of mirrors' through which the archaeologist can explore past societies, their perceived pasts, future aspirations and social identities.

Introduction

Social identity is a term employed by archaeologists in many different ways. It refers not only to personal perceptions of the self but also to the external categorisation of individuals and groups. Hence, social identities are a nexus of interpersonal and inter-group relationships. Furthermore, identities are rarely static, but shift depending upon context. They are created by the interaction between the existing structures of society and the agency of groups and individuals. They operate on multiple scales and are multi-vocal, having different meanings for different people. These meanings vary depending upon context and perceptions and are mediated by the senses. Consequently, identities are inherently social, complex and multi-faceted; they reside less within individuals and groups and more in the fields of interaction and boundaries between them.

However, it would be misleading to regard identities as arbitrary and constantly invented and reinvented. Identities are rooted in practice (Curta 2007; Jones 1997). Hence, material culture in all its varieties can serve in the construction, communication and transformation of identities as well as conveying them through time from generation to generation. Identities are embodied in the meaningful and mnemonic qualities of objects and materials (Sayer forthcoming; Williams 2006). What applies to portable artefacts can also be discussed with regard to other spheres of archaeological evidence, including the human body, food and crops, materials, substances, dwellings and buildings, texts and images, religious architecture, monuments and even landscapes. Material culture is central and active in the creation, negotiation, transmission and performance of identity.

Archaeologists have sometimes been unduly cautious in their attempts to use material evidence to reconstruct and chart the changing manifestations of social identities in past societies. Certainly material culture is not reflective of identity in a way that early twentieth-century archaeologists sought to apply ethnic or gender labels to pots or brooches (Lucy 1998). Yet, historical archaeologists should be optimistic about the potential to perceive past identities from the rich sources at their disposal, including archaeological evidence as well as texts, place-names and art. When studied within clearly defined geographical and chronological parameters and with sensitivity to context, archaeological data provide a rich environment in which to discuss the constitution and materialisation of medieval identities. The results of this research can hold implications that reach beyond the particular period or subject of study.

Some facets of medieval identities have received extensive discussion by archaeologists, including social status (e.g. Arnold 1980), gender (e.g. Gilchrist 1999), age (e.g. Crawford 2000) and perhaps most extensively and controversially, ethnicity (see Hills 2003). There has been a long tradition of debating these themes and they have been central to the work of Härke and many of his students (Härke 1989a and b; 1990a; 1992a and b; 1997a and d; Stoodley 1999a and b; 2000). Other identities have received less archaeological attention. These include sexuality (see Gilchrist in this volume), household identities and the role of kinship (see Sayer in this volume), religious identity (see Petts and Høilund Nielsen in this volume) and the identities of those excluded from society (Reynolds 2002) and those with diseases and disabilities.

A wide range of material culture can be implicated in the expression of medieval identities. Identities may be mediated by the *habitus* of daily life in settlements, churches and in the landscape (e.g. Gilchrist 1999), portrayed in the commemorative strategies of buildings and monuments (e.g. Hawkes 1999), and reflected in the production, styles, use and deposition of artefacts (e.g. Dickinson 1991). Yet burial data have a special and unique role with regard to medieval identities. Not only are graves a discrete context within which human remains and material culture are deposited deliberately in association with each other during a specific period of time and space, but burials are also the intentional outcomes of ritual processes (Härke 1997b). As such, mortuary practices have frequently been regarded by archaeologists as contexts for the display and constitution of identities in a discursive and overt manner. Moreover, funerals are arenas of identity-shift, for both the survivors and the deceased undergo ontological, social and cosmological realignments as they deal with and selectively remember and forget aspects of the deceased person (Williams 2006). They are also events implicated in identity conflicts between the different groups involved in the funeral and through claims over critical resources such as the inheritance of portable wealth and land (Härke 2001). In this way, mortuary practices are a context in which identities are rooted in the past. Yet through funerals, identities are created, recreated and transformed. Funerals also define identities in relation to aspired futures (prospective memories), both in this world and in the next (Williams 2006).

In recent years, there have been valuable syntheses and analyses of the theory and method of medieval mortuary archaeology (e.g. Effros 2003; Hadley 2001; Lucy 2000; papers in Lucy and Reynolds 2002; papers in Semple and Williams 2007; Gilchrist and Sloane 2005; Williams 2006) as well as debates concerning current and future directions in medieval mortuary research (Dickinson 2002; Scull 2000; Williams 2005; 2007a). These studies display contrasting approaches but they concur in suggesting that burial evidence must be understood within a social context. All elements of the burial ritual may have roles in the construction of identities; the manner in which a body is treated and displayed will affect contemporary perceptions of the identities of survivors and the deceased. The grave and the body may have been regarded as special, thus the medieval burial place was not simply an accrued collection of memorials. In this way, cemeteries affected the living through their links to the past. This approach sees cemeteries and landscapes not just as spaces within which funerals are performed and the bodies of the dead reside. They are regarded as fields of interaction between the living and the dead in the social and symbolic landscapes of medieval people.

Yet the focus on social identity has become something of a new orthodoxy. As well as studies that explore social identities in ever-increasingly sophisticated ways, others are revisiting existing themes such as the relationship of burial to religious identities, afterlife beliefs and cosmologies (Høilund Nielsen in this volume; Gilchrist and Sloane 2005; Petts in this volume; Williams 2001). There is considerable potential for further studies that integrate the mortuary analysis of social identities with the economic context in which social structures were negotiated and developed (e.g. Chapman in this volume). There is also potential in considering further how rituals negotiated myths and memories in the formulation of social identities (Thäte 2007b; Williams 2006). Others still are exploring the relatively uncharted waters of the aesthetic, emotive and performative aspects of medieval mortuary practices (e.g. Williams 2007a and c, and in this volume).

Meanwhile there is scope for the application of new approaches to identity in mortuary contexts. For example, the term 'personhood' is a useful concept in dealing with the fluid relational characteristics of identity in the medieval world. The term incorporates the relationships between people, materials, substances and environment (Fowler 2004) and focuses attention upon the material constitution of identities and their transformation in ritual contexts (see Back Danielsson 2007; Williams 2007b). The exploration of the roles of material objects in the exhibition and embodiment of identities through mortuary practice has only recently begun. The study of social identities is a key theme in ongoing debates in medieval mortuary archaeology from the fifth to the fifteenth century.

Death and identity in the archaeological research of Heinrich Härke

The range and character of Härke's contributions to the study of death and identity in the Middle Ages focus upon five themes: martial identities; identities on the move; identities in material and place; modern identities; analogies, methods and data. A sixth and final theme – changing directions – addresses Härke's past research outside of medieval archaeology, his ongoing research and its relevance to the volume's theme. In combination, these key ideas are currently driving research in the mortuary archaeology of medieval identities.

Martial identities: Warrior graves?

Härke is well known in British, Continental and Scandinavian archaeology for his influential study of the early Anglo-Saxon weapon burial rite. In a German language monograph (Härke 1992a), a series of research papers (Härke 1989a and b; 1990a; 1992b) and a co-authored book (Dickinson and Härke 1992), Härke outlined a clear thesis that weapon burial was a multi-vocal symbolic statement relating to the identity of the deceased. In doing so, he rejected the notion that weapon burials were 'warrior graves'. He achieved this through the analysis of the technical aspects of weapons themselves, the use of human osteological data, and the study of the burial context alongside the analysis of mortuary variability (Härke 1992a; 1995a). This took the form of a chronological and quantitative study on a national database of early Anglo-Saxon male inhumation graves from 47 excavated cemeteries.

Härke observed that there was an inverse correlation between the historical evidence for the frequency of warfare and the frequency of weapon provision in graves (Härke 1990a: 28–33). Investigating the combinations of weapons interred, he observed that they were often a dysfunctional selection with only some individuals receiving full combat weapon-sets (Härke 1990a: 33–35). Weapon provision was structured by gender, almost always occurring in male graves where osteological sex determinations had been made. Those interred with weapons were individuals of 'fighting age' but also younger and older persons who may not have easily wielded the items in combat. Using osteological evidence he noted no correlation between weapon provision and either the deceased's build or evidence of weapon-induced trauma upon the skeleton (Härke 1990a: 35–37). The variability in the provision of weapons was found to correlate not only with the age and sex of the deceased but also with the overall burial wealth and energy expenditure in the grave itself (Härke 1990a; 1992a and b).

Härke pursued studies of particular weapon types and construction including debunking the identification of a laminated shield from Petersfinger (Härke 1981). His study of shield bosses went beyond their physical characteristics and recognised the many facets to weapon symbolism. Shields could be studied with regard to typology, chronology, technology, their use in combat and role in both display and burial ritual (Dickinson and Härke 1992; Härke and Salter 1984). Even the length of knife blades seemed to correlate with the age and sex of the interred individual (Härke 1989b).

The provision of weapons was not the same between cemeteries, localities and regions suggesting variations in practice and social context (Härke 1989a). Furthermore, changes over time in weapon burial indicate a shift in the significance of the rite, particularly during the seventh century. Härke associated this change with the rise of kingdoms and an accompanying increased social stratification. The symbolism had changed from one of male adult identity to an identity bound up in status roles and linked to a process of politicised ethnogenesis (see below, Härke 1992b).

As a result of his analysis of the weapon burial phenomenon (Härke 1995a), he was invited to contribute to the publication of a number of Anglo-Saxon cemeteries from across Britain, notably Westgarth Gardens, Suffolk (Härke 1998a); Wakerley, Northamptonshire (Härke 1990b); Empingham II, Rutland (Härke 1996); Blacknall Field, Pewsey, Hampshire (Härke forthcoming a) and Butler's Field, Lechlade, Gloucestershire (Härke forthcoming b). The most notable of these studies, owing to the controversy it caused, was Berinsfield, Oxfordshire, where he argued that inhumation G110, an adult male with spear and shield identified as having *spina bifida*, would have been incapable of using his weapon in life. Unfortunately for Härke, this pathology was later identified as *spina bifida occulta*, a genetic condition that the sufferer may have been entirely unaware of during his life. Härke noted this at the end of the volume. This contribution has nevertheless made Berinsfield one of the most studied and commented on cemeteries in early medieval archaeology (see Stoodley 2000; Lucy 2000; Tyrell 2000; Williams 2006; Sayer 2007b for examples) even more remarkable because the excavations may only have revealed around three quarters of the total cemetery.

Härke's original thesis concerning the symbolism of weapon burial has been upheld and subsequent research supports his original proposal that weapons are found in the graves of people who may not have been able to use them (for example see Lucy 2000; Tyrell 2000). For while the Berinsfield instance of *spina bifida* proved irrelevant to the argument, Härke identified weapon burial afforded to individuals with severe osteoarthritis and broken bones that had healed badly. Thus the burial rite itself was an identity-related ritual practice which may not have directly reflected the martial abilities of the deceased, either at the time of burial or at any point in life. In conclusion, weapon burials were not simply 'warrior graves' but multi-vocal symbolic statements ascribed to the deceased by the survivors.

As an extension to the research on male weapon burials, Härke argued that weapons were part of an ideologically-oriented male gender display (masculinity, although he never uses this term; see Gilchrist this volume). Through this argument, he provided a response to the problems of male and female 'gender kits' in the graves of skeletons which have sometimes been identified interred with individuals of the opposite biological sex (Härke 2003a). This paper, first presented at a German conference, was an answer to a popular trend in British archaeology seeing these burials as evidence of a third or fourth gender in early Anglo-Saxon society – in other words adult females who dressed in male apparel and adult males who dressed in female clothing (see Lucy 1997; 1998; 2000). A sample of 1401 furnished inhumations was analysed and Heinrich Härke observed that 1.16% were men with 'female kits' and 0.24% women with 'male kits', figures not strong enough to support the existence of these extra genders. Incidentally, these figures fit well within the error margin (98%) for accurate skeletal sexing observed by physical anthropologists (see Molleson *et al.* 1993). Härke accepted that these additional genders have been recognised among other ancient societies, for example there are archaeological correlates to the supposed Scythian and Sarmatian 'Amazons', which, in contrast to the Anglo-Saxon cases, were female individuals interred with weapons and female dress artefacts. He argues that the rigid adherence to two genders displayed in the Anglo-Saxon furnished burial rite is due to a reaffirmation of sexual and gender boundaries as a result of the early Middle Ages being a period of ideological uncertainty and 'the blurring or even disappearance of traditional boundaries and distinctions can, in turn, lead to uncertainty about social norms' (Härke 2003a: 137; see also Stoodley 1999a).

Identities on the move: Migrations and ethnogenesis

Within British archaeology in the 1980s and 1990s, an anti-migrationist climate prevailed. Härke's work was widely perceived as controversial at the time by addressing the ethnic symbolism of the weapon burial rite. Enamel hypoplasia data provided no discernible differences in terms of the health of males interred with and without weapons. However, a small difference in the mean stature of the two groups of male graves suggested that those interred with weapons were those of Germanic descent whereas those without were native Britons. Härke found support for this in the observation that stature differences disappeared in the seventh century when these groups may have begun to coalesce. At Berinsfield, prior to the seventh century, males with and without weapons seemed to be members of different descent groups judging by the contrasting occurrence of a select number of non-metric skeletal traits (Härke 1990a: 40–42; Härke 1995a). This led Härke to suggest that in addition to the social symbolism of weapon burial, the rite also served to articulate an ethnic identity of immigrant Anglo-Saxons living alongside, but remaining separate from, Britons – a situation he argued was prevalent in Anglo-Saxon England until the seventh century. Later this argument was expanded using historical analogies to indicate the powerful ideological statement that weapons could make when employed in ritual displays (Härke 1997c). Here Härke identified that ethnicity was not determined by biology, but symbolically articulated through myths of origin.

This study was a springboard to a wider discussion of the long-running debate over the scale and character of the Anglo-Saxon migrations. Härke advocated that the pendulum of opinion had swung too far away from migration in early Anglo-Saxon studies (Härke 2002: 146). Based upon estimations of the archaeological and skeletal data drawn from his analysis of weapon graves, Härke promoted a view of a substantial immigration of Anglo-Saxon peoples in the fifth century. He estimated that perhaps 100,000 to 200,000 individuals moved across the North Sea, joining a much larger native population of around 1 or 2 million. At one level this immigration figure is much larger than many recent commentators had been happy to concede (e.g. Higham 1992; Hills 2003). On the other hand, Härke postulated a scale of British survival that sat uneasily with more traditional narratives for the period (reviewed in Welch 1992). In doing so, Härke's thesis might be seen as a compromise between extremes and yet simultaneously in contradiction to both staunchly pro- and anti-migrationist camps.

In a synthesis of the archaeology of early medieval Britain, Härke has contributed to the debate over the scale of the Scandinavian settlement of the ninth century AD (Härke 2002: 158) and the interaction of immigrants and natives in this period (Härke 2002: 159). He observed both clear similarities and contrasts with the subsequent impact of the Norman conquest (Härke 2002: 162–63). Härke saw parallels between early Saxon Wessex and early Norman England; both were 'conquest societies' albeit with different proportions and relationships between settlers and natives.

More recently, Härke has returned to the theme of migration and ethnicity. In response to a debate at the 2004 conference *Early Medieval Mortuary Practices: New Perspectives*, Härke reviewed and critically appraised both traditional and post-processual perspectives on ethnicity, forging a middle ground between these extremes. His view is of migration as a social and cultural phenomenon in the early Middle Ages and ethnogenesis as a political and ideological process (Härke 2007a). Härke has also promoted the use of analogies from the modern world (see below) and parallels with the Continent to discuss the 'invisible Britons' of the fifth and sixth centuries in lowland Britain (Härke 2007b). Moreover, drawing upon modern DNA evidence, Härke has expanded his view of societies in fifth and sixth century lowland England as multi-ethnic in character. He has suggested that there existed a form of cultural 'apartheid': a socially sanctioned co-existence between natives and immigrants who were afforded a different social, economic and legal status. While immigrants were in the numerical minority, they possessed greater opportunities to pass on their genetic (and hence their linguistic) heritage because of their socio-political hegemony (Thomas *et al.* 2006; 2008; Thomas *et al.* 2008; see Hills in this volume).

Härke's use of terminology has sometimes courted controversy and his ethnic interpretation of the weapon burial rite has been questioned (e.g. Gowland 2007; Hills 2003; Lucy 2000). Certainly a comparable clear-cut distinction in artefact provision and osteological data could not be found by Nick Stoodley in his analysis using the same national database to focus on female-gendered graves (Stoodley 1999a). Repeatedly, caution has been raised concerning the sample size and reliability of Härke's osteological data as well as the statistical significance of his osteological findings for stature and non-metric traits. For example, Tyrell (2000) is not unusual among critics of Härke's work in arguing that not enough is known about the origin of skeletal traits to propose a relationship with ethnic distinctions. However, no clear alternative explanation has been proposed. It is notable that similar albeit cautious observations have become more common in the analysis of early Anglo-Saxon cemeteries (see Malim and Hines 1998; Duhig 1998: 188–94; Anderson and Birkett 1993: 257; Boylston *et al.* 1998: 227; Sayer 2007b). Hence, there has been widespread acceptance of Härke's thesis that weapon burial was multivocal and served, in part, as a statement of group identity and origin myths (e.g. Lucy 2000; Stoodley 1999a; Williams 2006). Whether or not all weapon burials denote the graves of Germanic immigrants and their descendants, the connection between weapon burial and social identity has been firmly established. New osteological studies and the application of stable isotope data may further help to disentangle the complex message of the weapon burial rite (e.g. Budd *et al.* 2004).

Identities in material and place

Although Härke's research has focused on the analysis of weapon burial and the themes of migration and ethnogenesis; he has also addressed other topics relating to mortuary practice and social identity in the Middle Ages.

Drawing upon his approach to weapon burials, Härke combined archaeological evidence and written sources in the study of early Anglo-Saxon social structure. He adopted an explicitly ethnographic perspective and drew upon both historical and anthropological approaches (Härke 1997a). A similar theoretical direction is taken in his analysis of the circulation of weapons in Anglo-Saxon society from the fifth to the tenth century AD (Härke 2001). Here a broader perspective is charted and weapon burial is placed in the context of the changing nature of Anglo-Saxon society including conversion and kingdom formation. Consideration is given to the literary and historical evidence as well as to discoveries of weapons found in both graves and rivers. Härke appraises the ritualised circulation of weapons through grave-robbing, display, gift-giving, inheritance and ritual deposition.

Härke has also used his database of early Anglo-Saxon weapon burials to explore the different archaeological interpretations of grave goods. In doing so, he has contributed to wider debates over the interpretation of burial data in early medieval Europe (Härke 2000a; 2001) and to numerous cross-period and cross-disciplinary debates (Härke 1994b; 2003b).

The study of cemetery organisation was a part of Härke's study of the weapon burial rite (Härke 1992a; 1995a). However, he initially focused upon burials as discrete units of information for comparison. This perspective was complimented by his increasing interest in the landscape context of cemeteries and burial sites. This approach seems inspired by Härke's earlier work on the territorial significance of Iron Age princely graves (Härke 1979; 1982). It is also evident in his discussion of the location of a wealthy seventh-century barrow-burial on Lowbury Hill, Oxfordshire. Härke took part in the re-excavation of the barrow as part of a wider investigation of the ruins of a Romano-Celtic temple originally explored in the early twentieth century (Atkinson 1916; Härke 1994a). He saw the choice of burial location in relation to an ancient monument as a means of creating connections to the past at a time of kingdom formation as well as ethnogenesis. He linked this argument to his earlier work concerning the shifting significance of weapon-burial from an ethnic symbol to one of social status. He argued that previously separate native and immigrant communities in the upper Thames valley were becoming acculturated in the seventh century; barrows like Lowbury were symbols of a new social hierarchy employing weapons and burial mounds (Härke 1994a).

In response to an article by Eva Thäte on the reuse of prehistoric monuments as burial sites in the Continental homelands of the Anglo-Saxons and in England (Thäte 1996), Härke argued that monument reuse was a wider phenomenon and not exclusively practised for wealthy barrow-burials. Moreover, the significance of monument reuse varied over time, becoming more important in the seventh century (Härke and Williams 1997). Subsequently, a broader thesis was developed by Härke with regard to the significance of cemeteries as 'places of power' in early medieval societies. He proposed that the significance of cemeteries was greatest during times of social stress and culture change such as the shift from the Roman period to the Middle Ages

(Härke 2001). On a broader scale, landscapes were perceived by Härke as integral to the conflict and interaction of migrants and natives. He subsequently explored this theme in relation to the succession of early Anglo-Saxon, Viking and Norman conquests (Härke 2002).

Finally, Härke had a different interpretation for the connection between conflict and landscape in his excavation of a unique, quadruple weapon burial at Tidworth on the Wiltshire/Hampshire border. This seemingly isolated grave was interpreted as containing the victims of a local conflict. The four men may have died together and were buried in one grave in the mid to late sixth century A D. This is partly supported by the osteological evidence from one skeleton for unhealed trauma. In this instance, these may have been 'warriors' indeed, who were commemorated by burying the bodies with their weapons in a prominent location rather than a communal cemetery. Through either expedience or to make a symbolic statement, they reused a Roman lynchet on a spur that served to give the impression of a burial mound (Härke and Entwistle 2002: 50–51).

Modern identities: attitude problems and method

A fourth area of Härke's work which also touches on the theme of this volume is the relationship between modern identities and the history and theory of archaeology. As a German archaeologist who worked for much of his career within the British university system and published in both English and German, Härke has been uniquely positioned to comment upon the theories and methods used by the archaeological communities of both countries and their wider European and Transatlantic context (Härke 1989d; 1991; Härke and Wolfram 1993).

In a paper in *Current Anthropology*, Härke explored the contrasting attitudes towards migrations between different schools of archaeological thought (Härke 1998). He began by identifying the modern contrast in German and British archaeologists' responses to and criticisms of his own work on the Anglo-Saxon migration: British scholars criticised his migrationist approach while, Germans questioned his substantial estimates for the scale of British survival! Härke then investigated how different socio-political contexts, rather than the nature of the archaeological record, have encouraged different uses of migration as explanation. He used as case studies the 'migrationist' archaeologies of Nazi Germany and South Africa and the more immobilist tendencies of Soviet archaeology (Härke 1998). A range of responses was published and appended to Härke's article, illustrating the complex and contentious nature of this debate (especially when voiced by a German speaker). Indeed the transparent misunderstanding of one reply to the article by Martínez Navarrete prompted a stern but measured rebuttal by

Härke (Härke 1998: 39–40). Such debates only serve to highlight the important relationships between identity and politics in the study of the past today.

The relationship between politics, language and archaeological thought also comes to the fore in Härke's study of the similarities and differences between Anglo-American and German approaches to mortuary analysis (Härke 1997b: 19–21; Härke 2000a; 2000c). He observed the complete dysfunction between the two traditions, the language barrier meaning that 'the wheel had to be invented twice'. Here Härke is referring to the social analysis of mortuary evidence (Härke 2000a: 379). From his appraisal, it was possible to identify theoretical weaknesses in both traditions when contending with the same themes. Härke consequently advocated a closer dialogue between Anglo-American and German scholars who may learn from each other in terms of theory and method building.

Härke's interest in the politics of the past culminated in an edited volume dedicated to the history and socio-politics of German archaeology. In his introduction to the book, he explored in detail the politics and context of modern German archaeology both before and after unification (e.g. Härke 2000c; see also Härke 1989d; 1991; 1995b; Härke and Wolfram 1993). Härke challenged the ghettoization of the politics of the past as something peculiar to totalitarian regimes. More controversially, he compared the situation in British academia since the Thatcher era with that of the Nazi regime and post-war East Germany because, he maintained, academics in all three contexts faced the choice between resistance and collaboration in response to complex political pressures. For the UK, Härke identified the impact of a monolingual education system, the insularity of attitudes towards the past (and the themes of migration and ethnicity in particular) and the politicised management of research and research funding within universities. This final aspect was regarded by Härke to be 'undemocratic and incompatible with academic freedom':

> When I explained to a retired colleague who had worked for 30 years in Communist East Germany the structure of a British university department in which the Head has the absolute power to allocate administrative and teaching duties, he exclaimed in dismay and disbelief: '*Das gab es nicht einmal in der DDR*' ('That did not exist even in the GDR!'). (Härke 2000c: 26)

Not all British academics would agree with the severity of his portrayal of the university system, but Härke has repeatedly identified links between politics and identities in the present and the archaeological study of medieval burial data.

Theories, analogies, methods and data

In this review of Härke's research, it is necessary to discuss his theoretical and methodological approach in broader terms. Härke's explicit promotion of archaeological theory won him dissident status in the 1980s in West Germany (Härke 1989d). From a British perspective, his work might be described as theory-driven but data-orientated research. He has promoted the use of analogies from both ethnographic studies and modern Western societies in the study of archaeological data, regarding them as enhancing the development of his archaeological interpretations. For example, he observed the public use of weapons and martial scenes upon the murals in Northern Ireland during the 1980s and 1990s as a possible analogy for the use of weapons in early medieval funerary ritual: both were interpreted as displays of ethno-religious identity connected to perceived myths of origin (Härke 1997d). Likewise, Härke has used the vast and rapid shift in settlement, burial and material culture associated with the collapse of the Soviet Union as an analogy for considering culture change, migration and ethnogenesis in the early medieval period (Härke 1999; 2007b). Based upon long-term, first-hand observations of the changing nature of material culture in the Soviet Union, this approach sits between the traditional use of ethnographic analogy and the practice of ethno-archaeology.

Härke recognised the importance of analogies in order to escape from historical straitjackets and has shown how traditional historical interpretations can be questioned by theorised archaeological interpretation (e.g. Härke 1997d). However, he has equally rejected an anti-historical stance (e.g. Pader 1982) and his social and ethnic interpretations are geared to addressing both archaeological and historical questions. Moreover, he has deployed a range of literary and historical sources in his work, in his study of Anglo-Saxon social structure, the sources used ranged from the poem *Beowulf* to Anglo-Saxon wills, charters, and secondary sources like Herlihy's 1985 study of Frankish households (Härke 1997a; 2000b; 2001).

With many new theoretical perspectives evident in the study of medieval mortuary practices (for a review, see Williams 2007a) it is worth reiterating that Härke's work has broadly straddled the processual/post-processual divide. His interests have focused upon both the study of long-term socio-political and economic processes, including migration and ethnogenesis, that might be described as 'processual'. He has also developed an interest in the symbolism of graves and material culture, and the investigation of the socio-political context within which archaeological interpretations are generated, themes that are 'post-processual' in character.

An equally important facet of Härke's research philosophy is that post-modern archaeology requires an amalgam of methods and theories rather than a single, unified perspective. Härke encouraged archaeologists to see that: '… this variety is not only fashionable, it is also useful in that it provides a variety of angles on similar data' (Härke 1997c: 191). Moreover, Härke prefaces this statement with the argument that the lack of available evidence of a quantity or quality desired should not limit the questions we ask and the approaches we adopt:

> … inadequate data quality alone should never deter us from raising the questions we are interested in: only the realisation that new (or different) data are required will eventually lead to new data, and a better data quality. (Härke 1997c: 192)

Indeed even the absence of a clear answer should not discourage the scholar: '… it is failure that drives progress, in archaeology as elsewhere' (Härke 1997d: 191). In this regard, Härke might be cast as an innovator in archaeological theory and method through a decidedly liberal perspective on the adoption of new ideas and perspectives.

Härke is also clear in his view of theory 'in the abstract'. The stronger theories are those where a clear methodology can be applied and which can be investigated through defined bodies of evidence. With regard to method, Härke developed an approach for analysing funerary evidence during his own study of 47 cemeteries, aspects of which have been adopted within computerised studies (for example Ravn 2003: 39) and recent interpretations of cemeteries in East Anglia (Penn and Brugmann 2007). His methodology has been developed further by his students including Stoodley (1999a), Sayer (2007b) and Williams (2007b), who built on his observations and methodologies for Anglo-Saxon cemetery evidence and Petts (2004), who used similar methods of data collection to assess British cemeteries. Such studies are not unique to his students (e.g. Marzinzik 2003) and all these works depart to a greater or lesser degree from a rigid adherence to Härke's approach in both theory and method. Yet it is this diversity that serves to deepen our understanding of not just medieval society but also archaeological cemetery analysis.

His approach encourages a close combination of theories, analogies, methods and data but also stimulates question-led research. Indeed, without this last innovation, Härke implies that we are left to repeat the same questions with the same methods. Unsurprisingly this will often result in the same conclusions!

Changing directions

This introductory paper reflects Härke's contribution to medieval mortuary archaeology – the focus of this volume – but it would not be complete if we did not refer to the diversity of Härke's wider research. His Göttingen MA thesis investigated prehistoric bronze artefacts using spectral analysis (Härke 1978). His Oxford B.Litt. thesis investigated settlement patterns in the western central European Hallstatt of the early Iron Age (Härke 1979; 1982; 1983; 1989c). Indeed, it was not until his Göttingen Dr Phil that he focused on Anglo-Saxon weapon burials (published as Härke 1992a). But Härke is not just a research archaeologist, he demonstrates a willingness to get muddy and has conducted several cemetery excavations, notably in 1976, the excavation of a Roman cemetery at Münsterplatz in Neuss (Härke 1977; 1980), in 1992 with Mike Fullford at Lowbury Hill (Härke 1994a) and the elite barrow burial from the third century BC Scythian-Sarmatian transition, dubbed the 'Princess of Ipatovo' (Härke and Belinskij 1999; Härke *et al.* 2000).

His most recent interests derive from his collaboration with Andrej Belinskij, director of the Heritage Protection Unit 'Nasledie' in Stavropol, Russia. Their joint-directed excavations at Klin Yar, and the subsequent research project leading to the publication of the results, has been enriched through the accumulation of Härke's previous experiences in excavating cemeteries and investigating Iron Age and early medieval graves.

Härke's involvement at Klin Yar was to direct excavations between 1994 and 1996 in an Anglo-Russian collaboration. The site is located on the sandstone hills of the Russian North Caucasus. Excavations uncovered 350 inhumation graves, most of them dating to the Iron Age (Korban), but including about 100 Sarmatian and Alanic graves. This collaborative fieldwork also identified an elite plot of rich Late Sarmatian and Early Alanic catacombs. Klin Yar provides one of the largest samples of Alanic burials in the North Caucasus (Belinskij and Härke 1995; 1996).

Previous excavations had produced exotic items, including Assyrian helmets and Scythian artefacts. The settlements and cemetery at Klin Yar occupied a space between the steppes to the north, and developed civilizations to the south. The occupants of this zone survived and prospered, straddling upland and lowland zones and trade routes, as well as a branch of the Silk Road later in the Alanic period. Cultural contacts shown through grave goods indicate a wide-ranging network extending from Central Asia to Mesopotamia and Byzantium (Belinskij and Härke 1995; 1996).

The burials consist of three distinct cultural phases: the Korbans practised inhumation with grave goods in rectangular grave cuts and marked gender through burial on the left (female) or right sides (male). Artefacts included pottery vessels, found with most burials, weapons and tools (with males) and dress items (females). The second phase was Sarmatian, a burial rite characterized by a high degree of variation between the inhumations. The Sarmatian graves consisted of an underground chamber accessed by a dromos. The body was lain supine, extended and accompanied by some grave goods. The excavated dromos often contained the remains of a horse skin (head and hooves). In this phase, males were identified with weapons, females with dress items, and pottery and horse sacrifices were identified with both genders. The third phase, the Alanic, was similar to the Sarmatian, but with more elaborate features including larger pits or dromos, and with structures added to the fabric of the grave. In contrast to the previous phase, these pits were oriented north-south, serving to visually and spatially separate them from the Sarmatian burials. The Alanic grave goods were similar to those of the Sarmatians, although burials found in chambers were often in groups with clear indicators of continual additional interments added to existing graves. Härke has interpreted this evidence as the result of a transformation of the funeral rite to emphasise family relations though the use of collective family vaults.

Klin Yar is a cemetery with incredible continuity, encompassing burials from over 2000 years. However, it is the details of ritual change for which this site is most notable. Härke and Belinskij argue that the transformations from uniformity to variation and back to uniformity (if wealthy uniformity) marks changes in the subsistence strategies that people employed (Härke 2008). For example, there are no settlements known from the region that accompany the second phase, indicating that the Sarmatians (a cultural not an ethnic term) depended on a nomadic economy as evidenced through the importance of a horse sacrifice in this phase of the burials rite. The final Alanic phase was marked by its uniformity and, as with the Korban phase, was agrarian. However, significantly, the transformation in the burial ritual from the Sarmatians furnished-chambered-rite emphasize the importance of family connections (Härke 2008; Belinskij and Härke forthcoming). In short, the expression of identity and religious belief in the burial rituals at Klin Yar showed a connection with economic strategy and social circumstances driven by the requirements of food, wealth and accommodation not by gender, religion or immigration.

This study makes a valuable contribution to scholarship by locating archaeological research in a depth of context that extends beyond one cultural phase or period. It considers the expression of social identities in death as part of broader regional transformations in social/economic strategies, highlighting that questions of religious conversion or ethnic identities must be considered alongside questions that include a broader chronological and pan-cultural context for mortuary ritual.

Mortuary practices and identities in the Middle Ages

The previous section reviewed Härke's legacy to medieval mortuary archaeology in the study of social identities. This sets the scene for the contributions to this book.

Prehistoric perspectives

The volume begins with studies by two prehistorians and former colleagues of Härke that serve to set a context for the rest of the volume. In different ways, they show the potential of new theoretical perspectives and ongoing debates in medieval mortuary archaeology.

Robert Chapman, like Härke, recognises the potential of learning from non-Anglophone traditions of mortuary archaeology. Moreover, Chapman advocates a materialist stance in mortuary archaeology and suggests its applications to the Middle Ages. In particular, the importance of integrating settlement and burial evidence is cited by Chapman as one approach that might allow archaeologists to move beyond the 'idealist' search for meaning to look at social and economic conditions. This is an area discussed by Härke for both Iron Age Europe and Anglo-Saxon England (Härke 1982; 2002) and has considerable potential for future study.

Meanwhile, Richard Bradley picks up on Härke's use of analogy in his consideration of the Anglo-Saxon poem *Beowulf* and British prehistory. Bradley shows how engaging with the Anglo-Saxon poem and a wide range of prehistoric archaeological material allows new perspectives across the false divide between prehistory and historical periods. Bradley considers *Beowulf* as a means of identifying possibilities for how funerals in past societies employed material culture, monuments and landscape to define social identities and their relationships with real and imagined pasts.

Continental and Scandinavian perspectives

The next four chapters move the focus to the archaeology of the first millennium A D in Europe and Scandinavia, addressing important aspects of Härke's work on social structure (Burmeister), migration and the use of osteological data (Hakenbeck), understanding the meanings of burial ritual (Høilund Nielsen) and cemeteries as places of power (Thäte).

Stefan Burmeister considers the contentious debate concerning how to interpret social identities from furnished inhumation graves, the topic of much of Härke's own research. He provides a critique of previous attempts to regard princely burials of the third century AD as evidence for a static, coherent Germanic social structure. He explores an alternative explanation, using archaeological and historical evidence alongside anthropological models to interpret Roman high-status material culture in princely graves as statements of identity within a particular context of Germanic military success. In doing so, his paper provides a Continental perspective on both the interpretation of social structure and ethnogenesis through mortuary evidence.

Härke has recognised the importance of looking at both biological and cultural evidence to investigate early medieval graves (Härke 1997c). Susanne Hakenbeck addresses a topic that uniquely embraces both culture and biology by considering the practice of skull deformation in early medieval Europe. She also engages with debates over the relationship between death, identity and migrations by disputing the traditional association of the practice with the Huns and their invasions. In doing so, Hakenbeck promotes the contextual perception of identity when rooted in the management and display of the human body.

Many social analyses of early medieval burial data focus upon furnished inhumation graves. Meanwhile, cremation rites are often portrayed as uniform and intractable to the study of mortuary practices and mortuary variability (see also Williams 2007b). Karen Høilund Nielsen's contribution presents a case study that counters this view through a detailed appraisal of an important cemetery of cremation graves and stone settings dated to between the fifth and eighth centuries AD. The site in question was uncovered in the 1950s at Lindholm Høje in northern Jutland, Denmark. Høilund Nielsen demonstrates the potential of the re-analysis of older excavation reports and archive material in interpreting the cremation ceremonies practiced as a rite of passage. Like Härke, she also draws widely upon analogies from Roman and early medieval written sources to develop her interpretations of burial data.

Eva Thäte builds upon Härke's 2001 discussion of cemeteries as places of power. Her focus is the topography of death in Scandinavian during the later first millennium AD. She identifies a widespread series of themes and trends in burial location. These include associations with ancient monuments, water, routes and boundaries. She questions whether these were the results of social, religious or indeed, more deeply-rooted psychological conceptions of death and landscape (see also Thäte 1996; 2007a and b).

Early Anglo-Saxon archaeology

The book contains three chapters dedicated to the analysis of early Anglo-Saxon archaeology. They contribute to Härke's research interests in migrations and ethnogenesis as well as the politics of identity in the present (Hills), the analysis of early Anglo-Saxon social structure utilising archaeological and textual sources (Sayer), and the interpretation of furnished inhumation graves as symbolic texts (Williams).

Burials have long been employed in debates about the scale and character of the Anglo-Saxon migrations and Härke was one of the earliest archaeologists to recognise the potential of DNA studies within this debate. Ancient DNA has yet to reveal clear results but modern DNA has made an increasing contribution. Catherine Hills undertakes a critical review of the use and abuse of modern DNA evidence and its employment alongside burial data in interpretations of early Anglo-Saxon society. She cautions against the preliminary conclusions of much of the research and she challenges whether interdisciplinary work that combines DNA, archaeology and history has enabled the construction of stronger theories or has simply perpetuated age-old myths. By looking at how DNA studies and archaeology have been portrayed by the popular press, she illustrates the continued relevance of early medieval migrations to modern perceptions of identity.

Härke's core interest in early Anglo-Saxon furnished inhumation graves is represented in the volume by a case study on mortuary analysis by Duncan Sayer. Through a detailed chronological and social analysis of the two cemeteries of Mill Hill and Finglesham, both in east Kent, Sayer investigates how mortuary practices and contemporary law codes can be employed to investigate early Anglo-Saxon kinship. Sayer's focus upon kinship breaks new ground and allows his study to chart the changing expression of household and family identities between the sixth and seventh centuries AD.

Recent studies of early Anglo-Saxon furnished inhumation burials have theorised them as symbolic texts and public displays. For example, this approach was used by Härke in his study of weapon burials (Härke 1990a; Dickinson and Härke 1992). Howard Williams's contribution addresses the ways in which these graves are represented through archaeological illustrations and art. In doing so, he suggests that the manner in which graves are illustrated affects both interpretations of furnished early Anglo-Saxon graves and popular perceptions of mortality in the present.

Medieval identities

While early Anglo-Saxon furnished burials have received considerable attention in recent years, less attention has been afforded to the relatively sparsely furnished burials of western and northern Britain. David Petts challenges the scholarly perception that burial rites and inscribed stones in western Britain reflect a uniform British Christian culture. The distribution and character of inscribed stones, cemetery organisation and the deployment of artefacts in graves are considered to illustrate both shared connections and the negotiation of local and regional identities. In this sense, western Britain shows greater similarities to early Anglo-Saxon England than is often supposed.

Only in recent years have studies engaged with the mortuary practices of later Anglo-Saxon England (the eighth to eleventh centuries A D) in social and symbolic terms (e.g. papers in Lucy and Reynolds 2002). For example, the analysis of mortuary variability within early Anglo-Saxon cemeteries by Härke and others has now been matched by the study of later Anglo-Saxon cemeteries incorporating the analysis of both skeletal and cultural data (Buckberry 2007). Grenville Astill addresses this period by directly addressing Härke's interest in cemeteries as places of power and tackling the complex topic of burial location (Härke 2001). Astill suggests that the social identities of communities were manifest in the persistent location of cemeteries away from churches and in association with settlements and fields.

Analyses of mortuary practices have also emerged for the later Middle Ages including the study of burial rites, commemorative monuments and mortuary geography. These studies have explored the social significance of mortuary and commemorative practice as well as their religious context, including the dynamics of lay patronage, the expression of social identity and the constitution of social memories (Astill and Wright 1993; Daniell 1997; Finch 2000; Hadley 2001; Williams 2003). Most recently, the work of Gilchrist and Sloane has set a benchmark for research by compiling and analysing a large dataset in order to explore the role of mortuary practices in monastic communities (Gilchrist and Sloane 2005). Against this background and in direct response to Härke's work on the early Anglo-Saxon weapon burial rite and its influence upon the development of gender archaeology, Roberta Gilchrist investigates expressions of masculinity among both the lay and religious elites of the later Middle Ages. She argues that the approach of Härke has implications far beyond the fifth- to seventh-century furnished graves of southern and eastern England and his insights have an enduring relevance to new fields of archaeological theory and enquiry.

Conclusion

Collectively, the papers presented here provide examples of original research into the relationship between death and identity in the Middle Ages. They address the fragmentary, incomplete, partial, conceptual and selective natures of mortuary evidence (Härke 1994b; Härke 1997b: 22–23) by employing explicit theories and methods. In so doing, it is hoped that these studies go some way to providing an appropriate and lasting tribute to the contribution and scholarship of Heinrich Härke to the study of medieval burial archaeology. Certainly many of them bear the mark of Härke's influence as a colleague, a supervisor, an influential scholar in the field of burial archaeology and even, simply, as a critical friend. The benchmark has certainly been set for future debates that appraise burial archaeology's theories, methods and practice in the exploration of social identities in the Middle Ages.

Perhaps it is appropriate to end by considering a quote of Härke's in which he asserts a potential compromise between a social (processual) and symbolic (post-processual) approach to the interpretation of medieval mortuary data:

> Burials are not 'mirrors of life': if anything, they are a 'hall of mirrors of life' (Zerrspiegel des Lebens) providing distorted reflections of the past. The greatest challenge for burial archaeology is to identify in each case the degree of distortion, as well as to attempt to infer the reasons for the distortion. (Härke 1997b: 25)

Härke is here questioning the straightforward reconstruction of social organisation from burial evidence (the 'mirror' approach) as well as the study of mortuary practices as simply symbolic allusions abstracted from past social conditions (what might be called the 'mirage' approach: Samson 1987). Crucially, Härke situates the agenda for the investigation of medieval social identities through mortuary practices at the point of interaction between society and ideology, between image and allusion, between reflection and distortion.

He recognises that medieval identities can be identified within the intended image created for reflection within the grave. Yet the process of distortion is more than a bias to be overcome in the search for social structure. The multiple 'mirrors' placed in our way create distortions that are worthy of study in their own right, since they are, at least partly, the results of the decisions of the survivors as to how they wished the dead person to be remembered in death. In other words, mortuary practices materialise ideals and allusions in relation to social conditions.

This perspective sets the agenda for the volume as well as for future studies. Neither society nor ideology can be ignored in understanding both the form and variability of medieval mortuary practices and how they, in turn, condition the construction of social memories and the identities of past individuals and communities. The papers presented here negotiate the extremes of the 'mirror' and 'mirage' approachs to mortuary material, some expliclty influenced by Härke's analogy. The studies share an awareness of the 'hall of mirrors' that must be traversed when exploring medieval graves and the identities they constituted. The challenge for the future is to remember Härke's definition of the interpretation of mortuary data as a 'hall of mirrors', investigating the reflections we see, the distortions that have affected these images in the past as well as the process of how archaeologists interpret these visions into stories for people today.

Acknowledgements

Thanks to Roberta Gilchrist, Sonja Marzinzik and Eva Thäte for commenting on drafts of the chapter.

Chapter 2

Working with the dead

Robert Chapman

Abstract
This paper argues that the archaeological study of the disposal of the dead needs to articulate an appropriately materialist theory with a critical understanding of the nature of archaeological evidence and a dialectical analysis of the social practices of life and death. The materialist theory contrasts with the idealism that permeates current studies of mortuary practices. The archaeological evidence for treatment of the dead needs to be compared at similar scales with that for social differences revealed in evidence for production and consumption in settlements. Examples from prehistoric archaeology lead to suggestions of the relevance of this approach to medieval archaeology.

Introduction: personal and intellectual context

I must begin this paper with a statement about my personal and intellectual context as a prehistorian who has, on two previous occasions, been invited to participate in medieval research symposia. In 1979 I gave a paper at the Anglo-Saxon cemeteries symposium (published in Rahtz, Dickinson and Watts 1980), followed in 1987 by a Sutton Hoo invitation seminar, both held in Oxford. I was asked to bring some input on death and the disposal of the dead from theory-rich prehistory to what was then thought to be the practice-rich, but theory-poor, context of medieval archaeology.

Among the participants at both symposia was Heinrich Härke, who became a colleague at Reading in 1989. The following year we began teaching together a module on 'Burial Archaeology', followed by our participation in the short-lived, but highly successful, multi-disciplinary MA in Death and Society, organised by the sociologist Tony Walter, from 1998 to 2003. During this period, Härke published a series of insightful papers that challenged us to bring together theory and practice in 'burial archaeology' and to learn from other traditions of thought. For example, his paper on 'The nature of burial data' (Härke 1997b) took what he argued to be the 'theoretical advances' of post-processual archaeology as a challenge to examine the distinctive nature of our material evidence for death and disposal: the premise of his argument was that we need to understand the nature of our data if we are to fulfil successfully the theoretical agenda set before us initially in the context of prehistoric archaeology. Three years later (Härke 2000a) he provided a critical and informative analysis of debates on the social interpretation of burials in what he called the 'parallel universes' of Anglo-American and German archaeology. The demonstrable lack of communication between these two traditions of thought provided a classic example of linguistic barriers and intellectual endogamy and, he argued, had harmed the development of both traditions.

These two papers provide the stimulus for my contribution, which has three aims. First I want to ask briefly whether the tripartite typology of traditional, processual and post-processual archaeologies is the only way or the most productive way to divide up approaches to mortuary archaeology, and, indeed, the discipline of archaeology as a whole? Secondly I want to suggest what we can learn from a non-English speaking tradition of thought about the disposal of the dead. Thirdly I will focus on the scales of analysis we use in studying the dead, how we can move to finer scales of analysis, and what implications these finer scales have for our ability to compare how people lived and died in the past. I cannot cover all of these questions in the detail they require, given the space available, but I will try to build on arguments I have proposed in recent publications (e.g. Chapman 2003a; 2003b; 2005). I will also try to show the relevance of these arguments to both prehistoric and early medieval archaeology.

Different traditions of thought: making history

The history of approaches to the study and interpretation of past mortuary practices, especially in prehistoric archaeology, has been grouped into the dominant tripartite typology of the discipline of archaeology in the Anglo-American world: 'traditional/cultural historical', 'processual' and 'post-processual'. For example, Binford's 1971 cross-cultural survey of ethnographic literature on mortuary practices illustrated two of the key tenets of processual archaeology, namely that there were no inherent limits to our knowledge of the past and that culture was an integrated system and not a collection of moveable traits. The material traces of the disposal of the dead could be used to reconstruct past social systems rather than the diffusion of beliefs and practices. In contrast, Hodder (1980; 1982) used particular ethnographic observations on the Nuba of south-central Sudan to argue that the disposal of the dead was not a direct reflection of their social position. This was an important plank in the post-processual argument that symbolism, ideology, beliefs and ultimately culture were important sources of variation in human behaviour and its materialisation.

Despite the hegemony of this tripartite typology of archaeology as a whole, there are good reasons to be critical of its continued utility both within and beyond the Anglo-American world. As I have discussed this issue elsewhere (Chapman 2003a), I will summarise my argument briefly in the following points:

1 The effectiveness of the tripartite typology as a representation of consistently distinctive theory, methodology and practice has to be judged against, among other things, the extent to which it accommodates the theories, methodologies and practices of individual archaeologists.

2 Debate on this typology has focused more on boundary definition than internal variation.

3 There has been sufficient internal variation in post-processual archaeology to suggest that it cannot be accommodated within a single 'type' of archaeology (e.g. Hodder 1991b: 37; Preucel 1995: 147; Thomas 2000: 2, 18).

4 Individual archaeologists have changed their theoretical positions during the course of their careers, whether by an eclectic mix and match of new ideas (which has its risks in a possible lack of compatibility) or by a more fundamental shift of theory or philosophy (e.g. compare Chapman 1990 and 2003a).

5 Any 'schools' of thought in any discipline are historically situated and defined in the work of a critical mass of scholars in particular places and contexts, rather than created as doctrines on tablets of stone, to be followed without variation or re-interpretation.

6 Different 'isms' and theories within archaeology have 'histories of development through overlap and interaction' (Chapman 2003a: 28) and, instead of isolation, these 'isms' and theories find areas of convergence and conflict, and proponents of one theory use and reinterpret data produced by the fieldwork or analyses of proponents of a different theory (e.g. Hodder 1990 on Neolithic Europe).

7 The tripartite typology is of marginal relevance in many areas outside of the Anglo-American world (e.g. papers in Hodder 1991a; Ucko 1995 and Politis and Alberti 1999) although many similar issues (e.g. materialism/idealism, particularism/generalisation) have been debated locally and the tenets of processual and post-processual archaeologies have been subjected to critique (e.g. Gándara 1982; Vicent 1991).

This tripartite typology is now part of the history of archaeology, the study of which may be approached in different ways. Of the alternatives presented by Trigger (2006: 5–17), the most realistic is one of co-existing, rival traditions, the cyclical popularity of which is determined by a complex interplay of social and political contexts and the ability of archaeologists (given their available data and methods) to tackle particular problems at particular times. Rather than focusing on large-scale 'schools' of archaeology, each incorporating a variety of theories, we could trace the smaller-scale histories of competing theories and ideas about the aims and scope of archaeology, the popularity of materialist as opposed to idealist ontologies, differences in epistemology (that is, ideas on what we can know about the past, given the data at our disposal, and how we construct and evaluate what is claimed to be knowledge), all situated in their historical contexts. This smaller scale would, I suggest, give us a more dynamic, cross-cutting understanding of the discipline and practice of archaeology in the last 50 years than that which we get by grouping it all exclusively into three large-scale 'schools'. We should also be mindful of the way this understanding may change as we move from the short term (how debates were perceived in the late 1960s or the early 1980s) to the longer term (20 to 40 years on). I do not dispute that it is possible to recognise intellectual fault lines, such as those between the study of culture and behaviour, or materialism and idealism, but our understanding of them in their historical contexts would benefit from a more nuanced approach.

What is the relevance of this discussion of traditions of thought for the archaeological study of death and the disposal of the dead? One way to answer this question would be to examine critically how far the tripartite typology successfully helps us to divide up different approaches to mortuary analysis in archaeology: to what extent has 'convergence and conflict', or what Hodder (1999: 58) has called 'productive tensions', blurred these distinctions during the last 40 years? At the same time, we might question the extent to which different theoretical approaches have used different types, units and scales of analysis in their study of the material traces of mortuary practices during the last 40 years: in other words, how has theory related to practice (Chapman 2005)? How far has theory been used as a tool rather than an end in itself? Lastly we could consider what we might learn from approaches to the dead used outside of Anglo-American archaeology. For the purposes of this paper I will begin with an example of such an 'external' approach and then consider the relationship of theory to practice with regard to the nature and scale of archaeological data on past mortuary practices.

Beyond the usual polemic: a case for materialism

It is no longer a contentious issue to note that there is no unambiguous relationship between life and death that enables us to make direct inferences of past social relations from the material ways in which the dead were treated. There are now sufficient empirical case studies from ethnography (e.g. Bloch 1971; Parker Pearson 1982) and history (e.g. Whaley 1981) to show, for example, that social divisions are not simply and automatically reflected in mortuary rituals. Indeed the marked growth in analyses of death in disciplines such as history, history of art and sociology took place after the seminal archaeological studies of the processual and post-processual schools (for examples, see Chapman 2003b). The much criticised 'representationist' position, most clearly identified with the work of Binford (1971) and Saxe (1970), works better for some societies than others (Brown 1995), but cannot account for the range of variation we see in the relationship between life and death.

The reasons for this variation have, broadly speaking, been divided into materialist and idealist camps, although the Spanish archaeologist Lull (2000a) argues that the so-called processualist and post-processualist approaches to mortuary analysis are both ones of subjective idealism, centring on the individual as either object or subject, his/her social position being mapped in processualism or ideologically manipulated in post-processualism. Härke's own position that 'there can be no doubt that burial ritual is shaped by thoughts, concepts, ideas and intentions' (1997b: 24) sounds like the expression of an idealist philosophy. In contrast, Lull proposes a materialist argument by which mortuary rituals are the products of social labour, such that 'the values assigned in burial to different people or groups will be directly proportional to the community's economic capacity, expressed in terms of the development of the productive processes and the social relations of production' (2000a: 579). Although objects deposited with the dead have symbolic attributes and social life is permeated by symbolism, they are all still the products of social labour and all ideologies exist within material conditions. The allocation of labour and social products in mortuary rituals has to be studied within the context of the available labour and the demands placed upon it by production (c.f. the not dissimilar arguments proposed from a materialist but non-Marxist tradition by Brown 1995).

This line of argument has two important consequences. First, the clusters or groups defined by archaeological analysis of the disposal of the dead enable us to define 'social hypotheses' (Lull 2000a: 579). Second, it is only by a dialectical approach, moving back and forth between these hypotheses and those defined on the basis of the evidence of production and consumption in contemporary settlements and other contexts of deposition, that we can develop more robust inferences about the social relations of the period(s) under study (see also McGuire 2002: 187–212 for a comparable case study of the Hohokam site of La Ciudad in the American Southwest). There is also another dialectical relationship, this time between culture and biology, by which the hypothetical groupings proposed on the basis of the former can be evaluated by attention to the record of health and diet in the latter.

Theory to practice: working with the dead

Whether we are studying funerary or settlement data, culture or biology, we need to have a developed understanding of the nature of the data we are using, otherwise we risk asking unsuitable or over-ambitious questions, let alone finding unsubstantiated answers. Härke (1997b) gives us a start by defining five 'key characteristics' of funerary data, namely fragmentary (preservation/formation processes), incomplete (as a record of rituals), partial (as one form of ritual deposition/consumption), conceptual ('reflecting intentional, cognitive and emotional aspects of thought') and selective (objects chosen for inclusion in mortuary rituals). He then discusses how far such characteristics support the division into 'functional' and 'intentional' data. While clearly not wishing to make this a hard and fast distinction, his main contrast is between the 'functional' data of biology and the 'intentional' data of culture.

Two other rather self-evident characteristics of funerary data, as of all archaeological data, may be added to this list, namely that they are material and static. Behind the graves and cemeteries we excavate are complex relationships between social groups and practices on the one hand and biological populations on the other. We cannot assume that people who lived together were disposed of in the same manner and the same space. Neither can we assume that they all lived together for the same amounts of time. We know from cultural anthropology that there are different scales of movement and changes of location during the life cycle, whether in the context of genuine mobility, matrimonial residence (e.g. Fox 1983), group fission and fusion, demic diffusion and even migration. Within archaeology, recent research on isotopic and genetic markers offers the potential to identify examples of these scales of movement, from the ultimately large-scale movements involved in the spread of agriculture in Europe to the smaller-scale movements, as part of social practices involving changing residence and gender relations during the human life span (e.g. Price *et al.* 1998; 2001; Bentley *et al.* 2007). Any fixation on the individual cemetery obscures what may be a more dynamic, regional account of social life.

These questions lead us to consider the scales of funerary data in time and space. The main focus has been on the analysis of individual cemeteries of variable quality of preservation and excavation. Relative chronologies of burials have been constructed by analyses of vertical and horizontal stratigraphies, grave good associations and typologies, but we have long been aware of caveats such as the regional/local variations in artefact life-spans and (inter-generational) circulation times (e.g. Rowe 1962 and Gräslund 1987 on the construction of prehistoric relative chronologies using typologies and finds associations in the nineteenth century), and the heirloom effect. Olivier (1999) points out the difference of at least fifty years between the archaeological dates of the early Iron Age 'princely' graves of Hallstatt D1 in the north Alpine region of Europe and the dendrochronological dates for this period. Rather than these graves being tight 'closed finds', containing materials of simultaneous use and deposition, he demonstrates how the objects in one of the most famous tombs at Hochdorf had different life histories and different circulation times and intensities of use. The size and involvement of the mortuary ritual, coupled with the numbers of objects deposited in the burial chamber, may make Hochdorf an exceptional example, but it presents us with a challenge to take up in analysing burial assemblages. Härke (2000b) himself combines textual and archaeological sources in his study of weapon circulation in Anglo-Saxon England, noting among other things the use of some swords for up to a century after production, while Woodward (2002) discusses the heirloom and relic effects on the dating of British early Bronze Age burials.

Even when there are radiocarbon dates available for the cemeteries themselves, and/or their cultural context, the chronological scale of burials analysed together may cover several hundred years and 10–20 generations (for examples, see Chapman 2005: 27–28). This means that we may fail to distinguish more fine-scale variations in social practices for the disposal of the dead, and fail to identify what might be changing material representations of the same social structure. The conclusion must be that we need to establish temporal scales at a finer degree of resolution than is often the practice.

This gives us a dilemma which has been expressed concisely by O'Shea (1984: 14):

> a short use-life minimizes the potential for diachronic change, but may provide an insufficient sample for meaningful analysis, whereas the large cemetery, ideal for social analysis, often has the greatest potential for diachronic distortion.

In addition, the focus on the individual cemetery lacks context within the broader sphere of regional, social, economic and political relations (O'Shea 1995: 126). It may well be that the social practices for the disposal of the dead are highly standardised across a region, so that individual cemeteries are representative of this regional tradition, but this is an assumption which requires scrutiny in each case. If we are working at the regional scale, then the use of finer-scale chronologies may give us smaller samples for analysis within individual cemeteries, but larger samples of burials from the same time periods in different cemeteries across the region.

If we follow the argument proposed above by Lull (2000a), then the evaluation of the 'social hypotheses' from funerary contexts requires similar scales of chronological resolution in settlement as in cemetery contexts. In cases of intramural disposal, the dead are placed and may be stratified in relation to the indoor and outdoor spaces in which activities of production and consumption took place. The inference that the dead were disposed of in the same spaces, structures or compounds in which they lived can be strengthened by the identification of biological indicators (e.g. non-metric traits such as Carabelli's cusp) shared by the dead in these contexts. But if evidence is forthcoming to support this assumption, and we have the appropriate level of absolute chronological resolution through, for example, direct dating of the human bone, then we have the potential to compare directly the disposal of the dead with social asymmetries among the living. In the opposite scenario, that of extramural burial, we might achieve the same level of absolute chronological resolution, but the relationship between the dead and their living spaces is, both literally and metaphorically, a more distant inference.

The kind of investment that programmes of C14 dating on funerary and domestic contexts require, if we are going to be able to compare them at the same levels of resolution, will often be beyond the financial resources of research projects. Careful thought is required for the selection of samples for dating within the context of sampling for other kinds of analyses (e.g. isotopic studies of human bone). Different sampling strategies may be required for situations of intramural and extramural interment, or in situations in which either vertical or horizontal stratigraphies are absent. Whatever the contexts, sampling for dating is based on the evaluation of hypotheses based on the basic archaeological evidence (e.g. stratigraphy, grave good typologies and associations, spatial location). As I have suggested elsewhere (Chapman 1995: 39), a regional approach to the cemeteries might require intensive dating of burials from a well-excavated and important cemetery, coupled with the use of the results of this programme to devise more extensive dating in other cemeteries to evaluate the extent to which common disposal patterns were present more widely.

Let us consider two recent research programmes on the construction of finer chronologies for later prehistoric burials. One programme is based on largely individual, intramural burials and the other on communal, extramural interments. Other examples of such absolute dating programmes are also worthy of consideration, but there is no space to discuss them here (e.g. Randsborg and Christensen 2006 on the dendrochronological dating of oak coffins under Danish Bronze Age burial mounds).

First, we have the example of a dating programme on the intramural burials of the early Bronze Age in southeast Spain, centred on the settlements of Gatas and Fuente Alamo in the Vera Basin. Here, the dead were selected for mainly individual interment in artificial caves, pits, pottery urns and stone cists within domestic structures. Quantitative analysis of the grave goods and their containers undertaken on a 20% sample of tombs across a region of some 50,000 km² led to the inference of five levels of this Argaric society based on the unequal distribution of wealth and grave goods of social value: the 'social hypothesis' was that this was a class society (Lull and Estévez 1986). Disposal rites were standardised across the region.

This regional-scale analysis included burials over a 700–year period, during which time we did not know the extent to which social groupings remained constant or were symbolised in different ways. Subsequently, a programme of extensive AMS C14 dating on human bone was initiated. Samples were first taken from stratified settlements such as Gatas (Buikstra *et al.* 1995; Castro *et al.* 1999) and Fuente Alamo (Schubart *et al.* 2000) and then from selected burials containing specific grave good associations elsewhere in the region. The outcome of this programme was set within a wider context of conventional radiocarbon dating from settlements in south-east Spain (Castro *et al.* 1993/94; Lull 2000b; Chapman 2005). First, rather than being limited to successive chronological horizons, the dates showed that the burial containers were used throughout the Argaric period, although a much larger sample is needed to evaluate their relative frequencies through time and there are regional differences in their frequencies. Second, there are differences in the representation of burials by age-at-death at different chronological stages of the Argaric sequence (e.g. adults were predominant before c.1900 BC; infants, child and juvenile burials became more frequent c.1700–1550 BC), suggesting possible changes of inclusion in intramural burial through time. Third, there are contrasts in the duration of deposition of grave goods: some objects were selected for inclusion in burials over almost the entire span of the Argaric, while more restricted ones such as copper halberds, pottery chalices and swords may only have been deposited over a couple of hundred years. The wealthiest male burials were associated with copper halberds during the period c.2000–1800 BC, some six to seven generations, and then these were replaced by swords and axes. The social hypothesis is that the number of levels within society remained the same, but that in this case they were symbolised by different grave goods through time (this is not always the case, as we see for continuing female associations with copper axes and awls). Further analysis of burials from the type-site of El Argar (Lull *et al.* 2005) shows that there are differences in wealth consumption from as young as one month of age and that all five levels proposed for Argaric society are distinguished from six years of age. What then changes is the consumption of grave goods by the top level with age, with the deposition of objects such as halberds, swords and silver diadems restricted to inclusion only with adults.

The overall social hypothesis for Argaric burials, based on this finer-scale study, is of a regional society in which identity, as part of a small number of social levels, was consistently marked out through 700 years, but the material expression of that identity sometimes varied when it came to ritual consumption. The intramural nature of these burials enables us to compare how people were treated in death with how they engaged in production and consumption during life. The assumption that those buried inside structures had previously lived there has some support from inherited skeletal and dental features at Gatas (Buikstra and Hoshower 1994). But not all those who lived in houses were buried inside them, or indeed within the settlements. This is shown by the relationship between the overall number of burials within individual settlements, their length of occupation and estimated population size, the overall age and sex frequencies of those interred in settlements and by differences in age and sex frequencies by site occupation phases (e.g. Chapman 1990: 200–1).

The most intensively studied evidence for production and consumption is from the settlement of Fuente Alamo (Risch 2002: 267–74).

The burials proposed for the top levels in Argaric society were placed on the summit and eastern slopes of the hill where there were productive areas (e.g. metallurgy), storage facilities (e.g. a water cistern, possible grain stores, large pottery vessels) and evidence for the concentration of pottery forms for the consumption of food and drink. This contrasted with other areas of the settlement: for example on the southern slope there was specialised cereal processing, but little evidence for habitation, burial or storage. At a larger scale, within the Vera Basin as a whole (Castro *et al.* 1999; Risch 2002; Chapman 2003a), there was unequal access to cereal production between the primary producers on the valley floor and the cereal consumers on the hilltop settlements that surrounded the basin. The instruments of production, such as grinding stones and flint sickles, were concentrated within the hilltop settlements in numbers exceeding the needs of domestic production. What is inferred from this evidence of production and consumption is a regional, political system, what Risch (1998: 148) calls a 'system of vertical production', in which surplus production is channelled into political and economic activities and centralised under the control of those groups who deposited grave goods of the highest social value with their dead. In other words, the interpretation of the burial evidence is congruent with that of the settlement evidence.

The second example is taken from a recently published programme of radiocarbon chronologies for five Neolithic long barrows in southern Britain (Bayliss and Whittle 2007). Here, the disposal of the dead took place beyond the area of daily habitation, but like southeast Spain, an intensive programme of radiocarbon dating has been used to produce a finer-scale chronology: in this case up to 44 dates have been obtained from a single long barrow. The main conclusion is that, contrary to expectations, these Neolithic monuments were constructed and used intensively over a maximum period of 100 years, that is, between one and three generations. The dead were immediate rather than distant ancestors of the living.

This gives us a better understanding of Neolithic mortuary rituals in southern England but more of an imbalance between the chronologies of the dead and the living in that region. The detailed structural sequences of fourth millennium BC monuments in this region are not matched for contemporary settlements, traces of which are mainly artefact scatters, pits, tree-throw holes and middens, with only the occasional discovery of houses (Bradley 2007; Hey and Barclay 2007). The dominant interpretations are of monuments with structured deposition, ritualised behaviour, specialised and public events and even associated with practices aimed at inducing altered states of consciousness. Such 'cultural' approaches also spill over into discussions of contemporary settlement, for which there is comparatively little analysis of production. Bogaard and Jones (2007) recognise that the productive and ritualised aspects of agricultural production are not mutually exclusive, but acknowledge that the subsistence data from fourth millennium BC settlements suffer from specific taphonomic problems. The current outcome is that we have a detailed and refined sequence of Neolithic monuments in southern England and a coarser record of unevenly preserved productive activities. This makes it difficult to compare archaeologies of death and life as the basis for a representation of Neolithic society.

Implications for medieval archaeology

While my expertise lies with prehistory, the points I have made on the chronologies of the dead seem to be equally applicable to medieval archaeology, particularly the furnished graves of the early Anglo-Saxon period. Here, dating of graves within cemetery sequences has been dependent on the classic methods of relative chronology (e.g. Lucy 2000), while recent research by Duncan Sayer (forthcoming) has proposed a methodology for dividing early Anglo-Saxon graves into generation groups, based on the mean dates of artefact associations in graves and the ages of the deceased. Current research on high precision radiocarbon dating of Anglo-Saxon graves will also permit an evaluation of the accuracy of the archaeological dating (John Hines, pers. comm.). But the current state of knowledge and study of Anglo-Saxon settlements is based on small-scale excavations, often of poorly-preserved sites (with the honourable exception of a handful of sites like West Heslerton and Mucking: Powlesland 1997), giving us a much coarser chronological scale with which to work. We have to accept that we are not in a position currently to compare the living and the dead of Anglo-Saxon England within chronological scales of similar resolution. While we have situations in which cemeteries are spatially associated with individual settlements, we cannot relate patterning in graves within cemeteries to patterning in buildings or spaces within the settlements.

This means that our representations of Anglo-Saxon society are heavily based on the 'social hypotheses' derived from burials. This is particularly true of the fifth to seventh centuries AD. Härke himself has carefully evaluated the evidence for the disposal of the dead against the available settlement data and the textual sources (1997a: 140), arguing that:

> households formed the basic residential and economic units in the fifth to mid-seventh centuries. They comprised individuals and

groups of different status, most likely the family of the master of the household, and unfree or semi-free dependants (Härke 1997a: 148)

He infers an increase in social stratification by the seventh century, seen in a settlement hierarchy (rural settlements, trading sites, royal residences), more marked size differences in settlement buildings and the changing nature of grave goods placed with the dead. This inference, along with that of the emergence of early states or 'kingdoms' is widely shared (e.g. Scull 1997; Saunders 2000).

Although textual sources cited by Härke (1997a: 141–42) discuss the existence of social classes in early Anglo-Saxon society, the concept of class itself enjoys less currency among the archaeologists, who prefer the use of terms like 'stratification' and 'status'. This may partly relate to the lack of a full engagement with Marxist thought among early medieval archaeologists (for a notable exception, see Saunders 2000). But it could also be determined by a belief that inferences of class are difficult or impossible with archaeological data. Saunders' observation that class is 'a structural relationship, more precisely … a relationship of production' and 'not dependent on subjective attitudes and behaviour, or perceived individual status, but upon a social relationship formed in the process of production' (2000: 210–11) gives us a way forward. So does the argument that the institutions of the state guarantee the interests of the dominant class, especially private property (e.g. land, human labour, the means of production, products – see Lull *et al.* 1995 discussing class society in south-east Spain, as presented above). If class relations were present in the seventh century AD among the Anglo-Saxon kingdoms then it is the settlements that will provide the best evidence for production, the organisation of production, the division of labour, consumption and, essentially, who produced what and for whom? Did individual households and settlements consume what they had produced or did they consume what had been produced by the labour of others?

These are questions that can be asked of archaeological data from settlements, not only from the seventh century AD onwards, but also from the previous two centuries. If class relations were present in the seventh century AD, then they must have had a period of development. How long was this period? Can the absence of classes during the fifth to seventh centuries AD be robustly supported, given the paucity of settlement excavations and research strategies focused on production, and the reliance on social hypotheses based on the inference of individual status in burials? Were these centuries simply ones of 'relative political fragmentation' (Scull 1997: 273), an inter-state period which was essentially static in terms of social relations and defined largely by what it lacked (i.e. the economic and political structure of the Roman state: see Wickham 2005: 307)? Even if class relations were not present at this time, what were the social relations of production? Inspired by my research into prehistoric societies, I ask these questions and wonder whether a more rigorous comparison of life and death may take us some way to answering them for the medieval period.

Conclusions

The dead have played an important role in the theory and practice of archaeology, whether in prehistoric or historic periods. Theoretical debates, initially within mainly prehistoric archaeology, have polarised approaches to the study of the dead but have not given sufficient attention to how scholars agree rather than differ, how they have changed their positions, and how the source of polarisation is historically situated. The history and theory of the subject would benefit from a more nuanced, detailed and smaller-scale study, whether of archaeology as a whole or approaches to the dead in particular, than is given by adherence to the overarching tripartite typology. I would argue that these approaches to the dead (and the living) would also benefit from a greater dose of materialism, rather than focussing on culture and idealism: 'thoughts, concepts, ideas and intentions' have no existence independently of the material bases of life (Marx and Engels 1970). The archaeological inferences or social hypotheses that we derive from the treatment of the dead are best evaluated against the evidence for differences in production and consumption among the living. This inevitably raises problems of the nature and scale of the data we have from both contexts. These observations seem to me to be of relevance in working with the dead in both prehistoric and early historic archaeology.

Trigger (2006: 517–18) argues that historic archaeology has the potential to combine the study of behaviour and 'culturally specific beliefs', given its use of material and textual evidence, while prehistoric archaeology is best focused on past behaviour. In this way the full potential of post-processual archaeology is realised within historic rather than prehistoric archaeology, given the nature of the available evidential sources. This is part of what might be called a 'horses for courses' approach to the kinds of questions and problems that can be studied in relation to the nature of available methods and data. While there is merit in this approach and in the argument against 'unsubstantiated speculation' (Trigger 2006: 518), we should at the same time remember our obligation to keep pushing against the so-called 'limits' of inference, in the same way that processual archaeologists used burial and settlement evidence to reach past society. Such inferences may be strengthened by the availability of complementary sources of evidence, as in texts, but our overall understanding of the past, bringing together the individual strands of inference, is still best pursued through a materialist view of existence. Unlike the inferences we make, this view does not depend on the sources and methods of the different period specialisms within archaeology.

Acknowledgements

I would like to thank Duncan Sayer and Howard Williams for the invitation to write a paper for this volume. Richard Bradley read a draft of the paper and Gabor Thomas talked me through some relevant issues in Anglo-Saxon archaeology. I am indebted to John Hines for knowledge of his current, collaborative research on the chronology of early Anglo-Saxon burials. Above all else I thank Heinrich Härke for being an excellent colleague and an example in the pursuit of scholarship. I hope that he will enjoy this engagement with Marx!

Chapter 3

Beowulf *and British prehistory*

Richard Bradley

Abstract

Whatever its precise date, the Anglo-Saxon poem *Beowulf* has often been employed to shed light on the burial practices of the Migration Period. It has also provided a model for prehistorians who lack literary evidence of this kind. Several funerals are described in the poem, but their wider implications for an archaeology of death are seldom discussed. Whilst there are references to two cremation burials of the kind familiar in Bronze Age studies, there is also a funeral in which the body and the artefacts that accompany it are not buried at all but are sent out to sea in an unmanned boat. Still more troubling, Beowulf is accompanied to the grave by two entirely different sets of objects: those burnt together with his body on the pyre, and the contents of a hoard of treasure which had been deposited inside what is sometimes interpreted as an ancient tomb. This paper reflects on these issues and their implications for pre-Roman archaeology.

Prehistoric archaeology

Prehistory is a difficult term to define. When was the prehistoric period, and how is it identified from one region of Europe to another? In England the problem is easily settled, as prehistory ends with the arrival of the Romans, and the early medieval period commences when they leave. That raises problems in itself, and the scheme has less application to the archaeology of northern Britain, and none at all to Ireland. It has led to confusion. Whilst it is possible to speak of a Post-Roman Iron Age in Scotland (Harding 2004), Irish scholars sometimes refer to the same phase as the early Christian period (Charles-Edwards 2000). On one side of the North Channel this terminology reflects the continuation of an indigenous way of life; on the other, it records the adoption of a new religion.

To make matters worse, the Anglo-Saxon phase is also known as the Migration Period. That introduces a further complication. In those parts of northern Europe which remained outside the Roman Empire it is regarded as part of prehistoric archaeology. In Britain, on the other hand, it signals the beginning of an historical archaeology and of early medieval studies. It means that migrants crossing the North Sea to settle in eastern England left Scandinavia during the Iron Age and arrived in Britain during the medieval period.

There is a fault line running through prehistoric studies that is particularly relevant to the use of analogy by prehistorians. By definition, they cannot draw upon historical accounts of the past, so in most cases ethnography provides a major source of inspiration. But what happens when the prehistory of one area was set down in the origin myths of another? Here it is possible to make comparisons of two quite different kinds. One is between written accounts of the past and their material expression in the archaeological record. Another comparison is between the archaeologies of two different areas, one of them with literary evidence and the other without any sources of that kind. It is the second situation that is considered here.

The Old English poem *Beowulf* (Heaney 1999) brings many of these issues to mind, for it is distinctive in three entirely different ways.

Firstly, it has been interpreted as a Christian codification of an essentially pagan epic, whose character was transformed as it made the transition from an oral poem to a written text (Irving 1997). Similar problems are posed by the *Ulster Cycle*, which was apparently recorded by monks.

Secondly, *Beowulf* is set in the past and describes events that took place not in England, where the poem was written down, but in Northern Europe. The identification of the places mentioned in the text remains a matter for discussion, but a broad association with southern Scandinavia is generally accepted today (Overing and Osborn 1994; Niles 2007).

Thirdly, *Beowulf* is set in the Scandinavian Iron Age. In the local terminology it describes the prehistoric period and might have implications for prehistoric archaeology. But the text was written in England, although it is not clear when. Similarly, the narrative is set in the later first millennium A D, although it is uncertain whether it refers to the Migration Period or the Viking Age (Hills 1997). In either case studies of *Beowulf* cut across the conventional distinction between prehistoric and historical archaeology.

Beowulf has been used as a source in historical archaeology (Cramp 1957), but the events described in the poem could also be employed by prehistorians in the same ways as they use ethnographic analogies.

In that case it might have the potential to illuminate the archaeology of other periods and other regions than those described in the poem. This paper considers two of the funerals described in *Beowulf* and the problems that these accounts pose for the study of prehistoric archaeology in Britain. To keep the argument within bounds here the emphasis will be on the archaeology of the North Sea.

The ship of death

The association between ships and the commemoration of the dead is apparent from the first part of the poem, which describes Scyld's funeral (*Beowulf* v. 34–52, Heaney 1999: 4). This has had a major influence on the archaeology of the first millennium AD, but it can also be understood in relation to a much longer sequence which extends from the last hunter-gatherers in Northern Europe. Bodies are associated with boats or representations of boats in the Mesolithic period, the Neolithic and the Bronze Age (Crumlin-Pedersen and Thye 1995: 51–75). In Scandinavia, rock carvings depicting boats are associated with a number of Bronze Age cairns and are occasionally found inside burial cists (Nordenborg Myhre 2005: chapter 7). There are also a number of ship settings dating from the same period (Artelius 1996). They are usually associated with cremation burials. The smaller of these represent relatively modest vessels, but the largest is nearly 40m long. In the pre-Roman Iron Age a vessel of this size is the Hjortspring boat (Denmark). It is of a type depicted in the latest rock carvings and was associated with an important deposit of weapons (Randsborg 1995).

There is only limited evidence for similar concerns on the other side of the North Sea. An early Bronze Age burial in Scotland may have been placed in a coracle (Watkins 1982: 74–77 and 118–19), and there was another inside some kind of canoe (Cressey and Sheridan 2003: 51–52 and 78–79). Both were close to the sea, but a third example was discovered on top of the North York Moors, where the body was placed in another wooden canoe (Elgee and Elgee 1949). Three models of boats feature in later prehistory, but may not have played a role in mortuary ritual. A late Bronze Age example has been found in a bog in North Wales (Savory 1980: 69–70) and another dating from the early Iron Age comes from the Humber wetlands (Coles 1993). The Broighter Boat from Northern Ireland was accompanied by gold ornaments and deposited in a raised beach beside a lake. It dates from the first century BC (Warner 1982). None of these artefacts was associated with human remains, although isolated bones, particularly skulls, are often recorded from rivers and similar environments (Bradley 1998: chapter 3).

The specific practice of using boats in funerals is illustrated by the account in *Beowulf*, but can be misunderstood. Although the poem might shed some light on ship burials in Scandinavia and Britain, there is an important contrast between the archaeological evidence and what is described in the poem. The vessel may contain a corpse and be equipped with a rich array of funeral gifts, but it was never buried. Rather, it was launched into the sea without a living crew and there it was allowed to drift (*Beowulf* v. 48–49, Heaney 1999: 4).

That practice may be reflected in circumpolar ethnography, where boats are often associated with the travels of the dead (Zvelebil and Jordan 1999). They have no means of locomotion. They carry human figures, but there are no oars, paddles or sails. The same is true of many of the ship carvings of the Scandinavian Bronze Age, some of which are directly associated with mortuary monuments. These images depict boats, often with large numbers of people on board, but only very occasionally are they equipped with paddles. It seems as if these images depict the travels of the dead.

There is less evidence of similar concerns in Western Europe. A more appropriate comparison concerns the items deposited with the person in the boat, rather than the vessel itself. For well over a century prehistorians have commented on the relationship between the artefacts deposited in water during the Bronze and Iron Ages and those found in graves. There are cases in which artefacts were employed as funeral offerings in one region and placed in watery environments in a neighbouring area, just as there are sequences in which the provision of furnished burials alternates with the deposition of river finds (Bradley 1998: chapter 1). Often the very same kinds of material are involved, particularly weapons. *Beowulf* raises the possibility – and it is no more than that – that some of the larger collections might have been deposited as the contents of a boat which no longer survives. Curiously enough, something rather similar is suggested by Alice Samson (2006) in a recent reassessment of the evidence for Bronze Age shipwrecks in north-west Europe. These are usually postulated on the basis of collections of metal artefacts recovered from the seabed. None is associated with unambiguous traces of a boat. Samson comments that the supposed cargoes have the same composition as the collections of metalwork that are interpreted as votive offerings when they are discovered in lakes and rivers. The text of *Beowulf* raises the possibility that wrecked ships and offerings of weapons may have more in common than is usually imagined and that both may even be the result of funeral ceremonies.

That is consistent with the suggestion by Tim Champion (2004) that the Bronze Age boat from Dover had been deposited deliberately when its period of use was over. His argument extends to other examples from Britain, but it is based on a very small body of evidence. Even so, he draws attention to two finds of Bronze Age vessels which did contain items of metalwork. This is hardly significant compared with the contents of the Hjortspring Boat, but it suggests that a purely functional explanation of ancient shipwrecks may sometimes be inadequate.

Thus the epic poem *Beowulf* is unusual in suggesting a funerary context which has hardly been recognised in the archaeology of the pre-Roman period in Britain. It will be difficult to take this discussion further, but, in common with the ethnographic sources deployed by insular prehistorians, it makes archaeologists aware of a wider range of possibilities than they otherwise might have considered.

Beowulf's funeral

At first sight Beowulf's funeral poses fewer archaeological problems than that of Scyld, for the offerings burnt on his pyre would have left tangible traces behind and would be associated directly with the cremated body. But earlier prehistorians have expected such deposits to provide other kinds of information. They have seen the contents of individual graves as 'closed deposits' in which all the items were buried simultaneously, and on that basis scholars have attempted to build a chronology. They have also compared the contents of different graves with one another in an attempt to reconstruct ancient social organisation (Burgess 1980: chapter 7).

The poem *Beowulf* suggests that the first of these procedures may be more vulnerable than is often imagined. The artefacts buried with the king had their own biographies. Some were gifts from the living (*Beowulf* v. 3137–40, Heaney 1999: 77–78) and others may have been heirlooms from Beowulf's ancestors (*Beowulf* v. 2190–96, Heaney 1999: 56), and therefore there is no reason to suppose that they had been made simultaneously. Certain items may have changed hands several times, whilst others were newly made. In the circumstances it seems more important to work out why those cycles of gift exchange had ended and why certain objects were taken out of circulation. This evidence was considered by Bazelmans (1999) and by Heinrich Härke a year later (Härke 2000b).

A new research project is shedding light on some of these questions as they apply to British Bronze Age artefacts (Woodward *et al.* 2005). This is based on a detailed study of their condition and has found abundant evidence for use-wear and modification. This work is still in progress, but already it has achieved enough to show that most of the objects associated with the dead had a significant history. That makes the deposition of newly made objects, like some of the goldwork of early Bronze Age Wessex (Coles and Taylor 1971), all the more exceptional. At the same time, if objects had circulated over very different periods between their production and their final burial, their values and associations may have changed during the course of that history. Certain objects would have acquired a special renown though their association with people in the past, just as other objects may have been reduced to fragments and could have lost their original significance. For that reason it is unsatisfactory to suppose that every object had a fixed value in the past. That has worrying implications for the use of 'wealth scores' in burial archaeology. Even the simple procedure of counting the number of artefacts in different graves may be unreliable (Bradley 1988).

Beowulf's body was accompanied by two quite separate sets of artefacts, and these need to be distinguished from one another. One group consisted of pyre goods and was dominated by items of weaponry (*Beowulf* v. 3137–40, Heaney 1999: 77–78). As mentioned earlier, some of them might have been heirlooms that carried a significant history. But there was a second group of material that was deposited during the funeral but not consumed by fire, and this had a very different composition. It was the treasure that had been guarded by the dragon responsible for Beowulf's death (*Beowulf* v. 3163–65, Heaney 1999: 78). These objects included ornaments and metal vessels and are specifically described as antiquities (*Beowulf* v. 2231–41, Heaney 1999: 57). If, as it seems, they were added to the burial after the pyre goods had been placed with the body, the excavation of Beowulf's burial would encounter an inverse stratigraphy. The newer objects, including the weapons, would be directly associated with the remains of his body, whilst the older artefacts – the metalwork from the dragon's lair – would be found in a secondary context.

These deposits are very different from one another. The burnt weapons and other pyre goods can be regarded as gifts to the dead person, expressing the relationship between the donor and the deceased. Indeed, the use of heirlooms means that the process even extended back into the past. The unburnt treasure, on the other hand, is not a funeral gift. Like many other collections of valuables, it may have been buried because it was a source of danger or because its special significance had to be protected. It could not be dispersed as private wealth, and to safeguard its special character it had to be hidden or destroyed (Meillassoux 1968).

That seems plausible for two reasons. The theft of part of the treasure led to the crisis with which the poem ends. When one of the artefacts was removed from its original context the dragon took revenge (*Beowulf* v. 2287–2323, Heaney 1999: 58–59). The treasure was a source of danger that needed to be controlled. The defeat of the dragon had led to Beowulf's death, and now the hoard was unguarded. By placing it inside the king's barrow it was taken out of circulation.

The distinction between the pyre goods and the treasure has other implications for prehistoric archaeology. One group of artefacts can be defined as 'grave goods', whilst the other would normally be categorised as a 'hoard'. Indeed, it was in its guise as a hoard that the artefacts were protected by the dragon. Although some researchers have suggested that there was a close relationship between these two types of deposits, and even that both were ultimately associated with the dead, they are usually studied separately (Bradley 1998). The dragon's hoard is still more unusual because the poem shows how such a hoard was reused in a royal funeral.

The hoard is specifically described as ancient (*Beowulf* v. 2757–77, Heaney 1999: 69), and in this respect it seems to be distinguished from the weapons that Beowulf had inherited. It had been concealed inside a distinctive stone monument. The most likely context is the kind of Neolithic tomb known as a passage grave, many examples of which are recorded in Denmark and southern Sweden (Keiller and Piggott 1939). Its reuse as a storehouse for treasure is echoed by one of the runic inscriptions in the Orkney chambered tomb of Maeshowe (Barnes 1994: 71–77). The contents of the hoard contrast with the artefacts deposited on Beowulf's pyre – fine vessels seem to predominate, compared with gifts of weapons – but both accumulations relate to different conceptions of time and different notions of the past.

The hoard consisted of ancient artefacts and was buried in an ancient monument. If it really was a passage grave, it would have been constructed long before the use of metal vessels. The deposition of the treasure in Beowulf's mound removed those objects from circulation among the living and brought their history to an end. By contrast, the pyre contained goods inherited from known individuals as well as offerings made by the mourners to signify their own relationships to Beowulf. The poet makes it clear that by building a burial mound on a prominent headland, Beowulf was expressed his dying wish to be remembered by future generations (cf. Härke 2001; *Beowulf* v. 2804–08, Heaney 1999: 70).

The passage grave, if that is the correct identification, was also located on the coast, but the poem does not say whether the two monuments were near to one another (*Beowulf* v. 3033, 3136, Heaney 1999: 75, 77). Even so the coincidence of location is striking, and it may be that Beowulf's barrow was considered to replace the older monument (Williams 2006: 201). In that way his burial mound referred to the past as well as the future and may have evoked links with the structure where the treasure had been deposited. A poem that ends by contemplating an uncertain future also shows an ambivalent attitude to the past.

Conclusion

What are we to conclude from this exercise? There is certainly a need for greater dialogue between the people who practise the two prehistories: the shorter version favoured in the British Isles, and the more extended sequence studied in Northern Europe. Sometimes they share important ideas in common, but just as often they research similar material from entirely different perspectives. The use of literary sources – even such a contentious source as *Beowulf* – opens up new possibilities, whether or not it illuminates the burial rites of the Migration Period.

Heinrich Härke is a more recent migrant, who has studied both the pre- and post-Roman Iron Ages to great effect and can move between them with a dexterity that his British colleagues envy. He has examined Hallstatt settlements in Germany and Anglo-Saxon weapon graves in England. He has considered the relationship between social structure and the organization of cemeteries in both periods and has worked in the North Caucasus and even on the Berkshire Downs. He is well placed to cast a quizzical eye over the vagaries of archaeological theory from one part of Europe to another (Härke 2000a). He is a prehistorian in both the senses I mentioned in the introduction to this paper, and his work is quoted by both interest groups. He knows better than most that they share common concerns.

Chapter 4

Fighting wars, gaining status: on the rise of Germanic elites

Stefan Burmeister

Abstract

Ancient historians provide a picture of Germanic society with noble elites, princes and kings at the top. We learn about kings and other military leaders who commanded many thousands of warriors and were the archenemies of the Roman Empire. The archaeological sources seem to support this picture: burials such as those from Gommern and Mušov have been labelled as 'royal' owing to their richness and their exclusivity. However, appearances are deceptive. In this paper it is argued that the political documents of antiquity and a few outstanding burials provide a distorted picture of Germanic societies.

A different picture is presented here: the rule of Germanic elites was a regional phenomenon; ruling elites were in a precarious situation and were constantly endangered in their position by rivalries among the tribal nobility. Hence, the development of dynasties cannot be substantiated from the surviving archaeological and historical evidence. This situation, revealed by both historical and archaeological evidence, is the starting point for political processes in the Migration Period. It was in this period that, for the first time, Germanic rulers established their reigns over the remnants of the Roman Empire.

Introduction

> The Germanic world was perhaps the greatest and most enduring creation of Roman political and military genius. (Geary 1988: vi).

With these words Patrick Geary starts his book on the history of the Merovingians, in spite of the fact that the Germanic world was also one of the gravediggers for the Roman Empire. At the end of the sixth or the beginning of the seventh century AD, the Byzantine military strategist Maurice described the Germanic people as wild, impetuous and fearless warriors, who were, however, careless and disobedient to their leaders and despised tactics (Maurice: *Strategikon* 11, 3, Dennis 1981). In this point his assessment does not differ much from the characterization that Tacitus gave about 500 years earlier (Tacitus: *Germania* 3–4, Rives 1999). Maurice, however, wrote his military manual at a time when the Western Roman Empire had already collapsed and several Germanic kingdoms existed on former Roman territory. This would hardly have been possible if the Germanic people had really been so disorganized. Maurice's descriptions surely fall into the category of a Barbarian literary topos. This is even more apparent in his clear echoes of Tacitus' descriptions. It is clear that Maurice reproduced a handed-down essentialist and fictional protrayal of Germanic people created in earlier writings.

For centuries the relationship between Romans and Germanic tribes had been marked not only by constant conflicts, but also by the lasting integration of Germanic people into the Roman army. The reforms of Diocletian (AD 284–305) and Constantine I (AD 306–37) allowed Barbarians opportunities for a military career and to take high office. In the fourth century about half of the *magistri militum* were of Germanic origin (Waas 1965). Moreover, those Germanic leaders who founded their realms on Roman territory were often high-ranking representatives of the Roman military machine. For example, at the end of the fourth century, Alaric, the king of the Visigoths, was made *magister militum per Illyricum*. Childeric, the king of the Salian Franks (d. AD 482), was a Roman general as well as governor of the Roman province *Belgica Secunda*. Those Germanic leaders of war bands that sealed the decline of the Roman Empire were, though to varying degrees, familiar with Roman military tactics, logistics and administration. Only these skills enabled them to inherit Roman power.

In what follows I want to explore the conditions surrounding these developments and the role of the Germanic elites in the transformation of the Roman world. To introduce the subject, I will sketch some key figures known from historical sources.

We can begin as early as the first century BC. With his retinue, the Germanic leader Ariovistus interfered in Caesar's Gallic War and became one of his most powerful opponents. Roman texts name him as king of the Germanic people (Julius Caesar: *The Gallic War* 1, 31, Edwards 1917) or as king of the Suebi (Pliny: *Natural History* 2, 67, Jones 1951). It is said that he commanded more than 100,000 warriors (Julius Caesar: *The Gallic War* 1, 31, Edwards 1917).

Some decades later the Germanic leader Maroboduus received the title of king after he led a mixed band of Marcomanni and Suebi to Bohemia. By AD 5 he controlled several tribes, is said to have had an army of 70,000 foot soldiers and had at his disposal 4,000 cavalry (Velleius Paterculus: *Historia Romana* 2, 109, Giebel 1989). The Romans unsurprisingly perceived his realm as a great threat.

The numbers mentioned above suggest the considerable complexity of Germanic rulership. As Roman propaganda was aimed at affecting domestic policy, it is often thought that the estimates of the size of the armies are probably far too high. One historical incident seems to be more reliable. It is without doubt that the Romans lost three of their legions in Germania in AD 9. This experience was so drastic and the result so readily attested in the available sources that this record can be only regarded as credible. According to a cautious estimation the Romans lost more than 10,000 soldiers. Six years later in the course of their punitive expedition, thanks to the military fortune of their commander Caecina, the Romans narrowly escaped the loss of another four legions. In both cases the Roman legions were confronted with an allied army of Germanic warriors under the command of Arminius (Tacitus: *Annals* 1, 59–69, Church and Brodribb 1952), although the historical sources remain silent about their size. Even if we concede a certain home advantage and the element of surprise for the Germanic allies, it is obvious that this military success would not have been possible without an organisation and a number of troops comparable to that of the Romans.

Archaeologically, any evidence for this scale of military organisation is generally absent. The only exception is the site of Kalkriese in Lower Saxony, where the remains of a battle of considerable scale between Romans and Germanic people were found (Rost 2007; Wilbers-Rost 2007; Wilbers-Rost *et al.* 2007). Despite this lack, the historical incidents require complex organisational structures on the Germanic side which, so far, have not been tracked down in the archaeological record.

Roman historical sources, above all the *Germania* of Tacitus, also indicate a differentiated Germanic social structure. According to the degree of distinction discerned, we can envisage either a society of five estates (kings, princes, freeborn, freedmen and slaves) or three estates (nobles, free and serfs). However, these descriptions have to be viewed with caution: it is obvious that the five-estate system, as it is described by Tacitus for the Germanic people, reflects the structure of Roman society rather than being an accurate description of Germanic social structure (Lund 1988: 36).

Going wrong

There have been many attempts to detect the Germanic social structure mentioned in historical texts within the archaeological evidence. For example, Helga Schach-Dörges reconstructed a threefold structured society from the third-century cemetery of Häven, Ldkr. Parchim, in Mecklenburg-West Pomerania (see Fig. 4.2 10). At the time of her analysis nine burials in total, all inhumations, were known. Later, four more burials were uncovered. The wealthiest graves, with Roman imports, belong to the group of 'princely' graves of the late Roman Iron Age. Dörges suggested that the richest graves were those of the clan chiefs, the ordinary furnished graves were the *liberi* (the free) and that the only grave lying on the periphery of the cemetery, a young male without any grave goods, was the burial of a serf. These nine burials can be distributed according to this approach as follows: four individuals belong to the highest class, four to the middle stratum, and only one case represents the impoverished serfs (Dörges 1960: 242).

Subsequently, the physical anthropologist Herbert Ullrich (1970) argued by using epigenetic (non-metric) traits that all the individuals at Häven were possibly related. There are ongoing debates over the use of non-metric traits to identify biological affinities (see Sayer this volume), but such an observation casts doubt on Dörges' hypothesis: she had not considered an appropriate range of possibilities and the skeletal data was not given due consideration. Therefore, two of the nobles, a man and a woman, showed close physical similarities with the supposed serf. Of course, it can be objected that a 'prince' can father a son with a maid, and because of this liaison the offspring will receive a low status. Yet Ullrich sees another reason for doubting the social interpretation of the Häven graves. The supposed serf suffered from extreme bone atrophy, which may have caused his eventual death. This man must have suffered immense pain and probably had an unpleasant appearance. It is doubtful that, with these symptoms, this man could carry out hard work in the later stages of his life. Moreover, it is likely that he was not able to achieve success in his community because of his disease, perhaps explaining his burial without any goods at some distance from the other graves.

This example shows one thing very clearly: while the estate model borrowed from the historical sources may seem to be confirmed by archaeological evidence in the variable furnishings of graves, physical anthropology challenges this approach, although it does not disprove the estate model completely. There is also the difficulty that all we know about the community of Häven comes from just 13 graves. We cannot estimate how representative this cemetery population was of the living population. What remains is the conclusion that the estate model cannot be rejected or confirmed on current evidence. All we can suggest is that if we interpret the varied burial furnishing as an expression of diverse social ranks, we have to conclude that members of the same kin group held different ranks at the time of their deaths.

Germanic 'princes'

Our current understanding of Germanic social structure in the Roman Iron Age is determined by grave finds. They make up the bulk of the archaeological finds and are represented in all regions beyond the Roman Empire. The focus of archaeological study is mainly on the so-called 'princely' graves, which are distinguished by gold objects, Roman imports and lavish grave construction. These stand in clear contrast to the vast majority of burials, which are cremation graves and do not contain more than a very small number of personal items, such as a bronze fibula, an iron knife or a pair of scissors. Because of their outstanding appearance, the 'princely' graves are seen as belonging to the social elite.

The distribution of these graves in Germania is, however, confusing at first glance. In the early Roman Iron Age (i.e. in the first two centuries AD until the Marcomannic Wars of AD 166–80) we see a sparse scattering of these graves. The great gaps, both geographical and chronological, in which these graves are absent should not be overlooked. For example, although it was the Rhine-Weser Germanic peoples who defeated Varus in AD 9, the region has produced no evidence of princely graves (Fig. 4.1). Furthermore, it is remarkable that 'princely' graves are restricted to one or two interments. Cemeteries of wealthy burials that span several generations such as those at Hagenow, Kr. Ludwigslust (Voß 2005), are clearly exceptional finds.

In the late Roman Iron Age (i.e. from the Marcomannic Wars to the Hunnic invasion of AD 375) the picture changed completely. The 'princely' graves are concentrated in two regions: the Middle Elbe-Saale region and the Danish islands of Zealand and Funen (Fig. 4.2). Local continuity with those burials of the early Roman Iron Age is rarely found. In each case where early and late Roman Iron Age graves are found in close proximity there remains, nevertheless, a clear chronological hiatus between them.

I want to focus below on the 'princely' graves of the Middle Elbe-Saale region, the so-called Haßleben-Leuna group, and in particular on the 'princely' grave of Gommern (Ldkr. Jerichower Land in Saxony-Anhalt). All those cemeteries with more than 20 burials of this group date to the second half of the third century AD. They therefore

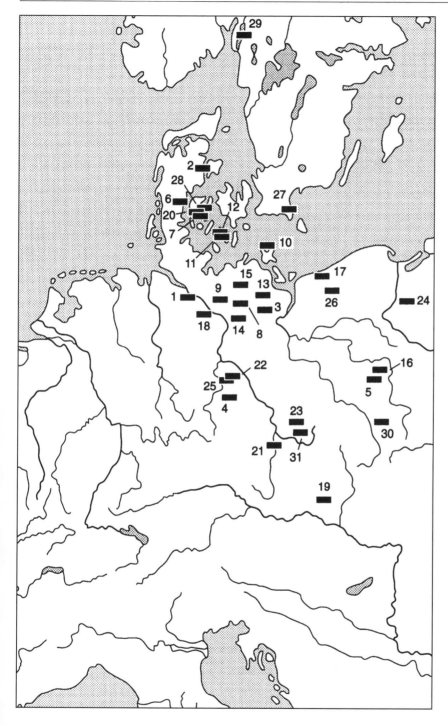

Fig. 4.1: Germanic 'princely' burials of the early Roman Iron Age: 1 Apensen; 2 Bendstrup; 3 Bietikow; 4 Bornitz; 5 Debe; 6 Dollerupgård; 7 Espe; 8 Groß-Kelle; 9 Hagenow; 10 Hiddensee; 11 Hoby; 12 Juellinge; 13 Klatzow; 14 Kossin; 15 Lalendorf; 16 Łęg Piekarski; 17 Lübsow; 18 Marwedel; 19 Mušov; 20 Nørre Broby; 21 Prag-Bubeneč; 22 Quetzdölsdorf; 23 Repow; 24 Rondsen; 25 Schladitzsch; 26 Schlönwitz; 27 Simris; 28 Skrøbeshave; 29 Store-Dal; 30 Wichulla; 31 Zliw (after Gebühr 1996: 186 fig. 25).

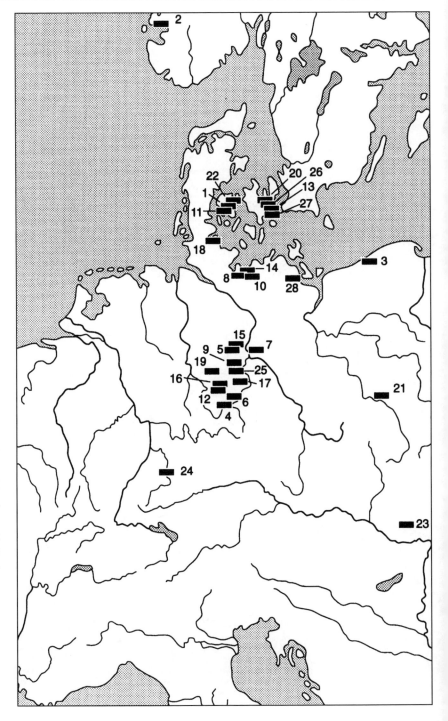

Fig. 4.2: Germanic 'princely' burials of the late Roman Iron Age: 1 Årslev; 2 Avaldsnes; 3 Balenthin; 4 Dienstedt; 5 Emersleben; 6 Flurstedt; 7 Gommern; 8 Grabow; 9 Großörner; 10 Häven; 11 Hågerup; 12 Haßleben; 13 Himlingøje; 14 Jesendorf; 15 Krottorf; 16 Leubingen; 17 Leuna; 18 Neudorf-Bornstein; 19 Nordhausen; 20 Nordrup; 21 Sackrau; 22 Sanderumgård 2; 23 Stráže; 24 Stuttgart-Eßlingen; 25 Trebitz; 26 Valløby; 27 Varpelev; 28 Woldegk (after Gebühr 1996: 187 fig. 26).

represent a relatively short-lived phenomenon in mortuary investment rather than a continuation of existing practice. Since they can be linked to historical events in the Roman Empire they allow interesting insights into key characteristics of Germanic societies in this period.

The most outstanding burial is without a doubt that uncovered in 1990 from Gommern (Fröhlich 2000). This burial was placed on a hill with a commanding view over the Elbe valley. The inhumation was placed about 3m beneath the ground surface within the remains of a wooden chamber. The inhumed male was between 25 and 30 years of age and was supplied with an exceedingly rich set of equipment. At the time of burial his appearance must have been magnificent. The most conspicuous objects were a golden torc, two golden fibulas and a golden finger ring. The torc alone weighs 500 grams and is one of the heaviest of its kind. It is heavier than the total amount of gold weight found in any other grave among all the European 'princely' burials of the Roman Iron Age. As the gold jewellery was complete and showed no traces of wear, and some even had clear and fresh production marks, it can be assumed that these pieces were produced for the burial.

Furthermore, the dead person wore a silver fibula and two belts with rich metal fittings. A third belt, splendidly decorated with gold leaf, lay in a wooden box near his feet. A pair of spurs, scissors and a knife (all made of silver), as well as a collection of Roman coins, were among the personal equipment placed in the grave. As in most Germanic 'princely' graves, offensive weapons such as spears and swords were absent. However, the man from Gommern was buried not only with three silver arrow-heads, but also with a splendid shield. The metal parts of the shield were made of silver. Most remarkable of all is the shield boss which was reworked from a Roman silver cup. The surface of the shield was multi-coloured. Its red and blue pigments had been imported from the Roman Empire. Furthermore, the front was decorated with numerous applications of gilded silver foil and glass inlays (Becker 2000a).

The burial also contained a valuable drinking service and a folding tripod. These items are likely to have originated from within the Roman Empire. Beside a Roman silver ladle–sieve set there was a Hemmoor-type Roman silver bucket. So far, there are only four silver buckets of this kind known from Europe. In the Gommern burial there were further wooden vessels, of which only the silver fittings survive. An indication of an elite lifestyle is provided by the presence of a game board and several glass gaming pieces (Becker 2000b).

The Gommern burial is the richest of the Haßleben-Leuna group and in supra-regional comparisons there are hardly any parallels. It was probably created no later than the second third of the third century, and belongs to the same chronological horizon as the other 'princely' burials of this group, which all date to the later stages of the third century. Gommern falls into the group of Middle Elbe-Saale 'princely' graves, although because of its much richer equipment it has been assigned to the top position within the class.

The differentiation in wealth between these elite burials and the common graves of the era can be interpreted as evidence of a social hierarchy in Germanic societies of the time. However, it is far from clear whether differences in wealth *within* wealthy burials reflect rank differences among the elite or, alternatively, whether they represent the expression of individual circumstances and the personal background of the buried person. For our understanding of social structure this question is of crucial importance. Was the person interred in the Gommern grave simply someone who was more successful and acquired more wealth, or did he acquire a separate social status above the other 'princes'? The two scenarios envisage societies with contrasting hierarchical depth and complexity as well as different strategies by which wealth and status were acquired.

Certainly, previous archaeologists have seen the differences in burial equipment as an indication of different social strata. Schlüter (1970) submitted a classification of the Haßleben-Leuna burials that has become widely accepted by archaeologists. He distinguished two groups (I and II), which he subdivided into five cumulative groups. The main distinguishing mark was the provision of burials with precious metal and Roman imports. Group Ia was defined as burials with gold, which he argued represented the richest graves. Group Ib were those with objects of silver and Roman imports. Group IIa–c differed in the provision of iron and bronze objects (IIa), non-metal objects (IIb) and the absence of artefacts (IIc). Schlüter did not address possible social reasons that might have caused this differentiation.

Joachim Werner (1973: 4) considered that group Ia represented burials of 'petty kings', group Ib those of the 'nobility'. His social model was based on Ammianus Marcellinus who differentiated the Alamanni in the fourth century into *reges, regalesque, reguli* [Ia], *optimatium globus* [Ib] and *populus* [II] (Ammianus Marcellinus: *Rerum gestarum libri*, 16, Rolfe 1952). Feustel (1984) saw in the richest burials the members of a royal dynasty, while he suspected that in the remaining burials of group Ia there were members of the high nobility which correspond with the *reguli* of the Alamanni. Group Ib he thought of as the burials of a clan nobility. Therefore, the common models used by archaeologists to interpret the Haßleben-Leuna group have been based on social ranking that implies a stratification *within* Germanic elites.

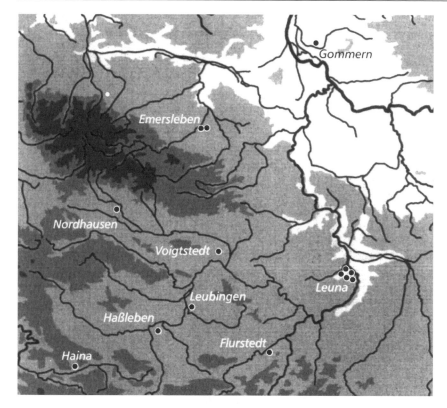

Fig. 4.3: 'Princely' burials in the Middle Elbe-Saale region (after Fröhlich 2000: 73).

At none of these find spots are found 'princely' graves that extend over more than two generations. The distribution of 'princely' graves shows that every 20 km there was a 'prince' (Fig. 4.3). This social upper stratum was, therefore, a localised phenomenon and the princes' notional territories were very small. Moreover, the phenomenon of the Haßleben-Leuna graves disappeared as quickly as it had appeared. Because of the short-lived character of these elite burials, we cannot see dynasties. It seems obvious that the buried individuals owed their wealth and their strong Roman contacts to a specific historical situation which favoured the local elite and gave them the desire as well as the opportunity to furnish their burials in such a manner, rather than persisting within existing social structures and burial practices.

The crisis of the third century

Any quick glance into the historical text books will show a clear historical context within which the Germanic elite could gain prestige and wealth during the third century AD through interaction with the Roman world. The Roman Rhine and Middle Danube provinces went through a severe crisis in the third century, which eventually resulted in the Roman retreat behind the Rhine and Danube by about AD 260. Germanic groups overran the Limes in several waves and raided through Roman territory, taking advantage of periods when Roman troops were deployed in remote parts of the Empire to fight other conflicts or were tied down by internal power struggles. It was frequently some years before the Roman military were able to stabilize the situation again. For example, in AD 233 the Chatti penetrated into Upper Germania. In the same year Raetia was struck by Alamannic invasions. Further Germanic invasions followed in AD 254 and 257. The Franks marched without hindrance through Gaul right into Spain, where they devastated Tarraco (Tarragona). In AD 259/260 the Limes collapsed because the frontier was overrun along a wide front, while in AD 259 Alamannic groups were outside Rome itself! In the following year (AD 260), the Germanic and Gaulish provinces were defenceless against raids, while the Roman usurper Postumus founded the Gallic Empire, which lasted until 274. In this period there were recurring internal Roman military conflicts which Germanic people exploited. The years AD 275 and 276 saw the most serious Germanic invasions at the Rhine and the Upper Danube that ever took place. The affected regions suffered extensively: many military and civilian places contain clear archaeological evidence of vast destruction in these years, and antique reports mention that several towns were destroyed.

Archaeologically, we have good evidence for the threat Germanic groups posed to the Roman provinces. Two finds in particular provide a striking insight into these events. In 1992 a Roman victory altar was found in Augsburg, Bavaria. The inscription refers to a battle between Semnoni or Juthungi and Roman military units – it is interesting to note that the Roman reporter was not certain about the identity of the Germanic enemy. The two-day-long fight was won by the Romans and 'many thousands of Italians' were subsequently liberated. The inscription indicates that the Germanic contingent returned from a raid in Italy heavily laden with booty. Since they held many thousands of captives it must have been an enormous contingent. The labelling of these Germanic people as Semnoni or Juthungi indicates that their origin lay in the Elbe region (Bakker 1993).

An archaeological find of a completely different kind is the so-called 'Alamannic booty' from Neupotz in Rhineland-Palatinate (Künzl 1993). In an area of over 200m in length c.1,000 metal objects have been dredged out of the Rhine by mechanical excavator. The greatest part consisted of Roman metal vessels (Fig. 4.4). A total of 297 vessels were made of copper, bronze, brass, silver or tin, and display a great variety of different types. Besides vessels there was a multitude of domestic,

Fig. 4.4: Small selection of metal objects from Neupotz (after Historisches Museum der Pfalz Speyer 2006: 15, fig. 4).

handicraft and agrarian tools, padlocks and chains. The metal from this assemblage weighs over 700 kg. The coins found make a date of deposition in the years around AD 260 most likely (Gorecki 2006). So far the find from Neupotz is unique in terms of its composition and scale. Three more hoards have been found in this part of the Rhine: Hagenbach (Kr. Germersheim), Lingenfeld (Rhein-Pfalz-Kreis) and Otterstadt (Rhein-Pfalz-Kreis). Each consists of a multitude of metal objects and, again, metal vessels form the principal component. These assemblages also date to the middle of the third century AD. Their significance is not simply that they date to the period of the Germanic invasions of the Roman provinces: some of the silver votive sheets from Hagenbach display Aquitaine name inscriptions which indicate that these finds originate in southern Gaul. Contrary to earlier assumptions, because of the regionally-specific objects and their bronze alloys, the Neupotz finds can be attributed a southern and central Gallic provenance. The composition of the hoards and their dating is reason to believe that we are dealing here with looted booty which was lost during the crossing of the Rhine. The remains of a number of wagons in Neupotz can be interpreted as those vehicles upon which the booty

Fig. 4.5: Germanic
invasions
AD 259/260 and
the origin of the
booties from
Hagenbach (I)
and Neupotz (II)
(after Historisches
Museum der Pfalz;
Speyer 2006: 204,
fig. 268).

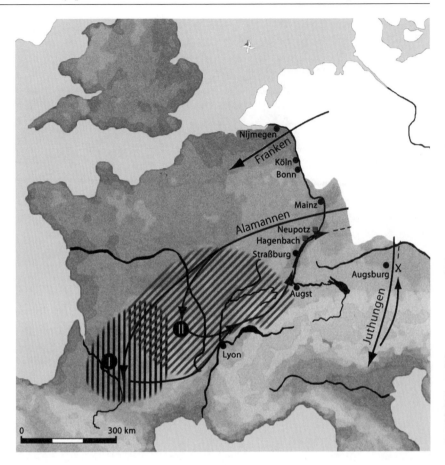

was transported. It is assumed that the Germanic looters were seized by a Roman Rhine patrol (Historisches Museum der Pfalz Speyer 2006). Germanic groups penetrated deep into the Roman Empire (Fig. 4.5) and gathered what they thought of as valuable. These finds from the Rhine are the materialized expression both of their intentions and (in these instances) their failure.

Even if not all expeditions into Roman territory were a success for Germanic people, we can assume that enough groups returned back into their homeland with booty. The objects from Neupotz could have easily supplied the wealth found in the 'princely' graves uncovered in Germania. The metal value of looted Roman goods alone would have been a significant economic factor; these goods certainly supported a social economy by stimulating the circulation of prestige goods. Furthermore, each successful incursion will have encouraged imitators. For Germanic people, the Roman crises in the third century were indeed prosperous times.

The Elbe region and the Rhine

Let us return to the Middle Elbe-Saale region. There is no clear evidence from within the Roman Empire for the military activities of these groups. The Alamanni were first mentioned in Roman sources for the year AD 213 and later settled in the abandoned province of *Agri Decumates*, to the east of the Rhine. Alongside the Franks, they were perceived as a major threat by the Romans in the third century AD. They were probably an amalgamation of different tribal groups who originated from the Elbe region. The Juthungi, named on the Augsburg altar, were described later as part of the Alamanni; they can be traced back to the Elbe region via elements of the material culture found among the Alamanni in the Rhine and Danube area (Schach-Dörges 1997).

Apart from lucrative raids, another field of activities was opened up for Germanic people. The Emperors of the Gallic Empire employed Germanic warrior groups in their fight against the Roman central power (Historia Augusta, Tyranni Triginta 6, Magie 1932), and Joachim Werner (1973) interpreted Roman coins in some of the Haßleben-Leuna burials as payments and hence an indication that these Germanic warriors had been in the military service of the Gallic Empire before returning to their homelands. Michael Erdrich (2001: 133) rejects this notion. He demonstrates that the quantitative relationship between Roman coins from the Gallic Empire and those from Rome is nearly balanced. It is very unlikely that Germanic troops would have been paid with coins from rival emperors. It is certainly not possible to come to a decision solely through the study of coins, however. As Erdrich emphasizes himself, besides coinage, payments in material goods, gifts as well as the right of plunder, were part of the income of Roman troops since Severan times. Especially in the third century, the fate of several Roman emperors was sealed by troops that were disappointed by the amount of booty they could acquire. Coins of rival emperors could also be booty and therefore might reflect an element of indirect pay. Certainly, Germanic contingents were put into Roman service and this is not contradicted by the raiding of Germanic groups. Two burials of the Leuna cemetery Saalekreis provide evidence for the use of local Germanic warriors in Roman troops – both contain fibulas, burial 2/1917 contained a silver example, and 5/1926 a gilded bronze one. These so-called Roman cloak fibulas belonged to the equipment of Roman military officers in the third century (Werner 1989). At least by the time of the Gallic Empire, Germanic contingents could have been recruited for pillaging rival Roman territories to weaken the enemy's situation.

The third century offered many incentives and opportunities to gain wealth and prestige. Germanic people certainly made use of Rome's weakness to get rich at its expense. This was a very specific situation and background against which the 'princely' graves in Germania have to be interpreted.

Germanic elites: a social anthropological perspective

To gain a better understanding of the nature of Germanic elites the discussion may be broadened further. The problems of power formation of the early Germanic elite can be clearly characterized using the careers of Maroboduus and Arminius. Maroboduus is described as king of a realm encompassing many tribes. He himself was not of royal descent but received royal dignity because in the face of threatening Roman subjugation when he successfully led the Marcomanni to a new settlement area. This multi-ethnic realm seems to be a misunderstanding by the Romans, as they did not appreciate the nature of the Germanic retinue system. Maroboduus would have been a military leader of a polyethnic retinue (Preidel 1972). Rivalries and competition within the Germanic elite for political dominance led in the end to Maroboduus' Roman exile; subsequently, the Marcomannic realm lost its political importance. A similar fate had been suffered by Arminius. He was a descendant of a royal Cheruscan family (*stirps regia*), although the Cherusci at that time no longer had a kingdom. Arminius was also in conflict with members of his family and other nobles of his tribe. It is insinuated in the sources that he strove for royal dignity (Timpe 1970), but by AD 21 he had been killed by a relative. The nobility was the greatest enemy of the king.

In her study on the principles of the Germanic kingdoms, Stefanie Dick (2004) comes to the conclusion that the term 'rex', as used, for example, by Tacitus, was not rooted in a monarchic institution in Germanic society. The *reges* originally would have been Germanic leaders who Rome regarded as representatives of their group and via whom the Empire negotiated its foreign affairs. It was Roman practice to bestow upon these leaders the title 'rex atque amicus'. As Roman–Germanic contact mostly took place in the course of military action, the Germanic negotiating party would have commonly consisted of military leaders. The imported title of king and the privileges associated with the relationship created with the Roman Empire will have enhanced the status of these persons, so that structures of power and the resulting authorization of power shifted with time. The usurpation of the royal title as it was used for Arminius is in the end the presumption of the claim to sole representation of the group.

In his seminal study of the genesis of the early medieval *gentes*, the historian Wenskus (1961: 339) drew structural parallels between Germanic and pre-state societies described by social anthropologists. Germanic social institutions were founded upon morals and customs rather than upon laws, and social relations were established by personal, not institutional, ties. Historical sources (e.g. Tacitus: *Germania*, 7, 11, Rives 1999) demonstrate the limited options open to leaders; they asserted their influence through conviction and charisma rather than institutional authority. Military leaders also lacked coercive power: they led by setting a good example. Germanic elites only had restricted opportunities to display power. Therefore, the social principle of leadership was based, according to Wenskus, on the war-band, sustained by the charismatic nature of individual leaders. Those who benefited from this system could assert claims to rank, but not to power as such. Consequently, despite outstanding rank one could not exercise command over other freemen – the nobility did not rule people, they represented people (Mitteis and Lieberich 1988: 34).

We have to ask how Germanic elites acquired their ranked positions and how they could consolidate their social position. The answer probably lies in an institution to which Tacitus gave the greatest attention and without which Germanic society and history cannot be understood: the retinue system (Tacitus: *Germania*, 13–14, Rives 1999). This was a voluntary amalgamation of warriors under the leadership of a charismatic military head. The followers were obliged to loyalty; the leader had to support them with goods. Gold and the opportunity for social advancement were the driving forces for the engagement in a retinue. This provided the retinue leaders with a fundamental problem. As Herwig Wolfram (1983: 18) emphasizes, the economy of a barbarian *gens* was an economy of scarcity. Considerable supplies of raw materials were not available and domestic production did not supply the surplus that would have been necessary to support a retinue.

The economic deficit could be compensated, however, with raiding expeditions. The booty obtained by these means could not be supplied by the home economy. The enormous importance booty had for the Germanic people is the subject of many historical descriptions (Hardt 2004: 161–87). Objects of value constituted the currency of this predacious economy, and with booty the retinues could be supplied. The prospect of rich booty and glory was thus a crucial motive in the decision to join a retinue. Military success – and with it booty and glory – was also a result of the size of the retinue. Apart from charisma and fortune, the military leader required the necessary means to tie followers together and this was enhanced by successful military campaigns. In this way the retinue system created for itself the cause of its own existence, providing the driving force for military activities. Here we see a structural element of Germanic society which had conflict as an integral part.

Let us now return to the third century and the Haßleben-Leuna group. The crisis of the Roman Empire offered the Germanic retinues a lucrative sphere of activities to acquire wealth and glory. Looking in this context at the 'princes' of the Middle Elbe-Saale region as successful retinue leaders and merited followers, we gain a much better understanding of the evidence. This would explain the appearance of this regional group in times of historically attested Germanic raiding campaigns and its obvious decline in the following period of Roman consolidation. Attempts to reconstruct different social strata from differing burial furnishings have provoked repeated critiques. Instead, wealth seems to have resulted from historically specific situations, which temporarily favoured certain groups who expressed their short-lived status in elaborate mortuary expressions and investment. On the other hand, individual wealth expressed personal success in the course of retinue activities. According to Wenskus' interpretation of Germanic social structure, this wealth did not set the differently equipped persons in a relationship that implies social or political hierarchy. The reconstruction of social strata using archaeological data within the elite of the Haßleben-Leuna group is therefore misleading.

Executors of Rome

Tacitus had already remarked that retinues had a strong appeal and attracted warriors from other tribes. We can suppose that retinues were often polyethnic war bands. The significance of polyethnic amalgams for the formation of new ethnic identities in the migration period has been widely discussed in recent years (e.g. Pohl and Reimitz 1998; Pohl 2004). War bands of the Roman Iron Age will have had a similar significance. The labelling of Germanic groups with certain tribal names by ancient historiographers mostly occurred at the interface of Roman–Germanic contacts and these were normally of a warlike nature. Ethnic names such as 'Alamanni' ('all men') only later developed into names of regional political formations. First and foremost they named war bands with which the Romans were confronted at certain parts of their frontier. In the course of the following events such polyethnic war bands could provide the starting point of the genesis of new *gentes* (Wenskus 1961; Steuer 2003). As already described, militarily successful retinues could steadily enlarge and in doing so could consolidate the power-base of the retinue leader. The declining Roman Empire offered successful retinue leaders opportunities to take on military and administrative executive duties, providing chances for the Germanic elite to establish their rule. The classic example of this scenario involved the Frankish king Childeric, as mentioned at the beginning of this paper. It was these groups who inherited the Roman Empire and founded realms on Roman territory. The rule was not primarily by kingship but, as Wenskus (1974: 44) emphasized, it was a situation whereby a retinue leader became a ruler who subsequently took on the title of a king.

The development of the Roman Empire from the third century onwards promoted the emergence of Germanic rulers. It is hard to believe that Germanic people would have reached the position that they had in the early Middle Ages without Roman impulse. So, we arrived again at the beginning of my paper and Geary's opening quotation: Germanic leaders who originally opposed the Roman Empire but ended as its executors could do this only because they were trained in Roman military and administrative offices. Maurice's characterization of Germanic people reveals itself once more to be a Barbarian topos – in such a manner Germanic groups would not have been successful in the long run. So I want to end with another quotation of Patrick Geary (2002), of a chapter heading in which he aptly hit the point: 'Barbarians and Other Romans'.

Acknowledgements

I owe a lot to Heinrich Härke who has always been an inspiring partner in numerous discussions and a friend. Some of the ideas presented in this paper result from a joint project on Anglo-Saxon migrations. I also thank Howard Williams and Duncan Sayer as well as two anonymous referees for their helpful comments. As I did not follow all their suggestions on ways to improve this paper the remaining shortcomings are my own.

Chapter 5

'Hunnic' modified skulls: physical appearance, identity and the transformative nature of migrations

Susanne Hakenbeck

Abstract

The distribution of modified skulls from the Black Sea to southern France has long been linked to the Huns. Historically, the advance of the Huns into Roman territory in the fourth and fifth centuries has been seen as the catalyst for the migrations of other barbarian tribes which ultimately contributed to the collapse of the Western Roman Empire. The archaeological evidence associated with these skulls provides a more varied picture of migrations and the effects they had on both the migrating and the receiving populations. First, the migration of nomadic peoples into the Roman provinces in the Carpathian basin was a gradual process that profoundly changed material expressions of identity there and led to the development of a 'hybrid' culture. Second, the distribution of women with modified skulls west of the Carpathian basin indicates directed movements of individuals, possibly in the context of an exogamous social structure. In a migration context, modified skulls are a clear physical reminder that a person is 'foreign' or has a history of migration, and the physical traits of the body in themselves become a source of identity. Individuals with modified skulls, and the manner in which they were buried, thus provide a case study for examining the relationship between physical appearance, identity and the transformative nature of migrations.

Introduction

In archaeology an unresolved conflict has been observed between the notion of ethnic identity as a cultural construct, which is based on self-identification with a group, and the physical characteristics of individuals or larger populations (Härke 2007a: 14f.). Härke (1998: 19) has drawn attention to the opposing and sometimes extreme responses by British and German scholars to his attempts to identify immigrants from the European continent in early Anglo-Saxon cemeteries by using certain skeletal markers, such as non-metric traits and calculations of body size (Härke 1990a: 38ff.; 1992a: 179–216). These reactions appear to be rooted in the different intellectual traditions of British and German-speaking archaeology. Much of German-speaking archaeology is situated within the 'ethnic paradigm' (Härke 1991: 188, 1995b: 54; Brather 2000: 163), according to which ethnicity is an essentially unproblematic social category that can be identified by certain elements of material culture or by morphological characteristics of the skeleton. Changes in material culture are therefore easily attributed to the migrations of ethnic groups. British archaeologists, on the other hand, have, in the past three decades, adopted an anti-migrationist position that favours the idea of autochthonous developments (Härke 1998: 20f.). In parallel, ethnicity came to be seen as an identity – as an internal sense of belonging – and the possibility of accessing it through material culture was therefore considered limited (Härke 2007a: 13). Thus, one perspective emphasises the internal nature of ethnicity, the other its external characteristics; neither acknowledges that there might be a relationship between the two. However, the physical traits of the body can become a powerful source of identity (Härke 2007a: 15). This is the case with the practice of skull modification

Individuals with artificially modified skulls (Fig. 5.1) occur in large numbers in late Roman and early medieval cemeteries in the Carpathian basin and as isolated cases in central and western Europe as far as southern France (Fig. 5.2). These skulls have long been interpreted as primary evidence for the Hunnic migrations into Europe. The practice of skull modification is thought to have originated in the central Eurasian steppes in the first century AD and to have been brought to central Europe with the Huns and other nomadic peoples (see Werner 1956; Kiszely 1978; Anke 1998a, 1998b for overviews). Isolated cases of modified skulls in western Europe have been explained as an effect of the sudden growth of the Hunnic power sphere which led to the temporary adoption of the practice (e.g. Werner 1956: 17, 93; Schmidt 1987: 474; Anke 1998a: 130; Huck 2007: 331). A more critical investigation reveals a more complex picture, where the association of

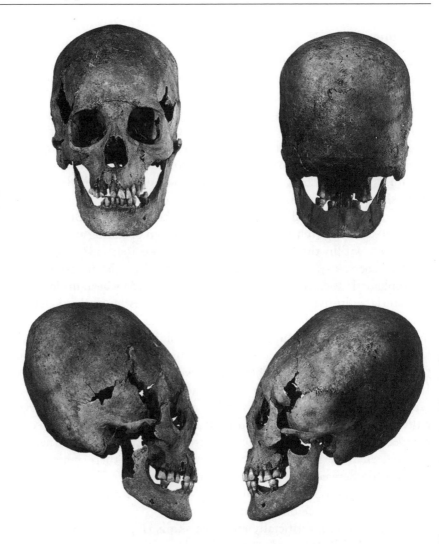

modified skulls with nomadic material culture is not always clear-cut, where skulls are often found in late Roman contexts and where skull modification west of the Carpathian basin is exclusively limited to adult women.

Artificial cranial modification is achieved through binding of the head, using boards, straps, cords or pads, during early childhood when the bones of the skull are still soft (Blom 2005: 4). After the age of about three to five years, the bones of the skull have fused sufficiently to make the cranial modification a permanent feature of a person's appearance. It was a highly regulated practice and may have been deeply tied up in notions of correct childcare, health and beauty.

Dingwall (1931: 88), for example, describes skull modification in Baluchistan in the early twentieth century as a complex process during which specific rules had to be observed and which required the use of special cloths and bands that were reserved for this purpose. Cranial modification suggests a view of the body as malleable and as needing to be improved from its natural state (Lorentz 2003: 10; Torres-Rouff and Yablonsky 2005: 4). The body of an individual is quite literally shaped by society; it becomes a symbol of both the personal and the social.[1] Unlike dress, a modified skull, like other aspects of physical appearance cannot be changed. It becomes part of a person's identity, of who they are and how they are perceived. Recent ethnographic and archaeological examinations of bodily transformations, such as cranial and dental modification, tattooing and scarification (e.g. Torres-Rouff 2002; Schildkrout 2004; Blom 2005; Torres-Rouff and Yablonsky 2005; Geller 2006), have drawn attention to the importance of these practices for generating and maintaining social identities, specifically ethnic or group identities. Torres-Rouff and Yablonsky (2005: 4) point out that skull modification in particular creates physical differences in a society where biological differences do not necessarily exist.

Background

Early work on skull modification in Europe was undertaken by anthropologists and anatomists who were primarily interested in the skulls' racial characteristics (see Schliz 1905; Dingwall 1931). Early medieval skull modification was first considered in its archaeological context by Werner (1956) in a comprehensive study of the archaeological evidence for a nomadic lifestyle during the time of Attila (the first half of the fifth century) in eastern and central Europe. In addition to mapping known examples of skull modification, Werner focused on material culture which he understood to be specific to the lifestyle of the Eurasian nomads, such as horse equipment and weaponry (especially the composite bow), as well as mirrors, diadems, bronze cauldrons and the so-called magical sword pendants. Some of these – notably the mirrors – matched the distribution of modified skulls very closely, while other artefact types, such as long swords or diadems, had a more varied distribution. Werner (1956: 11) identified the origin of the practice among the Mongolian Kenkol group from the Tian Shan and Pamir mountains, dating from the first century AD. He believed

---

[1] See Shilling (1993) and Synnott (1993) for more in-depth examinations of the 'social body'; see Meskell (1998), Joyce (2005) and Sofaer (2006) for archaeological approaches.

it then to have been transmitted to the Sarmatians and Alans in the third and fourth centuries A D and to have spread into central Europe with the Hunnic expansion in the early fifth century. According to Werner, skull modification continued into the sixth century among the Goths on the Crimean peninsula, the Gepids along the river Tisza in Hungary, the Langobards in Moravia, and among the Thuringians and Burgundians (Werner 1956: 17).

Operating within a strict historical framework, Werner assumed that all apparently nomadic material culture in the Carpathian basin dating from the first half of the fifth century A D was associated with the Huns. However, in line with contemporary scholarship (e.g. Jettmar 1953), he acknowledged that the archaeological study of the Huns posed particular problems, since they were to be considered as an ethnically diverse political confederation, rather than a homogenous group (Werner 1956: 1). He therefore focused on the evidence for a nomadic lifestyle and society more generally, rather than aiming to identify a distinct Hunnic material culture. Werner's Hunnic hypothesis has been widely upheld by more recent scholarship (e.g. Kiszely 1978; Anke 1998a; b). One exception is Crubézy (1990), who undertook a study of skull modification in France. Crubézy criticized Werner's exclusive attribution of skull modification in western Europe to Hunnic influences, his over-reliance on historical events, and his failure to take modified skulls from before the fifth century into account (Crubézy 1990: 195f.). However, while he emphasizes the heterogeneity of the practice, its continuity over time and the possibility of independent development, Crubézy nevertheless ultimately returns to the theory that skull modification was initially a foreign practice: 'We believe that discoveries [of modified skulls] dating from the time of the great invasions ... might eventually be related to the passage or settlement of Germanic tribes' (Crubézy 1990: 196).

These various approaches to skull modification in early medieval Europe track the changing attitudes to migration and ethnicity in archaeology over the course of the past century, beginning with an emphasis on race and followed by the almost exclusive reliance on material culture as an ethnic signifier and finally by a rejection of migration hypotheses in favour of autochthonous development (see Chapman and Hamerow 1997; Härke 1998; Härke 2004; Hakenbeck 2008). Recent years have seen a renewed interest in the (bio)anthropological and morphological characteristics of skull modification (e.g. Wiltschke-Schrotta 2004/2005; Teschler-Nicola and Mitteröcker 2007), though generally without a focus on its wider archaeological context. None of these studies entirely do justice to what is clearly a complex phenomenon, covering a large geographical area and time span. There are several reasons for this: on a methodological level, large-scale syntheses are rarely integrated with a detailed analysis of the archaeological context, since, in many cases, secure dates or information about the associated burial practices are not available. Further, archaeological approaches to migrations continue to be a matter of contention, in spite of a recently renewed interest in the subject (e.g. Burmeister 2000; Vander Linden 2007), partly brought about by developments in archaeological science such as stable isotope analysis and genetics (e.g. Schweissing and Grupe 2003; Price *et al.* 2004; Thomas *et al.* 2006). On the other hand, scholars who do study migrations frequently focus on those that are known from historical sources, and they fit the archaeological evidence – often simplistically – into a pre-existing conceptual framework. However, if we aim to move on from treating modified skulls simply as dots on a map that indicate the Hunnic advance, and towards an understanding of the social dimensions of this practice, then we need to address the complex relationship between the migration of people, the transmission of material culture and the effects of these factors on identity.

The eastern group: from the Black Sea to the Carpathian basin

The distribution of modified skulls in Europe falls into two distinct geographical groups, an eastern and a western one, which are roughly divided by a line running north–south to the east of the Alps and the Czech massif (Fig. 5.2). In the eastern group a great number of cemeteries contain individuals with modified skulls and the distribution of males and females is roughly equal. The Romanian cemeteries are among the oldest in this group. Four burials in Pogorăşti, with one modified skull, and the large cemetery of Tîrgşor, with more than 400 graves, of which six skeletons had modified skulls, date from the second and third centuries A D (Anke 1998b: 105, 136). These cemeteries have been associated with the Sarmatians, according to typological and historical interpretations, and they are thus thought to pre-date the Hunnic invasions (Kiszely 1978: 21). The cemetery of Dunaújváros (Roman Intercisa) in Hungary contained more than 2,000 inhumations. Its nine modified skulls date from the second and third centuries A D (Kiszely 1978: 28). Teijral (1974: 12) has suggested that such incidences of skull modification in late Roman cemeteries in Pannonia may also have been connected with late-Sarmatian influences. However, even in the following, post-Sarmatian, centuries, modified skulls are frequently associated with late Roman sites (see Anke 1998a: 134ff.), pointing to complex and ongoing interactions between individuals

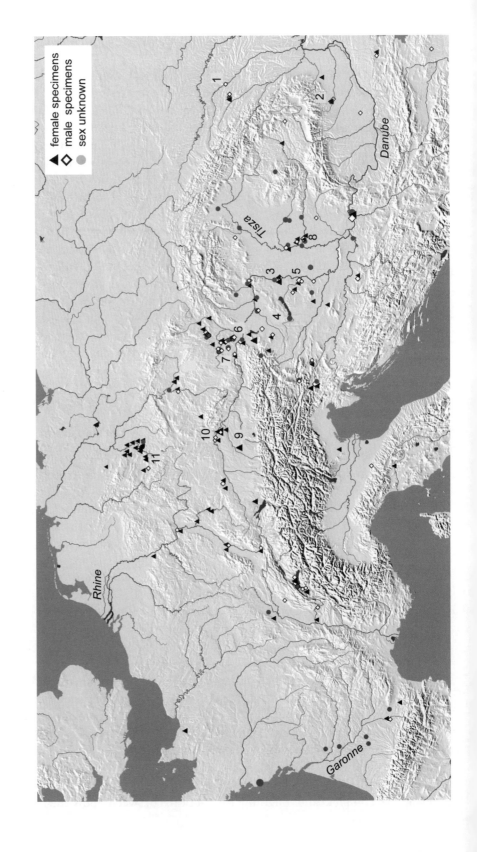

female specimens
male specimens
sex unknown

Rhine

Garonne

Danube

Tisza

1
2
3
5
4
6
7
8
9
10
11

with Roman and barbarian² associations at these sites. The eight cases from the fourth or fifth centuries at the Roman fort of Valcum on Lake Balatón, modern-day Keszthely-Fenékpuszta, Hungary (Müller 1987: 270; Anke 1998b: 61), are a good example of this.

South of Dunaújváros, the fifth-century cemetery of Mősz has been interpreted as a family cemetery (Salamon and Lengyel 1980). Of 28 individuals, 11 had modified skulls. Of these, six were female and five male (based on their grave goods); five were children. In this cemetery, the Roman practice of burying in brick-lined graves continued, with three of the four brick graves containing individuals with deformed skulls. The grave goods reflect a variety of influences, with some objects, such as iron brooches and earrings with polyhedric pendants, representing the Roman period in Pannonia, and others that have been identified with the Huns (Salamon and Lengyel 1980: 98). The spatial lay-out of the cemetery indicates that three generations were buried here. The authors suggest that an adult man introduced the practice of skull modification to the community in the second generation, while the other individuals with modified skulls belonged to the third generation (Salamon and Lengyel 1980: 103).

The majority of modified skulls from the area around Vienna, and from Lower Austria and Moravia, date from the first half or the middle of the fifth century. In this cluster, individuals with modified skulls on average make up between 10 and 20% of all inhumations. In the mid-fifth-century cemetery of Gaweinstal in Lower Austria five individuals out of a total of nine inhumations exhibited modified skulls (Winkler and Wicke 1980). Three of these were female, one male, and one was a child. Grave goods were limited to belt buckles and fragments of knives and strike-a-lights. The cemetery of Grafenwörth (Lippert 1968), also in Lower Austria, dates from the same period. Here two adult skeletons, one male and one female, out of a total of 18, had

OPPOSITE

Fig. 5.2: Location of modified skulls across Europe.

1. Pogorăști,
2. Tîrgşor,
3. Dunaújváros,
4. Valcum (Kesthely-Fenékpuszta)
5. Mősz,
6. Gaweinstal,
7. Grafenwörth,
8. Kiszombor,
9. Altenerding,
10. Straubing-Bajuwarenstraße,
11. Oßmanstedt.

---

² Naming the peoples of late antiquity is highly problematic, and no satisfactory and uncontroversial naming convention has yet been found. While 'barbarian' is a term that was employed by the writers of antiquity to describe peoples that were not Roman and was not used by the barbarians themselves, I consider it preferable to the alternative – 'Germanic' – which carries with it a different set of problematic meanings. In its artificiality, 'barbarian' conveys some sense of the 'other' that is useful in the context of studying identities. I have adopted the term 'barbarian' as a collective label for non-Roman material culture and for the identity of those people that were outside the Roman empire or operated along its frontiers. Some elements of this 'barbarian' material culture are more closely associated with a nomadic lifestyle (as listed by Werner 1956 and Anke 1998), while others have been classified typologically as 'Germanic' or 'east Germanic' (e.g. 'Gothic' brooches).

modified skulls. The burial practice in Grafenwörth combines a variety of influences: a sword appears to be of a western European type, the decoration on the pottery and a bone comb point towards the Black Sea, whereas wheel-thrown technology and burial in stone-lined graves are late Roman (Lippert 1968: 45). In the later fifth and sixth centuries, the practice of skull modification radiated out from the earlier centres in Hungary and Lower Austria/Moravia, the cluster of modified skulls along the river Tisza dating from this slightly later period. The multi-period cemetery of Kiszombor B in Hungary, with 11 modified skulls out of a total of 423, contained some of the latest examples in this area, such as a juvenile/young adult male from grave 234 dating to between the second half of the sixth and the early seventh century A D (Anke 1998a: 129, 1998b: 65).

Romans, nomads and other barbarians

Werner (1956: 16) interpreted the modified skulls from eastern Europe and the Carpathian basin as evidence that the practice of skull modification had spread from east to west, as a consequence of the Hunnic migrations into central Europe. However, subsequent research has shown that skull modification was a far more complex phenomenon that cannot simply be reduced to Hunnic influences. First, in Romania and at some sites in Hungary, skull modification pre-dates the historical arrival of the Huns. Further, the fifth-century heartlands of skull modification, Transdanubia and Lower Austria, correspond with the Roman province of Pannonia, and here many of the cemeteries with large numbers of modified skulls are associated with Roman forts and settlements. Both the practice of burial in stone- or brick-lined graves and the use of late Roman material culture as grave goods indicate that a new population was not simply making use of the late-antique infrastructure (as was suggested by Werner 1956: 92), but that there was close social and cultural integration. On the other hand, the material culture assemblage that Werner interpreted as nomadic is only rarely directly associated with individuals with modified skulls. Instead, the burial practice exhibits a variety of influences. Not only were grave good types of varied provenance used together, but the production and decorative styles of artefacts were also highly mixed.

The ways in which the practice of skull modification was transmitted across Europe are thus by no means clear. There is little indication that the practice came to the Carpathian basin in the wake of one defined migration event. The skulls provide evidence for migration only by proxy: the movement of the practice indicates a movement of people, but the extent to which specific individuals were mobile is difficult to gauge. The picture is complicated further by various elements of material culture that were also transmitted from eastern Europe and beyond, such as new types of weaponry and jewellery, mirrors, and new styles of pottery decoration. They indicate changes in social practices and lifestyles that were taken up in the receiving areas, particularly within the former Roman provinces, where a 'hybrid' society developed (Friesinger 1977; Tejral 2007: 107ff.). That a distinct 'frontier culture' encouraged the development of regional identities has also been noted elsewhere (e.g. Goffart 1989; Swift 2000; Hakenbeck 2006).

In the Carpathian basin, this was compounded by complex interactions between nomadic and settled lifestyles (Pohl 1997: 66f.; Anke 2007: 42). Environmentally, the Carpathian basin is at the periphery of the Eurasian steppes, and it lacked the conditions to support full nomadic pastoralism as it was practised in central Asia. It did, however, provide access to the portable wealth and luxury items that could be obtained in the Roman provinces through raids, trade and treaties, and offered the possibility of arable farming along the Danube (Pohl 1997: 70). On the other hand, raiding and warfare on horseback were an attractive choice even for settled populations, as is indicated by the ready take-up of certain types of weaponry and horse equipment (Bierbrauer 2007: 101ff.). This led to the creation of a new identity that drew on its nomadic origins, as well as the existing late Roman and barbarian identities. The spread of the practice of skull modification was one aspect of such a heterogeneous development.

The western group: from the Alps to the Pyrenees

In the second half of the fifth century A D, modified skulls first appeared west of the cemeteries in Lower Austria and Moravia (Fig. 5.2). They cluster in Bavaria, Bohemia, central Germany, the Rhine valley, around Lac Léman and in the valley of the Garonne in southern France. There is also a cluster in Slovenia and some isolated cases in Italy. Compared with the eastern group, several differences are immediately apparent: the skulls are distributed over a large area, they are fewer in number and, most importantly, 71% (77 of 109 sexed skeletons) are female. As far as they can be dated, most cases fall between the second half of the fifth and the first half of the sixth centuries (Werner 1956; Kiszely 1978; Schröter 1988: 263; Geisler 1998; Hakenbeck 2006: 260). The pattern in southern France seems to have been slightly different, since there is some evidence that the practice of skull modification may have begun in the Gallo-Roman period and continued into the eighth and ninth centuries (Crubézy 1990: 190).

None of the individuals from this western group has been identified

Age Distributions

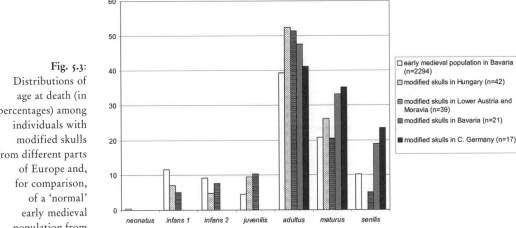

Fig. 5.3:
Distributions of
age at death (in
percentages) among
individuals with
modified skulls
from different parts
of Europe and,
for comparison,
of a 'normal'
early medieval
population from
Bavaria.

as a child or even a juvenile, apart from one case in Bohemia (Anke
1998b: 81). In fact, the proportion of older individuals is extremely high,
both compared to the eastern group and to a typical early medieval
cemetery population (Fig. 5.3). Overall, more than 98% (93 of 95
aged skeletons) belonged to adult or older individuals. In Bavaria and
central Germany more than half of the individuals with modified skulls
were classed as *maturus* or *senilis*, and the pattern within the smaller
clusters is very similar. Since children would otherwise be included in
the demographics, such an age distribution strongly suggests that skull
modification was not an indigenous practice. Furthermore, with the
exception of Bavaria, only one or two individuals with modified skulls
have been found in each of the cemeteries and the cemeteries often lie
far apart. Lorentz (2003: 10) has pointed out that skull modification
is a practice that requires considerable knowledge, commitment and
time investment by the mother or carers of an infant. Such an extended
package of knowledge, practice and belief cannot have been easily
communicated between isolated individuals. Both the demographics
and the relatively infrequent occurrence of the practice therefore
indicate that these individuals were not indigenous to the places where
they were buried. Instead, we can assume that they travelled to these
areas, possibly from Austria or Moravia or from even further to
the east where – as we have seen – a much larger proportion of the
population in the fifth and sixth centuries had modified skulls. The
location of modified skulls predominantly along the main river valleys
provides a clue as to the route these migrations might have taken.
The Danube and Rhine were not only frontiers but important axes of

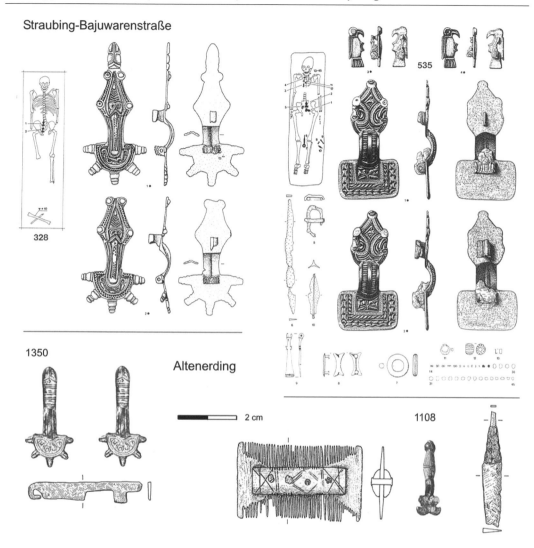

Straubing-Bajuwarenstraße

328

1350

Altenerding

535

1108

2 cm

Fig. 5.4: Grave goods of individuals with deformed skulls from Altenerding and Straubing-Bajuwarenstraße, Bavaria (from Sage 1984: plates 134, 158, 187, 188, reproduced with permission; ©H. Geisler, reproduced with permission).

commerce and communication and the routes connecting the Danube, Rhine, and Rhône were of fundamental importance for linking the Mediterranean with northern and eastern Europe (Werner 1961: 310f.; Harris 2003: 65ff.).

The women with modified skulls in this western group were buried almost exclusively according to the local burial practice, wearing local funerary dress. Only in exceptional cases was there evidence of eastern or nomadic influences. In southern Germany they were buried with elements of the assemblage typical there in the later fifth and early sixth centuries: a variety of brooches, a bead necklace, belt buckle, comb and knife. The five women in Altenerding (Fig. 5.4) were buried with grave goods that were entirely unremarkable in the context of the cemetery and the region (Losert 2003: 301). Even the fact that one grave contained a pair of 'Thuringian' brooches is representative of the variety of brooch types that was in use at this site (Losert 2003; Hakenbeck 2006). In Straubing-Bajuwarenstrasse (Geisler 1990; 1998) eleven women had modified skulls. The bow brooches include 'Frankish/Alamannic' and 'Ostrogothic' types, as well as two bow brooches with rectangular heads and rhomboid feet which are clearly reminiscent of northern European, even 'Anglo-Saxon', types (Fig. 5.4). These are not entirely unusual so far south: similar brooches have been found in Basel-Kleinhüningen, Switzerland, and in Schretzheim in southern Germany (Koch 1999: 175ff.). Such variability of brooch types was in keeping with wider practices during this time.

However, in exceptional cases, even the grave goods suggest a non-local origin for these women. The mid- to late-fifth century grave of an adult woman in Oßmanstedt (Fig. 5.5) is unique in the Thuringian area. It contained a gold and garnet eagle brooch on a gold chain, two gold earrings with garnet inlay, a gold and silver buckle with a plate with gold and garnet inlay, a gold finger ring, and a mirror fragment, among other items (Anke 1998b: 100; Huck 2007: 328). Eagle brooches have been found at sites in the Balkans and in Ostrogothic Italy, as

Fig. 5.5: The skull and eagle brooch of the adult woman from Oßmanstedt, Thuringia (Copyright S. Stefan, Thüringisches Landesamt für Denkmalpflege und Archäologie, Weimar, reproduced with permission).

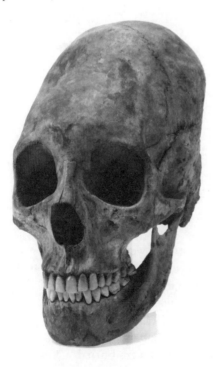

2 cm

well as in Visigothic southern France and Spain (Martin 2000: 137). In all these regions they were commonly worn *peplos*-style as a pair on the shoulders.[3] The way in which it was worn here, singly on a chain at the pelvis, is unusual, but more in keeping with the local practice. The high-quality gold and garnet work has been associated with nobility and was probably manufactured in the eastern Mediterranean (Arrhenius 1985). The mirror, on the other hand, is a component of nomadic-style material culture. Mirrors found in eastern Europe and central Asia were frequently broken before their deposition (Werner 1956: 19–24; Anke 1998a: 19). The fact that the mirror in this grave was also broken suggests that there was a common understanding of the significance of a broken mirror in burial practice in Oßmanstedt and in eastern Europe. All aspects of the assemblage therefore point to an origin in the Carpathian basin or northern Italy. It is difficult to assess why this woman was buried in a manner that made reference to her foreign origins when this was not the case with most other women with modified skulls, although her greater burial wealth and possibly higher status may provide an explanation. The purpose of her travels, her marital status or the manner of her death are impossible to determine, but these may have been factors that led to a non-local identity being expressed in her burial.

Migrations and transformations

It is attested in historical sources that royal and noble women frequently married far from their original home and travelled long distances to be with their in-laws (Nelson 2004: 186ff.). Guichard and Cuvillier (1996: 338) suggest that 'the practices of exogamy and homogamy were essential to [an ethnic] group's political expansion and social cohesion'. 'Mixed marriages' – in other words, marriages outside of one's original ethnic group – played a particularly important part in this. They established the cognatic ties (that is, the ties between a woman's husband and her family) which cemented political alliances. Thus Sidonius Appolinaris wrote in later fifth-century Gaul: 'The country

---

3   The *peplos-style* dress was typical for fifth-century Italy, eastern Europe as far as the Crimea, and the Iberian peninsula. In England it was still used in the sixth century and in Scandinavia it was worn until the end of the Viking period. In southern and central Europe it has been associated with the Goths (Bierbrauer 1971: 138; Koch 1998: 78ff.). West of the Rhine it had been abandoned by the end of the fourth century in favour of one or two bow brooches worn lower down on the body (Böhme 1998: 443ff.; Martin 2000: 134).

where our mother was born is still part of the fatherland' (Guichard and Cuvillier 1996: 326).

While little is known from historical sources about individuals from the lower echelons of society, archaeological evidence supports the notion of high levels of mobility among women, at least once during their lives. This evidence is not limited to individuals with modified skulls. A frequently cited example of individual mobility is the older woman from the cemetery of Altenerding (grave 421). She was buried wearing a *peplos*-style dress and with grave goods that all point to an origin in Scandinavia or the Baltic region (cf. Werner 1970: 78f.; Sage *et al.* 1973: 260; Losert 2003: 84f., 91f.). The manner in which she was buried is so homogeneously Scandinavian that migration seems the only explanation. However, such clear-cut cases are rare and not necessarily representative of wider practices. Usually, the evidence is more subtle. Measuring metric and non-metric traits in the skeletal material from Altenerding, Helmuth (1996: 36, 48) found that there were statistically significant differences between the male and female populations. He suggested that men and women could have originated among different population groups. A similar pattern was noted by Schweissing and Grupe (2003) in a study of stable strontium isotopes in the skeletal remains from a cemetery associated with a late Roman fort in Neuburg, on the Danube in southern Germany and not far from Straubing. They concluded that 68.8% (11 of 16) of adult and older women, compared with 37.5% (15 of 40) of adult and older men, had not grown up locally (Schweissing and Grupe 2003: 1377).

Exogamy as an explanation for the distribution of modified skulls in this western group is not entirely new, although it is usually employed simply as a convenient label for an otherwise unexplained archaeological pattern (e.g. Schmidt 1987: 474; Schröter 1988: 256). The implications of exogamous social networks for our understanding of migrations and mobility and of how they relate to people's identities have remained unexplored. First, the movement of these women clearly does not take a path into the unknown, but follows a meaningful direction. We can assume two-way connections between early medieval societies that were sustained across long distances, providing the reasons for the journey as well as the knowledge of the route and the destination (cf. Anthony 1990: 902; Burmeister 2000: 544). Second, such mobility of individuals appears to have had a limited effect in terms of the identity of the receiving population and a fundamental one on the identities of those who undertook the journey. Skull modification during childhood has a profound and permanent effect on appearance even in adulthood. Their altered physical appearance remained with these women as a permanent reminder of a childhood in distant lands and as evidence that they had travelled far during their lifetime. Nevertheless, they were buried according to the local practice, with local dress and locally-common grave goods. Usually nothing but their modified skulls marked them out as different in any way.

However, we need to bear in mind that both skull modification during infancy and the manner of the funeral lay outside the control of the individual and represented identities given by society at the beginning and end of life (cf. Härke 1994b: 32). One insight into how these women negotiated events in their adult lives is provided by the fact that they seemed not to have transmitted skull modification onto their children in central and western Europe. In contrast, the practice continued for several centuries in the Carpathian basin. Perhaps the practical knowledge of the childcare that was necessary for the modification of skull-shape was no longer available to them, or the receiving populations had an altogether different, more rigid, notion of the human body that was incompatible with the practice of skull modification. Not being able to continue with a practice that may have been a fundamental aspect of childcare to these women must have increased a sense of alienation from their childhood world, in addition to already being geographically removed from it. It also meant that the children would become physically more similar to the receiving population than to their mothers. On the other hand, the adoption of different childcare practices must have facilitated their incorporation into the receiving populations.

Conclusion

The distribution of modified skulls across Europe suggests two distinct modes of migration and mobility. In the eastern group, migration takes place on a larger scale, over a long period of time, and brings about a new 'hybrid' identity of the receiving as well as the migrating population. In the western group, this is replaced by evidence for the directed long-distance movement of a small number of individuals, mostly women, which may have been motivated by exogamous social practices. This second scenario in particular does not fit historical narratives of the early medieval migrations that focus on armies and the aristocracy as their principal agents. In such narratives, women's journeys are considered only when they were married from one *gens* to another to forge a political alliance. Otherwise they remain invisible: they are simply assumed to have followed in the baggage trains of the great migrations or to have been abducted or bought by travelling men. Paradoxically, archaeological approaches to migrations focus primarily on female dress accessories, especially brooches, as the main sources of information about the paths of the migrations (Hakenbeck 2006: 120). Population movements were thought to be visible in female graves because women conservatively maintained the ethnic identity of their origins (e.g. Koch 1998: 70ff.). That such approaches are fundamentally flawed is highlighted by the examples above, which illustrate that dress and its accessories were more strongly determined by the receiving population than by the original one. On the other hand, these examples also show that migrations and mobility can be interpreted from the archaeological evidence. We have seen that the movement of women was a widespread phenomenon across all social strata and was not primarily linked to known historical migrations. While the women were eventually buried as locals, their physical appearance was a constant reminder, both to them and to their new society, of a foreign childhood and a once-different identity. In the first mode of migration, the encounter with different material culture, practices and lifestyles generated a transformation of identities, but in the second the journey itself was the source of the transformation.

Acknowledgements

I would like to thank Howard Williams and Duncan Sayer for inviting me to contribute to this volume and for their editorial suggestions. I also extend my gratitude to Manuel Arroyo-Kalin, Hans Geisler, Catherine Hills, Marc Vander Linden, and two anonymous referees for their helpful comments.

Chapter 6

Rituals to free the spirit – or what the cremation pyre told

Karen Høilund Nielsen

Abstract
Burial finds are rare in southern Scandinavia during the sixth and seventh centuries A D. However, Jutland harbours the biggest southern Scandinavian cemetery of this period: Lindholm Høje near Aalborg. The 600 cremation graves from this site are not furnished with conspicuous grave goods; most artefacts have been burned down to hardly recognizable lumps. Furthermore, the cemetery was excavated back in the 1950s and the publication consists solely of a catalogue which in many ways is inadequate by modern standards. Despite the incomplete nature of the evidence, it is possible to deduce information on the various rites which took place during the funeral and afterwards. Using written sources concerning cremations from the same and adjacent periods, together with the archaeological information from the cemetery of Lindholm Høje, a wider understanding of the rites may be achieved.

Introduction

This paper was originally inspired by the art on the cover of the book *Burial and Society* (Jensen and Høilund Nielsen 1997a), which depicts a Viking cremation ceremony and is entitled 'Funeral of a man of the ar-rus people, as Niels Milan Pedersen imagines Ibn Fadlan saw it'. It also derives from my own work on Lindholm Høje, which has, until recently, focused on chronology and gender. *Burial and Society* was the result of an unforgettable seminar held at Aarhus University in 1994 at which Heinrich Härke was the central, inspiring, participant and discussant, as is also apparent from his own three contributions to the book.

Cemeteries and burial finds are rare in southern Scandinavia in the period AD 450–800. They form a very poor contrast in terms of both numbers and furnishings to contemporary graves from the Continent and Britain, including the furnished early Anglo-Saxon inhumation graves studied in detail by, among others, Heinrich Härke. However, the largest cemetery in southern Scandinavia of this period is located in Jutland: Lindholm Høje at the eastern Limfjord. Its c.600 cremation graves are not furnished with conspicuous grave goods, and the burned and barely recognizable artefacts make heavy demands on the imagination of archaeologists.

Cemeteries similar to Lindholm Høje that contain cremation graves combined with stone enclosures have been found elsewhere in Jutland. Examples come from Tømmerby in Thy, the islands Hjarnø and Als at the east coast of Jutland (Broholm 1937) and, most recently, Trustup on Djursland.[1] However, these sites are much smaller and less well preserved. A different type of cremation grave was found at Bjerre, south-east of Horsens. In the cemetery of 11 burials, the cremation graves showed traces of a fire at the bottom of the grave before the burial. Subsequently the graves were filled with large stones, often burned, mixed with soil, charcoal, a few burned human bones and in some cases also unburned grave goods (Madsen 1994). Finally, traditional cremation graves in urns are known, although very rarely, as for example at Okholm (five graves), close to Ribe (Høilund Nielsen 1998). In addition, about 12 inhumation graves have been found in Jutland: these are mostly single graves (Møbjerg and Møller-Jensen 2005; Ørsnes 1966). In general the graves are poorly furnished. On Funen, only about six graves, all inhumations, have been found. Meanwhile, on Sjælland about 12 inhumations have been recognised (Ørsnes 1966). These graves rarely form cemeteries. Only on Bornholm can graves of this period be counted in their hundreds, and these are inhumation graves that are often fairly well equipped with grave goods (Jørgensen and Nørgård Jørgensen 1997; Ørsnes 1966). Against this background Lindholm Høje stands out as something special.

Lindholm Høje was excavated back in the 1950s by Oscar Marseen (Aalborg Historiske Museum) and Thorkild Ramskou (Nationalmuseet). The excavation was financed by the Ministry of Labour and Economy as a job creation programme. The excavation results were never properly analysed. The very large number of graves, however, provides a fairly solid statistical basis for a discussion of the funeral rites. The aim of this paper is to analyse the archaeological evidence of the funeral rites at Lindholm Høje and discuss them in relation to some of the very

---

[1] My sincere thanks to Niels Axel Boas, *Djurslands Museum*, for information on Nordbakken at Trustrup.

rare written sources with detailed information about early medieval death rituals. These include the detailed description of an early medieval funeral by Ibn Fadlan as well as the four funerals included in the *Beowulf* poem; other sources will be employed only on a general basis.

Background

The Lindholm Høje cemetery (Fig. 6.1) was located at the Limfjord just north of Aalborg. The excavations uncovered *c.*40 inhumation graves, 581 cremation patches (of which 339 were associated with stone-enclosures) and 11 single pots without accompanying burial remains. The cemetery was covered by a thick and uneven layer of shifting sand which reached a depth of 4m in some parts of the excavated area. This preserved the cemetery from later disturbances. In the sand above the cemetery the traces of a settlement from the eleventh and twelfth centuries A D was found (Trolle 1994: 12–14).

Fig. 6.1: The Lindholm Høje cemetery seen from the northeast with the Limfjord in the background. ©Nordjyllands Historiske Museum.

Because of the area's huge quantities of sand and stones, the site had been a quarry for road building during the second half of the nineteenth century. This activity particularly damaged the southern periphery of the site. In hills nearby, pots and glass beads have been found on various occasions, indicating that the cemetery may once have been considerably larger (Ramskou 1976: 18; Trolle 1994: 7). The German occupation in the 1940s saw the site subject to the building of military defences (Johansen *et al.* 1992: 33), while looting by tourists and some 'amateur' archaeologists has had an impact on the surviving finds too. The cemetery was published only in a few interim reports during the period of excavation (primarily Ramskou 1953; 1955; 1957) and a summary catalogue (Ramskou 1976). The latter is unfortunately not up to the standards expected of modern archaeological work, meaning that the data does not allow us to fully explore many of the questions we might wish to ask about this important site.

Of the bones, only the animal remains were analysed and only in a preliminary fashion (Møhl in Ramskou 1976). In particular, the very large amounts of dog bone found at the cemetery are likely to have a much larger potential for further analysis than is presented in the excavation report. The human bones were recognized where present, but neither sex nor age were analysed, something that would have enhanced the value of the cemetery data for mortuary analysis.

The remains of the funerals at Lindholm Høje comprise cremation patches and their contents, including associated artefacts and bones, pots, traces of fire and stone enclosures. Almost all of the relatively small number of inhumation graves uncovered date from the Viking Age and thus were later than the cremations; they will not be discussed here.

The cremation patches

The size of the cremation patches or cremation deposits varied considerably and may have been influenced by a number of factors, such as the place and size of the pyre, the posture of the corpse, the presence of a soil or stone cover, preservation factors caused by the soil and weather, and social differences relating to the deceased and those conducting the funeral.

The excavator's interpretation of the cremation patches as pyre sites varied over time from 'they were not' (Ramskou 1953: 188) through 'unknown' (Marseen 1971: 7) to 'they were' (Ramskou 1976: 15). None of the features discovered at Lindholm Høje seem likely candidates as a separate pyre site, however (compare Artelius 2000: 147, 149). The cremation deposits included cremated bones, burned grave goods, sod and charcoal, which means that if this material was transported from pyre sites located elsewhere, it was not just the important items that were removed from the pyre and buried, but the whole lot.

If the pyres had been where the cremation patches were found, some traces of the high temperature's impact on the ground beneath and around the pyre should have been identified. However, experiments show that if pyres had been placed on the turf, the only impact on the sand and soil below would have been a thin grey layer. Only in places where flames had been in direct contact with the sand would a reddish-brown colour have been generated (Gräslund 1977: 367; 1980: 61). On the red clay, the only trace was a slight reddish tone down to a depth of 2cm (Becker *et al.* 2005: 120). Therefore, missing traces of reddishness in the area below the cremation patch does not exclude the grave from being the pyre site. The cremation patches were mostly round or oblong and fairly regular, which may suggest that the remains were swept together and the site made tidy during or directly following the cremation (cf. Gräslund 1980: 61; Vretemark in Sjösvärd 1989: 36). Such actions may have removed or blurred traces of the fire and the shape of the pyre.

In a number of cases – all ship settings – there were positive traces of the cremation having taken place at the burial site: the soil had clear traces of being subject to high firing temperatures (e.g. graves 1092 and 1124, 1125; Ramskou 1976: 15). Furthermore, a number of graves even had traces of a burned boat with clench-nails found in distinctive rows (graves 635, 1067, 1081, 1097; Ramskou 1953: 192), again suggesting that the grave had been the pyre site.

Six graves are probably of the *bustum*-type, where a pyre is placed over an oblong pit into which the bone and sod is afterwards backfilled (cf. Becker *et al.* 2005; Toynbee 1971: 49). Graves 1431, 1710, 1749 and 1752 were pits/graves of the same shape and almost the same size as inhumation graves, but contained all the remains from cremation pyres. Graves 1671 and 2207, which were more circular in shape, were of comparable size and construction, and were also probably *busta*. These graves either contained objects of fifth- to early sixth-century date or belonged to zones of the cemetery which were dated to this period (cf. Høilund Nielsen 1994: 35).

To accommodate a corpse, the pyre needs to be of a certain size, which is perhaps influenced by the posture of the body. For a supine or crouched posture the pyre ought to be at least 1.5m long; if seated, perhaps smaller (>1.25m?). At Lindholm Høje the diameter of the cremation patches varied from 0.25m to 8.0m; 71% were 1.5m or less and 53% were 1.25m or less. Only three oblong cremation patches were more than 6m long. This implies that most of them were smaller than would be expected of a pyre. The thickness of the patches was only rarely mentioned in the catalogue. Many were only a few centimetres thick, whereas a few were up to 15cm thick at the centre of the patch. At Vallentuna, Sweden, the actual remains of a pyre that accommodated a man, a horse, three dogs and several sheep, pigs, cattle and birds covered an area of 3m by 1.8m and was 0.3m thick. However, a thin (a few millimetres) layer of soot covered an area of 4m by 6m. Faint traces of a rectangular construction were identified (Sjösvärd 1989: 21, 30, 57). The difference in size compared to the patches at Lindholm Høje can be accounted for by the large amount of animals at Vallentuna and suggests that the cremation patches at Lindholm Høje may be the pyre sites even though they seem smaller than expected.

As suggested above the posture of the corpse may have influenced the shape and size of the cremation pyre. As with the inhumation graves, supine, crouched or seated postures are likely. Seated burials do occur in later Iron Age inhumation graves, as at Birka, Sweden (Arbman 1943: 221; Gräslund 1980: 37–39; Price 2002: 132–35), and this tradition cannot be excluded as also part of cremation practice at this time. Seated burials are also mentioned in Old Norse literature and are known in rare cases among the Germanic people on the continent (Gräslund 1980: 38–39 with further references; Price 2002: 134–35).[2] Interestingly, inhumation grave 1262 at Lindholm Høje compares with the Birka graves in that the deceased had been placed in some sort of chair. The types of chair known from the late Iron Age may easily pass unrecognized in cremation graves, and thus a seated corpse may also be missed.

No traces of pyre construction were found at Lindholm Høje, except of grave 1462. Underneath this cremation patch were found four postholes set in a rectangle *c.*0.4m by 0.7m.

Many of the cremation patches contained only a small amount of very fragmented bone, which was sometimes so disintegrated that it was impossible to collect the pieces (e.g. burials 1462, 1679, 1756). The sandy soils may be to blame for this poor state of preservation. Human bones, however, were identified even in the smallest cremation patch (Ramskou 1953: 193), and small dog bones from the tail and toes were common finds. It has been suggested that the small amounts of preserved bones in cremations may be explained as a *pars pro toto*, while mechanical fragmentation may explain the high degree of fragmentation. These ideas have been questioned as a result of

---

[2] A more exotic case is the cremation of Lama Kirti Tsenshub Rinpoche (a Buddhist lama) in 2006. He was cremated in Lotus posture in a *stupa* with a lid for five days: http://kalachakranet.org/kirti-tsenshab-rinpoche-health.htm and http://www.fpmt.org.

experiments which show that, in a slow open-air cremation, a cadaver with normal body tissue burns unevenly and thus cracks up during the burning process. Immediately afterwards, the bones are very brittle and break at the slightest touch, making it almost impossible to collect any larger piece of bone. Some of the bones disintegrate entirely (Becker *et al.* 2005: 140, 145–46).

The weather conditions in the area, combined with the landscape and soil, may also have had an impact (Fig. 6.2). The area is extremely exposed to the wind, and shifting and drifting sand is a severe problem as soon as the thin layer of turf is removed. The wind and sand seem to have periodically covered new burials and exposed old ones, thus causing a lot of erosion. In graves such as 1723, 2159, 2171, 2172, 2174, 2175, and 2184, the cremation patches were uncovered, and many others had only a thin soil cover (Ramskou 1953: 188). In these cases the winds that made the sand drift may have also damaged the cremation deposits and even blown charcoal and light and brittle bones away (Ramskou 1976: 17). Moreover, the smallest cremation patches (<0.6m) were all unmarked and therefore more vulnerable. The oval stone settings form the only group which is covered with a thick layer of soil or stone and could have retained an intact cremation deposit, depending on when they had actually been covered. Their cremation patches are relatively small, but never smaller than 0.6m.

Whether the cremation patches represent both the pyre and the grave cannot be proven beyond doubt for all the graves, but it seems likely for

Fig. 6.2: The thick sand-layers which covered the cemetery as seen during the excavation. Some of the graves were placed on original surface whereas others were placed at various levels in the sand layers and may quickly have been covered by new layers of sand. ©Nordjyllands Historiske Museum.

most cases. As noted above the patches consisted of cremated bones and grave goods as well as sod, charcoal and soil, suggesting that all parts of a pyre were present. Furthermore, the amount of material seems in most cases to equal what one might expect from a pyre. Therefore, either the grave contained the pyre or the entire pyre must have been moved to the grave. Very small bones would have easily been lost if the pyre material had been moved, but this is not the case, as the small bones such as toe and tail bones were found when the animal bones were analysed. Finally, at a number of graves the traces of intensive fire had left a pronounced reddish tone to the soil, while boats were sometimes revealed by the presence of clench-nails recovered in long rows following the planks of the boat. It thus seems most likely that the general tradition at Lindholm Høje was that the deceased were burned and buried in one and the same place. The small size of some of the cremation deposits seems to some extent to be a result of the weather and soil conditions in the area.

Grave goods

The temperature of the pyre must have been intense, considering the degree to which metal and glass have been transformed (Høilund Nielsen 1997: 189 with further references). This has a significant negative influence on the possibilities of analysing the range and character of the grave goods themselves and any subsequent questions about mortuary variability. Therefore, the grave goods cannot contribute to a discussion of rituals for single artefacts and particular grave contexts, but only in general terms as a group. For the same reason, chronology can be discussed in only very general terms.

When the objects were identifiable, the female accessories covered the same main types known from elsewhere in southern Scandinavia in this period, namely: beads of glass (152 graves), crystal (23) and bronze (56), bronze from brooches and other ornaments (102), spindle whorls (44), knives (43), buckles (37), toiletry (tweezers and combs) (23) and bronze bracelets (11). Of the graves, 36% contained female accessories, suggesting that the corpses were all fully dressed at the funeral. Toiletry, buckles and knives are used by both sexes in this period, whereas weapons, which in other areas are diagnostic of men, are present only in the form of a few arrow-heads. Attempts have been made to analyse gender differences at Lindholm Høje (Høilund Nielsen 1994: 31–33; Jensen and Høilund Nielsen 1997b: 58–59), with the result that also hone stones (13) and clench-nails (probably from boats) (14) were identified as male accessories.

Most common among the other grave goods were various iron

mounts (93 graves) which may represent the remains of wooden boxes or other wooden objects. Small nails (37) may represent the same category. Interestingly, an impressive proportion of graves contained gaming pieces (31). Overall, the range of grave goods indicates that in many cases the deceased were burned with more than just personal accessories.

Animal bones

The bones from 387 cremation graves were analysed by U. Møhl (in Ramskou 1976). Circa 36% (139) of this sample contained only human bones, whereas 64% contained both human and animal bones. Of the animal bones, dogs were recorded in 222 graves, horses in 19, sheep in 67, pigs in 10 and cattle in six graves. Furthermore, uncremated teeth were found in six graves. Of the analysed graves, 57% included bones from dogs and 23% contained horse, sheep, pig and/or cattle remains, whereas only 6% included large animals but no dog. This suggests that dogs were common companions for cremated individuals whereas other animals were much rarer. In addition, it is very significant that dog bones almost always occurred in fairly large numbers and many types, suggesting that the whole animal was placed on the pyre, whereas large animals were represented by only one or very few selected bones.

The 19 graves with horse bones came predominantly from triangular or ship-shaped stone enclosures; only three of them were undoubtedly female burials. In one of these graves (1308) the horse bone fragments were very small and there may be doubts about their identification. The other two graves were a very large ship setting with (parts of) a burned ship (grave 635), and an oval stone setting (grave 1727). The remaining occurrences were either from male graves or from graves without any gender-specific grave goods. Therefore, horses can be regarded as predominantly associated with male burials. Furthermore, only one grave with horse bones did not include dog bones, and 11 of the 19 graves with horse bones also contained the bones of sheep, pig or cattle, suggesting that horses were associated with male individuals of a certain status.

Comparative analyses can be made with two samples of animal remains from Swedish late Iron Age cremations, the first from chieftain's graves from the Mälar Valley (Sten and Vretemark 1992) and the second from all excavated cremation graves in the parish of North Spånga, just north of Stockholm (Sigvallius 1994). Both samples show that dogs were as common as they were at Lindholm Høje. However, in comparative terms, other animals seemed to have been much rarer at Lindholm Høje. Even sheep were half as common and for horses the frequency of 5% at Lindholm Høje was next to nothing compared to the 36% frequency for horse from North Spånga. In both Swedish areas, the lower legs and other body parts with a low meat yield predominated for the larger animals. Likewise, at Lindholm Høje 93 of 102 samples (*c*.90%) belong to these groups of bones. However, the situation differs with regard to horses because at North Spånga half of the horse remains suggest the conflagration of whole animals rather than just a selected part of the animal (Sigvallius 1994: 111–12) and the horse was predominantly found in male burials (Sigvallius 1994: 83). This suggests that the animal parts used as grave goods were not literally food,[3] and that large animals in general are much rarer at Lindholm Høje than at North Spånga.

The appearance of dogs is typical for Scandinavian (cremation) graves (cf. Gräslund 2004: 168–70). At Lindholm Høje, dogs could accompany both males and females on the pyre. In the cases of seven of the Lindholm Høje dogs, the report commented on their size, which probably means that they differed from the average: three dogs are described as relatively large, one as sturdy, three as small and one as very small. Both at Lindholm Høje and at North Spånga few of the dogs could be regarded as small in size. However, there seems to be a slight tendency for (very) small dogs to appear mostly in female graves (cf. Sigvallius 1994: 69). The small, even the very small, dogs may indicate that not all dogs were utility animals kept as guardians or for shepherding, carting or traction. Some might have been pets. The small dogs at North Spånga are of the size of modern Papillons, with a withers height of not over 28cm (Sigvallius 1994: 69).

Pots

Pots can be regarded as intermediate between grave goods and votive offerings because they may be part of both and it is hard to distinguish one from the other when the pot is broken. Pots occur in 394 graves (68%) at Lindholm Høje, the remains ranging from one sherd to a complete pot or even multiple pots. In almost half of the graves with ceramics, the pots were to some extent, if not totally, reconstructable. Eleven pots, some represented by sherds only, were scattered between the graves.

The term 'urn' has deliberately not been used. None of the graves were strictly urn burials, since the cremated bones (although some

---

[3]   In inhumation graves from the Danish Roman Iron Age the deceased is provided with proper food, such as a joint of meat.

may have been contained in pots) are always found in the cremation patches. Furthermore, the pots are often too small for this purpose. Urn burials were known in Denmark throughout the entire Iron Age, but they were most popular in the pre-Roman Iron Age. The urns of this period are 20–40cm tall (Jensen 2005: 47), a size that is very rarely found at Lindholm Høje.

In 170 burials the position of the pots is known. Generally, the pot was placed either directly on top of the cremation patch, slightly dug into it or dug through it (Fig. 6.3). These pots are likely to have been placed after the cremation. Any pot that was placed on the pyre was likely to have burst during the cremation (cf. Becker *et al.* 2005: 151) and will have to be sought among the shattered sherds sometimes found among the ashes. If some of the bones of the deceased were contained in the pot it would have to have been placed in the cremation patch after the cremation was over. Only six pots were found above the cover of the grave, indicating that they were definitely placed there after the actual cremation.

Smaller or larger amounts of cremated bone were found in 43 pots. In only four of these instances was the bone from pots placed above the cover of the grave. If the bone in these pots belonged to the deceased it is likely that it was placed there very shortly after the cremation. Food residues (excluding bone) were found in seven pots. Cremated

Fig. 6.3: Cremation grave 1755: a small mound. A standing stone was placed in the middle of the mound. This is one of only three cases in which the pot seems to have been either dug through the cremation patch or placed in the grave before the cremation took place. ©Nordjyllands Historiske Museum.

0   5   10 cm

Fig. 6.4: A selection of pots from cremation graves 1022 (oval stone enclosure), 1116 (ship setting) and 1319 (ship setting). ©Nordjyllands Historiske Museum.

bone in pots was found in all chronological zones of the cemetery but predominantly in the earlier graves, suggesting that this practice could therefore be the traces of an older ritual linked to urn burials of the Roman Iron Age.

Finally, 11 pots were found on their own scattered between the graves. These were only found outside the stone settings. One contained bones (dog and horse) and another only food residues, whereas the rest were found empty.

The pots found at Lindholm Høje were often rather small, the shape often unevenly round, and the fabric was coarse. Handles were rare and almost exclusively found in graves of the early Germanic Iron Age. A small number of pots, however, were vase-shaped and stamp-decorated. The heights of the pots varied between 4.9cm and 25cm, but most were below 15cm. Their widths vary between 5cm and 29cm, but most were less than 20cm. Many pots had been used before; some had food residues, others had evidence of old breakages when used at the funeral and very few stood out for their good condition (Fig. 6.4): they were included because they contained something important. Compared to the urn burials of the pre-Roman Iron Age mentioned above, the pot sizes cover the food vessels and cups found together with or in the urns, and were very different in size from real urns (Jensen 2005: 47–48). This indicates that probably none of the pots at Lindholm Høje were understood as bone containers, but were part of a different ritual. The smallest pots, equalling the sizes of the pre-Roman Iron Age cups, never contained bone or food residues.

To summarise: pots or sherds were either included as grave goods or they were placed on or in the cremation patch immediately after the cremation. In probably less than 25% of graves, some of the cremated bone was placed in the pot. However, it has to be kept in mind that wooden containers may also have been used, which would increase this percentage. The remaining 'empty' pots must have contained something, but this 'something' left no traces behind. Soup or drinks are possibilities. Cases indicating that the pots were part of post-burial rituals are very rare.

Secondary fires

In 31 burials (5% of the graves) fires that took place later than the actual cremation could be identified. The fires were situated either directly on top of the cremation patch (16 graves), or on top of a layer of soil covering (12 graves). In some cases a pot was found with the secondary fire. These fires usually consisted of one or more logs (Fig. 6.5) and, according to the excavators, it seems unlikely that the logs derived from the cremation itself. The fires are predominantly found on oval graves and mounds and most of these graves had identifiable female dress-accessories, whereas there were none with typical male grave goods. The fires appear in all chronological zones of the cemetery, but were predominantly from the seventh century. These fires therefore seem to be mortuary rituals for only a minor social group in the area and there was no indication that the fires took place later than at the funeral.

Fig. 6.5: Secondary fire in grave 1362, an oval stone-enclosure. The cremation patch was 5–10cm thick and covered with 10cm soil on which the charcoaled logs were found. ©Nordjyllands Historiske Museum.

The stone enclosures

A characteristic feature of the cemetery of Lindholm Høje is the large number of stone enclosures of varied size and shape. The 339 excavated stone-enclosed cremation patches included *c.*16 circles, 10 rectangles/ rhomboids, 67 triangles, 116 ovals and 130 ship-shaped features. In addition, there were 22 small mounds and 220 unmarked cremation patches, some of which may once have had a stone enclosure or mound.

The stone enclosures were probably introduced in the later fifth century AD, especially the triangular ones with concave sides; triangular, rectangular, circular and oval as well as early ship-shaped stone enclosures dominated the sixth and seventh centuries, while in the eighth century, oval and especially ship-shaped enclosures dominated (Høilund Nielsen 1994: 31). Furthermore, the shape of the stone enclosures and the gender of the deceased correlated: triangles and ships were preferred for men and rectangles, circles and ovals were preferred for women. In the later period rich women too were occasionally buried in ship settings (Høilund Nielsen 1994: 31–33; Jensen and Høilund Nielsen 1997b: 58–59).

The stone enclosures are often interpreted as conspicuous monuments placed to commemorate the deceased, but while the cemetery was still in use stones were already removed, and sometimes only shortly after the funeral (Marseen 1971: 9; Ramskou 1976: 18). Stratigraphic relationships clearly show this for a number of ship settings. Graves 600, 635, 1176, 1215, 1223, 1311, 1325, 1334, 1429 and 1525 all have empty stone pits that were cut by slightly later graves. These in turn were covered by an intact sand layer or by slightly later ploughed fields which had again been covered by somewhat later graves. Other cases of complicated stratigraphy are present at the site, indicating the removal of stones from older enclosures but without the stone pits actually being cut by later structures.

An obvious reason for the removal of stones from the burials would have been to use them for new burials. We might regard this as the desecration of graves, but to do so would also involve an assumption that the stone enclosures were meant as eternal monuments. On the contrary, the removal of stones by contemporary dwellers in the area suggests that the monuments' importance was only temporary. Had it not been for the shifting sand those enclosures which remain might have entirely disappeared through subsequent stone-robbing.

Especially in the earlier zones of the cemetery, standing stones or menhirs were sometimes found, usually in the centre of the grave. These were only associated with cremation patches lacking any stone enclosures, or with triangular stone enclosures or with mounds.

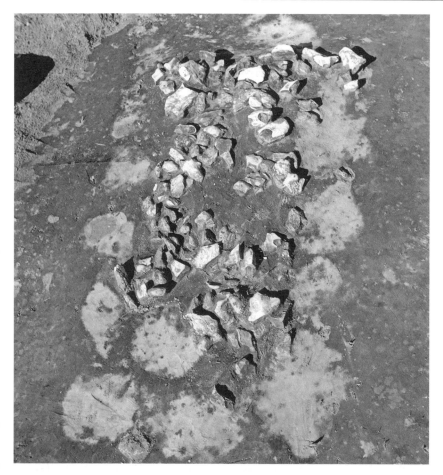

Fig. 6.6: Cremation grave 1685, a rectangular enclosure. The pits left by the stones, which were removed and probably reused in another enclosure, quickly filled up with drifting sand. The cremation patch covered the area inside the enclosure and is again covered with a 'carpet' of 'fresh' flint with cortex. ©Nordjyllands Historiske Museum.

The stone enclosures are often assumed to have been erected after the burial but evidence from other cemeteries indicates that they may occasionally have been erected before the cremation probably took place. Examples are known from Halland, Sweden, where the inner sides of the stones bear clear traces of fire, which suggests that the cremation took place within the stone circle (Artelius 2000: 115 fig. 52). In the oval stone enclosures and in some ship settings (e.g. grave 1293) the cremation patches covered the entire space enclosed by the stones (Ramskou 1953: 188) but no traces of fire on the stones are mentioned. The stratigraphy may indicate that some constructions – at least occasionally – had been in situ before the pyre was burned, as, for instance, in grave 2205, where the grave marker, now missing, seems to have been erected before the cremation. Meanwhile, in graves 1064 and 1124, the darkened layers surrounded the now-missing stones but such material was not recovered from underneath them (Fig. 6.6).

Other rituals

Some rare features may be interpreted as part of rituals associated with the mortuary process. Characteristic of many graves, but predominantly earlier ones, was the use of 'fresh' flint lumps with a chalk cortex. The presence of flint varied from one or a few lumps to an amount that filled the space inside the stone enclosure. The use of these flint lumps was clearly intentional because the closest location where they naturally occur is a couple of kilometres away (Ramskou 1976: 17). White stones are conspicuous and often found to have been used at cemeteries or other ritual places in later Iron Age southern Scandinavia (Artelius 2000: 174–75).

Mourner's intentions of returning to the grave can probably be seen only in grave 1520. This oval stone enclosure produced evidence of a small stone chamber erected within the enclosure and next to the cremation patch. The area within the enclosure was entirely filled with black soil except for the stone chamber, which was kept open and only later filled up with drifting sand. No finds were recovered and consequently the purpose of the chamber remains unclear.

Grave 1726 was a cremation patch with female-gendered grave goods and a pot that dated from the late sixth/early seventh century. The grave was located centrally within a house that measured 6.5m by 4.5m and had an open eastern gable and the remains of three pairs of roof-supporting posts. The large amount of charcoal in all the cut features of the house makes it likely that it was burned down (cf. Ramskou 1955: 181–82). Except for the grave's central position in the house, there is nothing to indicate the chronological relationship between the two features. The house may have burned down as part of the funeral ritual, but conclusive proof of this is lacking and the interpretation of the evidence was hampered by the fact that the area appeared to have been disturbed prior to excavation.

The funeral process at Lindholm Høje

Based on the above evidence, a typical funeral at the site was composed of a sequence of ritual procedures. Mandatory for any cremation seems to have been that the corpse was fully dressed, that wood for an appropriate pyre was available and that a pyre was built and burned, resulting in a cremation patch. Anything else seems to be optional, following rules that we can only sometimes recognize.

The archaeological evidence allows us to divide the funerals into three stages:

1) Preparation: laying out the deceased; providing grave goods; providing firewood and making the pyre; preparing the food and drink; possibly establishing or preparing the stone enclosure.

2) The cremation: placing the corpse fully dressed with accessories and the provision of pyre goods comprising objects, animal parts and drink; killing and placing a dog; kindling the fire and tending the burning pyre.

3) Post-cremation: tidying up the site; placing a pot containing either cremated bone or food/drink; make a fire on top of the remains; building the stone enclosure (if not already done); covering the remains (more or less).

Comparison with written sources

This funerary process can be understood in relation to written sources, although these are always from other regions and written down by people of different religious observances (including Christians and Muslims). Despite this, they do provide insights into the archaeological evidence encountered at Lindholm Høje. The most well-known sources – but also the only detailed ones – describing cremations among pagan (possibly northern Germanic) people are Ibn Fadlan's account of a funeral among the Rus (Frye 2005: 66–71) and the four funerals in the poem *Beowulf* (Scyld lines 26–52; Hnæf 1107–24; the Last Survivor 2252–66; Beowulf v. 2794–3182) (Owen-Crocker 2000; Porter 1991). They contrast markedly in the overall character of the funerals that are presented. Ibn Fadlan's description is very detailed, whereas the descriptions of the funerals in *Beowulf* leave out elements that might have been regarded as pagan and thus offensive to a Christian audience. Ibn Fadlan describes the whole process from death to the construction of the mound and the departure of the participants, whereas in *Beowulf* the information is more fragmentary and concentrated on the grave goods, the burning itself, oral presentations at the burning and the building of a monument befitting the narrative it was part of. Another difference is that whereas the Rus's death was peaceful, the deaths in *Beowulf* are predominantly violent and include two king's burials. We have no accounts of the funerals of females. To widen the perspective, analyses of Roman and later sources are also discussed here.

At Lindholm Høje the cremations are very consistent in appearance, as they are in other contemporary cemeteries of the region. The choice of wood, the method of pyre-building which enabled high temperatures to be reached (Høilund Nielsen 1997: 189) and the possible use of fluids and bellows suggest that the whole cremation process is likely to have been carried out by specialists (Becker *et al.* 2005 130, 138; Sigvallius 1994: 135). This is also suggested, to some extent, by the written sources. Ibn Fadlan mentions that the organizer of the funeral was a woman, the Angel of Death, who was assisted by her two daughters, whereas at Hnæf's funeral it is his sister Hildeburg (v. 1114–18; Owen-Crocker 2000: 48) and at Beowulf's funeral it seems to have been Wiglaf, his loyal retainer (v. 3103–13). The Romans used professional undertakers and a friend or relative (usually not the heir) acted as the organizer (Toynbee 1971: 45, 54). Ibn Fadlan writes that the possessions of the deceased were used to cover the funeral expenses (garments and mead) whereas another part of the possessions was given to the family. Having no son and heir, Beowulf gives his golden neck-ring, mail coat and helmet to Wiglaf, his only remaining kinsman (v. 2808–12). At Roman funerals it was usually the heir who paid (Toynbee 1971: 54).

At Lindholm Høje, the corpse was laid out and dressed in his or her garments with accessories before the cremation. Ibn Fadlan is more detailed. The body was placed in a preliminary grave (accompanied by mead, fruit and a lyre) until the cremation. In the meantime new garments were made for the deseased. At Lindholm Høje it is not easy to identify any places for a preliminary burial and no suitable empty pits have been identified. The body may, however, have been laid in his/her home, as was the tradition among the Romans (Toynbee 1971: 44–45), although it seems clear from the Icelandic sagas that a preliminary burial was the tradition in Scandinavia, as were certain other rites, such as the laying out of the body (Schjødt 2003: 344–46). For the deceased at Lindholm Høje, new garments may have been prepared, but the body may just have dressed in clothes different to those worn at death, as was also the practice among the Romans (Toynbee 1971: 44). In both cases the clothes may have been taken or made from the possessions of the deceased.

The large amount of wood needed for the pyre had to be provided for and the pyre had to be built. The amount of wood needed is, according to Becker *et al.*, estimated to be the equal of 1–2 entire large tree trunks or the amount of firewood required per person for 1–2 years (based on accounts from 1850–1900) (Becker *et al.* 2005: 128–29). This is a considerable investment compared to an inhumation. In some cases a boat was part of the pyre. The only mention of pyre wood in the written sources is that for Beowulf's funeral: it was brought by his subordinate chiefs (v. 3110–13; Owen-Crocker 2000: 85).

In the graves at Lindholm Høje, the bones of large animals and the presence of pots indicate that food and drink were part of the funerary rites. Probably a funeral feast took place, although there is no archaeological proof of this. Pots and cups with no bones or food residue may have contained drink and the animal bones were perhaps from the parts that were not prepared and eaten at the funeral feast. If graves with pots and/or bones of large animals are added together they account for 72% of the graves. The remaining 28% are not necessarily poorly equipped; rather, there may have been variations in the rituals or perhaps a drink was brought in a wooden container. If such a container had no metal frame and was placed on top of a grave it is unlikely to have left any traces. It is possible that, in fact, all graves were given food or a container with drink, either as grave goods on the pyre or placed in the remains afterwards, suggesting that this ritual is probably more common than accounted for in the finds.

If the meatless bones found in 23% of the graves are leftovers from animals which were killed and cut up to be eaten at the funeral feast (Lee 2007: 88), the bones thus indicate what was served at the funeral feast. In this scenario, the evidence suggests that food was only served at every fourth funeral, which is perhaps questionable. Bad preservation certainly reduced the identifiable numbers, however. The menu consisted of sheep six to seven times out of ten, with pig, horse or cattle employed only rarely. Horses probably indicated the funeral of a man of a certain status.

Ibn Fadlan describes that the mead drinking started when the slave girl was killed – which means when the pyre including the boat was ready – and the mourners drank day and night. In *Beowulf*, no feasting is mentioned. Among the Romans the meal at the grave took place just after the cremation and a pig had to be sacrificed before the grave was legally considered as such (Toynbee 1971: 50–51). In the Frankish areas in the early medieval period Christianity influenced many rituals but the church seems to have taken offence against the funeral feast only at a late stage. However, complaints about feasting at graveyards suggests that (pagan) funeral feasts actually took place at the grave and included a meal shared between the deceased and the mourners as well as drinking, singing and dancing. When it was forbidden by the church, the feast was substituted by a vigil before the funeral and/or a wake afterwards (Lee 2007: 89, 113, 126–27, 147).

The archaeology can provide material facts about a funeral but not about the actual performance. According to the written sources, songs/dirges, eulogies, elegies and music are part of the funeral rituals. At the Rus funeral there is a musical instrument in the preliminary grave, the slave girl sings and the men beat their shields. At Hnæf's funeral Hildeburg sings a dirge (v. 1117–18; Owen-Crocker 2000: 50–51) and at the Last Survivor's funeral 'harp's joy' is mentioned (v. 2262). Between the death of Beowulf and his funeral a whole series of eulogies is made and a Geatish woman sings at the burning pyre (v. 3150–55), while an elegy is performed by 12 of his men riding around the mound (v. 3169–77; Owen-Crocker 2000: 101–2). At Roman funerals there were processions with music and the relatives; friends called upon the dead by name just after his last breath and once more just before the cremation (Toynbee 1971: 44, 46–47, 50). As mentioned above, drinking, singing and dancing at the grave were a well-recognized 'problem' for churchmen during the early medieval period. It is therefore very likely that some sort of performance of song, music or recitations was part of the funerary ritual at Lindholm Høje also.

At the cremation itself, the dressed corpse, grave goods, animal parts and drink were placed on the pyre. In rare cases a boat was part of the pyre. If a dog was to accompany the deceased it was killed and placed on the pyre. In Ibn Fadlan's account, they carried the deceased to the pyre, whereas among the Romans a procession took place at night with torches and music (Toynbee 1971: 46–47). The Rus chief was dressed in his new garments, placed sitting in a bed on the boat and served food and mead. A dog was killed and placed in the boat followed by his weapons; horses, cattle and poultry afterwards. Finally, the chosen slave girl was killed and placed next to the dead Rus. In *Beowulf* the grave goods mentioned for Scyld's, Hnæf's and Beowulf's funerals are warrior's equipment; for the Last Survivor, however, they included a cup, a lyre, a falcon, and a horse (Owen-Crocker 2000: 69). At Roman burials, grave goods comprised gifts and personal belongings, but there was occasionally also a pet animal to accompany the soul (Toynbee 1971: 50).

Weapons were very rarely placed at Lindholm Høje, but the difference may be explained by the different contexts. Animal sacrifices are only indirectly mentioned in *Beowulf*, whereas the range of animal sacrifices mentioned by Ibn Fadlan echoes what we see in high-status Scandinavian graves. At Lindholm Høje the range of animal remains seems more modest, probably reflecting a different social context. An interesting aspect is the dog and the slave girl at the Rus funeral and the pets in the Roman funerals. The slave girl follows the Rus as a companion. It may be the case that the order in which things are mentioned in the text is significant. If so, it is striking that the dog is mentioned before the weapons. Perhaps the common presences of dogs at Lindholm Høje suggests they served the same role as the Rus slave girl and the Roman pet – a companion on the last journey – rather than that of sacrificed animals.

By analogy with the written sources, the funeral pyres at Lindholm Høje were probably set on fire by close relatives or heirs. At the Rus funeral the closest relative kindled the pyre and other relatives followed suit; at Beowulf's funeral it was done by his retinue (v. 3143–44). It has been suggested (Schjødt 2003: 358–60) that the act of kindling the pyre is related to a rite of passage in which the heir is initiated to the position of the deceased.

The pyre seems to have burned for at least 7–10 hours (Becker *et al.* 2005: 135). Twenty-four hours after the pyre was set on fire it would have been covered in a thick grey layer and still have been too warm to touch (Becker *et al.* 2005: 155). Ibn Fadlan mentions that the cremation lasted only an hour, although this is impossible. In contrast, Livia sat for five days at Augustus's cremation (Toynbee 1971: 59).

When the pyre had cooled down the site was tidied up; the remains were often swept together to form a round or oval patch. If the stone enclosure had not been erected before, it was possibly done now. A pot with either cremated bone or a drink was frequently placed among the remains and sometimes (for some female burials) a fire was burned on top of the remains. In very rare cases a pot was placed or a fire kindled after the remains were covered.

It seems that many of the Lindholm Høje cremation deposits had much less cover than described in the written sources. Ibn Fadlan mentions how a mound was built over the pyre-site and a wooden pole recording the name of the deceased was erected in the middle. At Beowulf's funeral a feature which may be interpreted as a mound with a stone wall at the foot is built on the pyre site. Roman graves could be simple or elaborate tombs sometimes adorned with decoration and inscriptions (Toynbee 1971: passim). In the early medieval period the occasional mound was still built, whereas a Christian influence can be probably seen in the use of stone markers (Lee 2007: 106).

The pots with food and/or drink and secondary fires placed on the remains at Lindholm Høje have no parallels in Ibn Fadlan's description or in *Beowulf*. The Romans shared a meal with the deceased at the grave just after the funeral, a ritual that was repeated regularly, the first time being nine days later. Each time offerings of food were left at the grave, which had a hole or pipe through which the food could be administered (Toynbee 1971: 51). At Lindholm Høje, however, there are no indications of meals shared with the dead after the funeral.

At Lindholm Høje some of the graves were left uncovered while others had a covering of soil or stone of varying thickness; there is hardly anything to indicate that rituals took place after the funeral was over. The place seems to have been left until the next funeral. At the Rus funeral the mourners also simply left after the mound was built, whereas at Beowulf's funeral some rituals seem to have followed the construction of the mound, which was also built as a beacon (but not as a place for rituals). There seems to be a clear difference to the Roman rituals, which created a sense of living together with the dead.

This difference is perhaps best expressed by Ibn Fadlan, who quotes that among the Rus the deceased was believed to be in paradise within the hour, and by Scyld's funeral in *Beowulf*, where the ship and the deceased leave for an unknown destination (v. 47–52). The dead were not thought to be in their graves after the burial ritual had been performed – they were separated from the known world, and through the cremation reintegrated in the 'other world' (Schjødt 2003: 359–63).

Conclusion

For Roman burials we can draw on information from archaeology, visual art and written sources. For northern Europe we are not so fortunate, but archaeological data can be compared with the few written sources available to open up some possibilities for understanding the coherence and meaning of funerary rituals. With regard to time, the Roman sources are earlier and *Beowulf* and Ibn Fadlan later than the analysed cemetery, whereas the early medieval Continental sources are much more indirect, which of course limits their value.

Some of the graves at Lindholm Høje are reminiscent of burial rites going back to the Roman period, which suggests that we are to some extent dealing with a changing ritual, so consistency in the ritual cannot be expected.

The large amount of wood and the long time needed to achieve a complete cremation of the corpse suggest that the funeral was a comprehensive and lengthy arrangement, in which the process itself seems to be central. The grave goods, the dog and the animal parts are burned almost beyond recognition. If we now turn to Ibn Fadlan, the burning is necessary to transfer the deceased as quickly as possible to the 'other world', and to convey with him his belongings and his companion. This means that the grave was relevant only during the funeral process; the bereaved were not supposed to be in touch with the deceased through the grave afterwards. The pots and the occasional secondary fire found on top of the remains are therefore probably not intended for the deceased. Instead, they may be part of the reintegration of the bereaved into society; the occasional mounds or more elaborate stone covers may also have served this purpose (cf. Schjødt 2003: 262).

Performance, eating and drinking are part of the ritual which is supposed to take the deceased to the 'other world'; a last supper (or banquet) is shared between the deceased and the bereaved. The whole scenario resembles a feast before a journey – a rite of passage.

The stone enclosures are without parallels in the written sources. The so-called wall around Beowulf's cremation remains that was built after the funeral is ambiguous. The uncertainty regarding the point during the process at which the stone enclosures were built means that there are many possible interpretations of their meaning in the ritual. The enclosure forms a closed space. Supposing that it was built before the funeral, the enclosure was thus a place which might be used for the preliminary deposition of the deceased in order to gradually segregate him/her from the bereaved. Ibn Fadlan describes how a man who has fallen ill is segregated in a tent, and in the same way the deceased Rus is segregated in a preliminary grave before he was actually cremated (cf. Schjødt 2003: 350). It ought thus to be considered possible that the deceased may have been preliminarily buried in an above-ground structure, such as a tent, within a stone enclosure.

If a funeral at Lindholm Høje is regarded as a process, a perspective is achieved which allows a better understanding of late Iron Age mortuary practices at Lindholm Høje and probably other sites in southern Scandinavia. The funeral was initiated by a feast including all proper preparations and culminated in an afterlife journey for the deceased. The rituals were staged in the same way that they would have been if (s)he was just moving away in this world. While the destination was in this case the 'other world', it may have been viewed as very similar to the world of the living. There is therefore also no real need for the covering of the remains after the cremation: the deceased had – almost literally – gone with the wind.

Chapter 7

Barrows, roads and ridges – or where to bury the dead? The choice of burial grounds in late Iron Age Scandinavia

Eva S. Thäte

Abstract
This article deals with the topography of Scandinavian burial grounds in the late Iron Age which in this region, is the period between AD 500 and 1000. In Denmark, Norway and Sweden people buried their deceased in or at ancient burial mounds, on high ground, close to water (rivers and coastal areas) and near roads or boundaries. The question is *why* did people choose a particular place for burial – or was it completely random? While the custom of reusing ancient funerary monuments for the dead may have had to do with hereditary rights to property in the first place, the historical sources show that the placing of cemeteries elsewhere in the landscape matches with concepts of the afterlife. Were some features more important than others? Are we seeing 'competitive topographies'? Modern studies on near-death experiences show that the aforementioned landscape features may be archetypes with a liminal meaning, and the theory is put forward that people chose sites which covered as many topographical features as possible.

Order my troop to construct a barrow
on a headland on the coast, after my pyre has cooled.
It will loom on the horizon at Hronesness
and be a reminder among my people–
so that in coming times crews under sail

will call it Beowulf's Barrow, as they steer
ships across the wide and shrouded waters.
(*Beowulf*, v 2802–8 ff, Heaney 1999: 72)

Introduction

The reuse of ancient monuments for burial in pre- and protohistoric
times is a mortuary custom which has become a field of archaeological
research during the last two decades. This burial practice has been
recognized in various parts of north-west Europe, in particular in
Great Britain, Germany and Scandinavia (cf. Bradley 1987; Holtorf
1998; 2000–2007; Semple 1998; Sopp 1999; Thäte 1993; 1996; 2007a;
Williams 1997; 1998a; 1998b). Research on this topic has shown that
ancient people probably used older monuments as burial sites in order
to link themselves or their deceased relatives to their own (or invented)
ancestors. One of the purposes of this custom was to secure the ruling
positions of elites. For example, in his interpretation of the location
of the seventh-century weapon burial beneath a barrow on Lowbury
Hill, Oxfordshire, Heinrich Härke addressed the barrow's proximity
to the visible ruins of a Romano-Celtic temple. He interpreted this as a
prominent means for the Anglo-Saxon elite to assert their relationships
with a native past as a means of establishing a common identity at
the time of the formation of the West Saxon kingdom and the ethnic
mixing with peoples of British and Germanic origin (Härke 1994a).

Another reason for reusing barrows for burial was to legitimate
claims to land and property. The *Gulathing Law*, for instance, which
dates back to the Viking Age, stresses the importance of genealogical
lines for the possession of land. The so-called *odal* was connected to
this law. The *odal* was hereditary land and this land could only be
called *odal* after it had been in the family for at least five generations
(Gulathing Law 270, Larson 1935: 178). This shows the importance of
ancestors for 'title to property'. Historical accounts also demonstrate
a link between ancestors, graves and land rights. A Welsh chronicle,
the so-called Book of Llandaff (the Ancient Register of the Cathedral
Church of Llandaff, dating to the twelfth century), mentions two kings
who granted land to the church whilst sitting or lying on the tomb of
their father and grandfather respectively (Ellis 1943: 107). In the Norse
sagas a similar case is mentioned: a Norse king who conferred his realm
to the king Harald Fairhair rolled himself down from a burial mound,
symbolizing with this action the loss of his kingdom (*Heimskringla* III
8, Laing and Beveridge 1930a: 55). Consequently, burying a deceased
relative in or next to an already existing grave mound may have
represented a claim to kinship and to hereditary property rights. Thus,

Fig. 7.1: The
frequency of
the late Iron
Age reuse of
earlier funerary
monuments
taken as a
percentage of
datable burial
sites from three
regions in
Scandinavia.

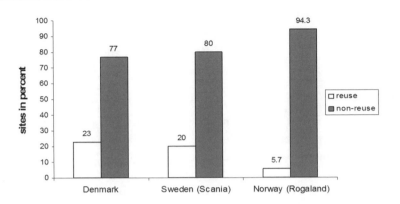

'ancestors' and 'legitimation' are the key words in this field of research,
and monument reuse has become an important focus for discussing the
roles of cemeteries as early medieval 'places of power' (Härke 2001).
Funerary monuments such as barrows, but also ruined houses, were
reused in such a way.

However, are different interpretations possible? If the legitimation
theory is right it would make sense if not everybody was buried
in ancient burial mounds. My research on late Iron Age reuse sites
(c.AD 500/600–1000) in Scandinavia, which included ancient Denmark
(including parts of North Germany), south Sweden[1] and south-west
Norway,[2] confirms this argument, and also supports the idea that there
is more to burial location than simply monument reuse.[3]

For example, in Rogaland in Norway (Fig. 7.1) there is a surprisingly
low percentage of reuse. This can be related to excavation methods
(most graves were discovered before the 1930s, i.e. before monument
reuse was a significant research topic). Excavations at this time were
often focused on the Bronze Age material in a mound, while other
finds were ignored. In the southern part of Viking Age Sweden, too,
the number of reuse sites is quite low.

Figures 7.1 and 7.2 demonstrate that a significant number of
monuments were reused, but also that a large number of burial sites
did not utilize reuse and that other landscape features played a role
in selecting burial location. This evidence raises doubt over whether

---

[1]   This includes the counties of Scania, Blekinge, Småland and Halland.

[2]   i.e. Rogaland, and samples from Hordaland, Sogn og Fjordane and Møre og
      Romsdal.

[3]   The term 'reuse' is defined here as funerary monuments that were used again
      for burial after a time gap of at least one period or at least after 200 years after
      their construction or prior use.

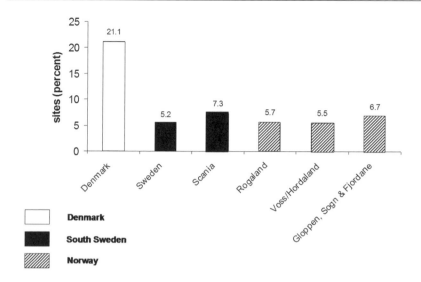

Fig. 7.2: The reuse of funerary monuments in south Scandinavia in the Viking Age (%).

monuments and the use of the past had really always been the most important factor influencing the placing of the dead. And it also raises a number of questions. *Why* did people choose a particular place for burial? Or was the choice of burial sites just random? Which other topographical factors apart from monuments may have influenced the choice of burial sites (see Williams 1999)? In order to see what was more important – monuments (such as barrows and houses) or other landscape features – I used the catalogue of Scandinavian reuse sites compiled for my doctoral thesis (Thäte 2007a) as a basis for research. The catalogue contains 162 cases of ancient funerary monuments

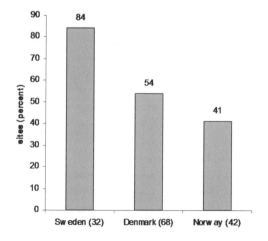

Fig. 7.3: Monument reuse sites related to other aspects of topography (%).

that have been reused by late Iron Age graves. It showed that a large percentage of sites had other topographical connections alongside their combination with earlier monuments (Fig. 7.3).

Where else besides into or close to earlier monuments did the ancient Scandinavians bury their dead? Three more significant topographical features appear relevant. These are: locations on high ground; watery locations; and associations with roads. Here, these features are investigated through the systematic analysis of a sample of burial sites from different regions of late Iron Age Scandinavia but they are found also elsewhere in north-west Europe (Bärenfänger 1988; Rötting 1985; Thäte 1993; 1996).

All three listed topographical features show some significance in relation to beliefs about the afterlife and may have been regarded as 'liminal' regions[4] between the inhabited world of the living and the supernatural. In what follows these features will be discussed. Boundaries also played a significant role. However, relatively little research has been done on the relation between burials and boundaries in Scandinavia, and since this would have been an extensive study in its own right which would have been out of the scope of this article this topic will not be discussed here (see Thäte 2007a).

High-ground locations

Figure 7.4 demonstrates that high-ground locations played an important role in all three Scandinavian countries (Sweden: 81.2%; Denmark: 50%; Norway: 38.1%). This kind of location could include shore embankments, but usually graves were placed on moraine ridges with a good view of the surrounding landscape. However, the visibility of the site from elsewhere will have been at least as important, as the Anglo-Saxon poem *Beowulf* demonstrates. Here, the hero wanted to be buried in a place where he could be seen so that people would remember him (*Beowulf* v. 2804–08, Heaney 1999: 88). Thus, visibility was an important factor for promoting the 'memory' of the deceased. In Denmark, in some cases the oldest or wealthiest graves were indeed placed on the highest locations. For instance, a social distinction becomes apparent at the cemetery of Kaagården on Langeland in

---

[4] The term 'liminal' can be probably best described as 'betwixt and between' or as 'not here and not there': it is a stage of transition and change. Liminal places comprise all kinds of borders and all locations people pass through but do not live in. Shores, rivers, mountains, roads, passes and bridges, for instance, are 'liminal', as are places which denote the transition from life to death – as grave mounds, for instance, do.

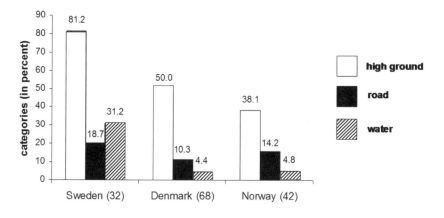

Fig. 7.4: Single topographical categories compared to reuse sites in the catalogue (%).

Denmark, where the richest graves were found on top of the hill, whereas the poorer graves had been dug further down (Eisenschmidt 1994: 125). This also applies to the exceedingly wealthy boat burial at the site of Ladby on the island of Fyn, Denmark, which contained around 600 artefacts. The boat was placed on the northern side of a plateau while the accompanying graves were located on lower ground on the opposite side of the hill. These graves were poorly furnished, and rarely contained more than a knife (cf. Müller-Wille 1987: 73, Abb. 24; 74). The ancient Scandinavians apparently had a conception of landscape and the afterlife which linked 'height' and 'status'. Indeed, several medieval Scandinavian written sources indicate that the top of a mound served as a 'high seat' for the king. John Meier describes how the subjects of a king had their seats on different levels according to their status when meetings on such a mound took place (Meier 1950: 23, footnote 2). Placing oneself on a lower level symbolized a loss of rank, as indicated in Snorri Sturlason's *Heimskringla*, which gives an account of two kingly brothers, Herlaug and Rollaug, who had built a barrow. When Harald Fairhair marched against them with his army, Herlaug went into the mound with drink and food, whilst:

> King Rollaug ... went upon the summit of the mound, on which the kings were wont to sit, and made a throne to be erected, upon which he seated himself. Then he ordered feather-beds to be laid upon the bench below, on which the earls were wont to be seated, and threw himself down from his high seat or throne into the earls' seat, giving himself the title of earl. Now Rollaug went to meet King Harald, gave up to him his whole kingdom, offered to enter into his service, and told him his whole proceeding. (*Heimskringla* III 8, Laing and Beveridge 1930a: 55)

The placing of graves may have even expressed a hierarchical distinction between men and women. For example, at Stengade, on the island of Langeland in Denmark, the upper part of a hill was used for men's graves while women were buried 1.60 to 3.30m below (Grøn *et al.* 1994: 159).

Apart from the secular aspects of visibility and status there is also a religious component. The idea that high-ground locations were chosen to facilitate contact with heathen supernatural powers is alluded to in the *Gulathing Law* (a Norwegian law of the tenth/eleventh century AD). It states that 'heathen sacrifices are also banned for we are not permitted to worship any heathen god, or (on any) hill, or (in) any heathen fane' (*Gulathing Law* 29, Larson 1935: 57). The *Landnámabók*, by Ari Froði Þorgilsson, in which the settlement of Iceland in the Viking Age is described, also gives accounts of Icelandic mountains being regarded as holy features in the landscape:

> Thorolf settled land from Staff river inwards to Thors river, and called all that part Thorsness. He had so great a reverence for that fell which stands on the ness, and which he called Helgafell [Holy Fell], that he enjoined that thither should no man unwashen look, and there was so great place hallowedness [sanctuary] that nothing should be destroyed on the mountain, neither cattle nor people, unless they should go away on their own accord ... That was the belief of them [Thorolf and his kinsmen], that they should die into the mountain. (*Landnámabók* II 12, Ellwood 1908: 53)

The kinsmen of Queen Auð, who was one of the first settlers of Iceland, also believed they would die into the hills which Auð had chosen as a place for her Christian worship (*Landnámabók* II 16, Ellwood 1908: 65).

The aforementioned passages demonstrate that high ground was not only linked to status but also to religious beliefs and afterlife concepts. It fits into a world-view in which hills and mountains were regarded as liminal places: they are thresholds between settled areas and the wilderness; they are unattractive places to live in and usually have to be crossed. Mountains were also places 'betwixt and between' the human and spiritual world: they were often considered as seats of gods and in Scandinavia they were also regarded as the habitat of supernatural beings such as trolls and other uncanny creatures.

The mountain as a liminal residence for kings and other men of high status is also known from myths and legends in other parts of north-western Europe. Examples from Germany include Charles V, who was said to live in Odin's Mountain near Kassel (Lyckner 1854: 5–7), Frederick Barbarossa in the Kyffhäuser Mountains (Grimm and

Grimm 1816/18) and Emperor Heinrich in the Sudemer Mountain (Kuhn and Schwartz 1848: 184–85). There are wider parallels still, with the legend of Arthur and his warriors sleeping in a hill at Craig-y-Dinas, Wales (Waring 1850) and St Wenceslas and his knights residing in Mount Blaník, the Czech Republic (Quitzmann 1860: 47). These are only a few examples of a larger range of legends which emphasize the significance of mountains, hills and other high-ground sites in the afterlife beliefs linked to the residences of heroes and ancestors.

Watery locations

The position of burial places on high ground was also frequently connected with water. Watercourses often run parallel to ridges (Bengtsdotter 1995: 8), while the locations may also provide vistas of lakes or bays. Especially in Norway, boat graves were generally situated along the coastline (Solberg 2000: 223; Næss 1996: 85) and in Rogaland they were usually placed in such a way that they provided a view over a river, brook or the coastline (pers. comm. O. Hemdorff, Arkeologisk museum i Stavanger).

Beowulf, the hero of the eponymous poem, wanted to be buried at a place where ships pass by, which shows a deliberate choice of such a site (*Beowulf* v. 2804–08, Heaney 1999: 88). Apart from his wish to be commemorated, the choice of a site near the water probably symbolised another concept of death: the travel across water in order to reach the otherworld. The Norse sagas mention funerals performed by setting loose a ship on water, although they do not give an explanation of the custom (*Skjöldunga Saga* XXVI acc. to Ellis 1943: 43; *Ynglinga Saga* I 27, Laing and Beveridge 1930a: 24; *Gylfaginning* 49, Wilken 1912; cf. *Beowulf* v. 34–52, Heaney 1999: 4). According to Emil Birkeli, a specialist in European ethnography, the basis for such a belief may have been descriptions of the residences of the gods in the sagas, which were said to be surrounded by water (Birkeli 1943: 116–17; cf. Ellis 1943: 45; Hedeager 2001: 503). In his *Gesta Danorum* the Danish historian Saxo Grammaticus (twelfth century AD) also mentioned a journey to the otherworld in which the travellers had to cross a 'river of blue-black water, swirling in headlong descent and spinning in its swift eddies weapons of various kinds' (Saxo Grammaticus I 30, Fisher and Ellis Davidson 1979: 31). A bridge that led across the water had to be traversed. The same scene appears in *Gylfaginning* (Gylfi's Bewitchment) in the Prose Edda: Hermod travelled to Hel in order to find there Odin's second son Baldr, who had died. On his journey Hermod came to the river Gjöll, which could be crossed on a golden bridge (Gylfi's Betörung XLIX, Neckel and Niedner 1942: 106).

Water was clearly regarded as a symbol of 'transition' and therefore had a liminal connotation. In Viking Age Iceland the liminality of watercourses was additionally emphasized by their frequent use as boundaries of properties. These boundaries were also used as places for burial (pers. comm. Adolf Friðriksson).

In the same way, Queen Auð's choice of a location for her burial appears doubly liminal:

> The next day she [Auð] died and was buried on the shore, between high and low water mark, even as herself had ordered, for this reason, that she would not lie in unhallowed earth being baptized. (*Landnámabók*, II 19, Ellwood 1908: 69)

Near the sea (liminal place 1), Auð had chosen a place betwixt and between for her grave: the border (liminal place 2) between land and sea. One may wonder if she still had some unconscious pagan concepts of death and afterlife in her mind. Was she aware of the Christian concept of only murderers and other social outcasts being buried in such places, as the *Gulathing Law* stated (*Gulathing Law* 23, Larson 1935: 51), believing that it was better to be buried in such a place than in unhallowed earth?

Nevertheless, the aforementioned cases show that the construction of King Olaf's barrow next to a river may not only have been a matter of practicality alone:

> Thorgils Halmeson and his son Grim had King Olaf's body, and were anxious about preserving it from falling into the hands of the king's enemies, and being ill-treated; for they heard the bonders speaking about burning it, or sinking it in the sea ... Then Thorgils and his men went with the body higher up the river, buried it in a sand-hill on the banks, and levelled all around it so that no one could observe that people had been at work here. (*Saint Olaf's Saga* 251, Laing and Beveridge 1930b: 383–84)

Roads

Roads and tracks are other features of importance in the placing of burials. This is not only a north European pattern: Elisabeth Schlicht believed that it was an Indo-European custom to place graves near main roads, noting that 'urn cemeteries as well as Iron-Age and Bronze-Age barrows are often adjacent to the ancient lines of communication in loose lines or groups' (Schlicht n.d.: 78, trans. E.S.T). Roman graves, too, were placed alongside roads (Hope 2003: 123; Kossack 1974: 15), and this was also common practice in Eastern Europe and Central Asia (Härke 2001: 15; Marschallek 1964: 419).

Unfortunately, there has not been much research on this topic in Scandinavia, probably because tracks are not as conspicuous as, for instance, Roman roads in England, and because dating trackways is difficult. Recent research on this topic, however, has been undertaken by the Swedish archaeologist Elisabeth Rudebeck who focused on the period between the late Neolithic and the early Iron Age. She highlighted the frequency of the combination of road and burial in prehistoric times in Sweden (Rudebeck 2001; 2002), and also pointed out another problem in the identification of ancient roads: many modern roads may cover ancient tracks today (cf. Rudebeck 2001: 95–97; for Germany cf. Marschallek 1964: 425). A combination of ancient roads, Bronze Age barrows and late Iron Age graves are often found on high ground, which makes it difficult to decide if such juxtapositions were only coincidental or deliberate. Nevertheless, there are cases which show a deliberate choice of roads as burial sites, two of which should be mentioned here.

One example is the cemetery of Fyrkat in Jutland: here, 28 graves were situated near a wooden track 40m long and 5m wide. The wealthiest graves (wagon grave 4, wagon grave 20 and double grave 22) were interred right next to the track, demonstrating that roads were apparently significant in terms of status (Roesdahl 1977: 77, fig. 86). Roesdahl suggested that this exceptional juxtaposition of road and cemetery indicates that the road had a 'ceremonial' function (Roesdahl and Nordquist 1971: 17; Roesdahl 1977: 145). It is, however, doubtful if this juxtaposition is really so unusual or if the scarcity of this combination is rather due to excavation methods and the aforementioned problem of modern roads overlying ancient tracks.

Another example dates to a somewhat earlier period but appears so significant that it shall be mentioned here. At the cemetery of Møllegårdsmarken, Gudme sogn in Svendborg amt in Denmark, a hollow way was used for funerary rites. The burials of the late Roman Iron Age and Migration Period respected the track, but at some stage a platform for a pyre was constructed on its western section. This construction and the hollow way had been in use contemporaneously. It is also significant that the way was close to a ford (Madsen 1995: 152), which emphasizes again the aforementioned relationship between cemeteries and watercourses (cf. Hedeager 2001: 503). Both cases show that roads may have been significant for rituals at cemeteries, and therefore had symbolic meaning.

The written sources do not often mention roads in association with mortuary beliefs. The *Heimskringla* (Olaf sagas), for instance, mentioned the burial of a child in a road:

Now when the coffin was set down, the street was broken up to see what was under it at that spot, and the body of a child was found which had been murdered and concealed there. (*Olaf the Quiet* XI 7, Laing and Beveridge 1930a: 245–46).

One may wonder if this had really been a case of murder or if people at that time interpreted an ancient burial in their own, by then Christian, ways. By way of comparison, in the Anglo-Saxon regions, for instance, there is clear archaeological evidence of burial into Roman road surfaces (cf. Thäte 1996: 109).

Another historical source is the *Hávamál* (Elder Edda), which says:

It is well to have a son, though he is born late after the death of his father. Seldom will memorial stones be seen by the roadside unless placed there by one relative for another. (*Hávamál*, v. 72, Clarke 1923: 61).

But roads are not much emphasized in the Norse sagas. Ellis has given some examples where the road was used as a means to travel to the land of the dead and there is some evidence of the road to Hel leading downwards and to the north: 'en niðr ok norðr liggr Helvegr' (*Gylfaginning* 49, Wilken 1912: 77; Ellis 1943: 172). There is one instance where the living hero of the story, Hadingus, travelled a country which probably represented a kind of pre-world or entrance area to the beyond: 'First they penetrated a smoky veil of darkness, then walked along a path worn away by long ages of travellers ...' (*Saxo Grammaticus* I 30, Fisher and Ellis Davidson 1979: 30) until they reached a wall which apparently represented the boundary to the otherworld.

Bridges as parts of roads seem to have been more important in the sagas. Here, the religious concept of crossing a river to the land of the dead may have played a role (Ellis 1943: 171; *Gylfaginning*, 49; Wilken 1912: 73 ff). But the road itself may also have been understood as a liminal feature. It is likely that roads near the boundaries of communal areas symbolized the transition between 'the known' and 'the unknown' (Rudebeck 2001: 107). There is also a mystic character associated with the 'distance' represented by roads and the process of travelling (Helms 1988; Herschend 2001; Rittner 1973). The liminal character of crossroads became particularly apparent in Christian times, when these locations were regarded as places of harmful supernatural powers (Griffiths 1996: 35; Reynolds 2002: 181).

Competitive topographies?

Having discussed the relevance of some topographical characteristics that were important for burial in late Iron Age Scandinavia in addition to the association with ancient monuments, let us turn to the original question of how important monuments were compared to these other landscape features. Are we dealing with 'competitive topographies' between different, contrasting, choices of burial location? There are indeed several examples which show that ancient monuments were not always the primary attractions for burial sites.

An interesting example is the Viking Age cemetery of Tollemosegård in Denmark (Fig. 7.5). Here, a megalithic grave on top of a ridge was apparently not the most significant focus for the later graves. Only a few graves were related to the dolmen, while a larger number of burials focused around an empty circular space in the centre of the cemetery some 40m away. This space may indicate the former presence of a ploughed-out barrow or a natural hill. One may wonder if the large and well-equipped grave Æ located some 20m from the ancient monument sought the vicinity of the megalithic dolmen or rather the prominent position of the place (Lai Sørensen 1998).

Fig. 7.5: Plan of the late Iron Age cemetery of Tollemosegård in Denmark (after excavation plan; reproduced with the kind permission of Museet Færgegården, Jægerspris, Denmark).

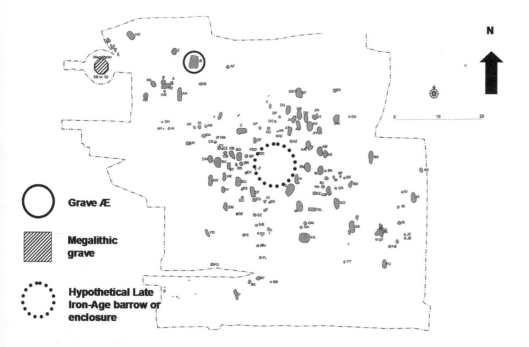

O Grave Æ

▨ Megalithic grave

⬭ Hypothetical Late Iron-Age barrow or enclosure

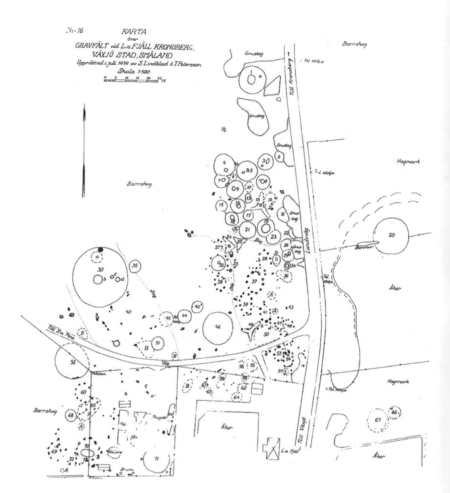

Fig. 7.6: Plan of the cemetery of Fjäll Kronoberg in Småland showing the juxtaposition of a Bronze Age barrow (no. 30), a late Iron Age cemetery and a (modern) road. (Karta över Gravfält vid Lia Fjäll Kronoberg, Växjö Stad, Småland, Nr. 16; S. Lindblad and T. Petersson 1939; reproduced with the kind permission of Smålands museum, Växjö).

In the case of the Lousgård cemetery on Bornholm, Denmark, the most prominent position was taken by one of the largest and wealthiest graves: the grave of a woman. However, this grave was also close to an ancient monument, a Neolithic stone setting (Lyngstrøm 1989).

The same issue arises at some burial sites in Sweden. At the site of Fjäll Kronoberg in Småland (Fig. 7.6), some Bronze Age barrows, a late Iron Age cemetery and a (modern) road were all juxtaposed. These features were located on top of a large moraine ridge. Again, only a few structures were close to the supposed Bronze Age mound (Martin Hansson, pers. comm.), while most of the late Iron Age graves extended along the road for a length of c.750m. It is debatable if they were related to an ancient road or if the graves only followed the direction of the extension of the ridge. However, since the road formed the boundary

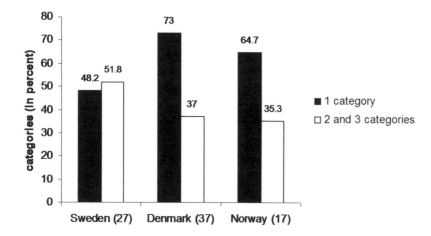

Fig. 7.7:
Combinations
of topographical
categories of
Scandinavian
cemeteries in the
catalogue (%).

of the cemetery it is very likely that the graves respected an earlier feature, a road or track, at this place.

At Ljungbacka in Scania, Sweden, the same pattern is apparent. The cemetery was located on a low ridge and right next to a Bronze Age barrow. However, the main part of the cemetery stretched out along an invisible boundary. Interestingly, this boundary matches the historical route of a former road (Samuelsson 2001; 2003).[5]

In Norway, too, the juxtaposition of roads and burial sites is apparent, although there are not many examples in my own research area in Rogaland (probably because in the old excavation reports topographical aspects are not often mentioned). Arne Skjølsvold observed a juxtaposition of ancient roads and Iron Age burials in the highlands of southern Norway. These graves were placed alongside the same roads several kilometres from each other (Skjølsvold 1980: 154). Heid Gjøstein Resi, too, noted that graves were often positioned close to roads or tracks (Resi 1989: 20).

All these examples – chosen from a larger number of cases – show that ancient monuments, although important, were not always the most significant feature of cemetery location where reuse occurs. The ancestors, although essential for legitimation, had to share their importance with other religious, mythical or spiritual concepts

---

[5] Samuelsson pointed out that roads sometimes had a supra-regional character. Main routes possibly stood under the control of a king – and this road was the main route leading to an important central place called Uppåkra near Lund. So roads may have had some significance as royal constructions, and this may have made them attractive for burial also in terms of status (Samuelsson 2003).

and ideas. High-ground locations seem to have been exceptionally interesting, as already pointed out at the beginning of this article. Figure 7.7 shows examples where topographical categories are combined in burial location. It becomes apparent that a large percentage of sites included more than one additional topographical category (beyond the presence of earlier monuments). In Sweden 52% of the reuse sites have more than one category; the percentages are 37% in Denmark and 35% in Norway. Is there a possibility that people looked for such combinations rather than these topographical categories being in competition with each other?

All of the aforementioned topographical categories – high-ground locations, roads, water and boundaries (although the latter had to be neglected here) – can be linked to liminal, supernatural and religious aspects. One should not forget that the belief in ancestors (who are buried under barrows) also has religious or supernatural characteristics. Barrows as entrances to the otherworld, as mentioned in the Norse sagas (Ellis 1943: 193), were clearly liminal and the way people dealt with their ancestors shows a belief in a life after death. An early medieval written source, the *Vita Vulframni*, demonstrates the importance of the ancestors for the pagan people. When the Frisian King Radbod was about to get baptized he asked if he would meet his ancestors in heaven. The answer was 'no' – and Radbod then rejected the whole ceremony as he could not do without this community and did not feel like sitting around in heaven with a bunch of poor people (*Vita Vulframni* 9, Levison 1910: 668).

The *Beowulf* poem, too, supports a deliberate choice of a combination of topographical features for burial: Beowulf wanted his barrow to be built on high ground, next to a supposedly megalithic barrow (*Beowulf* v. 2409–13, Heaney 1999: 76; Semple 1998: 109) and near a watercourse. Since he gave no reasons for his choice of place it seems likely that the poet anticipated that his audience would recognize that the decision over burial location was carefully considered.

The choice of places for burial: a psychological approach

Why did the ancient Scandinavians choose these places for burial? Where did these liminal landscape concepts come from? A special, probably psychological, phenomenon may provide an answer to these questions: the so-called near-death experience (Gebühr 2001).

The term 'near-death experience' describes the condition of people who are clinically dead but during this time have an out-of-body experience and often a glimpse on the 'otherworld'. The sense of a bright light or the entering of a tunnel are sensations that are often reported. But there are more aspects involved. Obviously, the individuals who could talk about their experience sooner or later had to reach a return point. These return points are often described as a kind of boundary. These boundaries can be invisible but they can also appear as fences, walls, doors or gates. In some cases mountains or water have to be passed or crossed to reach the beyond (cf. Kellehear 1996; 2007; Moody 1977; Zaleski 1987; see also Long and Long 1999, near-death experience archive; Gebühr 2001). A relative of mine who had a near-death experience recounted that she could not cross the water that was between her and the other side. Here, the boat or ship may be a vital element. Several accounts of near-death experiences include journeys on a ship or a boat (cf. Moody 1977; Long and Long 1999: nos 807 and 805). Roads, too, belong to the set of topographical features seen during such experiences (Long and Long 1999: nos 1379, 774, 699, 600, 418, 353, 335). In one case it was a crossroads which served as a boundary: to the right was death and to the left was life (Long and Long 1999: no. 241). Many accounts mention the appearance of already-deceased relatives and even unknown ancestors (Moody 1977; Long and Long 1999). Gebühr, who analysed a catalogue of 116 near-death experiences (compiled by Sabom 1982), suggested that people who do not go to church meet their relatives in the otherworld rather than God or Jesus (Gebühr 2001: 194–95). This could explain the close linkage between pagan people and their ancestors.

Explanations for near-death experiences vary; they have been discussed in medical, psychological, religious and sociological disciplines (see Parnia 2006). However, this article does not aim to discuss whether near-death experiences are genuine afterlife journeys or not. It is only relevant that people who experience them *believe* their experiences are real. When comparing the archaeological evidence it is striking how Viking Age concepts of locations for burial and topographical features linked to the otherworld match the findings of thanatology today. Is it possible that there is a link between them? Is it possible that individuals in the Viking Age had similar 'death visions' to those of modern people?

This suggestion is supported by earlier accounts of near-death experiences reaching back to medieval times and still earlier periods (cf., for instance, *The Dialogues of Gregory the Great*, parts of the *Gilgamesh* epos or Plato's *Republic*: Zaleski 1987; Parnia 2006: 15–17). The sociologist A. Kellehear believes that they might reach as far back as the Stone Age (Kellehear 2007), and notes that they seem to be also a cross-cultural phenomenon (cf. Kellehear 1996; Parnia 2006).

The universality of this phenomenon may be best explained by the fact that the aforementioned recurrent features and landscapes of 'the otherworld' have archetypal characteristics in psychological terms.[6] Archetypes are part of the human unconscious and can, for instance, appear in dreams. Although people who describe a near-death experience usually state that it was not dreamlike, their body was in an 'unconscious' condition, and, for those who have not experienced it the closest analogy to this state of body and mind could be sleep.

The Swiss psychiatrist C.G. Jung, the founder of analytical psychology, established the archetype theory. He has defined the term 'archetype' as follows:

> A more or less superficial layer of the unconscious is undoubtedly personal. I call it the personal unconscious. But this personal unconscious rests upon a deeper layer, which does not derive from personal experience and is ... inborn. This deeper layer I call the collective unconscious. ... The contents of the collective unconscious ... are known as archetypes. (Jung 1968: 3–4)

These features he identified as 'primordial types' and 'universal images' reaching back into distant times (Jung 1968: 5). This would mean that such images can appear in people's minds at any time and in any place no matter if they know about them or not. This knowledge would be *a priori*.

Jung described all the aforementioned landscape features in his book on *Archetypes and the Collective Unconscious*. Moreover, he put them into spiritual context, which matches the 'otherworld' aspect of such features in near-death experiences. Two dreams he described contained most types of topographical categories mentioned in this article. First, he illustrated one of his own dreams:

> I was climbing slowly and toilsomely up a *mountain*. When I had reached, as I imagined, the top, I found that I was standing on the edge of a *plateau*. The crest that represented the real top of the mountain only rose far off in the distance. Night was coming on, and I saw, on the dark *slope* opposite, a *brook* flowing down with a metallic shimmer, and two *paths* leading upwards, one to the left, the other to the right, winding like serpents. On the crest, to the right, there was a *hotel* [reminiscent of the house – cf. Thäte 2007b]. Down below, the brook ran to the left with a *bridge* leading across. (Jung 1968: 193; emphases E.S.T.)

---

6   Tore Artelius, for instance, explained the use of the boat in prehistoric Swedish burial rites by using Jung's archetype theory (Artelius 1996). Gebühr, too, refers to the recurrent images of near-death experiences as archetypes (Gebühr 2001, 196).

Jung pointed out that this agrees with patterns in an ancient text from 1602, and suggested that the recurrent images were likely to be archetypes (Jung 1968: 193–94). He mentioned another 'archetypal dream' with 'spiritual content' which was described by a theologian:

> He saw on a mountain a kind of *Castle* [the house?] of the Grail. He went along a *road* that seemed to lead straight to the foot of the *mountain* and up it. But as he drew nearer he discovered to his great disappointment that a chasm separated him from the mountain, a deep, darksome gorge with underworldly *water* rushing along the bottom. A steep *path* led downwards and toilsomely climbed up again on the other side … (Jung 1968: 19; emphases E.S.T.)

If such landscape features really represent archetypes it is likely that the same images occurred in people's minds in the late Iron Age in Scandinavia (and also elsewhere). The aforementioned stories about Hadingus, who travelled on a road and Hermod, who saw the river Gjöll and the golden bridge across it, are experiences that particularly resemble near-death experiences and Jung's archetypal dreams.

Conclusion

The archaeological evidence suggests that various topographical features apart from monuments were important for the placing of burial grounds. The archaeological evidence and the historical sources demonstrate that the ancient Scandinavians regarded high-ground locations and water, as well as roads, as significant for burial. Boundaries, too, seem to have played an important role for burial, although there has not been much research on this topic in Scandinavia yet.

Secondary burial in mounds and the use of high ground and roads for burial were all apparently linked to status. While one aspect of monument reuse was linked to claims to land and property, the use of high-ground locations may have had to do with visibility and the wish to be commemorated. It is also possible that the idea of a protector and guardian was of significance here. Roads, too, were clearly important in terms of visibility. It is likely that individuals of high status were in the position to claim the best locations close to these landscape features.

Although high-ground locations were clearly preferred for burial, there are indictions that combinations of landscape features were sought. Apart from status-related explanations, cosmological concepts played a crucial role, as the historical sources suggest.

It is not unlikely that cosmological concepts relating to the afterlife were based on stories of people who claimed that they had seen the otherworld. The theory of archetypal images in near-death experiences might explain why there was such a variety of choices for a burial place for a pagan Scandinavian individual in the late Iron Age. It is likely that places where several topographical features were available were chosen deliberately in order to match as many concepts as possible. It may have also been important to have a choice between several kinds of boundaries to the otherworld in order to prepare for possible alternative afterlife destinations. Stories of the otherworld – which, quite probably, were not told as often as nowadays for medical reasons – may have influenced the choice of location and changed preferences.

The reuse of ancient burial mounds can also be tied into this idea of afterlife beliefs: several sources show how important the ancestors were especially for people of higher status, and meeting deceased kinsmen after death was part of the afterlife concept, as the *Vita Vulframni* demonstrates. Thus, next to the legitimation of claims to land and property, it may have been as important to be physically close to the ancestors in death in order to be able to meet them in the otherworld.

Acknowledgements

I am grateful to Duncan Sayer and Howard Williams for inviting me to contribute to this volume. Many thanks to Howard Williams and Tony Walter for their helpful comments and advice on this paper. As this article is based on a chapter of my PhD thesis I would also like to thank Heinrich Härke, who was my supervisor, for his support and encouragement, and for proofreading earlier versions of this text.

Chapter 8

Anglo-Saxon DNA?

Catherine Hills

Abstract

In recent years, geneticists have turned their attention to population
movements in the past, including that of the Anglo-Saxons to Britain.
The conclusions proposed have been contradictory, ranging from genocide
of Britons by invading Frisians during the fifth century to the arrival
of Germanic speaking peoples before the Romans. What sense can we
make of this, and how far has this really advanced our understanding
of what happened in the North Sea region during the fifth and sixth
centuries A D?

F OR MUCH OF HIS ACADEMIC CAREER Heinrich Härke has
worked on the archaeology of Anglo-Saxon burials, with particular
interest in the question of the identification of immigrant Anglo-
Saxons as opposed to native Britons. In 1991 he appeared in an episode
of the Channel 4 TV programme *Down to Earth*, introducing a project
to extract ancient DNA from Anglo-Saxon burials. He explained his
thesis that in 'Anglo-Saxon' cemeteries men of British and Anglo-
Saxon descent could be distinguished. This argument rested partly on
his demonstration that weapons were buried with males who might be
too young, old or disabled to bear arms, so they had been chosen to be
buried with weapons on grounds other than that they were able-bodied
men of fighting age. He also used osteological evidence which seemed
to show that weapon-bearing males were taller than those without
weapons, to argue that they might belong to a different ethnic group:
tall robust incoming Germanic warriors with weapons, as opposed to
small native Britons without (Härke 1990a, 1992b). This thesis attracted
criticism from various directions, which Heinrich Härke discussed in

an amusing paper which compared the differing reactions of English and German scholars to his findings: the latter were surprised there was any doubt that there had been large-scale invasion, the former rejected the idea that there had been any significant population change (Härke 1998). This divergence, as Härke showed, had more to do with recent scholarly and political histories than with the fifth century A D. Also, amongst British scholars, confidence in the traditional equation between material culture and ethnicity has been undermined in recent decades, partly through awareness of anthropological research in this area. Another recent paper by Härke (2007b) develops this theme by showing that there has been change in material culture in the former Soviet Union during the past decade of the kind archaeologists might once have attributed to invasion. Osteology seemed a safer, more neutral, means of approaching the subject. Epigenetic traits could indicate family groups, and studies of tooth morphology suggested that population continuity could be identified in southern England (Gowland 2007; Lloyd-Jones 1997). However, the skeleton is subject to environmental and even cultural influences (Sofaer 2006): stature is not wholly genetically determined and so a difference in height does not necessarily mean a difference in ancestry.

At the time of the TV programme it seemed that a new scientific method, the extraction of ancient DNA from excavated bones, offered the possibility of a definitive answer to the questions Härke was asking. The presenter (Roberta Gilchrist in a telegenic orange jacket), explained the principles of the process in an upbeat way, set against a backdrop of excavated skeletons, laboratories and a throng of modern people. At one point in the programme it looked as if Germanic and British genetic codes were unrolling side by side on the screen.

The results were discussed briefly in two papers (Richards *et al.* 1993; Richards and Sykes 1995). The first paper referred to tentative results (Richards *et al.* 1993: 23) while the latter paper, a discussion of the problems involved in extracting ancient DNA, explained that one sequence was identical to that of one of the operators. While it seemed that the DNA of pig bones from the Mary Rose could be identified, the Anglo-Saxon and Romano-British human bones were subject to a high risk of contamination: the DNA being amplified was possibly that of recent excavators or scientists, not of Anglo-Saxons. The high hopes of the TV programme were not fulfilled and Heinrich Härke's thesis based on early Anglo-Saxon burial evidence remains debated and not, so far, substantiated by ancient DNA evidence.

Research continues into ancient human DNA, but most recent genetic research relating to British populations has been based on modern DNA. It is important to remember this; some of the general public who write in to Bryan Sykes in Oxford to find out which of his ancestral 'Eves' they are descended from not unreasonably believe these to be ancient excavated women who have been carbon-dated and whose DNA has been extracted (Sykes 2006: 131). They are not: they are an extrapolation backwards from modern genetic patterning. All of the research discussed below derives from samples taken from living people. The most complex parts of much published research are the mathematical calculations used to arrive at interpretations of maps of genotypes of modern populations in terms of ancient population history. In many papers, models are tested to provide a best fit for the results. Again, this is not direct evidence and the most important aspects of a model are the premises on which it is based. If those are invalid then so are the conclusions. A model does not in itself prove anything: it simply demonstrates that, given the data presented, and the parameters within which it is analysed, the conclusions have a calculable range of probability.

In this paper I shall try to review some of the recent research into the genetic history of the population of Britain, especially in relation to the origins of the strongly felt differences between English, Scots, Welsh and Irish. This work is difficult for non-scientists, like this author, to access and to assess, but it is important that we make the attempt if we are not to abdicate from intellectual control of our own research. It is difficult for the obvious reasons that it includes both genetic analysis and complex mathematics, in which few archaeologists are trained. Also, this is a fast-developing field in which different specialists are pursuing different lines of enquiry, and publishing in scientific journals not often on the reading lists of archaeologists – though at least they are mostly online and so relatively easily accessible. Scientific papers tend to be published far more quickly than more traditional academic books and journals, so that our discussion lags behind the scientists and we may be reacting to conclusions which have already been superseded.

Another problem is that the media are interested in anything to do with human origins, genetics and, in Britain, the origins of the English, as opposed to the 'Celtic' peoples. They report simplified, and sometimes misleading, summaries of scientific research in an often confusingly contradictory manner, as a selection of online news pieces from the past few years demonstrates: 'English and Welsh are races apart'; 'research supports the idea that Celtic Britain underwent a form of ethnic cleansing by Anglo-Saxon invaders' (BBC news 30 June 2002); 'Teeth unravel Anglo-Saxon legacy'; 'new scientific research adds to growing evidence that the Anglo-Saxons did not replace the native population in England' (BBC news 17 March 2004); 'British have changed little since Ice Age, gene study says'; 'the genetic makeup of today's white Britons is much the same as it was 12,000 years ago' (National Geographic July 19 2005); 'Britain had apartheid society'; 'Anglo-Saxons ... wiped out almost all of the British gene pool' (BBC news 18 July 2006). So you pay your money and take your choice: there is no ancestral difference between the English and the Celts, all are and always have been 'British' – or, alternatively, the English are descended from brutal Germanic invaders who wiped out the British men and took over their women in what became England. Science has 'proved' both conclusions. All of these, and other reports, have sparked off debate which has often added to the confusion. The letters pages of archaeological magazines contain recurrent exchanges on this topic between enviably confident correspondents, to whom their own favoured conclusions are usually blindingly obvious.

Popular presentations of the issues draw on academic literature in which discussion of this period has often been dominated by perceptions shaped by historians (Hills 2007). Archaeological support for some of the simpler historically derived accounts has waned in recent decades, especially in the light of anthropologically orientated interpretation. Now, it seems, modern science can overturn the unnecessary complications introduced by archaeologists with a straightforward dialogue between historians and geneticists producing a clear, simple story (or several different ones ...).

We could decide to ignore the whole topic, or at least the media reports, and/or wait until consensus has been achieved amongst the geneticists. But the examples I have listed above all come from respectable news media, likely to be read by an intelligent public including academics and prospective students forming their ideas about the subject. Also, there seems no reason to suppose that this branch of scholarly enquiry, which currently certainly includes a fair amount of internal disagreement, is any more likely than others to draw a final line under a debate which clearly does have a great deal of underlying energy, for reasons I have reviewed elsewhere (Hills 2003). Another important point is that the premises on which the scientific projects are based, and the interpretation of their results, are strongly conditioned by the models of the history of the period which they have drawn from historians and archaeologists. The choice of historians/archaeologists as advisers/contributors means that the points of view of those specific scholars are incorporated in the research design – and the conclusions – thus genetic debate replicates historical/archaeological debates and will not independently resolve them. This is sometimes obscured by the apparently clear and uncontroversial presentation of historical and archaeological evidence in the introduction to scientific papers whose authors may not realize that their interpretation is open to question. We must try to distinguish between new scientific data and its interpretation in old and possibly debateable terms. As archaeologists we need to work out what geneticists are saying and understand how what we say influences their work before we can begin to assess what we have already learnt and might in future learn from their research. This paper is a preliminary attempt in that direction. For the purposes of this exercise it is assumed that the genetic and statistical analyses have been carried out accurately, by competent scientists.

Genetic research is a large and expanding field, fuelled by considerable resources and driven not only by pure research but also by medical, commercial and political imperatives. Genes are the new explanation for all aspects of human biology and behaviour – not only are there genes for hair colour and hereditary disease, but it has been claimed they can also be found for sexuality, criminality and obesity. A new version of Calvinism – predestination by genes rather than Divine Grace – has provoked dispute as to the relative roles of culture and biology in human behaviour. Advances in methodology since the 1980s have transformed all aspects of genetics, including research into the history of human populations. Samples can be taken and analysed quickly, and larger and larger databases are being amassed. An early paper on DNA and the Frisians (Richards *et al.* 1994) drew on samples from 123 people, whereas in a recent book Bryan Sykes (Sykes 2006) claimed he had used a database of 50,000 samples. Inevitably some earlier research has been superseded by later, as more data invalidates earlier conclusions.

The history of human populations is a significant part of this research field, but starting by looking for Anglo-Saxons in the fifth century A D is to focus in on a very small part of a large picture, like enlarging a small part of an old-fashioned newsprint picture: spots with hints of barely coherent pattern are all that can be seen. Most research has been directed to broad questions relating to the evolution of modern humans and their dispersal around the world, and within Europe to the development and spread of farming populations. Two broad approaches have so far been taken. The first, developed on the basis of blood samples, which became increasingly available during the twentieth century, plotted the geographical distribution of different gene types and their frequencies in different populations, as determined by immunological assays and protein electrophoresis techniques. It might be argued that populations cannot be securely separated, as they have fluid boundaries. The key publication in this field was the compendious volume published in 1994 by Luca Cavalli-Sforza and his colleagues (Cavalli-Sforza *et al.* 1994). Their maps showed different patterns across Europe for different gene loci. Cavalli-Sforza concluded that: 'the major genetic differences in Europe reflect older events', in other words, events of Palaeolithic and Neolithic date, and that overall central Europe shows 'substantial genetic homogeneity' (Cavalli-Sforza *et al.* 1994: 301). A tree of genetic relationships between 26 European populations (Cavalli-Sforza *et al.* 1994: fig. 5.5.1) grouped Scots and Irish together, putting English with Dutch and Danish. A series of maps showed the distribution of summary statistical values which represent a synthesis of the variation in gene frequencies across many loci. Some of these values group all of Britain together, others show divisions. Cavalli-Sforza pointed out that 'it is often difficult to link a cline of gene frequencies with a precise historical expansion' (Cavalli-Sforza *et al.* 1994: 294), although this did not stop him trying to do that himself, suggesting the spread of middle-Eastern farmers and the Kurgan culture as probable explanations for some of his maps.

Other researchers produced more detailed maps of genetic boundaries in Europe. One showed England, Scotland and Wales as one unit, separated from Ireland, Scandinavia and the Netherlands (Barbujani and Sokal 1990: fig. 1), another identified divisions within Britain including unexpected boundaries running east–west across Lincolnshire and Suffolk, neither of which corresponds to historical, geographical, linguistic or material culture divisions (Falsetti and Sokal 1993: fig. 5). The dividing line in Suffolk was suggested to relate to a difference between Angles and Jutes, putting the Jutes some distance from Bede's location of them in Kent. No explanation was offered for the line across Lincolnshire. A more recent paper (Rosser *et al.* 2000) analysed Y-chromosomes across Europe, including the British Isles. A plot of genetic distances amongst the populations used in this paper shows a cluster in western Europe including the British Isles and Iberia. Within Britain, there is a difference between west and east, with East Anglia closest to Denmark with links also to Dutch, Belgian and Bavarian populations. Exactly when and how these differences arose remains to be established but it seems so far to add more weight to the argument that populations on either side of the North Sea had a similar genetic inheritance long before the fifth century A D.

The other approach has become possible only in recent years with techniques allowing characterisation of the 'sequence' (the genetic code) of specific sections of DNA. This research looks at the history of hypervariable regions of DNA and therefore the history of the people who have carried, inherited and passed on this DNA. Sequence data from two regions of the human genome have dominated recent research: mitochondrial DNA (mtDNA), and the Y-chromosome. Research using mtDNA started first, but in the last few years research using Y-chromosomes has also become possible. Both these regions have the advantage that they are inherited as discrete blocks, in which the fundamental order of the DNA sequence is unchanged from generation to generation, in contrast to the other chromosomes of the human genome. mtDNA is transmitted from mother to child, Y-chromosomes from father to son, so separate patrilineal and matrilineal lines of descent or lineages can be traced. Occasionally changes, or mutations, take place which result in alterations in the DNA sequence, and these mutations accumulate over the generations of inheritance. This is what allows the identification of lineages: individuals with the same pattern of mutation had a common ancestor at some point in time, and genetic relationships can be expressed in trees or networks. This principle is clear: what is less easy for the non-specialist to understand is how the comparison of sequence differences is translated into absolute time of population divergence. Calculations of time start from the known mutation rate, but how is that known? Is the 'molecular clock' a reliable tool? Often a given rate of mutation is quoted without explaining how this has been calculated. For the purposes of this paper the time spans seem too short, and the margin of error too great, to be confident that any suggested dates are reliable. Disentangling genealogies is a direct approach to genetic evidence which two recent writers, Sykes and Oppenheimer, have used for comprehensive reviews of the early population history of Britain to which I shall return later in this paper. Most research using modern samples tries to minimize the overlay of recent population movements to any pattern of ancient movements by selecting people whose grandparents were born close to their present place of residence.

Looked at from the wider perspective, population movements around the North Sea in the first millennium A D look less significant and more difficult to identify than some of the headlines suggest. The British Isles have been continuously populated by modern humans for a relatively short time in comparison with, say, the peopling of Europe and the rest of the world. Recent research suggests it is only since the end of the last glaciation, about 11,500 years BP, that there has been continuous human settlement in Britain, for a shorter time still in Ireland (Stringer 2007), although there had been earlier periods of occupation. Initial settlement was of a peninsula of Europe, where eastern England was joined to a land christened Doggerland which now lies beneath the North Sea (Coles 1998), and so to the north European plain. The earliest populations of England were not separated from Europe by the sea, and mobile hunter-gatherers would not have respected later frontiers in their movements. If any signature of their population history remains today in their genes a similarity between those of East Anglia and North Germany would be expected, as remnants of the same population.

The development of archaeogenetic studies in relation to Britain was reviewed by Martin Evison as a contribution to a volume on the interaction between Anglo-Saxons and Scandinavians (Evison 2000), and more recently by Sykes (Sykes 2006). Skull formation and hair colour were replaced during the twentieth century by blood groups as the favoured means for distinguishing between people of different ancestry. This did not always lead to clear conclusions, as Evison notes: 'it may seem surprising that Scandinavian connections seem able to be supported in some way whatever the level of blood group A frequency of the donating or receiving populations' (Evison 2000: 281).

In fact, research into the Scandinavian contribution to British genes has made progress, as has investigation into the genetic origins of the Celts, whereas the impact of the Anglo-Saxons remains more problematic. It is worth considering why this should be so. Research using Y-chromosome analysis has been carried out at UCL, producing a number of papers, not all arriving at the same conclusions (Capelli *et al.* 2003; Weale *et al.* 2002), and also featuring in a TV series. This was *Blood of the Vikings*, a BBC programme presented by Julian Richards in the autumn of 2001 (was the title a deliberate echo of the title of the series this author presented in the 1980s: *Blood of the British?*). A key element in this was the genetic research carried out for the programme by the UCL team, led by David Goldstein, which showed that many of the male population of Orkney had Norse ancestry (Wilson *et al.* 2001). Later research on Orkney by a team based in Oxford looked at both Y-chromosomes and mtDNA (Goodacre *et al.* 2005). Although they identified a smaller proportion of Norse males of Norse origin than the earlier study they found a similar proportion of Norse females, suggesting substantial settlement of whole families from Norway. In other regions like the Western Isles, there was some male Norse settlement, but little female. Most interesting is Iceland, where the expected 'Norse' population, historically recorded as settling an empty island in the ninth century, has produced a population where, although a majority of males can trace their ancestry to Scandinavia, a majority of females derive from elsewhere, probably the British Isles.

Identifying a substantial Scandinavian element in the populations of the north Atlantic is not a surprise in itself, but genetic research here is providing new information as to the scale and character of that contribution, and seems to be proceeding towards comprehensible conclusions which can be incorporated into historical and archaeological debate. The situation is simpler than in England, especially in Iceland, where there has been only 1,000 years of human settlement, without large-scale subsequent migration or invasion.

In the paper (Wilson *et al.* 2001) that reported the Orkney results, other populations were compared with British, identifying similarities between Welsh, Irish and Basque Y-chromosome patterns and concluding that these 'Atlantic' populations represent the original human population of the British Isles. It was also suggested that later cultural transitions, such as the Neolithic, might have left stronger traces on female than male lines. This line of research has been developed by others (e.g. McEvoy *et al.* 2004), who argue that both Y chromosomes and mtDNA show shared ancestry from Iberia to Scandinavia, including the British Isles, dating back to the last Ice Age. This has been taken as support for the arguments against the traditional identification of the Celts as invading Iron Age warriors from central Europe. Rather, the modern 'Celtic' populations of Ireland and western Britain are largely descended from prehistoric people who moved up from Iberia after the last glaciation.

The history of England, and the interpretation of its genetic evidence, is more complicated. An early paper using mtDNA gives some indication as to why. This addressed the question of the Frisians (Richards *et al.* 1995; Forster 1995). Samples were taken from North Germany, including some from Ostfriesland and the island of Fohr, off the coast of Jutland, together with some from Denmark. The study was supported by a historical summary by Peter Forster reviewing the context for migration or population movement in the region during recorded history. Results showed the sampled populations to be not dissimilar to other European populations in terms of relative frequencies of different genetic types. However, one genetic type was identified among the North German but not Frisian samples. A later extension of this research compared the results with samples from southern and central England and identified this genetic type as common in Germany but rare in England. The conclusion was that there had been no large-scale replacement of the Romano-British population by immigration. This research was referred to by Evison in *British Archaeological News* (Evison 1997), who also argued that genetic evidence did not support the hypothesis that the native population had been displaced by Germanic invaders. It was also included in a later paper by Forster *et al.* (2004: 107) but has not figured largely in recent discussion.

This raises the question of the relationship between medieval and modern peoples and regions with the same names, which is more problematic than it always appears. Discussion of 'Frisians' is not always geographically precise, which undermines confidence in the identification of differences between them and neighbouring – or overlapping – peoples such as 'Saxons', 'Jutes', 'Angles' or 'Danes'. All these groups are recorded as occupying parts of the coastal regions from the Rhine mouth to the Jutland peninsula, in modern terms the northern Netherlands, North Germany and southern Denmark. Ethnic and geographical distinctions between these peoples in the past are sometimes taken as having been more precise, and more stable, than is likely to have been the case. Most papers give details of the modern population sampled for that project, but synthetic papers, using existing databases, may simply describe populations as 'Frisian' or 'Norwegian'. Except for the Frisians there is not usually a problem in identifying modern geographical sources: the difficulty arises when the data is interpreted in terms of early peoples. There is the tendency to assume that we know exactly where those peoples lived and understand their relationship to later people with equivalent names who may or may not be living in approximately the same place. Classical and medieval authors do not give maps with precise boundaries for the territories attributed to the peoples they name, some of whom they may not have known much about. Frequently both frontiers and names have changed over time. Some recorded names disappear, and new ones emerge: this could be because new people have taken over the territory, because previously separate groups have combined, or because the existing people have changed their name. The two main sources deployed in discussion are Tacitus (Rives 1999), who wrote in Rome towards the end of the first century AD, and Bede (Colgrave and Mynors 1969), writing in Jarrow (Northumberland) in the eighth century. Excellent scholar though each was in their contemporary context they did not have first-hand knowledge of everything they discussed, and although Bede gives sources for some of his statements he does not do so for the famous passage in which he identifies the Saxons, the Angles and Jutes as the continental ancestors of the Anglo-Saxons.

On modern maps, 'Friesland' relates to specific coastal regions and islands off the coast of the Netherlands and Germany, reaching as far as the modern frontier of Denmark. Tacitus located the Frisii at the mouth of the Rhine, while in the seventh century AD 'Frisia' may at its maximum have included much of the modern Netherlands and the North German coast, before conquest by the Franks in the eighth century (Heidinga 1997). The study by Richards and Forster used 'Frisian' samples from modern Germany, whereas another paper (Weale *et al.* 2002: 1010) included 'samples from 94 males in Friesland (northern Netherlands)'. If 'Frisian' samples are used in other studies it should be clarified precisely what that means, especially before embarking on comparison with 'Dutch' or 'North German' populations.

If we look at the other peoples we see that there are further uncertainties. The Anglii were listed by Tacitus as one of a series of peoples not very precisely located in more remote regions of Germania. Bede located the Angles as living between the Jutes and the Saxons, in 'Angulus', which has been equated by later scholars with a modern district of Germany: Angeln. This region occupies part of the Jutland peninsula, a small region to the south of the modern Danish border but to the north of the medieval Danish border. Modern inhabitants of Angeln are German and any samples of their DNA would therefore be included under the 'North German' heading. Their ancestors, up until the Prussian invasion of 1864, were living in Denmark, and so would have been Danish. Distinctions in material culture between different regions within Jutland during the Roman Iron Age and Migration Period have been identified, and such distinctions might reflect separate named groups. Early Anglian culture or influence has sometimes been seen as extending to most of modern Schleswig-Holstein, to the island of Fyn, and into north-east Germany. Bede claimed that Angeln lay deserted until his own time because its inhabitants, the Angles, had migrated to Britain, and it has been argued that archaeological evidence does in fact show depopulation in Angeln during the sixth and seventh centuries A D (Gebühr 1998). If that were true there would be no genetic links between the later incomers to the deserted land and the descendants of those who had left and settled elsewhere, so we would not find genetic links between the two places. This hypothetical problem has not received much attention, although it is one possible explanation for the difference in mtDNA between North Germany and southern England detected by Forster *et al*. The 'Anglian' culture, identified in England, mostly dated to the sixth century, seems to be a new creation within England, drawing on components of material culture from around the North Sea, rather than consisting of a package transferred from Angeln during the fifth century.

Neither Saxons nor Danes were mentioned by Tacitus, though other classical authors refer to Saxons. Lower Saxony, between the Elbe and the Weser, is usually identified as the homeland of the Saxons who came to England. The appearance of similar houses, burials and pottery further west, into the Netherlands, during the fifth century, has sometimes been interpreted as colonization of Frisia by Saxons, just as appearance of similar material in eastern Britain has been seen as supporting accounts of the arrival of Angles, Saxons and Jutes. This would make it even more difficult to distinguish between Saxons and Frisians.

Danes appeared first in sixth-century sources, notably the *History of the Franks* by Gregory of Tours (Thorpe 1974) and thereafter in Frankish sources, as hostile neighbours. There may have been a process whereby smaller groups combined into larger groups and adopted new names: Saxons may have replaced Chauci, Angles and Jutes may have been subsumed within a new larger Danish grouping. It is difficult to be sure how precisely we can or should distinguish between these peoples, whether in terms of history, archaeology or genetics. It is even more difficult to know how far we can or should go in connecting ancient and modern named peoples: that after all, is the theme of this paper.

One UCL paper (Weale *et al.* 2002), directed specifically at the question of Anglo-Saxon migration, has had considerable impact and therefore deserves particular attention in this discussion. This was based on analysis of Y-chromosomes. Samples were taken from small long-established market towns in an east–west transect across England and Wales, from men whose paternal grandfathers had been born within 30km of those towns. The results were compared with samples collected in Friesland (defined as north Netherlands) and Norway. This showed that the Welsh samples were very different from the English and that the English were not close to the Norwegians, but 'statistically indistinguishable' from the Frisians. The conclusion was that the findings were best explained by a mass immigration of Anglo-Saxon males from the continent. The media reports on this referred to 'ethnic cleansing' of Britons by Anglo-Saxons, as 50–100% of the indigenous male population was wiped out.

I will not engage with the technical aspects of this paper, except to note that the interpretation is based on the model which seems to the authors to best fit their results, and that the sample size is still fairly small – 313 men from seven towns. I have two different kinds of issue to explore. One is the Frisian/Anglo-Saxon distinction. The two names are used interchangeably in the paper, which is confusing but, as explained above, may actually reflect the original situation. Frisia, however defined, was a thinly populated region or series of regions. Recent research in the Netherlands has suggested a hiatus in occupation of at least one major site during the fourth and early fifth centuries, possibly reflecting a more general phenomenon (Besteman *et al.* 1999). However significant the role played by any invading Frisian chieftain, he would have needed to recruit more widely than his immediate homeland to have had an army sufficient to make an impact on Britain. Groups drawn from the rest of the North Sea coastal region would have included the peoples discussed above and historically recorded as participating.

My second point arises from the first. If other peoples, as well as Frisians, were involved, some (i.e. Angles and Jutes) came from Denmark, which is also the origin of the Scandinavian Viking settlers in eastern England, as opposed to the Norwegians, who headed for Orkney and the north Atlantic. All the English towns sampled lie in the Danelaw, land subject to settlement by Danes in the ninth and tenth centuries. The authors recognize this and admit that it may prove difficult to distinguish between ninth- to tenth-century Danish Viking and fifth- to sixth-century Anglo-Saxon incomers.

A further paper (Capelli *et al.* 2003) included data from other parts of Britain, Ireland, Denmark and Germany. This paper repeated the findings of Norwegian influence in the northern areas, but found southern England predominantly indigenous. Little difference was found between Danes, North Germans and Frisians, underlining the difficulty of distinguishing between Anglo-Saxon and Danish Viking immigrants/invaders – and it was suggested tentatively that the Danes might have had a greater demographic impact on England than the Anglo-Saxons.

One of the UCL team, Mark Thomas, has reaffirmed the conclusions of the Weale *et al.* paper (Thomas *et al.* 2006), and has tried to reconcile the difference between the high genetic contribution from Frisian (?=Anglo-Saxon) immigrants to the modern English male population argued by Weale *et al.* with the low numbers of immigrants suggested recently by historians and archaeologists. He proposes a form of apartheid – a term already used by Alex Woolf in this context (Woolf 2007) – as the mechanism whereby a relatively small, but dominant, immigrant group of males could make an overwhelming eventual genetic contribution to the later population. The incoming Anglo-Saxon males had more sons, more of whom survived to become fathers in turn, and so on, so that over five generations, in Thomas' calculations, the genetic contribution of an immigrant male population could rise from less than 10% to more than 50%. Thomas supports his argument both by the historical evidence for differential treatment of English and Welsh in Anglo-Saxon England, by Heinrich Härke's research into weapon burials outlined at the start of this paper (Heinrich Härke is credited as a co-author of this paper), and by genetic studies in other parts of the world. For example, a population in Columbia has strongly contrasting male and female ancestry: 94% of the Y-chromosomes are European, 90% of the mtDNA indigenous (Carvajal-Camona *et al.* 2000). This is genetic confirmation of the historical record, where European men are recorded as fathering children with women indigenous to the various countries colonized in the early modern period. It might be thought that distinguishing between European and Amerind could be simpler than between different groups of North Europeans, but certainly this shows that Thomas' model could reflect reality. Thomas' paper attracted wide media coverage and its conclusions are likely to appear, probably as demonstrated fact, in the secondary literature for years to come. However, his paper is a reconstruction of what *might* have happened, given certain basic starting points – it is not a demonstration of what *did* happen. This is a vital distinction, but one easily lost. The basic premises are that the findings of Weale *et al.* are correct, that is that modern English male populations are indistinguishable from Frisian populations, and that this is best explained by migration from Frisia to England during the fifth century. Thomas therefore stands or falls with Weale *et al.* Neither has resolved the Anglo-Saxon/Danish Viking issue, they are not clear about the different ancient peoples around the North Sea, nor do they allow for any underlying prehistoric similarity between peoples on either side of the North Sea. This is not to say their conclusions are wrong: but that they have not yet been clearly demonstrated.

One problem with interpreting present genetic patterns in terms of specific episodes of movement in the past is that no allowance is made for changes in the rate and direction of mixing in the past. Weale *et al.* did look at, but discard, alternative scenarios, including continuous migration from Frisia since the fifth century, but modelling the undoubted complexity of real population movements demands very complex statistics. Bill Amos (Amos *et al.* 2008) has begun to develop ways of simulating patterns of mixing in a series of time slices in the past. This work is still in progress, but one point Amos makes is that so far Frisian and North-German/Danish populations look very similar in his analysis.

Another experimental approach to the subject is through language, always a major bone of contention. Why do we speak English if there was not a large Anglo-Saxon migration? Here I only want to refer to a recent contribution by a geneticist to this discussion. It is perhaps not surprising that this has been greeted with disbelief or even outright hostility by some linguists. Peter Forster has applied the network analysis he uses in genetics to ancient languages to suggest that English diverged from other Germanic languages at a very early date, indeed, before the accepted fifth-century date for the Anglo-Saxon migration (Forster *et al.* 2006). As a tool for exploring relationships between languages this seems a valid and interesting technique, but the evidence for early Celtic and Germanic languages is fragmentary and less clearly interpretable than DNA, and dating language change is even less straightforward than dating genetic splits (McMahon and McMahon 2006). *Beowulf* might well look different to the prose of Alfred's day, but it is an epic poem with poetic vocabulary, and of uncertain date of composition. The conclusion that English developed early as a separate Germanic language is interesting and worth further investigation, although the subsequent history of English as a language with much contact with both French and Latin has contributed to its difference from other Germanic languages. Forster does not himself suggest where this early development took place, and his estimates for its date are extremely broad. But his idea has been taken up by Oppenheimer to argue that a Germanic language might have been spoken in Britain before and/or during the Roman period – which as Oppenheimer admits is 'contentious', as it is at variance with all other scholarship (Oppenheimer 2006: 415). Research has instead focused on the extent to which Latin was spoken by ordinary people in Roman Britain, assuming their native language was Celtic, and it has also recently been argued that there was a distinctive Lowland British version of Celtic (Schrijver 2007). However, it is true that we do not really have much evidence for the language(s) spoken in Britain during the Roman period (or before) and maybe this argument should be considered seriously, perhaps with more detailed linguistic input.

The genetic origins of the British are the topic of two books, both published in 2006, by Oxford professors. These are *Blood of the Isles* by Bryan Sykes and *The Origins of the British* by Stephen Oppenheimer. Neither refers to the other. Both are aimed at a popular audience, both are readable. Sykes has no bibliography or references, whereas Oppenheimer is fully referenced and has a large bibliography, useful to the academic but perhaps intimidating to the general reader. It is easier to assess Sykes' book: the genetic sections are based on the research of the author and his team, and so constitute a presentation of original research, while the sections on history and geography are summaries. Oppenheimer's is a mainly synthetic work, based on extensive reading in various fields of scholarship, drawing especially on a wide range of genetic research of all kinds, with some re-analyis of genetic data by the author. This is interesting and very useful, as it brings so much material together, but where I know the source material well I have reservations. For example, I am puzzled by the caption to figure 9.3, which seems to suggest that cruciform brooches are not found in Lower Saxony; this is not true as indeed his own map shows. Nor am I quite sure what is being plotted on the same map as 'early Scandinavian type runes'. I am not competent to decide whether the captions of his genetic maps are fully justified, though I would like to believe them: examples include 'maternal representatives of the LBK line reach England' (fig. 5.3a) and 'Scandinavian mothers in northern and western Britain during the Neolithic?' (fig. 5.3b).

Both books emphasize the long durée and argue for a substantial prehistoric contribution to the genetic ancestry of modern Britons. Both are interested in Celtic history and myth, both use genetic markers as evidence of ancestral history. They personalize their genetic lineages – Ursula, Sigurd, Rory and Rob – in a way which may make their work seem less serious than perhaps it should. Neither author sees any evidence for Celtic migration from central Europe; this is in fact one of Oppenheimer's main targets. He identifies a difference between west and east in the British Isles, but traces this to early prehistoric settlement history, not to the Anglo-Saxon period or later. In this regard he is influenced by Barry Cunliffe who has identified prehistoric connections along the Atlantic seaboard from Spain to Scotland, and also takes on board Forster's arguments for the early development of Old English. Where Mark Thomas quotes Heinrich Härke's research on weapon burials as evidence for separate ethnic groups, Oppenheimer draws on Francis Pryor's presentation of the case for long-term British continuity (Pryor 2004). Pryor, as a prehistorian, would not himself claim authority on the Anglo-Saxons.

To me, the most important aspect of Oppenheimer's book is his stress on the long-term processes of settlement, including significant input from the very first prehistoric settlers and also others arriving at different times and from different directions. The genetic traces of any Anglo-Saxon invasion need to be disentangled from that earlier population history. It is not necessary to agree with all the specifics of Oppenheimer's data presentation and argument to accept this as a valid and important principle. Another conclusion is that there: 'is a deep genetic division between peoples of the west and east coasts of the British Isles' (Oppenheimer 2006: 406). In other words, Oppenheimer argues that the English are different from the Scots, Welsh and Irish but sees this as result of different prehistoric population histories, long before the fifth century A D. This is, however, not the conclusion Sykes reaches.

Sykes' book has some synthetic elements and is frustratingly lacking in references. The linked webpage has data but not more detailed scientific presentations of the arguments, which remain, therefore, to be fully substantiated. However, this is a very readable and clear account of research which does seem to advance the argument in a straightforward way. Many samples have been taken from people across the British Isles, both by Sykes' team and in other projects. The numbers involved do seem sufficient for real patterns to be demonstrated, not accidental results of sampling bias. The resulting maps, whether glossed as historical lineages or not, do appear to show very similar distributions across Britain of most of Sykes' male and female 'clans'. These maps do not show a strong east–west division and only some of the less common genetic types show some geographical clustering. Sykes argues that 'the genetic structure of the (British) Isles is stubbornly Celtic' (Sykes 2006: 287). The matrilineal history of Britain is both ancient and continuous: 'on our maternal side, almost all of us are Celts' (Sykes 2006: 281). On the paternal side this is also true, but there is some evidence for Saxon and Dane, which Sykes does not feel able to discriminate between. He estimates that in the south of England approximately 10% of men have Saxon or Danish ancestry, while this rises in the Danelaw, to as much as 20% in East Anglia. Another point Sykes makes is that there is, overall, less male genetic diversity than might be expected. One explanation would be that the similar groups are recent arrivals, descended from comparatively recent ancestors. However, another interpretation, which Sykes favours, gives a different slant to the 'apartheid' argument. He suggests that dominant males, of whatever ethnic background, have greater chances of reproducing 'powerful men [to] monopolize the women' (Sykes 2006: 285). So their lineages prosper whereas others die out, and maybe we are all descended from our mythical clan chief, whether Hengist or Cerdic. While this fits feminist perceptions of male behaviour we can see that historically this does not always work out – Henry VIII has no legitimate descendants despite his six wives, and not even many recorded illegitimate offspring.

The stress by both Sykes and Oppenheimer on long-term prehistoric genetic history is welcome but another aspect seems hardly to have been taken into account so far. This is later population history, from the Norman Conquest to the twentieth century. Why jump back from the present to the first millennium A D without taking account of the second millennium? Mobility at all times and in all places needs to be taken into account. For example, the small town of Barton-on-Humber grew rapidly during the nineteenth century, so that in 1851 more than half the population had not been born in the town (Rodwell 2007: 10). People whose grandfathers were born in East Anglia might have more distant ancestors who came as Huguenot refugees in the sixteenth century: by 1582 there were 4,679 immigrants in Norwich, mostly from the Low Countries, fleeing from religious persecution and predominantly engaged in the textile industry. This is estimated as a third of the population of the city (Rawcliffe and Wilson 2004: 221). 'Frisian' genes could have arrived then rather than 1,000 years previously. Modern demography, which draws on an extremely rich and detailed database, must also have conclusions we should take account of. The popular interest in family history has not only encouraged the accessibility of documentary resources, but it has also begun to draw on genetic data. Detailed comparison of historical and genetic data for recent populations might suggest new ways of thinking about the reconstruction of early populations.

So far, the picture presented by Sykes seems to me the most persuasive, partly because it is based on actual distributions of genetic types within Britain, but also because it is an undramatic picture from an archaeological standpoint. According to Sykes, much of the population of modern Britain, east and west, is descended from prehistoric settlers. Male and female lines have histories which differ in some respects. There is evidence for Norse settlement in Orkney, for Saxon/Danish in East Anglia. This all seems plausible, but because this research has not yet been fully published, these conclusions can only be taken as provisional.

Meanwhile, a return to the scientific examination of ancient skeletons has recently been driven by research into stable isotopes. This is clearly a work as much in progress as the study of DNA, but it is interesting that here we see a return to direct analysis of ancient bones to see what information can be derived about the diet and possibly the origins of the people whose skeletons these are. Research into ancient DNA also continues, mostly in relation to prehistoric burials. We may not have the key to Anglo-Saxon DNA which the TV programme hoped for, but it may yet be that some answers will come from the bones themselves.

Acknowledgements

I am very grateful to my colleagues, Tamsin O'Connell and Harriet Hunt, of the McDonald Institute, Cambridge, as well as Martin Richards, of the University of Leeds, who took the time to read and comment on a draft of this paper from a scientist's perspective. Remaining errors and misunderstandings are of course my own responsibility.

Chapter 9

Laws, funerals and cemetery organisation: the seventh-century Kentish family

Duncan Sayer

Abstract

Archaeological studies of kinship have been scarce in recent scholarship. Anglo-Saxon archaeology has tended to assume kinship was important without considering how or what the kindred's role was within society or the burial rite. Recent studies of burial archaeology have focused on topical issues like age, gender or group identity without the context within which they exist: the family and household. This paper will begin to redress this imbalance by comparing the archaeological evidence of two Kentish cemeteries, Mill Hill and Finglesham, with the seventh-century legal sources, also from Kent. I will focus on cemetery organisation by considering grave location, burial wealth and grave structures. This paper builds on research by Heinrich Härke (1997a) who successfully combined written sources and material evidence to offer an insightful and vivid picture of Anglo-Saxon social structure. I will offer the hypothesis that the seventh-century final phase burial rite involved not just a reduction in grave goods but also a transformation in the funerary rite and in the use of cemetery space. I will suggest that this is because the emphasis of the funeral changed from expressing the unity of an extended household to emphasising familial relationships. This shift took place in a time when wealthy kindreds were increasingly in conflict with a newly powerful system of kingdoms.

Introduction

Early Anglo-Saxon England (here taken to mean c.AD 450–700) is usually considered a period with furnished burial but without extensive and reliable written sources for reconstructing social structure. It is perceived to be a dark age, only accessible to historians through later writings like those of the Venerable Bede or *The Anglo-Saxon Chronicle*. By contrast archaeological evidence is abundant and the data from furnished graves has been employed in discussions of the character of social organisation and local identities (see Lucy 2002). However, it is the argument of this paper that it is through the combination of these two types of evidence, texts and mortuary data, that it might be possible to advance our understanding of early Anglo-Saxon identities. In particular, it is suggested that an interdisciplinary perspective sheds new light upon an under-investigated but crucial topic: the early Anglo-Saxon family and household organisation.

A number of useful texts for reconstructing kinship have survived from later Anglo-Saxon England c.AD 800–1100 (see Wareham 2001, Herlihy 1985, Drew 1988 for the uses of different types of source). These include wills, charters and laws, all of which have specific uses for considering Anglo-Saxon family and social organisation. Unfortunately for the scholar of the fifth to seventh centuries, these sources are of limited use as they were mostly written after society had undergone a number of social and religious transformations; including the conversion to Christianity, the centralisation of power structures, the foundations of what was to become later Anglo-Saxon kingship and multiple shifts in settlement structures and location. These changes mean that social structures during the later centuries of the Anglo-Saxon period were likely to have differed from those in the early period. However, one class of historical source can be of specific value in providing insights into contemporary kinship structures: the seventh-century legal codes (e.g. Härke, 1997a). Most of these laws date to the latter half of the century but the law of Æthelbert (king of Kent) dates to the early seventh century. This class of evidence was first written down during the time when furnished burials were being interred within the cemeteries of the Kentish coast. Indeed, many of the richest and most striking of the burials from Finglesham and Mill Hill – the sites investigated in this study – were interred during this period. Likewise, the late seventh-century burials from Finglesham were contemporary with the laws of Ine and Withred. Consequently, when alive, the individuals within these graves were agents within both the written and unwritten legal systems of the period.

Although they are different types of evidence, the laws and the cemetery data are contemporary. The law codes of the seventh century were, as Reynolds (2009) discusses, not just passive documents or part of the regalia of kingship. They were active legal codes used in response and relation to contemporary society. Successive codes did not substantially revise or supersede their predecessors but rather added to the range of stipulations made by written law.

Härke (1990a, 1997a, 2000a) and Hines (1994) have championed the use of both primary and secondary written source material to study early Anglo-Saxon archaeology. Härke (1997a) particularly focused on the early Anglo-Saxon laws, as well as the later charters and wills, not as a reaction to the anti-historical approaches of scholars like Pader (1982) but as a means of enriching the archaeological evidence with information that specifically deals with the broader issues debated in both disciplines. Indeed, archaeologists and historians have approached their respective evidence to answer similar questions; for example we might cite the work of Stoodley (1999a) and Crick (2000). Stoodley investigated questions of the social role of women, their inherited status and funerary expression using the furnished burial rite as evidence. Meanwhile, Crick used the information from the late Anglo-Saxon wills to consider questions of differences between the wealth, inheritance and expressions of social status in documents referring to women's property. Similar debates have covered comparable topics, namely: identity, age, gender, life course and household organisation. Consequently, this tradition increases the potential gains in interpreting the seventh-century laws alongside contemporary mortuary evidence and through their combination to achieve a greater appreciation of early Anglo-Saxon society.

However, interpretation of the laws is not straightforward. They come to us today through a later proxi, having often been copied and annexed to the twelfth-century document, the *Textus Roffensis* (see Whitelock 1955 for the individual laws). Moreover, they were part of an incomplete tradition and related only to certain Anglo-Saxon kingdoms (namely Kent and Wessex). Furthermore, just four law codes have survived from the seventh century. These collections of law codes were succeeded by a dearth of written laws (or at least surviving laws) until the ninth and tenth centuries when, among others, Cnut and Wulfstan issued legislation. This was followed by another more limited gap in the written laws during the early and mid-eleventh century under Edward the Confessor and the Norman kings, although several special codes may date to the eleventh century. The four seventh-century laws are very limited documents and seem not to have been intended as self-contained and complete laws. Many of the rules people lived by (or flouted) must have been assumed and dealt with by customary oral traditions and therefore not subject to records set down at the king's court.

Similarly, the cemetery evidence is a data-set fraught with interpretative challenges. Understanding furnished graves is hampered by the conditions of preservation within a site and many cemeteries have only received partial excavation. The quality of preservation can vary dramatically between graves situated in close proximity, making interpretations of mortuary variability problematic. The character of mortuary practices is dependent on the decisions made by survivors, decisions that went into the preparation of a grave for burial and for funeral display. Mortuary variability incorporated the expression of local identities (Lucy 2002) as well as broader regional and nationwide traditions in the expression of, for example, gender and status. Consequently, archaeologists view early Anglo-Saxon society through a mirror reflecting the aspirations and ideologies that the living chose to represent in death rather than having access to a direct view of social organisation at a particular period of time (see Härke 1997b; Williams and Sayer in this volume).

The combination of different sources, burials and written evidence has often been seen as problematic or misleading. However, if properly considered, such combinations provide an interlocking mesh of shared themes relating to the expression of social ideals and aspirations. In this way, the laws and burial rites can be used to interpreted specific questions – providing an informed context for their interpretation is established. Therefore, just as historians have increasingly turned to archaeological evidence to inform and support their conclusions (e.g. Blair 2005; Smith 2005), archaeologists can integrate written material into their detailed analyses of mortuary data.

Added to the problems associated with the historic and archaeological data is the difficulty of reconstructing social institutions. This is further complicated by the limited and partial nature of the evidence. Indeed if scholars of this period hope to understand satisfactorily principles such as kinship then it is a combination of written and material evidence that will provide the most reliable means. The cemetery data provides material placed by survivors, and the historical sources can help to reconstruct the legal and social context within which those survivors made their decisions, providing a means to discuss social interpretations in more detail.

These themes have a particular pertinence for the analysis of Anglo-Saxon society in the seventh century. Overall the seventh century was a time of change, of conversion to Christianity, and of the transformation of old traditions (such as furnished burial). Because of this, and the potential to combine physical and textual evidence, the seventh century is an important gateway to understanding the organisation of society on both sides of this watershed for scholars of the past. The survival of rich archaeological evidence alongside written source material makes this a period key to understanding the nature of the changes in the funerary tradition which, in reflecting the relationship between living and dead, can be viewed as manifestations of social relationships. This interaction between the deceased and the mourners – who were likely to have shared kinship bonds – can be extended to include the social participation, co-operation and mutual obligations between the survivors, structured through their own personal relationships.

In this article I will consider the general collection of legal evidence with reference to specific codes from three laws. The laws of Æthelbert, king of Kent (AD 602–603), Hlothhere and Eadric, also kings of Kent (AD 673–685) and Ine, king of Wessex (AD 688–694), will be examined in relation to the organisation of two cemeteries, Mill Hill and Finglesham (Parfitt and Brugmann 1997, Grainger and Hawkes 2006). These cemeteries were chosen because they were found in east Kent (see Fig. 9.1), an area with good cemetery evidence and which has been the focus of recent studies. Both burial sites have received extensive excavations yielding good biological and material evidence. Each burial site revealed a large number of intact and systematically investigated graves that produced a wealth of artefactual evidence. These data simultaneously provide social information about how the dead were adorned by the survivors, and valuable material for the construction of reliable internal chronologies. There is one other law from the seventh century from Withred, king of Kent (AD 695) (Whitelock 1979: 396–97). This law is mostly concerned with outlawing the practice of heathenism, punishment for crimes, preserving church law and the Christian formalisation of marriage and manumission (the freedom of slaves). In this way, key social institutions were reflected in this very late seventh-century law. Despite this paper's focus on Kent, Ine's seventh-century Wessex law code has been included as it is an important document for understanding interpersonal relationships and its absence in a study of this type would be conspicuous. The combination of written and burial data provides the greatest potential for reconstructing household and family structures; structures that can be simultaneously regarded as the best known and least understood of early medieval social institutions.

Archaeology and kinship

The analysis of cemetery data to outline social organisation has been a widespread theme in the burial archaeology of the last four decades (Bartel 1980; Binford 1971; Brown 1971; Chapman *et al.* 1981; Childe 1945; Hodder 1980; O'Shea 1984; Tainter 1975). Anglo-Saxon archaeology has both borrowed from, and contributed to, these studies and debates (e.g.

Arnold 1997; Härke 1990a; 1997a; 2000a; Pader 1980; 1982; Scull 1993). This may be, at least in part, because cemetery evidence is by far the most prolific type of data available for the study of early Anglo-Saxon society. However, for burial archaeology generally, non-material social relationships such as kinship are very difficult to see archaeologically and have for many years been studied by anthropologists who are able to interview living people. Earlier pioneers in an explicitly social approach to mortuary archaeology, such as Lewis Binford, aspired to use ethnographies to inform archaeological interpretations: they saw material cultural remains as not only a means of studying artefacts, migrations and culture but also as an indicator of sociological factors. Binford argued that material culture was used within a set of culturally defined contextual relationships which consisted of less visible characteristics such as socio-economic complexity, kinship and social differentiation. Consequently he postulated that it was possible to extrapolate from the depositional contexts, by means of an interpretive framework, more anthropological explanations of human societies across different time periods:

> Granted we cannot excavate a kinship terminology or a philosophy, but we can and do excavate the material items which functioned together with these more behavioural elements within the appropriate cultural sub-systems. (Binford 1962a: 218–19)

As Parker Pearson has recognised (1999: 110), Binford was one of the first to attempt to reconstruct kinship elements in one of the earliest case studies of the 'New Archaeology'. Because their principal focus was upon the analysis of prehistoric mortuary data, these early studies tended to borrow more readily from anthropology than history to perform these reconstructions. Binford's studies (1962b, 1972) used the dis-articulated skeletal elements recovered from Galley Pond Mound, Illinois (early tenth century AD) to reconstruct societal residence patterns. A different approach was conducted after excavation work in 1961 on a cemetery discovered on Charter Ranch, a Pueblo site from eastern Arizona. Longacre (1964) applied a statistical reduction analysis to 175 design elements of ceramic vessels from the cemetery. He correlated the deposition of three stylistic groups of pots with the three spatial groups of burials that made up the cemetery. From this study Longacre (1966), supported by Hill (1966), suggested that the village consisted of two or three unilateral descent groups. Both Longacre and Binford concluded that the societies studied were matrilocal and matrilineal, that is, the women stayed where they were and the men married or moved into the community from elsewhere with the house and property being the only form of inheritance which took place through the female line. Beyond the obvious problems of small sample size and data quality issues, there are a number of difficulties with these studies. Because they were built on the work of Deetz (1960), all three sets of results are surprisingly similar given that the societies under investigation were separated by so much distance and time. All three ended in very neat studies of female residence patterns where they assumed that female residency and agency was linked with kinship. Alternative explanations or the flexibility of male kinship patterns were not considered. Indeed, Longacre's pottery assemblage seems to contain more variation than similarity and may be indicative of mobile female agents adding to a pool of local styles.

In fact these archaeological investigations are not analyses of kinship at all, a problem which may stem directly from the use of anthropological terminology. In 1971, Allen and Richardson published a scathing anthropological critique claiming that archaeologists cannot determine residence, inheritance or kinship patterns in the fashion attempted by Deetz, Binford and Longacre. They argued that these studies relied on the belief that a set of pre-prescribed descent systems guide the actions of a society's members who do not waver or step outside of this system. Since archaeologists cannot determine individual resident choices, socially cohesive actions, or choices in life, and since the incorporation of individuals into descent categories can occur through affinity, adoption, or complimentary filtration, it cannot be assumed that descent was the primary influence upon traditions in material culture.

However, to understand Allen and Richardson's reaction it is necessary to see the broader academic context of this work. Both Binford's and Longacre's articles (1962a and 1964 respectively; incidentally, both were entitled: *Archaeology as Anthropology*) were a response to Willey and Phillips' statement 'American archaeology is anthropology or it is nothing' (1958: 2) described by Binford as 'apt' (1962a: 217). In essence they were an attempt to justify archaeological theory through its union with anthropology. It is unsurprising that as part of this package, American archaeologists adopted anthropology's terminologies, often applying them uncritically and inappropriately to a range of data-types.

Subsequently, archaeologists in the Anglo-American tradition seem to have abandoned the theoretical study of kinship or residence patterns and have turned to quantifiable studies of social hierarchy. Certainly, kinship remained of interest in American archaeology. However, it was not pursued through the study of mortuary practice but through physical anthropology. This was based on the assertion that physical characteristics can be used to identify differences between human populations (Brothwell 1959). Lane and Sublett (1972) attempted to study this difference using skeletal non-metric traits. Corruccini (1974) and Ortner and Corruccini (1976) developed the technique by employing the use of skeletal and dental measurements in combination, a method more widely employed in American archaeology (Bartel 1980: Corruccini *et al.* 1982). Although these studies rarely seem to have fed into a mainstream theoretical discussion, many claimed to have moved beyond simple skeletal studies. For example, Howell and Kintigh argued that:

> [... we] take a step beyond recent studies by coupling age and sex compositions, spatial information, and biological measures of genetic distance (dental morphology) to examine kin group membership. (Howell and Kintigh 1996: 539)

Despite this failure to engage with Anglo-American theoretical archaeology, or theoretical archaeology's failure to satisfactorily employ appropriate empirical evidence, these studies were picked up by European archaeologists. Bondioli (*et al.* 1986) applied the principles to the non-metric skeletal traits found within an Italian Iron Age cemetery and Jørgensen's (1987, 1991) early medieval (Scandinavian late Iron Age) case studies ambitiously combined the science with the cultural/theoretical side of this problem, although with a heavy focus on the identification of a martial elite. This European debate also underwent somewhat of a transformation through the integration of well-preserved non-metric dental traits by Alt and Vach's study of remains from the Iron Age cemetery at Kircheim, Germany (1991, 1995 and with Jørgensen *et al.* 1997). English studies, until recently, have been more conservative and were summarised in a paper by Tyrell (2000). He argued that while there is a biological inheritability in the frequency of some non-metric traits among family groups, the extent of this inheritability is, as yet, unknown. Environmental factors may hide traits that would normally have formed, and we do not as yet understand the mechanisms for this inheritability. This approach can be understood partly as a response to the early American physical anthropological studies (cited above) and Heinrich Härke's (1995a) discussion of Berinsfield Anglo-Saxon cemetery in which he suggested that kinship groups could be identified through the combination of archaeological data and non-metric traits (Williams and Sayer this volume). However, Tyrell's paper was meant as a critique of Härke's discussion of ethnicity and group identity rather than engaging directly with the question of kinship relations.

One of the biggest problems for studies claiming to investigate kinship in archaeology remains their tendency to instead address issues of residence or ethnicity, in other words themes related to, but not synonymous with, kinship. They focus on social or physical anthropological approaches and terminologies, and even studies within the ambiguous pre/proto-historical periods tend to avoid direct engagements with relevant historical sources.

When kinship has been discussed within Anglo-Saxon archaeology, much is assumed about the nature of such family organisations. For example, Scull's approach identified burial as an expression of a basic family unit, suggesting that furnished graves were those of the heads of families or clan chiefs, and an indicator of lineage units or descent groups 'which might include nuclear families in any one generation' (Scull 1993: 73). This elite-focused approach takes a simplistic and static view of society, modelled as a network of '...broadly-equal, internally-ranked patrilineal, patrilocal descent groups farming or exploiting their own territories' (Scull 1993: 73). It is an approach close to the 'Teutonic ... peasant commonwealth' (Campbell *et al.* 1982: 168) of nineteenth-century scholarship. Historical anthropologists such as Murray (1983) and Goody (1983) have rejected such simplistic interpretations, but as part of the wider anti-historical traditon, Scull did not engage with the more balanced and historically fluid scenarios of kinship relationships that a multidisciplinary approach might have offered.

To conclude this appraisal of approaches to kinship, archaeological interpretations can benefit from creating a dialogue engaged with both anthropological and historical sources, if only to prevent the use of interpretations already rejected by historians and to guard against misapplying anthropological terminology. It is to avoid making assumptions about Anglo-Saxon kinship in order to deal with its context that this paper will focus on the archaeological and historical source material and will leave more detailed discussions of individual cemetery organisation and biological characteristics to more appropriate publications elsewhere.

The historic literature discusses the nature of kinship within Anglo-Saxon society but significantly does not question the importance of it. By contrast, within recent archaeological discussions kinship has remained absent. The organisation of society has formed the backdrop for demographic studies (Brothwell 1981) as well as approaches to understanding the operation of gender in life and its representations in the burial rite (Härke 1989a; Härke 1990a; Lucy 1997; Stoodley 1999a). Particular attention has been paid to how these aspects fitted into the burial treatment of individuals of different ages or at different points within their life course (Crawford 1999; 2000; Härke 1997a; Stoodley 2000). For example, Stoodley (1999a) addresses these points as well as discussing household organisation, or specifically the role of gender within it. He outlines a system in which females played an important role that was manifest through the inclusion of specific grave goods within the burial, just as had been outlined previously for males interred with weapons (Härke 1990a). Even in discussions of community and group identity (see Härke 1997a; Hines 1994; Lucy 1998; 2002; Williams 2002; 2006), the inclusion of a sophisticated discussion of the role of kinship relationships within society or simply within a specific funeral is notable only by its absence. If gender, age and identity are all important aspects of community cohesion, funeral ritual, and social organisation, then kinship must also play an important role. These parts of an individual's identity all intersect and affect how people interact on a daily basis just as they may dictate specific behavioural differences between the funerals of a friend and that of family members.

Anglo-Saxon kinship

Anglo-Saxon society was transformed between the fifth and the eleventh centuries; it was not a static entity but one constantly being remoulded by both internal and external forces. There are a number of changes noticeable in the historic record which relate to kinship systems, including the development of a partrilineal royal descent system by the tenth century (Wareham 2001). Wareham based this observation on the study of wills, which are a useful source but perhaps not appropriate for application to the seventh century as they usually date to between the ninth and tenth century.

Other scholars have approached this question not by using uniquely English documents, like wills, but relying instead on European source material. For example, the Frankish Lex Salica 62 (AD 793) (see Murray 1983: 115–34) describes the situation pertaining to the killing of a father; his son or sons should collect half of the wergild[1] and near relatives from the mother's or father's side collect the rest. The Lex Salica 68 further complicates this arrangement by breaking down the fraction of the wergild that specific named members of the kindred received, resulting in a split of 6:2:1. A split depended on the degree of relationship that kin had to the deceased and whether this relationship passed though the matrilineal or patrilineal side. Approaches to this Continental evidence deal with broader concepts of Germanic kinship but are much more familiar with the European material than with the Anglo-Saxon. Moreover, they tend to focus on specific legal sources like the *Lex Salica*, which is written in a different tradition to the

---

[1]   Blood price payable by a slayer to his victim's family.

English legal sources. Also, the Continental sources outline the extent of relationships while Anglo-Saxon sources do not (e.g., Charles-Edwards 1972; Goody 1973; Herlihy 1985; Drew, 1988: 265; Murray 1983; Phillpotts 1913). These scholars have investigated the problem on a national or regional scale and their conclusions rarely escape from this rationality.

In other words, the focus has been on clan, tribe and kingdom rather than the specific nature of individual kinship relations. Consequently studies have more in common with archaeological discussions of regional identities and ethnicities than with the localised dynamics of kin. Moreover, tribe and clan have much more in common with ethnicity than parent-child and sibling relationships. Many clan ties are based on the appreciation of a common, possibly mythical, ancestor (Charles-Edwards 1997) rather than specific interpersonal relationships. While clan and tribe are aspects of kinship systems, they are not the only aspects available for study.

However, a number of authors do approach the topic of family and household organisation. For example, Wareham (2001) advanced a system which consisted of male-based inheritance replacing an older system of individual-focused kinship in later Anglo-Saxon England. This older system was dependant on personal relationships and not upon a wider family or gender relations. Goody (1973: 230) also describes society as personal as opposed to ancestor-oriented, where it is a person's kindred who were responsible for supporting them during a feud just as it is they who received wergild payments (as in the Lex Salica). Unfortunately, this direct evidence for kindred from the Continent is not found in the Anglo-Saxon laws (Drew 1988) where there is more reference to friends and associate family members as, for example, in Edmund's Late Saxon Law code (A D 939–49):

> 1. If henceforth anyone slays a man, he himself [is] to bear the feud, unless he can with the aid of his friends [*frēondas*] in twelve months pay compensation at the full wergild, whatever class he [the man slain] may belong to. (Whitelock 1955: 391)

This emphasis on the Old English term *frēond*, etymologically the origin of the modern term friend, may be misleading. Green (1998: 57) has suggested the term refers to kindred, although not exclusively. Therefore, family, kindred by marriage as well as friends (who may be like kin) could also have been included in the use of this term. In contrast to the Continental codes, this non-specific terminology is apparent early in the English material. The laws of Hlothhere and Eadric (clause 5) refer to the legal assistants of a defendant as so-called 'free oath-helpers' not specifically as kin, although this could refer to free kin. The laws of Ine mention specifically the importance of the baptismal sponsor in forming relationships:

> If anyone kills the godson or godfather of another, the compensation for the [spiritual] relationship is to be the same as that to the lord; the compensation is to increase in proportion to the wergild, the same as the compensation for his man does which has to be paid to the lord. (Whitelock 1955: 366)

Indeed, clause 40 of the laws of Ine mentions directly relations between neighbours and the fencing of land as do clauses 42, 42.2 and 49. These clauses refer to compensation received from damage to property by a neighbour's animals and demonstrate that non-kindred members of society were living in close proximity.

As Lancaster (1958: 373) pointed out, the day-to-day co-operation of a group depended on constant communication. A personal kinship system required that in any given family unit (i.e., parents with at least one child) there were at least three differently-experienced yet interdependent kinship networks in operation: the mother's, the father's and the child's (not only does the child have different parents to its mother and father but in elite families it may be fostered out for a time). This was a model of a highly complex and idealised community. In contrast and as noted above, the Anglo-Saxon laws use terms like *frēondas* referring to kinsmen, family by marriage, and probably more occasionally friends (Green 1998: 57; Charles-Edwards 1997: 172). This form of non-specific expression highlights the importance of flexible relationships at an everyday level, a flexibility which may not be delivered by distant kindred. After all, it is the *frēondas* of the dead who probably attended the funeral and laid out the corpse, not simply the family. Charles-Edwards (1997) reports that kinship systems were different between kings, freemen, and the un-free, although his paper focuses on the relations of kings and may be a political, idealised kinship system not reflected in the inherent flexibility of the lower social ranks.

Some of the earliest laws we have are also unclear about the exact nature of the kindred's role. In the Laws of Æthelbert, King of Kent (AD 602–3), clause 21 states: 'If anyone kills a man he is to pay as an ordinary wergild 100 shillings … of which 20 are to be paid at the open grave' (Whitelock 1955: 358). This may mean at the grave itself and suggests that a funeral may have been delayed until after the settlement of feud or to allow distant kindred time to travel. Certainly such a clause has implications about who actually attended a funeral. Indeed the identification of fly and insect pupa within some grave contexts (Halliwell 1997; Hirst 1985: 31) support the idea that graves may have been left open for some time after the placing of the body and grave gifts. In clause 23 of the same law it is indicated that if the man (i.e. the slayer) absconded, his kin were responsible for half the wergild. Presumably this law is meant to place responsibility for keeping the slayer present among his kin group and use the kin as a tool to reduce the escalation of feud. However, who these people are remains ambiguous, just as there is no indication of who was present at the open grave of the deceased or who would have received the 20 shilling first payment. In the Laws of Ine (AD 688–94) it is indicated that if a foreigner was slain then a third of his wergild would go either to his son or his kinsmen (Whitelock 1955: 366) and the rest to the king. If he had no kinsmen then it was to go to his *gesith*, which Whitelock (1955: 366), interpreted as the man under whose protection he lived: his lord. This shows how kingship and lordship could have started to encroach on the important functions of kinship ties. It is the kin group that would demand compensation and so provide a form of insurance, deterring violence or at least slaying. Under these laws the king or lord offers the same deterrent and insurance to those with no kin – or far away from a useful kinship network – and thereby undermines a reliance on kinship ties while at the same time allowing free movement and encouraging commerce.

It is not until the later Laws of Alfred (AD 871–99) that we start to see evidence of the sharing of wergild payments between kin (Whitelock 1979: 407–16). Even Alfred's laws are ambiguous though; in clause 30, Alfred seems to be calling the maternal kin, and to a lesser extent associates, to be responsible for an individual's payments should he have no paternal kin (Whitelock 1979: 413). This is a law whose very existence suggests that the maternal kindred were either not previously recognised as responsible for this payment, or, as a result of attempts to dismantle powerful kindred and feud, were subsequently trying to avoid wergild. That kindred formed an important part of a person's supportive network is in no doubt, and can be seen in an extract from Edmund's law code (AD 939–49):

> 1.1 If, however, the kindred abandons him, and is not willing to pay compensation for him, it is then my will that all the kindred is to be exempt from the feud, except the actual slayer, if they give him neither food nor protection afterwards. (Whitelock 1955: 391)

This extract is arguably a smart piece of social engineering, designed to remove the tight kindred connection and undermine the support that personal kindred may provide. However, considering *The ordinance of the bishops and reeves of the London district* (VI Athelstan: Whitelock

1979: 423), also from the tenth century, there is no doubt that the kindred were strong:

> 8.2 And if it happens that any kindred is so strong and so large, within the district or outside it, whether men of twelve-hundred wergild or two-hundred wergild, that they refuse us our rights and stand up for a thief, we are to ride thither with all our men with the reeve in whose district it is.

> 8.3. And also we are to send in both directions to the reeves and request help from them of as many men as may seem to us suitable in so great a suit, so that the guilty men may stand in greater awe on account of our association; and we are all to ride thither and avenge our injury and kill the thief and those who fight with him and support him, unless they will desert him (Whitelock 1979: 423).

Far from having been dissolved, the tenth-century kin groups were still large and powerful and may have required sizable armed forces to disband. As with Edmund's law, it seems to have been the desire of Athelstan to neutralise the power held by the kindred, perceiving them as having posed competition to the rule of kings and dividing important loyalties between family and the emerging state. In combination these codes suggest that there is a constant conflict between kingship and kinship and that both legal and physical action was required on behalf of increasingly powerful kings to neutralise the ever present network of personal kindred and to maintain the rule of law.

The written evidence for early Anglo-Saxon kinship is ambiguous at best and does not stand out as clearly as the Continental sources. The concept of kinship, if not the detail, is undeniably important and remains so from the advent of child care, witness Ine:

> 38. If a husband and wife have a child together, and the husband dies, the mother is to have her child and rear it; she is to be given six shillings for its maintenance, a cow in summer, and ox in winter; the kinsmen are to take charge of the paternal home, until the child is grown up (Whitelock 1955: 366).

However, important kinship relationships may not have been an everyday community structuring principle. While important at a person's death for the dissemination of land, goods and people, there is little evidence to suggest that kinship was the only source of significant relationships in the sixth and seventh centuries. Indeed, the term *frēond* may help to highlight this ambiguity but also the range of people that the extended kindred may have been able to call on for support in conflict.

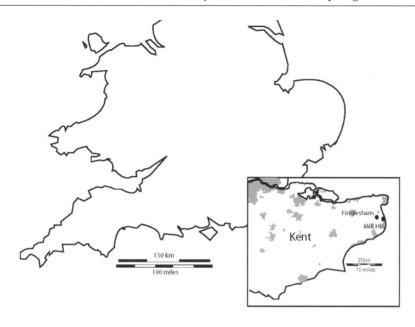

Fig. 9.1:
Location map
of the excavated
cemeteries
investigated in
the paper: Mill
Hill, Deal and
Finglesham, east
Kent.

In contrast to the written evidence, the archaeological evidence may not be able to address questions of terminology or degree of relationship, nevertheless a cemetery is the product of those who survived the deceased, people who had relationships with the deceased in life just as they did in death. As already discussed, Anglo-Saxon cemeteries have been used to successfully identify differentiation in age, gender and identity but not in kinship as an inseparable part of community organisation. Using the historic source material discussed above it is possible to create a context within which to interpret the cemetery evidence. This combination is particularily pertinent because both Mill Hill and Finglesham were in use during both the sixth and seventh centuries, with Finglesham remaining in use to the very end of the seventh century. In other words, the sites are partly contemporary with the written evidence. Both sites are located in Kent (Fig. 9.1) a region in which there are a number of recent studies of cemetery data, social structure, and landscape (Brookes 2007a; 2007b; Richardson 2005).

The archaeology of two Kentish cemeteries

Mill Hill

Mill Hill site is located on the east Kentish coast and in the outskirts of modern Walmer and Deal (Parfitt and Brugmann 1997: 1–6). It was fully excavated between 1986 and 1989 to make way for a housing estate. The cemetery consists of two distinct areas of burial in the first phase, referred to as A and B in the publication, located on either side of a large circular ditch which was formerly the perimeter of a large prehistoric barrow. The complete excavation of this site revealed a cemetery comprising of 76 graves, many of which were in closely packed rows. Like other Kentish Anglo-Saxon cemeteries, this was a rich burial ground consisting of a mixture of English and Continental grave goods.

Mill Hill was in use during the sixth and the early seventh centuries, making it an important site for understanding social changes during the early Anglo-Saxon period. The slight extension of dates to include the seventh century is based on a reassessment by Sayer (2007a; 2007b), suggesting that an early seventh-century date is more appropriate for the eastern burials, many of which include seaxes and other seventh-century paraphernalia, and is consistent with the revision of dates proposed by Hines *et al.* (forthcoming). The skeletal preservation was good and in combination with the archaeological evidence there are some convincing patterns within the cemetery which are consistent both with the spatial areas outlined within the excavation report and with those recently discussed by Williams (2006).

Williams (2006: 64; fig 2.12) looked at the pattern of weapon burials and observed their close proximity. He interpreted this proximity as the result of the reproduction of a remembered burial ritual in subsequent funerals, a system that relied on memory and visual mnemonics to recreate and build associations with past inhumations. These patterns describe the proximity of weapon burials but in this cemetery there are also localised distributions of artefacts not traditionally associated with ethnicity, for example, fire steels, pins and keys. Figure 9.2 illustrates this similarity, highlighting three clusters of burials at this site. These are labelled as plots A, B and C. 'C' is the separate group of inhumations buried in lines on the eastern side of the barrow ditch. Interestingly, fire steels are clustered in plot A, whereas pins, possibly in combination with keys, are clustered in the south of the cemetery and are focused on plot B. Plot C contains more tweezers and swords than the rest of the cemetery. Figure 9.2 also plots the probable dating of these burials. The dating is obtained by combining the relative dates of each object to derive the smallest possible date-range for each grave.[2] The two sixth-century plots A and B contain individuals of

---

[2]   As this study is dependent on developing a finite internal chronology within the cemeteries it is necessary to reduce artefact data to absolute chronologies dependent on the combinations of artefacts in one grave (Hines 1997; Mortimer 1990). Individual artefacts may have a date range spanning 30, 50 or even 150 years, but they can be used in combination to reduce the range in which

mixed wealth, age and gender spatially clustered together and separated slightly in the detail of their funerals.

By contrast, the linear group of burials in plot C is later than the other two plots, dating to the late sixth and seventh centuries. If this illustration of spatial organisation is compared with the plot of the wealth[3] in the graves (Fig. 9.2), then it is notable that wealthier inhumations are interred in plot C. There are four inhumations with my 'A-wealth' classification in plot C; this is far more than in either of the other two plots. This later sixth- and seventh-century phase also has some less wealthy inhumations, although these remain in the original plots A and B. These burials include numbers 29, 100, 101 and 103 and although these are not directly datable because of the absence of artefacts, their construction cuts through earlier inhumations. Of these burials, 100, 101 and 103 all cut burial 104, which was interred in the mid-sixth century, so they must all have been interred after this date. This implies that these interments were contemporary with the burials of plot C. These intrusive burials were, like plot C, a continuation in the use of the cemetery by the late sixth- or seventh-century population. They also represented the rejection of the previous burial traditions, just as plot C was the rejection of the previous two spatial areas of the cemetery. Plot C consisted almost entirely of wealthy interments, unlike the two earlier plots. This new funerary tradition rejected the mixed-wealth plots of the sixth-century choosing instead to separate different groups by wealth.

This is a significant transformation from the earlier phase of burial within this cemetery. Among the early graves there were burials of mixed wealth in close proximity, but they also clustered around two

---

burials may have been interred. For example, grave number 73 at Mill Hill – a female grave – is buried with an annular brooch (AD 450–700?), a button brooch (class L; AD 450–500), an animal brooch (AD 500–550), a type I.4 buckle (AD 480–550) and group A2 glass beads (AD 480–580): these objects in conjunction give an early sixth-century date. The same is true of male burials, but usually relies more heavily on a combination of spear, shield and buckle typologies (see Sayer 2007b and forthcoming for the detailed discussion).

[3]   This is a development of previous studies of wealth based on Shephard (1979) and Stoodley (2000) using divisions of wealth to identify the higher status groups and gender to distinguish the lower status groups – although I will refer to this as wealth rather than social status. The groups are labelled as follows in figures 9.2 to 9.4. A – graves with highest wealth in the cemetery, swords, shield and spears or pairs of gilt brooches, other jewellery and precious metal. B – spear and shield, pair of brooches and jewellery. C – gender-specific objects i.e. spear or a pair of brooches. D – objects in modest number and form. E – no objects surviving.

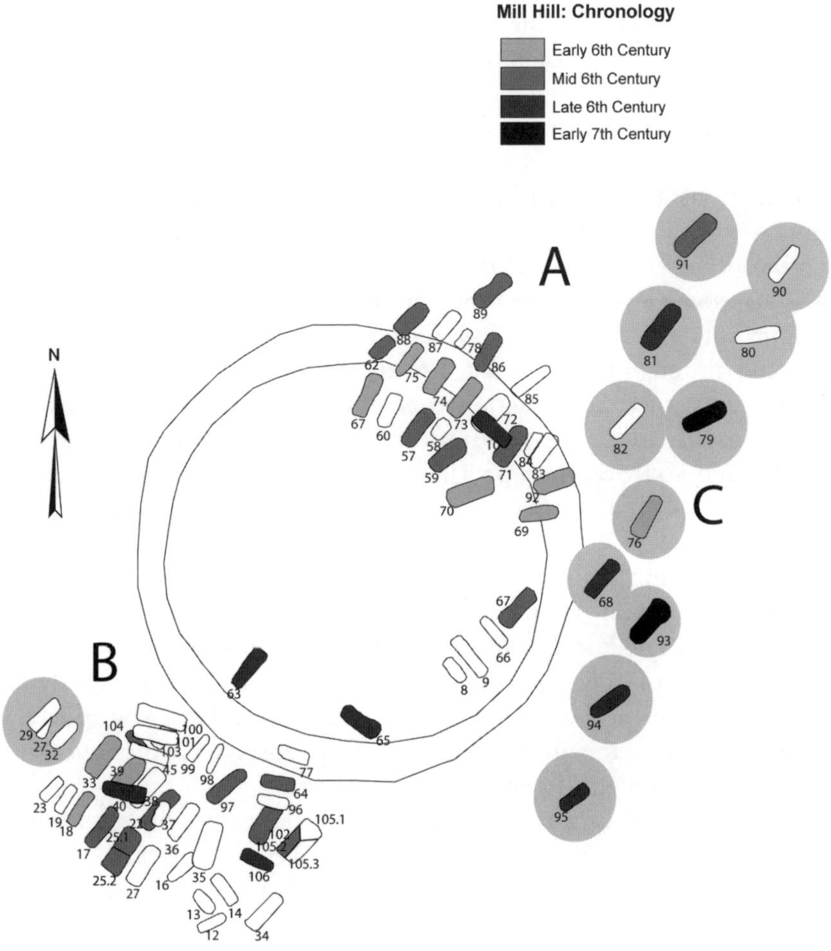

Fig. 9.2: Mill Hill cemetery. Plans of the chronology and relative wealth of the inhumations at Mill Hill. Redrawn by the author after Parfitt and Brugmann 1997.

separate groups focused on a small number of high-wealth burials. In Plot A, inhumations 67, 73 and 92 were all early sixth century and inhumations 86, 89 and 71 were mid-sixth century. This implies that in a period of some 60 years, there was one high-wealth interment (A or B) for every 10 years or so. A similar situation existed for plot B, where graves 18 and 33 date to the early sixth century and 17, 25.2, 102, 97 and 64 are mid-sixth century, following a similar pattern of one burial interred approximately every 8.6 years. These inhumations seem to be the foci of the plots: the burials of the highest wealth were surrounded, although not uniformly, by lower wealth inhumations. The graves were quite regularly placed in these dense plots or clusters. The difference between the fifth- to sixth-century burials and those of the sixth- to seventh-century revolves around what aspects of an individual's

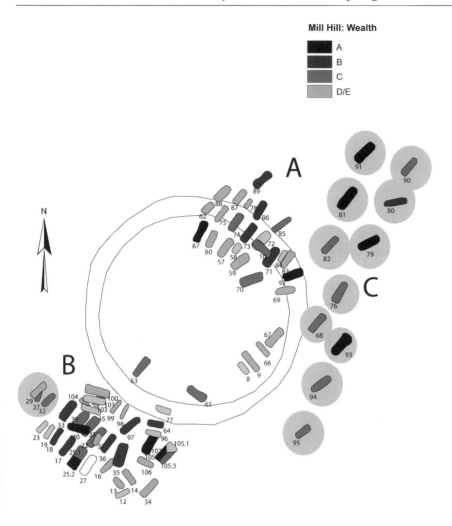

identity were expressed in the burial rite, who was afforded furnished burial, who was placed in the focal points and whether earlier burials were respected by subsequent graves. The unfurnished burials did not respect the previous interments, suggesting that there was at least an ideological separation between these two groups. The furnished burials were all in one new plot and similarly furnished with males to the north of the plot and females to the south. This was the plot that was important as a chronologically-distinct, high-wealth area as noted by Williams (2006: 64). The uniformity suggests these burials utilised a mnemonic system in which a specific repertoire of funerary provisions were used to identify the deceased as a member of a particular family unit or household unit.

Finglesham

The second site comprises a large cemetery located just south of the village of Finglesham in east Kent. According to Hawkes (1982: 24), the village's name is Old English and is derived from Þengels-Hām, meaning the 'prince's manor'. The word 'Þengel' occurs in line 1507 of *Beowulf*, referring to the hero. The cemetery itself contains over 250 inhumations (Hawkes and Grainger 2006) and has an exceptionally long life-span from the late fifth to the early eighth century AD. This makes it one of the longest-lived cemeteries in early Anglo-Saxon England and the site is key to an understanding of changing cemetery organisation over this period. The first 38 inhumations to be discovered at Finglesham were investigated by William Stebbing and William Whiting in 1928 to 1929, with further, large-scale excavations taking place in the 1950s by Sonia Chadwick Hawkes. Despite the site's importance, only limited analysis has been forthcoming comprising studies of individual artefacts and cursory interpretations of the site as a whole (Hawkes 1977; 1981; 1982; Hawkes *et al.* 1965; Hawkes *et al.* 1966; Hawkes and Pollard 1981). The final report on the excavations, including a more complete catalogue, has recently appeared in print, but since it is intended simply as a catalogue, it contains limited interpretations of the burial rites and cemetery (Hawkes and Grainger 2006). The discussion here is therefore based on an original and systematic analysis of the data by the author.

Finglesham is a rich cemetery but the wealth is heavily concentrated in a small number of affluent inhumations. The burials have a mean artefact date in the eighth century and were identified by artefact combinations which included Brugmann's (2004) type C beads, a broad seax (Böhner 1958; Dickinson 1976) or a Marzinzik (2003) type II.26 buckle. The graves may be more realistically considered as late seventh century (based on an ongoing scientific re-dating project using AMS dates, Bayliss pers. comm.) although I have left them labelled as early eighth century here, following the terminology of this author's doctoral thesis (Sayer 2007b). It is evident that artefact typology supports a very late seventh- or early eighth-century date for these wealthy graves and in all likelihood they were probably interred around the end of the seventh century. Despite the problems of precise dating, as with Mill Hill there is a very clear contrast between the sixth- and seventh-century burials.

Along the lines of Mill Hill, I have identified three plots at Finglesham – A, B and C – within which burials of successive phases can be found (Fig. 9.3). This chronological interpretation replaces that of Härke (1992a: 171; 258–59) who described Finglesham as a cemetery with a single core expanding in one direction based on the data available to him at the time of his study. Hawkes (1982) dated the burials broadly to the sixth and seventh centuries and suggested that inhumation 204 was a rich male founder's grave from the early sixth century, with the seventh-century burials all to the south of this high-wealth, sixth-century area. The basis of this dating scheme holds up, as plot A to the north of the site is generally earlier than plot C, and, as discussed above, burial 204 is early sixth century, as is burial H2. There are also a number of mid- and late sixth-century inhumations in this area (Fig. 9.3). Even though plots A and C clearly overlap, both having inhumations from the late sixth and early seventh centuries, the general trend is for plot C to replace A as the favoured burial location. By contrast, plot B contains late fifth-century burials 117 (based on a B2 Swanton 1973; 1974; spear head) and 134 (based on a Myres-type tall pot: Myres 1969; 1977) and seems to have been continuously used through to the more northerly seventh-century burials, including 1, 7, 8, 9, 14, 15, 16, 18, and 20 (Fig. 9.3). The identification of these plots is partially based on this chronological difference but also on the distribution of wealth within the site, which is clearly focused on plots A and C (Fig. 9.3) and the similar distribution of grave structures (Fig. 9.4). This suggests that plot B is a separate, less wealthy, burial plot. Such a conclusion is supported by a higher concentration of skeletal damage (fractures and arthritis) within this area (Fig. 9.4).

The distribution of richer grave goods in this site is focused on plots A and C, which may be part of the same group with C following on from A. What is interesting about these two plots is that they contained most (if not all) of the small barrows that Grainger and Hawkes predicted on the basis of the cemetery's layout (Hawkes 1982). Indeed, when these mounds are plotted, a number of burials seem to wrap around spaces where barrows may have been (for example, burials 39, 69, 87, 88, 89, 90, 91). The transformation of burial practice from the sixth to the seventh century is characterised by the contrast between plot A and C and the presence of burial mounds and other funerary structures within the cemetery. The seventh-century inhumations of plot C include more types of burial than the other two plots. Different levels of expenditure in external mortuary monuments accompanied different wealth burial. Hence burials could consist of the following combinations: barrow + high wealth, barrow + moderate wealth, ledges + moderate wealth, ledges + low wealth, no structure + no grave goods. Crucially, high expenditure does not necessarily accompany high wealth. The sixth-century plot A is similar to the two early plots at Mill Hill, as indeed is the southern area of plot B. There are a small number of high-wealth burials surrounded by groups of much lower wealth burials – in the case of plot A there are 8 or possibly 9 (if 22 is

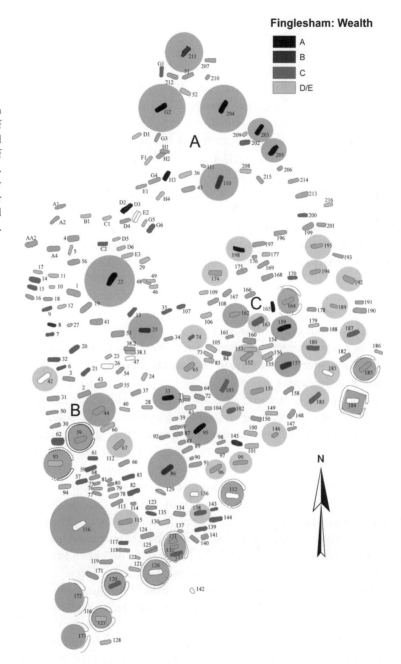

Fig. 9.3: Finglesham cemetery. Plans of the chronology and relative wealth of the inhumations. Redrawn by the author after Hawkes and Grainger 2006.

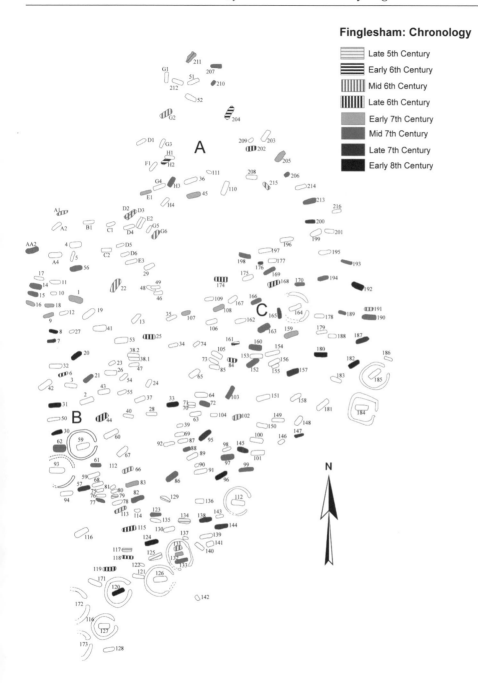

Finglesham: Chronology

	Late 5th Century
	Early 6th Century
	Mid 6th Century
	Late 6th Century
	Early 7th Century
	Mid 7th Century
	Late 7th Century
	Early 8th Century

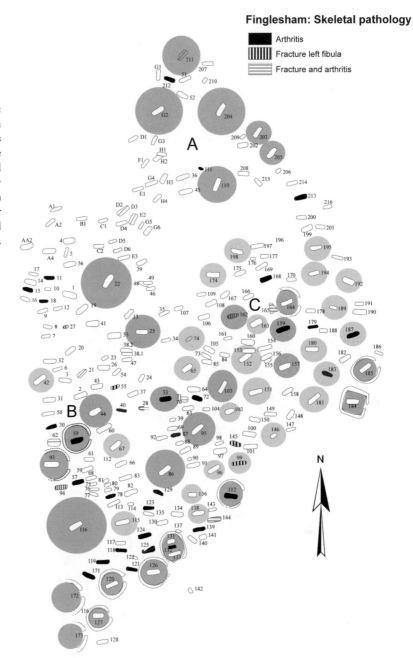

Fig. 9.4:
Finglesham
cemetery. Plans
of the grave
structures and
skeletal pathology
present. Redrawn
by the author
after Hawkes and
Grainger 2006.

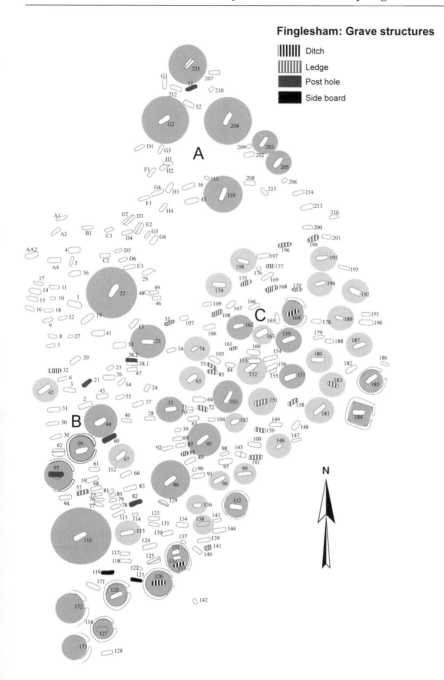

Finglesham: Grave structures

part of this group) high-wealth inhumations from the early sixth to late sixth century. This represents an average of about one burial for every 11–12.5 years. Plot A is interesting because, like Mill Hill's plots A and B, there is an obvious contrast between the wealth of its inhumations that distinguishes the core members of the household from less key participants.

Plot C does not exhibit the same level of contrast: these burials are separated visually in terms of the funeral rite since almost all of the burials with gendered grave goods are interred in areas with space around them, and according to Grainger's interpretation (as published by Hawkes 1982: 24–25) originally had barrows over them. In addition, many of these burials have lower wealth satellite burials around them. The contrast is still there but not all of the 'barrow' burials are wealthy; instead all have gendered grave goods in contrast to the satellite burials. The interpretation of this pattern is that barrow burial in all plots is a way of distinguishing members of the 'free' household: the kindred; whereas grave goods remain a means of identifying key members within that kindred. Other expressions, such as the use of grave structures, distinguish between members of the surrounding household. This might have included, for example, the semi-free or the unfree. Notably this burial strategy distinguishes non-kindred from the kindred, a characteristic which was not true of the sixth-century phase either at Finglesham or at Mill Hill, where only key members of that kindred were distinguished with wealthy burials rites.

The burial rite at Finglesham, as at Mill Hill, was transformed between the sixth and the seventh century. Again the key aspect of this change was the expression of social identity. Plot A showed a single wealthy grave every few years. Plot C showed fewer wealthy graves than at Mill Hill, but a uniform burial style among the graves with comparable wealth. The presence of enough space around the grave to position a barrow in a densely packed cemetery may not be definitive evidence of a barrow, but it is a strong indication. In support of this inference, the burials with artefacts but without a gender association were buried in graves with ledges. This demonstrates a further use of grave structures to display aspects of social identity that were not previously expressed during the fifth and sixth centuries and equally, were not associated with the wealthiest graves. The transformation is thus in the visual expression of grave-form at the grave side rather than burial contents in the seventh century. The individuals with gendered grave goods were interred in a similar way, creating a visual uniformity and standardising a burial system reserved for a uniformly wealthy elite: the rising Middle Saxon elite family.

Conclusion: Mortuary practices and changing expressions of kinship

As Figure 9.2 shows, it was speculated that Mill Hill may also have had barrows focused on the plot C graves, regardless of the wealth of those burials, in contrast to plots A and B, which simply did not have enough space to allow for barrows. Although there is strong evidence in favour of these small barrows, it is of no consequence whether or not they existed for the argument presented here. Whether or not capped by mounds, a change in organisation of the cemeteries is evident in the spatial arrangement of graves. This took place at some point between the late sixth and early seventh century, and is an early example of a wider change to funeral display often called the Middle Saxon 'final phase' burial rite (Arnold 1997: 199–210; Hyslop 1964; Meaney and Hawkes 1970) as defined by Leeds (1936) and studied in greatest detail in recent years by Geake (1997). It is characterised by the reduction in the numbers of grave goods and the transformation in the type of these goods. What is apparent about these two sites is that this change also indicates a transformation in the funeral rite itself (as demonstrated by Boddington 1990). A lessening in importance in the number of grave goods does not indicate a simplification in the modes of expression. On the contary, these later burials are more complex and use more external visual identifiers to express different aspects of social identity. A similar phenomenon is also taking place in Merovingian burials in the seventh century (Halsall, 1995b). Another characteristic of the final phase inhumations, at least for these two sites, is that these burials were separated from the earlier sixth-century plots. At both these sites this took place through the creation of a third burial plot. A notable aspect of these changes is the lessening in importance of the single wealthy grave that represented every generation and a comparable reduction in the importance of a centralised area for the burial of a wealthy individual. The use of visual identifiers had previously been reserved for that special role-related social rank, perhaps the head of the household for every generation. This indicates a fundamental change in the decisions that went into selecting which individuals were afforded wealthy funerals in rites of the seventh century.

The middle and late Saxon historical material indicates that there was an enduring and strong kinship system in place, despite the attempts of the state to undermine it. Scholars have suggested that this system existed before the introduction of the seventh-century law codes, which were, at least in part, meant as a form of social engineering designed to control and limit these kindred. The early laws are ambiguous about the importance of kindred; they refer to free oath helpers (and later *frēondas*): terms which could include the kin but need not have done. They point to living arrangements where kindred members need not have lived in close association. They also highlight responsibility for childcare and the widow of a dead father/husband, as if this was previously ambiguous. In these instances, the nature and strength of the family and kindred is unclear. Similarly, the burial plots in the sixth-century phases of the two cemeteries focus on a small number of wealthy inhumations. These inhumations are divided up into plots of mixed wealth with a single wealthy burial every 8–12 years or so. This arrangement suggests that the burial areas were the focus of extended households and that the funeral of a single member of that household, possibly the head, was an important event for that community and so justified special treatment.

The archaeological evidence also points to a change in the way social identity was expressed at this time, moving from an emphasis on a single elite person to a group of elite people, a transformation in expression from a head of a household to a whole family. This is not to say that the family was not previously an important part of society, but that it was not the principal component highlighted in the representation of social persona that took place during the furnished funerary rite. The combination of historical and archaeological evidence can be used to advance Lucy's (2002) observation that cemetery evidence is about the expression of local identities and to suggest that one aspect of this identity, the household had a key role in funerary practice in the sixth century. This social structure was later augmented or replaced by the display of family identity. If the legal codes can be construed as the beginning of the suppression of elite kindred's freedoms by the state, it is noteworthy that this is also the point at which the funeral rite changes to express family identity. Indeed, changes in the funerary rite suggest that an increased importance was placed on the internal stratification of household hierarchies, highlighting the free element more openly and emphasising a single, wealthy family unit at its core.

Society in the seventh century had greater vertical stratification, a situation created by increasingly powerful kindreds who occupied less-than-stable positions between the king and the members of free society. However, the expression of family identity within a funeral rite can only result in the strengthening of that family identity. Anthropological and sociological studies tell us that the funeral is where a community recreates itself after the loss of an individual, where old alliances are reformed and old bonds strengthened (Metcalf and Huntingdon 1991; Walter 1999). Indeed, expressions of household versus family identity within the burials rites of the sixth and the seventh century have some interesting implications for the nature of social relationships on both sides of this transformation. However, one thing is clear: Anglo-Saxon society did not consist of simple nuclear units. It was a transforming social institution consisting of *frēondas* and extended households with free families at its core. It consisted of interpersonal relationships, all of which contributed to a more uniformly expressed identity within the seventh-century elite family, an identity threatened by conflict with the growing power of kings and state, but one which was also important for the continuity of kingly families (Charles-Edwards 1997). The law codes undermined the power of the free family but they also introduced aspects which preserved it by outlining who was responsible for childcare should members of that family die. Unimportant members of a family, those who may have simply passed into the household, were preserved as important members of a kinship. The laws actively sought to preserve and maintain kinship identities while undermining their freedoms.

An integrated approach to the past can tackle complex social problems; it can be used to witness period-specific institutions like the expressions of social relationships. This is best done within an interdisciplinary research framework. However, to progress within this field effectively, research must utilise its strengths rather than relying on the terminologies and methodologies of external debates. Archaeology is good at identifying social transformation; it can outline aspects of wealth, vertical and horizontal differentiation, sex and gender, as well as patterns within the funerary space. The advent of written records may have begun as part of the regalia of kingship, but its details defined who belonged to which family groups and contributed to an increase in levels of social stratification. It is the combination of these sources from which it is possible to witness a transformation in social expression in the seventh century, that allowed household and family identities to become increasingly visible.

Acknowledgements

The author would like to thank John Hines, Howard Williams and the external readers for their very helpful comments on drafts of this paper and Heinrich Härke, without whom this research would never have taken place. I would also like to thank Meredith Carroll and Eva Thäte for editorial comments and in particular to thank Howard for his patience, attention to detail and constant assistance with editorial issues.

Chapter 10

On display: envisioning the early Anglo-Saxon dead

Howard Williams

Abstract

A variety of images are employed in the archaeological interpretation of past mortuary practices, including plans, sections, photographs and artists' reconstructions of graves and funerary scenes. Addressing early Anglo-Saxon furnished inhumation graves, I argue that the role of images in archaeological interpretations requires both greater recognition and critical appraisal in the archaeology of death and burial. The paper questions an exclusive focus on early Anglo-Saxon furnished inhumation graves as symbolic texts and visual displays. This view is over-dependent upon a snapshot impression of funerals as static displays derived from archaeological conventions of grave-recording and perpetuated in many artists' and museums' reconstructions of graves and funerals. The relationships between images of early Anglo-Saxon graves and modern perceptions of death and mortality are also appraised.

Introduction

> ... the representation of archaeological knowledge has been seen as relevant, but not central, to archaeology's analysis and understanding of itself. (Moser and Gamble 1997: 185)

Images are integral to every stage of the archaeological process, from field recording to the public dissemination of archaeological interpretations. Mortuary archaeology is no exception, but has a specialized role in depicting the remains of people: their bodies, the artefacts interred with them and the contexts in which they are found. Indeed, the portrayal of funerary discoveries – be they Bronze Age urnfields, Egyptian mummies, Roman sarcophagi or medieval tombs

– has been practised since the earliest antiquarian studies (see Schnapp 1996). These images have been an important part of antiquarian and archaeological recording, interpretation and dissemination. Once created, images have life-histories, influencing subsequent academic and popular perceptions of the past for decades and even for centuries to come (Moser 1998). Yet despite there being well-established debates among archaeologists concerning the ethics and socio-politics of digging up, displaying and storing mortuary remains (e.g. Swain 2007: 147–68), there have been no studies dedicated to the history and theory of envisioning death in archaeology.

It is appropriate to focus upon images of furnished inhumation rites dating to the fifth to seventh centuries A D from southern and eastern England. Early Anglo-Saxon inhumations have been subject to a rich and varied tradition of archaeological interpretation and visualisation. Furthermore, the interpretation of these burial rites has repeatedly hinged upon their role as public displays in which the furnished grave served as a tableau – a composed scene – that was read like a symbolic text by those attending the funeral. Moreover, early Anglo-Saxon inhumation graves have a prominent place in popular books, the media and museums, and so they have taken on a widespread and enduring presence in British popular culture during the later twentieth and early twenty-first centuries. Therefore, this case study in the envisioning of the archaeological dead provides a critique of the use of images to interpret past mortuary practice as well as allowing an assessment of the roles of the archaeological dead in contemporary British society.

Images of the early Anglo-Saxon dead

The very first discoveries assigned to the 'Saxons' were made by James Douglas in his *Nenia Britannica* of 1793 (Fig. 10.1). Douglas was himself an artist and his illustrations focused not only upon the grave goods recovered but also the burial context itself (Douglas 1793; see Marsden 1999: 16–19; Piggott 1978: 50; Smiles 2005). In particular, Douglas' plan of a weapon burial was to provide the inspiration for archaeologists of the nineteenth century, such as Charles Roach Smith and John Yonge Akerman, who were keen to write the earliest history of the English using archaeological remains (Williams 2008; Fig. 10.2). Alongside detailed renditions of artefacts and some cemetery plans, archaeologists were increasingly motivated to use Saxon graves to explore the roots of Queen Victoria's nation and empire, the grave plans illustrating the principal perceived racial characteristics of England's Germanic forebears. Unsurprisingly, it was usually 'warrior graves' that were depicted; early examples include those from Ozengall (Kent, Fig. 10.2),

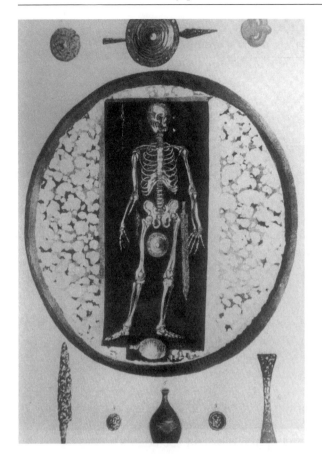

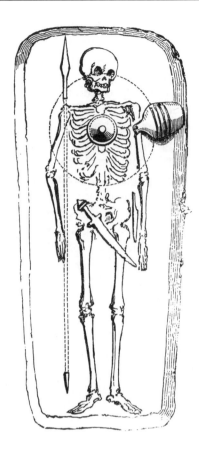

Fig. 10.1:
Illustration of
an early Anglo-
Saxon weapon
burial unearthed at
Chatham Lines and
illustrated by James
Douglas (after
Douglas 1793).

Fig. 10.2:
Illustration of an
early Anglo-Saxon
weapon burial from
Ozengall, Kent
(after Roach Smith
1852).

Long Wittenham (then in Berkshire) and Fairford (Gloucestershire) (Williams 2008: 79–84).

Through the Victorian and Edwardian periods, most illustrations of early Anglo-Saxon graves focused on the characteristic artefacts recovered. Yet, occasionally, plans were drawn and published for exceptionally wealthy graves. Examples include the Taplow chamber-grave (Welch 1992: 94) and the Lowbury barrow-burial (Atkinson 1916; Fig. 10.3). Indeed, the detailed and famous plan of the chamber within the ship beneath mound 1 at Sutton Hoo can be seen as at the culmination of this tradition of publishing only exceptional burial contexts (Phillips 1940).

It is only from the 1930s that more 'typical' furnished graves were regularly illustrated and published. Early and innovative examples include the sketches of selected graves in T.C. Lethbridge's reports on his excavations at Holywell Row (Lethbridge 1931: 46), Burwell (Lethbridge 1931: 54, 61, 69) and Shudy Camps in Cambridgeshire

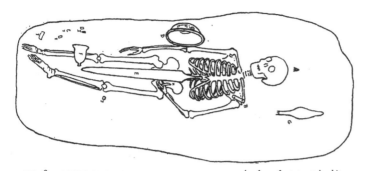

FIG. 8. DISTRIBUTION OF OBJECTS IN SAXON GRAVE (scale 2 feet to 1 inch).

A, Skeleton. B, Cloak-fastener. C, Comb-case. D, Bronze Bowl. E, Sword. F, Shield-boss.
G, Spear-head. H, Knife lying on pelvis. I, I, Ironwork of Shield. J, Iron ring.

Fig. 10.3: Plan of a seventh-century weapon burial excavated at Lowbury Hill (after Atkinson 1916: 16).

(Lethbridge 1936: 4, 11, 13, 16, 20, 24; Fig. 10.4). However, grave plans remained scarce in this period, with the focus remaining upon the objects retrieved rather than their context (e.g. Leeds and Atkinson 1944).

Recording practices became more systematic after the Second World War. Grave plans and photographs were regularly used for field recording during the 1950s and 1960s and were being published with greater regularity, albeit selectively (e.g. Knocker 1956; Meaney and Hawkes 1970; Hope-Taylor 1977). Accompanying the dissemination of rigorous excavation methodologies and the use of scientific specialists,

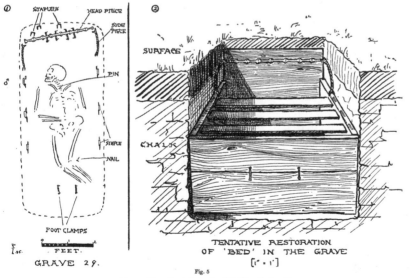

TENTATIVE RESTORATION OF 'BED' IN THE GRAVE [1 . 1]

Fig. 5

1. Diagram of Grave 29. 2. Restoration of 'Bed' found in Grave 29.

Fig. 10.4: Annotated plan of a seventh-century furnished female bed-burial together with a sketch-restoration of the bed, excavated at Shudy Camps, Cambridgeshire by T.C. Lethbridge (after Lethbridge 1936: 11).

it was only from the 1970s that the publication of all early Anglo-Saxon graves, regardless of burial wealth, became a standard practice (e.g. Aldworth 1979; Gingell 1978). This trend facilitated more sophisticated analyses of grave contexts and mortuary variability (see Arnold 1997; Lucy 2000).

By the 1980s, the established formula for the publication of early Anglo-Saxon cemetery reports was defined for both older sites dug from the 1950s onwards (e.g. Evision 1987; Hirst 1985) as well as recently excavated sites (e.g. Cook and Dacre 1985). These standard methods of field recording have developed over the last two decades (e.g. Haughton and Powlesland 1999; Malim and Hines 1998), the only exceptions being cases where poor preservation made the recording of detailed grave plans impossible (Sherlock and Welch 1992) or where the archives of older excavations have been mislaid or damaged (e.g. Holbrook 2000).

During the same period, the increasing use of photography, artist's reconstructions and three-dimensional models can be recognised. These have become widely produced, used and reused for archive reports, printed and electronic publications by field archaeologists and academics, museum displays, heritage interpretation boards, television and the internet. Early Anglo-Saxon furnished graves are now found in many contexts, even popular books and newspapers.

For many sites and graves, as well as for the period as a whole, it is these photographs and two- and three-dimensional reconstructions of graves and funerals that *are* the early Anglo-Saxon period. For both academic and popular audiences, artefacts derived from funerary contexts (most famously the Sutton Hoo helmet), but also the images of graves and funerals, have *become* icons that embody the historical processes of migration, kingdom formation and conversion to Christianity that constitute the 'story' of the early Anglo-Saxons. Therefore, images are more than simply distillations of archaeological information simplified and condensed for public consumption. Artist's reconstructions (or 'simulations', see James 1997) are an active and sophisticated medium for the articulation and communication of interpretations in early Anglo-Saxon archaeology. They are also a medium that archaeologists can never fully control following their dissemination beyond the discipline.

Interpreting early Anglo-Saxon mortuary images

How have early medieval archaeologists commented on these images? The answer appears short and simple: they have not. There have been discussions of the representation and reconstruction of early medieval artefacts, buildings and landscapes in museums and heritage sites (James 1997: 24; Fowler and Mills 2004; Lucy and Herring 1999). Equally, studies of the history of archaeology have referred to illustrations of early medieval finds (e.g. Piggott 1978: 50; Schnapp 1996: 281–82). However, the distinctive nature of early medieval grave images and reconstructions has escaped scrutiny in both the history of mortuary archaeology and the contemporary context (but see Redknap 2002: 43). This is in spite of their widespread use to accompany archaeological texts (e.g. Arnold 1997; Hadley 2001; Lucy 2000; Williams 2006).

It is understandable that archaeologists, unless they are trained artists themselves, may wish to reserve comment on these reconstructions beyond discussions of authenticity and basic comments upon their artistic merit. For museums, these images tend to be costly to produce and hence there is a pressure to utilise them for many years after their production despite any awareness by curators that they may be dated or inaccurate. Alternatively, they may prove popular with the public long after curators are aware they have become dated (Tim Pestell pers. comm). What is clear is that early medieval archaeologists are exposed to a charge of 'logocentricism' in their reluctance to critically comment on images and their persistence (this author included) in using grave images as supplementary and subservient to textual argument. So it appears that, despite the long tradition of using images to record observations and communicate within archaeology, there remains a prejudice against acknowledging the influence of, and employing, images in an active and interpretative way that might challenge or detract from text (James 1999: 118; see also Cochrane and Russell 2007).

Therefore, it is the contention of this paper that the importance and influence of images of early medieval graves and funerals has been neither fully acknowledged nor appraised. While I am not a field archaeologist, illustrator, artist or museum archaeologist, these images are important to me. From the perspective of an archaeologist who uses these images for both teaching and research, I have long found it odd that there is very little comment about them. Their profound impact upon both the archaeological interpretation and the public perception of early Anglo-Saxon mortuary practices, including my own ideas, suggests that we treat these images both seriously and critically. It is important that we recognise and explore how images have the potential to be more powerful and problematic even than the terms that we employ. If long-used concepts like 'warrior graves' (see Härke 1990a) can be subject to deconstruction and reinterpretation, so must the images employed in the study, interpretation and illustration of the early Anglo-Saxon period.

Given that this paper addresses both the interpretation of early

Anglo-Saxon furnished inhumation graves (e.g. Härke 1990a; 1992b) and the relationship between archaeological theory and practice in the modern world (see Härke 2000a), this seems an appropriate subject to honour the influential work of Heinrich Härke in both these fields of scholarship.

Plans, sections and photographs

Within modern conventions of field recording and publishing early Anglo-Saxon inhumation burials, grave plans (usually drawn at a scale of 1:20) have become ubiquitous in early Anglo-Saxon cemetery publications. Sometimes they include details of complex grave assemblages and numbered annotations (Fig. 10.5). Most published plans are now created from field drawings and photographs using computer drawing software. A survey of early Anglo-Saxon cemetery publications reveals considerable, if subtle, variety rather than a strict adherence to uncompromising conventions.

These different 'ways of seeing' (Bradley 1997) have many causes. Differences reflect the varying levels of preservation encountered as well as contrasting scales and circumstances within which fieldwork takes place. The idiosyncrasies, experiences and methods adopted by different excavators, excavation projects and field units also play a part. Moreover, computer technologies have become increasingly used in the post-excavation analysis and publication of early Anglo-Saxon cemeteries and they have changed the way images are produced and subsequently appear. These 'craft traditions' (Bradley 1997) of grave-recording are evident in the contrasting records for very similar archaeological deposits, such as, for example, those of Sewerby, East Yorkshire (Hirst 1985), Apple Down, Sussex (Down and Welch 1990: 122–33), Mill Hill, Deal, Kent (Parfitt and Brugmann 1997), and West Heslerton, North Yorkshire (Haughton and Powlesland 1999). The tradition has been adapted to more schematic attempts at grave-plan drawing in cases where human remains have survived only as soil-stains, as at Harford Farm, Norfolk (Penn 2000: 7–42), or in instances of disturbed and poorly preserved graves, as at Norton, Cleveland (Sherlock and Welch 1992) and Croydon, Surrey (McKinley 2003; Fig. 10.6). Other variations include the increasing use of bi-colour and multi-colour plans to allow more detailed annotations and the recording of artefact-positions and body-positions (Boyle *et al.* 1995; Boyle *et al.* 1998; Malim and Hines 1998).

Despite these subtle variations and the publication of sections, plans of a similar form provide the dominant mode of recording early Anglo-Saxon inhumation graves. This largely two-dimensional

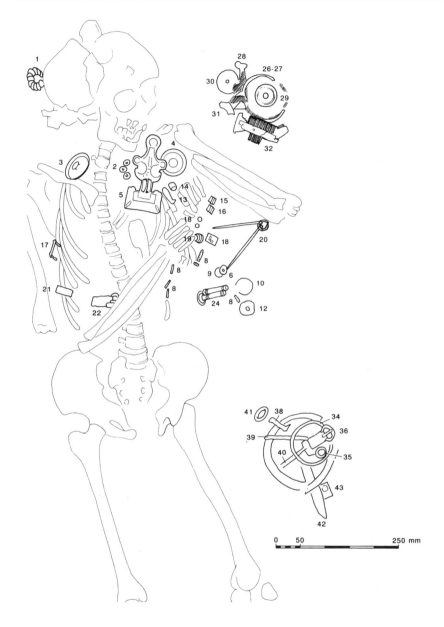

Fig. 10.5: A close-up plan originally reproduced at a scale of 1:5 of a rich adult female grave excavated at the Butler's Field cemetery, Lechlade, Gloucestershire. A reconstruction of this grave has been created within the Corinium Museum, Cirencester (after Boyle *et al.* 1998: 154). Reproduced with kind permission, ©Oxford Archaeology.

approach to furnished graves is one of the principal influences upon their interpretation. Yet there are some exceptional and important uses of section drawings in reports. For example, the careful recording of poorly-preserved inhumation graves from Spong Hill, Norfolk, used the juxtaposition of sections and plans to good effect. In doing so, the report portrayed many additional aspects of burial practice beyond the creation of a burial tableau at the bottom of the grave. These

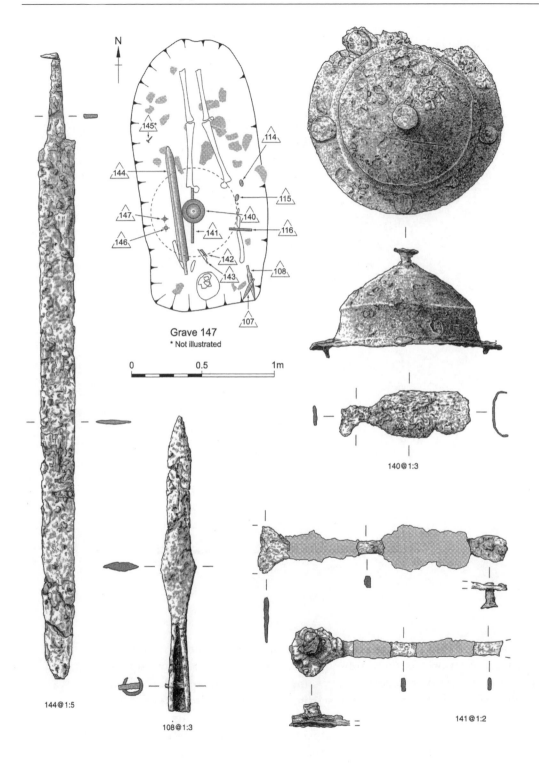

N

145*

144

147

146

114

115

140

141

116

142

143

108

107

Grave 147
* Not illustrated

0   0.5   1m

144@1:5

108@1:3

140@1:3

141@1:2

included the presence and character of coffins and chambers (Hills *et al.* 1984: 81, 109) and the locations of artefacts, such as pots and weapons, within the grave-fill (Hills *et al.* 1984: 57, 106, 110). Sections were also used as part of the careful recording of organic deposits in grave-fills at Snape, Suffolk. Here, the combination of sections and multiple plans during the excavation of each grave revealed evidence for the sequence of grave preparation, including the placing of grave-linings and structures, the burial of the clothed cadaver, artefacts and offerings, and, finally, rituals connected with the back-filling of graves (Filmer-Sankey and Pestell 2001: 236–50; Fig. 10.7). This serves to show that the quality of the data revealed, and the images produced, direct the subsequent possible archaeological interpretations. Where single grave plans are used – conflating the sequences of actions that comprised the composition and back-filling of the grave – it becomes

OPPOSITE

Fig. 10.6: A schematic grave plan of a poorly-preserved weapon grave 147 from Croydon, Surrey (after McKinley 2003: 36). Reproduced with kind permission, ©Wessex Archaeology.

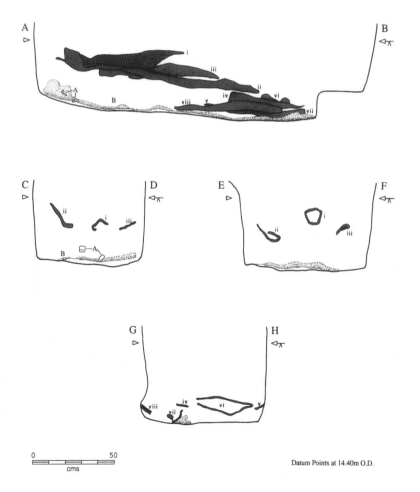

Fig. 10.7: Section drawing of early Anglo-Saxon inhumation grave 9 from Snape, Suffolk. The careful recording of the grave in section reveals rituals associated with the closing of the grave including the laying of burnt oak timbers over the cadaver (after Filmer-Sankey and Pestell 2001: 38). Reproduced with kind permission of Suffolk County Council Archaeological Services, ©Suffolk Council Council.

more tempting to regard inhumation graves as a single act of deposition rather than a mortuary process.

The same point applies to photography. While photographs provide the most visceral engagement with the early Anglo-Saxon dead, they have been employed only sparingly, even in very recent reports. This seems largely due to the costs of their reproduction in print since while photographs are widely used in field recording they are sometimes absent despite the rise of digital printing (e.g. Williams and Newman 2006). In modern contract archaeology, photographs are valuable as an important stage of the field recording process; in cases where graves must be excavated rapidly (especially given the threat of looting), photographs are the primary record: plans are produced only at the post-excavation stage (McKinley and Roberts 1993: 4). However, when photographs are employed in publications, they can reveal important additional details such as the complex three-dimensional positioning of bodies, objects and structures found in grave 41 from Sewerby (Hirst 1985: Plate IIB). More recently, photographs have been employed in innovative ways in reports to depict a range of other information, including excavation methodologies, grave contexts, artefacts and human remains. A good example of this is the report for Edix Hill, Barrington, Cambridgeshire (e.g. Malim and Hines 1998). Photographs are also essential for recording organic deposits and other ephemeral features that do not survive the excavation process. Examples include the coffins and body-stains at Snape, Suffolk (Filmer-Sankey and Pestell 2001: 26, 105, 109, 200). Moreover, photographs have been widely used as a medium for disseminating the character of archaeological discoveries in popular books on early Anglo-Saxon burial (e.g. Lucy 2000), in museum displays (e.g. Stevenson 1998: 52) and on the internet. Diggers are sometimes also portrayed: providing a scale or in 'heroic' action pose. Despite their potential, however, the most common use of the photograph is to emulate the grave plan, once again providing a somewhat two-dimensional view of early Anglo-Saxon furnished graves.

Plans, sections and photographs have tended to be separated out in excavation reports. Over the last decade, facilitated by computer databases, GIS technology, illustration and publication software packages publications have begun to change this tradition. This development has encouraged the depiction of the grave context itself as the primary archaeological focus of study rather than its constituent elements of finds, bones and their relative positions at the grave-bottom. For example, the use of GIS recording for the West Heslerton cemetery allowed plans, sections and photographs of graves to be integrated with artefacts and X-ray radiographs within

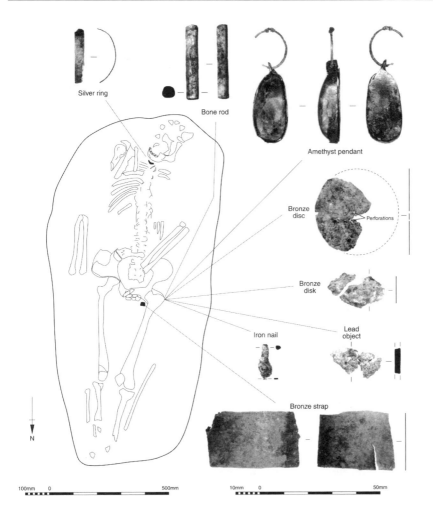

Silver ring

Bone rod

Amethyst pendant

Bronze disc

Perforations

Bronze disk

Lead object

Iron nail

Bronze strap

100mm 0   500mm   10mm 0   50mm

N

Fig. 10.8: An isolated seventh-century furnished grave of an adult, probable female, excavated at the Eton Rowing Course (after Foreman, Hiller and Petts 2000: 33). Reproduced with kind permission, ©Oxford Archaeology.

the grave catalogue (e.g. Haughton and Powlesland 1999: 122–24, 244–48). Other examples of this trend include the publications of Croydon, Surrey (McKinley 2003: 36), and St Mary's Stadium, Southampton, Hampshire (Birbeck 2005: 27–47). Meanwhile, Oxford Archaeology have recently used multiple colour photographs of individual graves in plan, using different scales to illustrate the detail of the skeleton and artefact positions (Booth *et al.* 2007: 188). They have also used traditional black-and-white grave plans annotated by colour photographs of the individual finds (see also Booth *et al.* 2007: 189–92, 389; Foreman *et al.* 2002: 33; Fig. 10.8).

In combination, facilitated by computer technology and digital publication, these varying styles of illustration provide more detailed and vivid portrayals of early Anglo-Saxon graves than traditional line-art depictions. Yet despite the potential for the illustration of excavation reports to reveal the finer details of the early Anglo-Saxon burial tableau, the burial process and mortuary variability, most early Anglo-Saxon graves remain represented principally through the publication of the two-dimensional grave plan.

Graves

Having discussed the more traditional media for recording archaeological discoveries, it is now possible to move on to consider artists' attempts to envision graves and funerals. Some artist's reconstructions have adopted what I would call the 'living dead' approach: portraying the appearance of early Anglo-Saxon people whilst alive based on the contents of graves. This approach has been particularly widespread for studies of early Anglo-Saxon costume (Owen Crocker 2004: plates D, F and G; Walton Rogers 2007: 181–83, 215–16). Sometimes these 'living dead' images combine grave-finds with forensic facial reconstructions as for the television series *Meet the Ancestors* (Richards 1999: 130–51).

However, our foci here are attempts to reconstruct the grave context itself. Isometric reconstructions of early Anglo-Saxon burial structures are relatively rare and are restricted to bed-burials (Speake 1989: 95), burial chambers and ships (Carver 2005: 177–99). Schematic reconstructions have also been employed in visualising mortuary monuments such as ring-ditches (Hedges and Buckley 1985: 18) and four- and five-post structures associated with cremation burials (Down and Welch 1990: 207; Lucy 2000: 26, 84; Welch 1992: 67).

More common have been attempts to reconstruct the burial tableaux of furnished inhumation graves. These images usually attempt a snap-shot of the grave as it may have appeared immediately prior to back-filling. The skeleton is re-fleshed and textiles and other organic finds are reconstituted in relation to the traces of artefacts recovered.

In many ways these reconstructions emulate the situation in the nineteenth century in so far as they do not illustrate unfurnished or poorly-furnished graves, nor those of moderate wealth. It tends to be the wealthiest, most complex or most distinctive inhumation graves which are selected for reconstruction. Examples include the seventh-century bed-burial 18B from Edix Hill, Barrington, Cambridgeshire (Malim and Hines 1998). This reconstruction, drawn from an oblique angle (as if from the perspective of an onlooker at the funeral), affords a sense of the layers and coverings of textiles that would have obscured body and bed. While attention is here paid to both the organic and inorganic finds, this burial was far from typical for the cemetery, in terms of both the burial wealth and seventh-century date.

Meanwhile, the rich chamber-grave from Prittlewell, Essex (Hirst 2004: 22; Fig. 10.9), illustrated by Faith Vardy, emphasises the three-dimensionality of the burial chamber, which includes objects suspended from its walls as well as laid on the floor. The complexity of the burial deposits here would be rendered difficult to comprehend in a traditional grave plan.

Both these examples demonstrate the role of grave reconstructions in communicating early Anglo-Saxon graves to a wide audience: the Edix Hill bed-burial adorns the front cover of the report while the image of the Prittlewell burial was completed soon after the excavation and widely disseminated in the national press and in popular archaeological texts (Pryor 2005: 229).

Fig. 10.9: The reconstruction by Faith Vardy of the chamber grave uncovered at Prittlewell, Essex. The image was widely used to disseminate the discoveries in the British media (after Hirst 2004: 22). Reproduced with kind permission of Faith Vardy and the Museum of London Archaeological Service, ©Museum of London.

Fig. 10.10: The reconstruction of the wealthy female burial with the burial of a child at the foot of the grave from grave 205 from Kingston Down, Kent, by Simon Bean. The image is based upon the written records of the Reverend Bryan Faussett's 1771 excavations. Reproduced with kind permission of and ©National Museums Liverpool, World Museum Liverpool.

Another use of an artist's grave reconstruction accompanies a display panel for the Faussett Collection of Anglo-Saxon antiquities in the Liverpool World Museum. Here the challenge was to illustrate the grave in which the famous Kingston brooch was found. The early seventh-century wealthy female burial had been recovered from grave 205 on Kingston Down, Kent, by the Reverend Bryan Faussett on 5 August 1771. However, Faussett did not illustrate his graves and he has left behind only a written account of the character of this burial (Smith 1856: 77–78; Fig. 10.10). The museum's visual interpretation of Faussett's account therefore allows viewers to visually locate the brooch in its burial context for the first time in over 200 years.

Exceptions to the rule of envisioning only the wealthiest graves are instances where unusual, 'deviant', burials are illustrated. Well-known examples include the 'live burial' from grave 41 at Sewerby, the reconstruction of which was used to adorn the cover of the excavation report (Hirst 1985) and has subsequently inspired a cartoon for popular consumption (Deary and Brown 2001: 70). Likewise, execution victims from Sutton Hoo were afforded detailed reconstructions to demonstrate the unusual postures in which the bodies were found (Carver 2005: 330; see also Redknap 2002: 43).

Whether portraying wealthy furnished graves or those of distinctive or deviant burials, these reconstructions have a power to distil and communicate archaeological interpretations in a fashion that traditional archaeological recording cannot easily achieve. Simultaneously, a clear limitation is that single graves illustrations offer the misleading impression that they are 'typical' and representative. They offer a normative stereotype that detracts from an appreciation of mortuary variability and encourages a view of burial rites as uniform 'customs' indicative of the period and region in question. In this regard, many illustrations are 'culture-historic' rather than processual or post-processual in their intent or result.

These biases have been remedied only in rare instances. Notably, the finances, public orientation and longevity of the *Time Team* television programme have afforded multiple opportunities for the artist Victor Ambrus to illustrate more typical early Anglo-Saxon inhumation graves. Ambrus has drawn graves from numerous sites and has chosen to visualise graves from both oblique and vertical perspectives. His accumulated portfolio from sites like Winterbourne Gunner, Wiltshire (Ambrus and Aston 2001: 53), and Breamore, Hampshire (Ambrus 2006: 39; Fig. 10.11), are examples of his work. While this has still not allowed Ambrus to illustrate a full range of burial variations known from the archaeological record for different age, gender and status groups for any given cemetery, he certainly provides a more representative portrayal of early Anglo-Saxon mortuary variability than hitherto.

Ambrus is also sensitive to the need to differentiate between aspects of his reconstructions that were revealed directly in the archaeological record and those elements that are more speculative. He has done this by using colour for the artefacts that were found and black-and-white for other elements, such as hairstyle, clothing and organic remains. Ambrus alerts the viewer to the nature of the original evidence as well as the process of interpretation.

Another example of this awareness of the artist's role as an interpreter concerns gender: one skeleton attributed as female by the osteologist was illustrated by Ambrus as being interred with a knife and shield. He therefore made the decision to portray the individual in female dress rather than depicting the burial as a male weapon-burial or a female warrior (Ambrus 2006: 41).

The advantage of this style of reconstruction is that it is interpretative and yet stays focused within the grave and hence close to the data recovered by the archaeologist. In this sense, it is tempting to regard these images as effective because of the seemingly 'accurate' or 'realistic' impressions they provide. This is, however, simultaneously their greatest disadvantage. By focusing on a single tableau they share

Fig. 10.11: A grave reconstruction by artist Victor Ambrus, from Breamore, Hampshire (after Ambrus 2006: 39). In the original image, Ambrus rendered the finds recovered from the grave in colour to distinguish them from the more speculative aspects of the reconstruction such as flesh, hair and clothing. Reproduced with the kind permission of Victor Ambrus.

with traditional grave plans the conflation of the burial process into a static, composed scene.

Funeral scenes

Many renditions go beyond artist's reconstructions of graves to attempt to portray funerary scenes. This kind of reconstruction image is often expensive and complicated to commission. They are also open to many levels of assumption and therefore, as ideas shift, they tend to date relatively quickly. Each choice made by the artist concerning which stage of the burial sequence to portray and the number, character, gestures and actions of the mourners, pose a wide range of interpretative problems. In particular, there is the tendency to impose upon mourners emotions and behaviour – reflected in their stances, spatial groupings and activities and expressions – that often reflect recent or modern British funerals rather than being supported by early medieval evidence. Choices are made over how 'familiar' and how 'exotic' the funeral should appear. Moreover, the problem remains (see above) that only a single funeral is depicted, which serves to stand for the site, period and/or culture in question. Issues of temporality remain challenging; the site is shown at one static moment, and the funerary rituals successively orchestrated over months, years and decades cannot be depicted.

Simultaneously, funerary scenes have their advantages over grave reconstructions: they provide among the most powerful and memorable images derived from archaeological research and are employed widely beyond academia. They also begin to situate the grave in relation to those that created it: the survivors and mourners, who make appropriate postures, gestures and emotional expressions. This style of reconstruction allows the living to become visible and tangible. Funerary scenes do assist more than grave reconstructions in presenting the burial tableau as only one stage in a complex mortuary process, and this can sometimes be achieved by the perspective adopted. Allusions might be made to rituals that took place earlier, as well as hints of activities that will follow the burial.

Let us consider some examples of these funerary scenes. More traditional reconstructions tend to focus on the grave-side scene, usually just before the grave is back-filled. In doing so, the focus remains upon the display within the grave itself following composition. Examples of this kind include depictions of sixth-century funerals of wealthy female individuals designed for museums from Glen Parva, Leicestershire (James 1999; Glasswell 2002: Fig. 10.12), and Portway, near Andover, Hampshire (Dark 2000: plate 7). Both take a similar view on wealthy female furnished graves of the sixth century: the body

is surrounded by a family group once the majority of mourners have departed for a settlement in the distance. Likewise, Victor Ambrus has illustrated funerary scenes for graves from Winterbourne Gunner, Wiltshire (Ambrus 2001: 54), and Breamore, Hampshire (Ambrus 2006: 38; Fig. 10.13) in addition to his grave reconstructions from these sites. Deborah Miles-Williams takes a different perspective in relation to the recently excavated early Anglo-Saxon graves from Cossington, Leicestershire. Given the evidence for cooking indicated by hearths close to the burials, her scene depicts both the burial tableau and some form of modest funerary feast taking place (Miles-Williams pers. comm.; Thomas 2008: plate 4).

A clear advantage afforded to Ambrus because of his involvement with Channel Four's *Time Team* is that he has the opportunity to portray multiple stages of the same funeral. For Winterbourne and Breamore, his scenes provide a sense of the cemeteries' location and topography as well as close-up graveside scenes. At Breamore, Ambrus draws a scene showing the cemetery's topographical location set on a Bronze Age barrow with a funerary procession approaching the site through earlier graves. He then provides a view of a funeral 'in action', with a weapon being placed into a double grave of a man and a woman (Fig. 10.13). For Winterbourne Gunner, one image shows a lone male mourner standing beside a freshly back-filled grave amidst an established cemetery; this is a different stage in the funeral to the open-grave burial tableau also depicted.

The commissioning of multiple images for the same archaeological site also has the advantage of showing different perspectives and interpretations of the same funeral. Such images have yet to be produced for a 'typical' Anglo-Saxon cemetery, but they exist for mound 1 at Sutton Hoo by virtue of the fact that, over the years, different artists have been approached to illustrate the site. These have included Alan Sorrell, Peter Dunn (Welch 1992), Victor Ambrus (Carver 2005) and Kelvin Wilson (Plunkett 2002). The contexts in which these images were produced vary slightly, but each serve, perhaps more than text-based archaeological discussions of the site, to evoke the theatre of the funeral (see Carver 2000) and the complexity of the funerary process.

Dunn's image was commissioned for the English Heritage series of popular archaeological books published by Batsford. His colour illustration focused on a cut-away view of the chamber within the ship together with attendant mourners. The scene focuses upon the process of composing the burial tableau, while the perspective allows the viewer to gain a sense of actions leading up to the funeral, including the dragging of the ship from the river Deben (Welch 1992).

Ambrus' images were commissioned for a popular book of the excavations by Martin Carver. Ambrus provides a series of artistic impressions illustrating the different types of funerary rites taking place at Sutton Hoo which have been used to illustrate both popular and academic texts (Carver 1998; 2005). These multiple scenes are valuable in that they provide a sense of the variability of the mortuary practices uncovered at this unique site, rather than addressing mound 1 in isolation. Ambrus is also effective in affording a sense of the mortuary process itself, and evokes the public nature of the funeral by depicting different sets of people: family, retainers, servants/slaves and a broader audience of onlookers (Fig. 10.14).

Kelvin Wilson, likewise, provides vivid scenes of cremation rituals, boat-burials and a child's burial at Sutton Hoo. Designed for the National Trust Visitor Centre at Sutton Hoo, Wilson also visualizes scenes from the lives of the individuals interred at the cemetery. However, most striking of all is Wilson's illustration a spectacular night-time scene showing mound 2's ship burial. This is a rare and effective instance where the completion of the burial is portrayed as still

Fig. 10.14: The funeral culminating at mound 2 at Sutton Hoo by Victor Ambrus (after Carver 2005: 176). Reproduced with the kind permission of Victor Ambrus.

Fig. 10.15: A night time view of the funeral associated with mound 2 at Sutton Hoo by Kelvin Wilson. The boat is being hauled into position over a chamber-grave (after Plunkett 2002: 19). Reproduced kind permission, ©Kelvin Wilson.

in progress rather than having reached the stage of a static tableau. The ship is being hauled over the burial chamber beneath it. In the chamber, only a glimpse of the body, grave goods and the mourners within are shown. This decision reflects archaeologists' caution over interpreting a grave that was plundered by antiquarians and heavily disturbed by Basil Brown's investigation. Yet through this choice of portrayal, more is left to the imagination of the viewer and a sense is given that the grave and the ship may have had a role in the funeral in concealment as well as in display. The choice to recreate a night-time scene further enhances the sense of spectacle and serves as a rejoinder to the daytime ceremony of the modern West. Wilson also evokes the complexity of the ritual process and the different experiences of contrasting groups of mourners. This is achieved by portraying the public elements above ground and hinting at activities of a more private or concealed nature going on within the chamber itself (Plunkett 2002; Fig. 10.15).

New technologies and innovative approaches will allow new ways of portraying early medieval graves and funerals. For example, Aaron Watson has integrated photography and art to computer-generate a

series of four images of different funeral scenes (Fig. 10.16), employing his philosophy of emphasising the experience of ritual practices in past societies (see Watson 2004). As with many of those above, the final products are the result of close dialogue between the artist and archaeologists. In this case, Aaron and I discussed in detail the overall impression that should be conveyed of the funerary scene, including a sense of dynamic action, emotion and spectacle. To emphasise this it was decided to focus on the perspective of someone attending the rites, rather than a bird's eye view. The reconstructions also aimed to move the focus away from the burial tableau to other stages in the mortuary process.

With this intention, the images attempted to illustrate an explicit theoretical approach to early medieval mortuary practice linked to the book in which they appear. They focus upon how the combination of artefacts, ritual technologies and the cadaver created an emotive force during successive stages of funerals. These engagements were ways by which the identity of the dead person was transformed through selective remembering and forgetting. Such an approach emphasizes transformation and staged engagement with the corporeality of the dead as much as it explores the funeral as a ritualised, public display (see Williams 2006; 2007b and c).

Fig. 10.16: An artist's reconstruction of a funerary scene by Aaron Watson (after Williams 2006: 198). The grave and location are inspired by the discoveries of female seventh-century barrow-burials like that upon Swallowcliffe Down, Wiltshire (Speake 1989). Reproduced with kind permission, ©Aaron Watson.

Three-dimensional and virtual reconstructions

There is a final form of the envisioning of early Anglo-Saxon inhumation graves that demands our attention. Many museums and heritage centres portray the finds from early Anglo-Saxon graves in traditional display cases and with discussions of their mortuary context provided by text and perhaps also by an artistic impression of a grave like those discussed above. Examples of this approach include (until recently) the Asmolean Museum, Oxford, and the Museum of London. Other museums adopt the 'living-dead' approach, utilising the evidence from graves to reconstruct how people lived, including aspects of their dress, tools and weapons, as demonstrated by the West Stow Anglo-Saxon Village (Anon. 2000; Lucy and Herring 1999). In addition to these manikins, 'live reconstructions', in which modern people dress up with costumes inspired by burial finds, can be seen as the ultimate extension of the 'living-dead' approach (Glasswell 2002; Owen-Crocker 2004; Walton Rogers 2007). Yet a number of museums and heritage centres have decided to portray the grave context itself: in a sense they attempt to bring early Anglo-Saxon death 'to life' in the museum context (Swain 2007: 162–63). These three-dimensional reconstructions represent the most expensive, elaborate and definitive ways of visualizing early medieval graves (see James 1999). They might be considered as one manifestation of numerous attempts by museums to contextualise, and sometimes sacralise, the ancient dead (Swain 2007: 163).

Many displays use the actual human remains and artefacts arranged in the fashion of their discovery. Sometimes these arrangements are placed within a mock grave. At Bede's World a replica of a sixth-century weapon burial uncovered from the excavations at Norton, Cleveland, is displayed vertically within a cabinet (Anon. 2004: 2). The relationships between bones and artefacts create a striking display and the vertical orientation facilitates its incorporation into

Fig. 10.17: Reconstruction of a seventh-century weapon burial depicted as discovered during excavations at Ford, Laverstock (Musty 1969) and displayed in the South Wiltshire Museum, Salisbury. Reproduced with kind permission, ©Salisbury and South Wiltshire Museum.

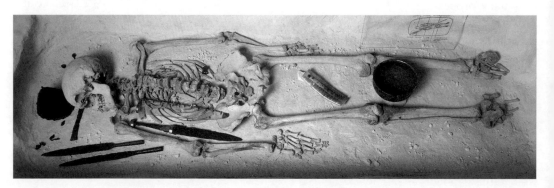

the visitor centre. In other museums a horizontal arrangement of bones and objects is preferred, mimicking the original grave context. One example, placed behind a traditional display case, is the reconstruction of a seventh-century weapon burial uncovered at Ford, Wiltshire, and on display at the South Wiltshire Museum in Salisbury (Musty 1969; Fig. 10.17). Likewise, at the Corinium Museum in Cirencester, Gloucestershire (see Swain 2007: 243–44), an arranged skeleton and grave goods reproduce a weapon burial. This example differs from the Salisbury display, with further attempts made to evoke a sense that the visitor is viewing an 'authentic' grave during excavation; archaeological tools (including a trowel, brush, bucket, planning frame and ranging rod) are placed around the skeleton together with ancient artefacts interred with the deceased (Fig. 10.18).

Fig. 10.18: A mock-up weapon burial 'during excavation' at the Corinium Museum, Cirencester. Reproduced with kind permission, © Corinium Museum.

A different strategy was adopted by the Norwich Castle Museum, to deal with the poor preservation of Norfolk cemeteries: the displayed furnished burial consists of a rare instance of a well-preserved eighth-century body with sixth-century grave goods and context in order to communicate the essence of an early Anglo-Saxon furnished grave (Tim Pestell pers. comm.). A further strategy to evoke the funeral context can be seen at Saffron Walden Museum, where the traditional display case is abandoned in favour to embedding the 'grave' into the floor itself so that visitors can walk over and look down onto the dead.

These examples can be contrasted with attempts at three-dimensional reconstructions of how the grave may have originally looked at the culmination of the burial rites and prior to back-filling. The 'Glen Parva Lady' in the Jewry Wall Museum, Leicester, is one example of this rendition (James 1999: 119). In addition to the artistic reconstructions commissioned by Kelvin Wilson for the display, the Sutton Hoo Visitor Centre near Woodbridge, Suffolk, incorporates a display of one of the 'sand men' (middle and later Anglo-Saxon deviant burials found only as stains in the sandy soil) as well as a reconstruction of the chamber from mound 1. In this way, the Centre encapsulates the dichotomy already identified between the visualisation of 'deviant'

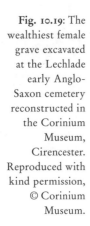

Fig. 10.19: The wealthiest female grave excavated at the Lechlade early Anglo-Saxon cemetery reconstructed in the Corinium Museum, Cirencester. Reproduced with kind permission, © Corinium Museum.

and 'high-status' graves. The design of the chamber makes clear to visitors something of the wealth and complexity of the burial, including both the organic and inorganic finds. However, the arrangement is a conceit designed to afford the public with a view of all the artefacts simultaneously on display. This spectacle is at the expense of including the possible presence of a coffin and innumerable textile coverings that would have sequentially concealed many of the grave goods during the burial process (Carver and Wainwright pers. comm., see below).

Along similar lines, the Corinium Museum in Cirencester offers the burial tableau of the wealthiest sixth-century grave excavated from a cemetery at Lechlade, Gloucestershire (Figs 10.5 and 10.19). Facial reconstruction, replica clothing, grave goods and grave structure are here afforded to a cadaver with a painted backdrop modelled on the reconstructed Anglo-Saxon village of West Stow. Two touch-screen computers allow the viewer to explore an interactive database of information about the grave and the society it represents. This display renders the reconstruction both physical and virtual. It provides the viewer with a rich and interactive appreciation of the interpretative process behind the model as well as putting the single grave in its wider context.

An attempt is made to render the grave with an identity and a personality in the present. Labelled 'Mrs Getty', using the term employed by the excavators in recognition of the grave's exceptional wealth, the composed grave embodies an identity that connects the visitor to the display, the process of excavation and an imagined personality for the human remains. Fleshed bodies tend to receive such nick names, and this is but one example of this widespread archaeological practice of humanising dead individuals through naming (Swain 2007: 154–55). The process of composition using the museum setting, science and replica objects is very much akin to the staged display of the body and material culture during the early medieval funeral itself (see below). However, rather than the fleeting snap-shot of display created in the early medieval funeral that would be subsequently concealed from the view of the mourners, Mrs Getty remains on display. She is frozen in time, receiving a form of post-mortem immortality, for generations of visitors to gaze upon (see also Beattie 1999; Curtis 2003; Nordström 2007).

The choice at Cirencester of the richest grave found in the Lechlade cemetery perpetuates the use of single burials as iconic representations of sites, periods and cultures, as discussed above for other forms of envisioning. This tendency for the selection of wealthy burials at Salisbury, Leicester and Cirencester is far from universal, however: the graves displayed at Norwich Castle and Bede's World might be regarded as more 'typical' in terms of wealth and burial arrangement. Moreover, the Corinium exhibition gets round this criticism and offers a more balanced portrayal by ensuring that the 'Mrs Getty' tableau is not set in isolation. As mentioned above, there is also a weapon burial portrayed as if freshly unearthed. There are also (living-dead) manikins with reconstructed costumes based on grave-finds and forensic facial reconstructions based on the skulls recovered. These are interspersed with traditional display cabinets of finds and information boards. This combination of different display methods provides a more rounded view of the mortuary evidence and offers the viewer alternatives for its interpretation.

More than any other media, three-dimensional models – whether physical or virtual – provide complex and diverse ways of exploring early Anglo-Saxon furnished graves and communicating them to the public. However, as with some artistic reconstructions of graves and funerals, the focus remains on a static image of death. In many ways, the two-dimensional artistic impressions have a greater potential to articulate the temporal and spatial aspects of early Anglo-Saxon mortuary practices than these three-dimensional museum exhibitions that enshrine and fossilise the dead into a single moment of either discovery (for skeletons arranged with artefacts) or prior to the back-filling of the grave (for reconstructions of the grave with the fleshed corpse).

Image and display in the early medieval grave

So far, this paper has sought to review the varied representations employed in interpreting and disseminating archaeological discoveries that are consumed by both specialist and popular audiences. What are the implications of this assessment for the study of early Anglo-Saxon mortuary practices?

First of all, let us consider how the evolution of images reflects changing archaeological paradigms. In crude terms, the style and choices of images employed reflect the successive influence of antiquarian, culture-historic, processual and post-processual modes of thought. Antiquarian and early archaeological images from the Georgian, Victorian and Edwardian periods focused primarily on isolated artefacts with only occasional uses of grave and site plans. When graves were illustrated they tended to be warrior graves which were employed to give an iconic image of the martial and racial qualities of the pagan and barbarous Teutonic settlers. Culture-historic (early and mid-twentieth-century) images retain their focus on artefacts although they extend their emphasis to grave assemblages. Little attention is paid to the bones, grave structures and mortuary context. The processual era might be recognised in the fully matured site report with specialist scientific reports and attention paid to the full recording of each archaeological context. Finally, the increased emphasis upon contextual information in site reports as well as the increasingly innovative ways of visualising mortuary scenes might be seen as reflecting (indirectly rather than explicitly) the reflexivity of post-processual ideas. In this sense, images commissioned for and by field archaeologists and illustrators reflect – albeit in only general terms – the intellectual climate of their times as well as the technologies at their disposal. The same point applies to the museum archaeologist, with the increasing focus upon thematic displays, interaction with the public and even the integration of art and archaeology in exhibitions. These are approaches that (to this writer's knowledge) have yet to be fully applied to early Anglo-Saxon grave displays.

However, the alternative argument can also be made: that images are active rather than passive results of theoretical trends. Images might be seen as directing, restricting, simplifying and even hampering interpretations because of the choices made in the portrayal of the archaeological evidence. We have seen how the persistent emphasis upon a single rich grave detracts from a fuller appreciation of *mortuary variability*. Rich graves visualised as iconic representations of a particular period and culture are therefore an emblematic way by which culture-historic paradigms have been perpetuated in academic discourse and popular culture (see also Lucy and Herring 1999).

We can also identify the impact of images in the pervasive attention given to furnished early Anglo-Saxon graves as a visual and symbolic text in recent theoretical discussions. This is an idea that was developed in the 1980s, when early post-processual studies attempted to regard mortuary practices as more than reflections of social structure. Instead, they regarded graves as symbolic messages composed by the survivors to communicate to a wider audience (Pader 1982; Richards 1987). This approach has had an enduring appeal since it prioritizes the operation of furnished graves as public social statements that were intentional and symbolic in their content. One version of this approach can be found in Heinrich Härke's (1990a; 1997b, c and d) study of the early Anglo-Saxon weapon burial rite.

Martin Carver (2000) has developed the artistic analogy further, likening graves and the funerals of which they were a part to a 'text with attitude', reflecting and affecting their audience. With the wealthy ship-burials of Sutton Hoo in mind, Carver regards funerals as artistic works like poems and theatre; complex compositions performed to particular groups at certain times. His explicit use of the term 'tableau' further emphasises his artistic interpretation of the early medieval furnished grave. Likewise, Guy Halsall (2003) has further provided the link to art and theatre in his interpretation of Merovingian furnished graves which he regards as concerned with the creation of memorable scenes through brief public spectacles (see also, Williams 2006: 118–21).

This approach has many advantages over regarding graves as an assemblage from which social information can be extracted. Yet, equally, there are numerous inherent and unquestioned problems with it. All these writings directly or indirectly regard graves as intentional and meaningful compositions following the intentions of 'composers'. As such their focus is on graves as a form of visual display equivalent to an artwork; the 'grave' is ostensibly an art installation. It is an installation directly accessible to the excavating archaeologist and subsequently permeating the archaeological literature through its recording via the visual media discussed above. Indeed, it is no coincidence that this perspective regards early medieval mourners as undertaking a similar task to the archaeologist; both are seen as artistic and creative thinkers making informed decisions about how to place artefacts and the cadaver with aesthetics and display relating to complex religious and socio-political concepts at the front of their minds. While the mourners perform and materialize their complex informed decisions into the grave, the excavator's careful methodology and decisions concerning what to record transforms the grave into visual information and documentation for publication. In doing so, this research tradition interacts with a particular way of seeing graves as well as particular way of viewing archaeological labour. This is not manifest in a single visual medium, but in the combination of the different media discussed above, from line illustration to photographs and artworks (Bradley 1997). Indeed, the entire approach might be seen as facilitated by, and the product of the way we dig graves and use grave plans in excavation reports rather than the complex sequences of actions and practices that these plans have distilled.

The argument here is not to suggest that a focus on display within the grave is refuted by its derivation from the archaeological process and the data it produces – the contrary is true. However, the dogged focus by interpretations upon the visual media and the burial tableau detracts from other elements of early Anglo-Saxon mortuary practice for which there is equally ample evidence. What is not regularly envisioned is the landscape context (increasingly identified as an important aspect of early medieval funerals: e.g. Härke 2001), beyond its depiction in a site location map or as a backdrop to some artistic reconstructions. Few images capture a sense of the many stages to the funeral and the potential for many places and actions that sequentially and simultaneously created the burial tableau and the actions that would have come afterwards (see Halsall 2003). In other words, in the same way that archaeologists' focus is upon the composition of the grave in archaeological publications, interpretations of past mortuary practices dwell on the display of the dead in the grave rather than either the rituals leading up to the burial or the commemorative rites that may have subsequently focused upon graves after the funeral.

The focus on display in modern art and archaeological illustrations also overlooks the fact that the mourners of the early Anglo-Saxon dead seem to have paid considerable attention to the staged consignment, concealment and closing off of visual information alongside carefully orchestrating mortuary displays within the grave. Early Anglo-Saxon funerals involved acts of destruction and dissolution as well as composition and representation. Many items found in graves were not on view for survivors to see in the final stages of the grave's composition but may have been associated with earlier stages of the mortuary process (see Williams 2006: 123–34).

Likewise, the focus upon visual display suppresses consideration of the other senses; archaeologists cannot restrict their interpretations of the significance of past mortuary practices to vision alone. Moreover, the material investigated has clearly identifiable non-visual properties that can be subject to analysis. The potential for important symbolic and mnemonic roles for aromas (both to mask the smell of decay and to create distinctive impressions), tastes (including the consumption of particular foods and liquids), sounds (including elegies and the acoustic impact of all manner of ritual activities, from grave-digging to animal sacrifice) and touch (including the importance of intimate gestures during funerals as expressions of bereavement, such as dressing the corpse and the placing of objects) need to be integrated into archaeological interpretations. The effects of these senses as well as the exclusion of different groups from such practices and engagements may have been as important as visual display. There is ample evidence for some of these: the choice is made, however, to prioritize visual display. Moreover, the focus upon the richest graves emphasises spectacle over more emotion-laden engagements with dead bodies of all ages, genders and status groups during early Anglo-Saxon funerals (Williams 2007c).

The process of interpretation is therefore both helped and hampered by the visual media that archaeologists employ. Exploring new ways of envisioning early Anglo-Saxon mortuary practices should therefore accompany the development of new interpretative approaches to the data available to the archaeologist. Innovations may take the route of computer-based technologies or simply the creation of different images within established illustrative media and modelling. One example might be the employment of the popular and widely understood genre of the comic strip in order to illustrate sequences of actions, characters and scales of activity often lost in a single, static reconstruction image (e.g. Artelius 2000; Schülke 1999). Mortuary variability might be evoked by using computer technology to envision multiple grave reconstructions from each site rather than a 'token' example to 'stand for' the rest. Meanwhile, different interpretations of grave reconstructions might be attempted for the same graves and funerals (see James 1999: 119). Likewise, it will be interesting to see whether virtual reality modelling of mortuary contexts, like that attempted on the Museum of London website for the Prittlewell chamber-grave, will reflect and affect future interpretations.

Finally, the injection of alternative emotions other than sombrness into illustrations of early Anglo-Saxon funerals might question our preconceptions of their tempo, mood and level of formality. This has been achieved to good effect elsewhere, with a comic portrayal of the tenth-century Viking cremation witnessed by Ibn Fadlan adorning the cover of an edited volume by Kjeld Jensen and Høilund Nielsen (1997)! I do not advocate a single direction, but would emphasise the potential for innovation by linking archaeological theory and artistic talent in the pursuit of novel, meaningful and perhaps challenging renditions of early Anglo-Saxon graves and funerals.

Images of the early medieval dead in the present

If the recent obsession with the visual display of the burial tableau is taken as a reflection of the interaction between the archaeological process that focuses on the two-dimensional grave plan and the kinds of images and art produced for and by archaeologists, these images of early Anglo-Saxon graves also interact with wider popular attitudes to the past and mortality. Through archaeological images and displays the early Anglo-Saxon dead reside visually and physically in our society.

There are certainly well-established discussions of the socio-politics of the use and abuse of mortuary data retrieved by archaeologists (e.g. Crist 2002) as well as the ethics of displaying and curating the archaeological dead (Curtis 2003; Swain 2002; 2007). Some attention has been paid to the emotional and personal experiences of archaeologists when encountering human remains (e.g. Kirk and Start 1999) and the engagements between mortuary archaeology and modern experiences of death and identity (Crossland 2000; Curtis 2003; Williams and Williams 2007).

Viewing remains of the ancient dead has rightly been accused as containing elements of voyeurism. More positively, the public display of ancient bones and mortuary artefacts has been promoted as primarily educational. Graves and bodies have a unique power to humanize and personalize the past, allowing the individual in the past to be tangible for the public. The display of mortuary remains might be seen as serving to spiritualize death for a secular culture by portraying death in a past ritual context and treating human remains as sacred (Swain 2007: 148–49). A further significance might be located in the ability of the archaeological dead to be uncanny, challenging or even subverting the attitudes towards the past and mortality (Moshenska 2006). Certainly, there is no single and universal modern response or attitude towards images of the early Anglo-Saxon dead in British society. Indeed, the power of the ancient dead for today resides in their multivocality and this requires further study (see also Williams and Williams 2007). It cannot be denied that the envisioning of mortuary archaeology is one element of modern death culture, portraying as it does both dead human beings and ancient mourners dealing with death and the dead.

Since the Middle Ages, timeless, static images of death have been widely deployed in mortuary practice and commemorative art. There are innumerable examples, from medieval effigies to early modern paintings of death-bed scenes, from Victorian photographs of the dead to the display of the embalmed body in funeral parlours and open-casket funerals (Hallam *et al.* 1999: 20–42; Llewellyn 1991).

In many ways, it is this evolving tradition of death-art, which has been adapted into the secular world of modernity, that provides the context within which archaeological portrayals of furnished graves may be understood. Indeed, the tradition of technical antiquarian and archaeological illustration that developed between the late eighteenth and early twentieth centuries might be seen as one way in which death-art has straddled major shifts in British attitudes to mortality over the last two centuries.

The role of mortuary archaeology as death-art needs explaining. During the last century, commentators frequently argued that we exist in a culture in which death is out of bounds, detached from experience and corporeal engagement. Death is medicalized, secularized, individualized and privatized. Simultaneously, death is increasingly tied to the demise of the individual body and the self (Howarth 2006; Mellor and Shilling 1993; Walter 1995). While natural dying and death are kept at a distance by hospitals and undertakers, violent deaths and fictional deaths are visible for all to see through the media. In response to this trend, in recent decades a constellation of practices and rituals have developed that constitute a 'rebirth' and re-location of death in Western culture in the absence of any shared religious system or cult of ancestors (Howarth 2006).

It is in this context, as one strategy of relocating death and the dead in modern society, that the appeal of mortuary archaeology's envisioning of death can be understood. Archaeology provides a medium that renders death visible, tangible and corporeal, and hence also real and meaningful, to modern people through the display of individual bodies. The precise 'message' may vary, and values attached to human remains are complex; but their power in modern society cannot be denied. This is achieved not only through the revelation, recording and display of human remains but also by rendering death in photographs and art. Death is depicted as managed by our ancestors through formal, sombre and exotic funerary procedures. Death is also viewed as 'tame' (mirroring the view of Ariés: see Floersch and Longhofer 1997), noble and natural (Walter 1995) through ritualization among the 'savages' and 'barbarians' of the past. Ironically, by placing death within history (particularly among those groups like the Anglo-Saxons, who are perceived as among the 'ancestors' of the modern British), death is rendered timeless and traditional – outside of history. Death joins the realm of the universal: an inevitability in the past, present and future. The past and our ancestors are therefore portrayed as like ourselves through a common, shared bond of mortuary management, while simultaneously romanticized as having conquered the problems and anxieties of dealing with death. This provokes the question: by celebrating their deaths, do we hope to come closer to transcending our own?

However comforting these images are for a grieving modernity in which death is privatized and secular, lacking the guidance of traditional religion and communal ritual, this may not be in itself the crux of the appeal of mortuary archaeology. The attraction of the archaeological dead may instead reside in the inherent contradictions of mortuary remains from the perspective of the modern viewer. The archaeological dead are simultaneously distant and anonymous while being close and individual. This tension is manifest in the way we display the archaeological dead. Death is individualized in the popular culture of mortuary archaeology through the 'rich and famous' – as with the 'Prittlewell Prince' – as well as through more modest personages. If their names are not known, archaeologists invent new ones for them, whether they be an Egyptian mummy (Spencer 1982), a bog body (Glob 1971), the Ice Man (Swain 2007) or the frozen body of John Torrington of the failed Franklin Expedition to find the North-West Passage (Beattie 1999). Archaeology creates such immortals (Nordström 2007).

Equally it is the sheer quantity and corporeality of unnamed human remains and the stories about individuals and communities that capture the public's interest. As well as the tombs of past 'celebrities' such as pharaohs and kings, the interest lies in the mortal remains of 'us' in the past (the average person) and the stories archaeologists can tell from their bones and artefacts. This is an emotional connection to past life histories and deaths as much as an interest in mortuary remains as a scientific and historical resource for decoding the past and the portrayal of past personalities.

The media of envisioning discussed above render the dead corporeal rather than abstract and ethereal. Unlike most displays of death in modern culture, archaeological death is fact, not fiction. The dead are close to modern people who are able see beneath the skin and handle (or at least view close-up) artefacts and contexts associated with the bones. Indeed, people living today can view, scrutinize and even touch through art and display the archaeological dead of the distant past more easily than they may a dying or deceased close relative.

Through the paradox of their distance and closeness, envisioned early Anglo-Saxon deaths are drawn into modern mortuary culture by archaeologists. Indeed, the archaeologist 're-wraps' bones with the interpretive text, artistic reconstructions and museum displays. Archaeologists are contextualizing burials within narratives about past lives and deaths as well as socializing the ancient dead into our own society. We are conducting a form of archaeological embalming following exhumation; socializing ancient bodies through archaeological practice (see Hallam *et al.* 1999: 131–38). It is in archaeological publications and museums that death is most tangible, managed in a public setting and situated within the 'tame' environment of the ancestral past.

The project of early Anglo-Saxon burial archaeology is therefore as much about constructing a vision of past mortality in relation to present-day experience and practice as much as it is about shedding light upon the past for its own sake. Early Anglo-Saxon graves have a unique position in this regard, between prehistory and history, between the pagan and Christian Middle Ages. Burial archaeologists may be even regarded as one further category of funerary specialist in the Western world. In this regard, perhaps archaeologists are 'artists' after all! The envisioning of death through field recording and archaeological illustration is a key element of this process. Just as the transformation and treatment of cadavers and material culture constituted early medieval identities, images of early medieval skeletons and graves mediate modern mortalities.

It may be for this reason that the majority of Western people do not strongly object to the excavation, curation and display of mortuary remains (see Swain 2007). Archaeologists and the public share the conceit that excavations serve to 'save' and 'preserve' the dead and with them ancient, ancestral mortuary practices. The reality is that archaeologists have created a tangible medium and place for dealing with contemporary loss and mortality through the controlled destruction, recording and envisioning of ancient graves.

Conclusion

> The power of the visual image needs to be understood, its ability to select and organize knowledge, to compress time and space, to insinuate conclusions, and to tidy away the inconvenient and the complex in the interests of a compelling vision is as true now as it has ever been. (Moser and Smiles 2005: 6)

From simple grave plans to three-dimensional reconstructions, images of early medieval graves are diverse, sophisticated, essential and integral media by which knowledge and interpretations of early medieval mortuary practices are represented, communicated and disseminated among both specialist and popular audiences. It is also the contention of this paper that these images are one element of a broader archaeological contribution to the visual identity of the dead in modern Western culture. Hence this is a topic that touches upon debates in the archaeological theory and method, the context and ethics of mortuary archaeology, interdisciplinary studies of mortality, heritage and museum studies as well as archaeological methodologies, recording techniques and illustrations.

By recognising the potential interpretative power and dangers of images (the ability to help and hinder archaeological interpretations), this paper challenges archaeologists to use images of early Anglo-Saxon graves in innovative ways. Rather than seeing archaeological illustrators and artists as subservient and secondary to text-based interpretations created by archaeologists, future studies of early Anglo-Saxon mortuary archaeology might consider recognising the importance of greater dialogue between archaeologists and illustrators and artists in the choices made over how to portray and reconstruct graves and funerals. This study has focused on early Anglo-Saxon furnished inhumation rites, but further studies are needed to explore how these images compare and contrast with those employed for other types of early medieval burial and to examine the interactions between illustrations, archaeological theories and archaeology's socio-political and popular context. Here are some key themes that I feel require further study:

1 The envisioning of early Anglo-Saxon cremation graves is a greater challenge than the portrayal of inhumation burials. Cremation leaves more ephemeral and fragmented traces and has tended to receive less attention in archaeological field recording (Høilund Nielsen, this volume). Subsequently, the rite and its variability is much more difficult to reconstruct and, unsurprisingly, fewer technical and artistic reconstructions of the rite have resulted (e.g. Leahy 2007: plate 4). New ways of visualising early Anglo-Saxon cremation practices are required, given the dynamic interaction of display and transformation integral to this disposal method (see Williams 2007b).

2 The relatively unfurnished early medieval burial traditions of western and northern Britain – as well as post-Conversion inhumation practices – are much more varied than is often supposed (e.g. Hadley 2001; Astill, this volume; Petts, this volume). However, perhaps because of a lack of 'grave goods', these rites have received far fewer published plans and artistic reconstructions than early Anglo-Saxon furnished inhumations (see Carver 1999: 22–23, 49). The reasons for this contrast may extend beyond data quality and require further critical examination.

3 The vivid and diverse envisioning of British and Scandinavian Viking-period furnished interments (including boat-graves, cremation ceremonies and chamber-graves) in excavation reports,

archaeological studies, museum displays and other media may provide a useful set of comparisons and contrasts with the portrayal of early Anglo-Saxon graves (e.g. Ambrus 2006: 44; Hall 2007: 132; see also Price 2002: 131, 136–7, 141, 153). What are the similarities and differences in the portrayal of early Anglo-Saxon and Viking burials, and what factors might explain these?

4 Wider comparisons and contrasts should be sought with the archaeological illustration of prehistoric, Roman, medieval and post-medieval mortuary practices to identify how these eras and their varying mortuary practices are visualized. Are there overriding similarities to or differences from the images discussed in this paper? If there are differences, do they reflect the nature of the archaeological and historical record or do they reveal differences in modern perceptions of these eras as either 'familiar' or 'other' (see Swain 2002)? Do periods regarded as more exotic and primitive nowadays receive contrasting portrayals to those thought to share modern sensibilities and emotional responses to death and mortality?

5 Finally, and perhaps of most interest to Heinrich Härke, it would be informative to compare the visualisation of early medieval graves within different regional and national academic traditions and to consider whether these images reflect alternative modes of archaeological thinking, socio-politics or attitudes towards death, commemoration and mortality. For instance, do Scandinavian, German or Russian (for sake of argument) archaeological images of early medieval furnished graves differ from British modes of envisioning the dead? If they do differ, why is this (see Härke 2000a)?

These topics can be combined with five further themes that constitute a provisional agenda for the further study of early medieval mortuary images:

1 New studies are needed into the history and traditions of the envisioning of early medieval graves (Smiles 2005; Williams 2008).

2 Future work should recognise and support the interpretative significance and innovative use of art during archaeological projects from their inception, through field-based investigations and excavations, to publication and dissemination.

3 The critical appraisal of mortuary illustrations must go hand in hand with attempts to use new technologies and media as ways of

communicating archaeological ideas through images and models (see also Cochrane and Russell 2007).

4 Innovative approaches to early medieval mortuary images must engage with new theories in mortuary archaeology. These might consider furnished graves as more than a public display and symbolic text focusing upon the tableau so often represented. This view must be qualified by an emphasis, where feasible, upon transformation, emotion and experience in rituals surrounding death (Watson 2004; Williams 2006; 2007b and c).

5 Future studies need to consider the interactions between Western (and in particular British) attitudes to death, the ethnographic and historical analogies that archaeologists often exploit in their interpretations, and the representation of early medieval graves.

By identifying this research agenda for the future, this paper is commended to Heinrich Härke in honour of his considerable impact on the field of early medieval mortuary archaeology.

Acknowledgements

The paper has benefited considerably from the comments and criticisms of many archaeologists, archaeological illustrators and artists who have provided support, discussed ideas and read drafts of the manuscript: Victor Ambrus, Anders Andrén, Tanya Berks, Anne Dodd, Peter Dunn, Liz Gardner, Erica Hill, Catherine Hills, Cornelius Holtorf, Simon James, Margaret Matthews, Deborah Miles-Williams, Tim Pestell, David Petts, Duncan Sayer, Sam Smiles, Eva Thäte, Angus Wainwright, Tony Walter, Aaron Watson, Elizabeth Williams, Kelvin Wilson and the anonymous referees. I am also extremely grateful to the following illustrators and artists for granting permissions to reproduce their work: Victor Ambrus, Simon Bean, Mike Codd, Faith Vardy, Aaron Watson and Kelvin Wilson. Finally, I would like to thank the following institutions for generously granting me permission to reproduce the illustrations: Corinium Museum Cirencester, Jewry Wall Museum Leicester, World Museum Liverpool, Museum of London Archaeological Service, Oxford Archaeology, Salisbury and South Wiltshire Museum, Suffolk County Council Archaeological Service and Wessex Archaeology. All errors remain my responsibility.

Chapter 11

Variation in the British burial rite: AD 400–700

David Petts

Abstract
This paper highlights the variation found in the early medieval burial rites of western Britain. Whereas archaeologists working on Anglo-Saxon mortuary practices have emphasised the extensive regional and local variability found across England, an overly simplistic model of British funerary traditions is still common, with the burials being characterised as lacking in grave goods and often laid out in regularly planned cemeteries. Whilst some cemeteries do conform to this stereotype, this paper demonstrates that there is more mortuary variability to be found in western Britain than is often assumed. It recognises that such variation is apparent in many aspects of burial, including the use of inscribed burial monuments, the organisation and planning of cemeteries and the presence of grave goods. By highlighting the complexity of funerary behaviour in western Britain we are able to start asking more subtle questions of the archaeological data, and develop increasingly nuanced models of early medieval British society.

Introduction

The mortuary record of early medieval Britain (AD 400–700) is dominated by the burials and cremations of the Anglo-Saxon tradition. Usually accompanied by a range of grave goods structured around age, gender and status lines, these graves are clearly part of a wider pan-European tradition of accompanied burials associated with the incoming Germanic peoples that moved into the Western Roman Empire in the fourth and fifth century AD (Halsall 1995a; Lucy and Reynolds 2002: 1).

However, this tradition was not the only one found in Britain at this time. In western and south-western England, as well as in Wales, another burial rite dominated. In contrast to the Anglo-Saxon burial rite, this is usually characterised as consisting of burials interred without grave goods laid in a predominantly west–east alignment (Petts 2004). This can be seen as reflecting the other side of the wider cultural fault-line that crossed the former Roman province of Britannia in the early medieval period, with the east and south dominated by a pagan society drawing many of its cultural traditions from Germanic incomers, whilst the west and north were the domain of a predominantly Christian British society deriving some of its cultural identity from late Romano-British society (Dark 1994a). Many of the archaeological analyses of the political and cultural developments of the fifth to seventh centuries A D are predicated not only on internal conflict between competing Anglo-Saxon polities, but also of a profound clash of culture between Anglo-Saxon society and the British, often characterised as an ethnic conflict in the face of migration (Lucy 2002; Goffart 1989; Higham 1992: 1–16; Hills 2003).

Despite a perceived broad unity in Anglo-Saxon culture, it has long been recognised that there is considerable diversity in the archaeological record, particularly in the burial rite. The difference between areas where cremation and inhumation dominate is apparent, often identified with a distinction between Anglian and Saxon areas of settlement respectively. However, recent work has started to dismantle these larger cultural blocks and highlight the evidence for increased regional, sub-regional and even inter- and intra-site variability (e.g. Lucy 1998; Lucy 2002; Härke 1990a). Alongside and related to this shift in perception has been a rise in critiques of models of early medieval society based on ideas of mass migration and ethnic replacement, emphasising the socially situated nature of ethnic and other identities (e.g. Geary 1983; Härke 2007a; Lucy 2002; Pader 1982; Stoodley 1999c). The debate over the extent and impact of Anglo-Saxon migration still rages despite recent advances in the analysis of blood groups, DNA and trace elements in bone diagenesis (e.g. Topf *et al.* 2006; Thomas *et al.* 2006; Montgomery *et al.* 2005; see also Hills this volume).

Despite these advances in Anglo-Saxon archaeology, the study of the British component of the population of England and Wales has followed a different course. The main discourse in recent years has been over the extent of continuity (and discontinuity) from the Roman period into the early Middle Ages. Although this notion has its origins earlier, the debate was stimulated in the early 1990s by the work of Ken Dark, the strongest advocate of the continuity thesis (Dark 1994a; Dark 2000). Despite some continued strong opposition to this thesis (e.g. Faulkner 2003; 2004) there has been increased interest in the concept of continuity, and the notion of western Britain being part of a wider Late Antique *koine* has been gaining ground in recent years (e.g. papers in Gerrard and Collins 2004; Esmonde Cleary 2001; Harris 2003). This debate has undoubtedly revived the study of the early medieval 'British', but the focus on continuity has had its less favourable consequences. Principally, while much emphasis has been placed on teasing out threads of physical and ideological continuity from the Roman world, less effort has been spent on highlighting the immense regional and chronological variability across the British cultural world. Little work has focused on highlighting the differences between, for example, Somerset, Cornwall and Pembrokeshire in the sixth century. In contrast there have been innumerable studies of local and regional variability considering the differences between Kent, Oxfordshire and Northumberland in the same period. In other words, whilst analyses of social change in the early medieval period are alive to the complexity inherent in Anglo-Saxon societies, it is still common to find the inhabitants of western Britain lumped together as an undifferentiated cultural mass known simply as 'the British', whose cultural traits include a shared exposure to imported Mediterranean material culture, hill-top fortified elite residences, Christianity evidenced in holy sites and inscribed stones as well as a shared milieu of Insular art and artefacts (e.g. Snyder 1996; Thomas 1971). This paper aims to highlight the diversity in the archaeology of early medieval British society by exploring several aspects of the burial record. The elements considered here are funerary epigraphy, cemetery organisation and the use of grave goods. By doing so, the paper demonstrates the possibility of writing a more textured archaeology of the British that will correspond with the increasingly subtle analyses of the varied and changing nature of early Anglo-Saxon society.

Epigraphy

The early medieval British burial rite, whilst seemingly lacking in grave goods (though see below), is blessed with a significant epigraphic record. A range of carved stone funerary monuments are known from Cornwall (with outliers in Devon, Dorset and Somerset), south-west and north-west Wales (with outliers particularly in Glamorgan and Breconshire) and to a lesser extent the Scottish borders (Nash-Williams 1950; Edwards 2007; Redknap and Lewis 2007; Okasha 1993; Forsyth 2005). These relatively unadorned monuments usually carry simple inscriptions recording an individual (usually with patronymics) and more rarely have some additional epitaph (e.g. [A]NNICI FILIVS [H]IC IACIT TECVRI IN HOC TVMVLO; 'The Stone of Anniccius, son of Tecurus. He lies here in this tomb', Abercar, Breconshire; Nash-Williams 1950: 41). Whilst a boundary marker function has been suggested for some (Handley 1998), this is not incompatible with a funerary function, which is indicated by the use of the phrase *Hic Iacit* (Here lies) on many stones of this type (e.g. CARAVSIVS / HIC IACIT/ IN HOC CON/GERIES LA/PIDUM; 'Carusius lies here in this heap of stones', Penmachno, Caernarvonshire; Nash-Williams 1950: 101). Crucially, it seems that this fifth- to seventh-century flowering of early medieval epigraphy is drawing on two distinct models. Many stones are in Latin and the choice of phraseology indicates they are drawing on contemporary epigraphic practices in the Late Antique world, although Handley has demonstrated that this influence was not specifically from south-west Gaul as previously supposed (Knight 1999; Handley 2001). Another, equally important influence, however, comes from Ireland with the use of ogham script; the presence of Irish names on these stones indicates not only Irish influence, but the presence of at least a small number of Irish settlers (Swift 2007).

While their relatively high archaeological variability, particularly compared with the relatively sparse nature of other aspects of early medieval archaeology in western England and Wales, has meant that these stones have attracted much research (e.g. Nash-Williams 1950; Edwards 2001; 2007; Knight 1992; 1999; Dark 1992; Handley 1998; 2001; Redknap and Lewis 2007; Tedeschi 1995; 2001; Sims-Williams 2003), relatively little consideration has been given to their wider geographical distribution. The use of ogham and the presence of Irish names have been used to suggest that they are indicative of areas of primary or secondary Irish migration in the early medieval period, though this has seen relatively little critical analysis. Whilst ogham stones are certainly found in areas close to Ireland, particularly Pembrokeshire and north-west Wales, it is in precisely these areas that we might expect to find pre-existing Irish contact and settlement. It is possible that the presence of ogham may merely be the first diagnostically distinctive element of Irish influence that had a longer prehistory during the pre-Roman and Roman Iron Ages (cf. Campbell 2001).

The advent of Irish settlement as an explanation for the rise of epigraphy in western Britain also suffers from another difficulty. It fails to explain the simultaneous appearance of the Latinate epigraphy in the same areas. Instead, the evidence for trade links with Gaul and other areas of the Late Antique world are usually used to explain this sudden appearance. Handley has also noted that the presence of Latinate gravestones in Britain in the fifth century AD reflects the wider reassertion of the epigraphic tradition across the Western Roman Empire (Handley 2001). Although the overall chronological distribution of Roman epigraphy in Britain seems to confirm Handley's hypothesis, there is still a real problem in explaining why this re-emergence of epigraphy fails to occur in the areas of Britain that had been home to earlier Romano-British epigraphy, but in areas far removed from the most Romanised areas of *Britannia*, in the far west and north. All other indicators mark these regions as peripheral to the spread of *Romanitas*. Despite the evidence for significant sub-Roman activity at some Roman towns (and the testimony of the *Vita Germani* c.16: Hoare 2000) we do not find this post-Roman epigraphy in St Albans, London or Colchester, but on the coast of Pembrokeshire, the Lleyn peninsular and Breconshire; the outliers at Wroxeter and Silchester (i.e. located in former Roman towns) are the exceptions that prove the rule (Fulford *et al.* 2000).

Despite the fact that it is unlikely that the emergence of Irish-influenced epigraphy and Latinate epigraphy at the same time and the same place is purely coincidental, there have been no satisfactory attempts to explain this convergence of commemorative practices. Rather than seeing this epigraphic horizon as occurring as a result of the intersection of two distinctive epigraphic traditions, we should instead consider how the social dynamics of the areas where this re-emergent tradition was strongest required funerary epigraphy to be used at all.

There is extensive literary evidence from Ireland pointing towards the use of ogham stones as both burial markers and boundary stones. For example, ogham stones were a way of 'testifying that it is one's land' and that one way of marking a claim to territory was through the 'testimony ... which is in the land, the ogham in pillar stone'; inheritance could be 'engraved in ogham' (Binchy 1978: 74, 746, 1566; translations from McManus 1991: 163–66; for other examples see Handley 1998: 345). It is clear that ogham stones were also used for burial, as over twenty references to standing stones or ogham at graves in the *Ulster Cycle* indicate (Handley 1998: 345, n.35). This documentary evidence appears to be corroborated by the archaeological record, such as the discovery at Ballinarig (Co. Kerry) of several ogham stones, graves and bone fragments (Cuppage 1986: 250–52).

Thomas Charles-Edwards has outlined a particular rite of claiming land known as *tellach* which has to be carried out on the ancestral burial site which is assumed to be on the boundary of the land in question (Charles-Edwards 1993: 84). However, whilst this rite is attested in Irish legal texts there are no exact Welsh equivalents (and it is from Wales that we have our only known British law codes). However, he has suggested that this or a similar practice may well have been carried out in Wales.

Handley has continued this exploration of the relationship between inscribed stones and land tenure, supplementing the evidence of the inscribed stones with material from the Llandaff charters and other documentary sources (Handley 1998). He argues that the paucity of direct indications that the stones were funerary monuments – for example, *hic iacit* inscriptions (81 out of a total of 242) – means that most were primarily boundary markers, and that stones with names in the genitive should be read not as '(The memorial) of X son of Y', but '(The land) of X son of Y' (Handley 1998: 348). He does, however, accept the possibility that such stones could have a dual burial/boundary function. This seems more likely considering the Irish evidence, and the possible broad parallels with Pictish inscribed stones which have been found associated with burials (Mack 1998: Appendix B; though see now Clarke 2007).

Handley argues that it is possible to recognize a chronological change in the relationship between the burials and boundaries (Handley 1998: 353–54). He notes that only two out of the ten inscriptions datable to the fifth century do not have explicit memorial formulae, whereas in the later fifth and sixth centuries stones with simple inscriptions in the genitive outnumber those with explicit memorial formulae. He suggests that this indicates a change in the use of stones from burial markers to boundary stones. However, the archaeological evidence, such as the placement of a slab reading simply ERCAGNI over a stone cist at Arfryn, Bodedern (Anglesey) (White 1971–72), suggests that stones using simple formulae with the names in the genitive case may well have been used to mark burials. Furthermore, it is easier to date stones with memorial formulae than those with simple genitive descriptions and consequently it is not clear if Handley's interpretation can be borne out with the current dating evidence at our disposal. Charles-Edwards has also suggested that the importance of burial on boundaries was reflected in later literary traditions which record the burials of kings on boundaries or facing the territories of their enemies. He has argued that burial on boundaries was 'designed to defend inherited land from the claims of outsiders …' (Charles-Edwards 1993: 262–63).

The clusters of both Irish and Latinate epigraphy in Wales clearly relate to the core areas of the known historical kingdoms of Gwynedd, Deheubarth, Brycheniog and Glamorgan. Whilst the precise boundaries and spheres of influence of individual kingdoms could ebb and flow with the successes and failures of royal élites and dynasties, the key areas of Anglesey and lowland Caernarvonshire, coastal Pembrokeshire, central Breconshire and south Glamorgan were consistently the home territories of a series of influential and successful Welsh kings. Rhys Jones has pointed out that these areas are, not surprisingly, also the largest areas of good-quality agricultural land in Wales. Inevitably the ability to assert control over agricultural surplus, whether through formalised tributary relationships or ad hoc raiding and extraction by force would have formed a key platform of early medieval kingship in Wales (Jones 1998). The social stress provoked by the struggle for control of land would have been exacerbated by the potential population increase caused by Irish immigration into these areas. Mapping early medieval epigraphy can thus be seen as more than an exercise in plotting contact zones or identifying islands of *Romanitas*; instead it is possible to begin to use the distribution of investment in monumental structures to explore the political and social tensions that prevailed in early medieval Wales. This is an approach well utilized by scholars of Anglo-Saxon archaeology (e.g. Carver 2002), but still to be developed for the western material. The rise of epigraphy in the fifth and sixth centuries may be not a simple, uniform phenomenon being driven by a single social factor; it was likely to have been a complex reaction with the need to express a range of social identities in a fluid and complex social landscape.

Cemetery organisation

In the late Roman period two distinct burial rites are apparent. One is a tradition in which burials are placed with grave goods, regularly aligned north–south and are often associated with unusual practices such as post-mortem decapitation and prone burial (e.g. Petts 2004: 77–80; Philpott 1991: 224–27; Quensel-von-Kalben 2000). This contrasts with a tradition of east–west aligned burials with no burial goods, often arranged in regular or semi-regular rows; their apparent spatial order led Charles Thomas to call them 'managed cemeteries' (Thomas 1981: 232). Whilst there has been much debate as to whether these 'managed cemeteries' represent the burial places of Christian communities (e.g. Thomas 1981; Petts 2003; Watts 1991) it is clear that in many areas of sub-Roman Britain the tradition continues into the fifth and sixth centuries, by which time they were located within a clearly Christian cultural context. Examples have been excavated at Cannington and Henley Wood (both in Somerset), Caerwent Vicarage Gardens (Gwent), Llandough (Glamorgan) and Queenford Farm, Dorchester-on-Thames (Oxon) (Rahtz, Hirst and Wright 2000; Campbell and MacDonald 1994; Holbrook and Thomas 2005; Chambers 1987). The author has argued elsewhere that this burial rite can be linked into a wider Late Antique Christian burial rite found widely distributed across Spain, Gaul, North Africa and beyond (Petts 2004). This broadly reflects the distribution of Latinate memorials as identified by Handley (2001).

However, as with the memorials, it is important not to underestimate the amount of local variation within the former province of Britain in the fifth to seventh centuries AD.

Increasingly a group of sites showing a distinctly different spatial layout is becoming visible in the archaeological record. Rather than having burials laid out in more or less tightly arranged rows, these cemeteries can be defined by the presence of focal graves, often marked out by square or rectangular ditched or fenced enclosures. Cemeteries of this type have been found in the south-west of England at Kenn (Devon), near Exeter, where partial excavation of the cemetery identified 111 graves in at least seven definable clusters (Weddell 2000: Fig. 11.1). In four cases, individual graves were surrounded by small ditched enclosures, and in an additional case one enclosure surrounded three separate grave cuts. This site was dated to the fifth to eighth centuries by radiocarbon dating (Weddell 2000: 51). In Somerset, excavation on part of a cemetery of uncertain extent at Stoneage Barton Farm, Bishop's Lydeard, uncovered at least three ditched enclosures (Webster and Brunning 2004). This site was dated by radiocarbon to the mid-seventh century. Ditched enclosures at both sites had small entrances or causeways at their eastern ends. Other excavated examples of similar burial enclosures are known from Wales, at Plas Gogerddan (Cardiganshire; Fig. 11.2) Llandegai (Gwynedd), Tandderwen (Denbighshire), Trefollwyn (Anglesey) and Capel Eithin (Murphy 1992; Lynch and Musson 2004; Brassil *et al.* 1991; White and Smith 1999). In addition to these excavated examples, these cemeteries are also now being identified through their distinct cropmarks, with examples being recognised in Wales at Bryn y Garn, near Margam (Glamorgan), Croes Faen, Bryn Crug (Gwynedd), Corwen (Denbighshire), Penrhyn Park (Gwynedd), Tyddyn Pandy (Gwynedd) and Fynnon, Llangoedmor (Cardiganshire) (details from National Monuments Record of Wales).

In previous discussions of these two burial rites it has been argued that their geographical distributions are quite distinct, with the sub-Roman managed cemeteries being found mainly in south-east Wales and west Wessex, particularly Somerset, with outliers as far east as Oxfordshire, whilst the cemeteries with focal graves are found mainly in the west, in areas that were never extensively Romanised in the first place (Petts 2004). The situation may, however, not be so simple; the cemetery at Kenn (Devon) is only 5km from the Roman town at Exeter, where sub-Roman burials are known from the site of the cathedral. Meanwhile, Stoneage Barton Farm (Somerset), in the heart of an area of south-west England that had been thoroughly Romanised, was only around 15km from a cemetery at Cannington (Somerset) which shows characteristics more typical of a managed cemetery.

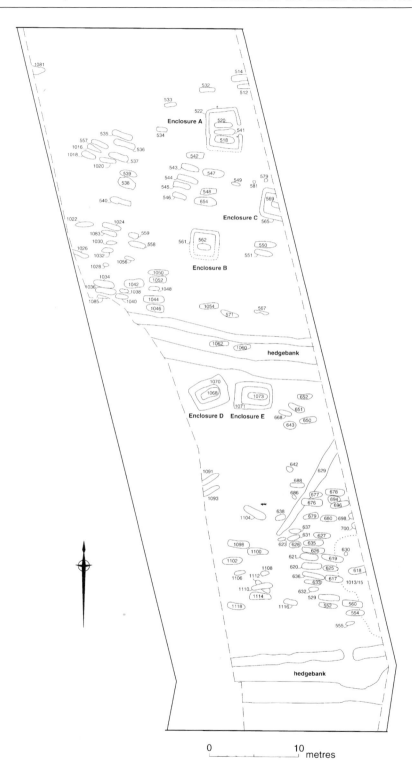

Fig. 11.1: Early medieval cemetery, Kenn (Devon). From Weddell 2000 ©Devon Archaeological Society.

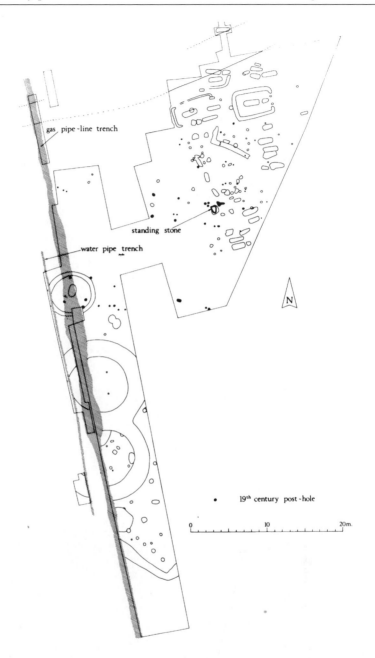

Fig. 11.2: Early
medieval cemetery,
Plas Gogerddan
(Cardiganshire).
From Murphy
1992 ©Dyfed
Archaeological
Trust.

gas pipe-line trench

standing stone

water pipe trench

N

• 19th century post-hole

0   10   20m.

Cannington is in itself more complex than it appears, for while it
may appear 'managed', there are focal graves in the later phases of its
use. It is noticeable though that the cemeteries with focal graves tend
to be in rural locations, whereas the managed cemeteries are located
close to sites that had been important in the Roman period. For

example, Queenford Farm, Dorchester, and Vicarage Orchard Garden, Caerwent, are located outside Roman towns with strong circumstantial evidence for continuity of some level of activity into the early medieval period (Campbell and MacDonald 1994; Chambers 1987; Knight 1998). Meanwhile, Llandough is adjacent to the site of a large Roman villa (Knight 2005). Although there is little evidence of direct continuity of occupation on the villa site from the Roman into the early medieval period, the juxtaposition of a major ecclesiastical site with a substantial Roman site has a clear symbolic resonance (Bell 2005). We may be seeing a distinction between communities who deliberately choose to associate themselves with sites with clear links to Roman culture in an attempt to harness the ideological associations and symbolic power associated with the Roman world and those who preferred to create novel histories focusing upon the invented connections with prehistoric monuments and focal graves. The extent to which Roman sites were reused in the early medieval period, in both British and Anglo-Saxon contexts, is becoming increasingly apparent (e.g. Bell 2005). In this context the reoccupation of hillforts at Dinas Powys (close to Llandough, Glamorgan), Cadbury Congresbury (adjacent to Henley Wood, Somerset) and probably Cannington (Somerset) is an interesting juxtaposition of images of power, making links with both the Roman past but also expressing status in a distinctly British manner through the refortification of hillforts (Dark 1994b; Alcock 1963). There is also an intriguing contrast between the association of power centres, whether in the form of hillforts or sub-Roman enclaves associated with Roman towns, and cemeteries where, spatially at least, personal identity is subordinated to a wider group identity. This may reflect the ability of elites to impose control over mortuary practices, preventing the expression of power in the mortuary sphere. This contrasts with focal burials, often found in places away from major centres of power, where power might be more commonly expressed through kinship and reflected in the presence of focal graves and possible family groupings within the cemetery. Rather than looking for broad regional or national patterns, it is likely that we need to be searching for explanations for these contrasts in the spatial layout of cemeteries and the way in which power is expressed at the local level (cf. Lucy 1998).

Grave goods

It is commonly assumed that one of the key differences between British/ sub-Roman burials and Anglo-Saxon graves is the presence of grave goods in the latter. The former are assumed to contain no accompanying items; a difference regularly attributed to an unfounded perception that

Christianity prohibited the use of grave goods (Bullough 1983). A closer examination of the archaeological record does not bear this out.

At Cannington (Somerset), the majority of objects found in graves are likely to have been residual; however, the excavators did identify a number of artefacts that were securely stratified with the skeletons, and thus have a reasonable likelihood of being grave goods (Rahtz *et al.* 2000: 84). The most common objects found were knives, which were located in eighteen graves, whilst beads were found in three graves and pins in eight graves (Rahtz *et al.* 2000: 85–86, Table 4); other items included a buckle, a belt appliqué, a bracelet and a ring. Most items were alone in the grave, but a small number of fifth- to seventh-century graves contained several items, including Grave 99 (spoon, bead), Grave 5 (comb, iron objects), Grave 402 (knife, buckle, Roman coin), Grave 405 (glass bead; penannular brooch) and Grave 407 (bracelet, vessel, Roman coin, amber bead) (Rahtz *et al.* 2000: 84ff). At Llandough, a very similar range of objects were also found in some graves, including knives (Burial 34; Burial 898) and beads (Burials 40, 547, 624, 851 and 934), all of pre-eleventh-century date (Holbrook and Thomas 2005: 20–22).

An early medieval cemetery at Bromfield (Shropshire) reusing an Iron Age ditched enclosure was interpreted by the excavators as a Saxon burial ground on the basis of the grave goods (Stanford 1995: 132; Fig. 11.3). However, out of thirty-one excavated graves, the only grave goods were a knife and buckle in F40, an amber bead and brooch (a fragmentary penannular brooch) in F104 and a knife in F33. This range of items is similar to the material found in the graves at Cannington and Llandough. It appears an Anglo-Saxon ethnic identity was given to the burials on the assumption that British graves had no burial goods, and despite the fact that the penannular brooch and the amber bead fit best in a sixth-century context, the cemetery was interpreted as a 'final phase' burial ground (Stanford 1995: 139–40)

Similar types of objects are found at a low level in a range of other early medieval cemeteries from 'British' areas. Knives were found in the graves at Ulwell, Swanage (Dorset), and Whithorn (Dumfries and Galloway) (Cox 1988; Hill 1997: 74), a saw blade was found at Portesham (Dorset) (Valentin 2004) and a Type G penannular brooch was found associated with the burials at Vicarage Orchard Garden, Caerwent (Campbell and MacDonald 1994: 83). At Queenford Farm, Dorchester-on-Thames (Oxon), one burial (F11) within an enclosure that cut through the silted-up ditch of the main cemetery enclosure contained a bone comb (Chambers 1987: 58).

The danger when looking at early medieval burials in western Britain is to assume that the presence of grave goods, even if only at low levels and

OPPOSITE

Fig. 11.3: Iron Age enclosure reused for early medieval cemetery, Bromfield (Shropshire). From Stanford 1995 ©Shropshire Archaeological Society.

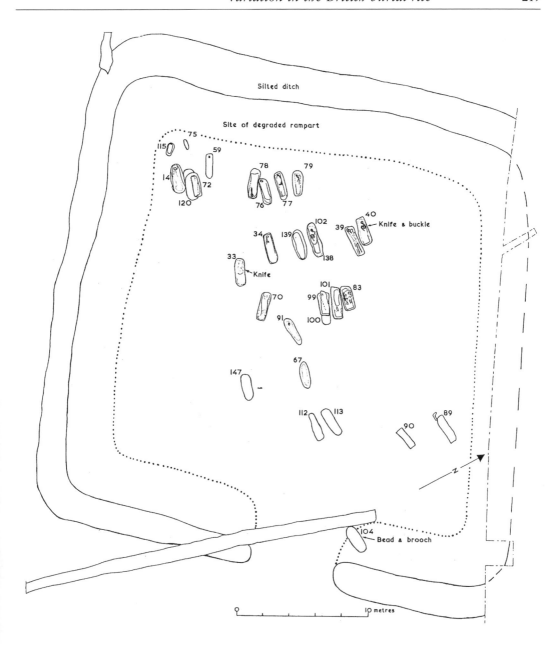

consisting of material that is not generally seen as culturally diagnostic, indicates that the graves are 'Anglo-Saxon'. This was seen in the case of the Bromfield cemetery. The similarity of some seventh-century 'Anglo-Saxon' burial assemblages to the range of material being used in British graves makes it particularly important not to make simple statements about the 'ethnic' nature of particular burials (Geake 1992). This problem can be seen acutely in some areas, such as Dorset, where Anglo-Saxon political take-over appears to be occurring in the mid-seventh century. It is tempting to point to cemeteries, such as Ulwell, which have seventh-century radiocarbon dates and link them to this process.

It is obviously wrong to characterise the sub-Roman burial tradition as lacking in grave goods. A range of objects, including dress items and knives appear in early medieval British graves, albeit at a relatively low frequency. It appears that these items were usually worn, presumably implying that the body is being buried dressed, rather than wrapped in a shroud. In this sense the British and early Anglo-Saxon burial rites are more broadly similar than sometimes realised. The key difference is in the relative 'wealth' of British and Anglo-Saxon burials. It is not sufficient to explain the apparent limited nature of British burial assemblages in terms of the 'poverty' of material culture in the west. The surviving metalwork from Wales, western England and Ireland includes a significant level of decorative metal dress items, including penannular brooches and dress-pins (Youngs 1989). In life, individuals in western Britain were clearly expressing status through the wearing of brooches and other dress items, just as those in Anglo-Saxon areas were. However, whilst in the east it was culturally appropriate to place these objects in the grave, in the west it was only a rare occurrence. Even though individuals in these areas were being placed in the grave dressed, there was a clear process of selection relating to which dress items entered the funerary record. There was clearly a deliberate decision by the British not to include high-status dress items, even though they were worn in life. There are also other clear differences in the use of grave goods between British and Anglo-Saxon burials; the former use mainly consists of dress items, whilst the latter incorporated a range of other objects, particular pottery, metal, wood and glass vessels. These differences are likely to lie in attitudes to the display and consumption of wealth, rather than relative wealth/poverty or religious dogma.

Conclusions

This paper has not attempted any over-arching synthesis of early medieval British burial rites. Instead, I have attempted to highlight the extensive variation that is visible in a funerary tradition that is often dismissed as highly uniform. This variation is apparent at a range of levels; differing attitudes to monumentality whether in the form of epigraphic habit or constructing focal graves can be seen at a regional, as well as local level. The presence of ditched rectangular graves within cemeteries highlights intra-group social distinction, as may the use of grave goods.

This variation could have been explored in other ways, such as the variation in the use of coffins or stone cists, a practice which shows extensive diversity in the archaeological record (Petts 2001). Although the use of lead and stone coffins seemingly ceases at the end of the fourth century, the use of wooden coffins does continue in some cases. Of the eight fifth-century burials from the sub-Roman phase on the villa site at Bancroft (Bucks), three contained iron coffin nails and possible soil-shadows indicating a wooden coffin (Williams and Zeepvat 1994). Further evidence for nailed wooden coffins is found at Queenford Farm, Dorchester-on-Thames, where 47 graves (out of 160 excavated) contained coffin nails or fittings, one of these graves having a radiocarbon date of AD 380–650 (Chambers 1987). These are the only examples of definite early medieval British burials with iron coffin fittings. Obviously such coffins are rare, and rely on good preservation and careful excavation to reveal them. In Wales wooden coffins are known from 22 of the graves found at Tandderwen (Clwyd) (Brassil 1991) and nine graves from Plas Gogerddan (Powys) (Murphy 1992). One of the coffins from Plas Gogerddan gave a radiocarbon date of AD 340–620, whilst at Tandderwen dates of AD 430–690 and AD 770–1160 (at two Σ) have been obtained. It was felt possible to identify soil-shadows of wooden coffins at the cemetery at Bromfield in Shropshire (Stanford 1995).

Both the Bromfield coffins and those from Wales seem to be of simple plank construction, and in Grave 50 at Tandderwen separate elements of the side and base of the coffin could be recognized, whilst the Bancroft and Queenford Farm coffins had metal fittings; again there are clearly regional differences here, which need further exploration.

It is important that archaeologists consider the way in which these and other variables can be used to gain a better and more sophisticated understanding of early medieval society in western Britain, especially as this variation may have contributed to the creation of distinctive social identities at the local and regional level. Archaeologists working on British material need to take their cue from the work of Heinrich Härke (e.g. Härke 1990a; 1992b) and explore the ways in which burial was used to construct a range of identities, based on gender, ethnicity (beyond a simple British/Anglo-Saxon opposition) and religion amongst the societies of Wales and western England. An increased emphasis on variation within the western British archaeological record will allow this and help to break down perceptions of a uniform British (or indeed Celtic) culture in contrast to the complex and highly variable Anglo-Saxon record.

Chapter 12

Anglo-Saxon attitudes: how should post-AD 700 burials be interpreted?

Grenville Astill

Abstract
This paper reviews the evidence for field cemeteries from the south of England in the context of contemporary land use and settlement evidence in order to understand the development of early medieval social identities. The survey of the cemeteries shows that they are more diverse than is usually acknowledged, particularly in terms of date range, size and location. A significant number continued in use until the tenth, eleventh and perhaps later centuries, which may conflict with the usual interpretation of these cemeteries as going out of use with the development of churchyards from the tenth century onwards. An alternative interpretation is offered where the cemeteries are related to the developing settlement pattern from the eighth to eleventh centuries and which also suggests that such cemeteries were part of an identity based around the rural settlement and its fields – the developing 'village community'.

H EINRICH HÄRKE has made some important excursions into post-seventh-century Britain and Europe in both his teaching and publications (e.g. Härke 2002); in recognition of this, the following reviews one aspect of later Anglo-Saxon burial, particularly with regard to developing social identities relating to the connection between changing settlement patterns and burial location.

The practice of furnished burial is usually thought to have ended in this country by about AD 720–30 (Geake 1997: 125; Geake 2002: 150), although a recent analysis shows it had largely disappeared by the late seventh century (John Hines pers. comm.). Variety in the form of burial, however, continued, indeed probably increased, over the next 300 years. Some of this variety is seen in a material way – stone packings, wood coffins, charcoal burials – and was probably associated with high-status burials at minsters from at least the eighth century (e.g. Thompson 2004: 35, 117–31). But another aspect of this variety was in an elaboration of ceremony either at home or by the graveside or both and perhaps overseen by priests (Hadley 2002: 226–28). Such differentiation was a way of reinforcing social identity, but whose? Conversely, there is a certain consistency in terms of location in that there are concentrations of burials close to a focal point, such as a minster, but there were also smaller, satellite, cemeteries in the vicinity. At present this pattern, however, is more apparent in the north (summarised in Hadley 2002: 211, 216–18; but Dorchester-on-Thames may be a possibility, Blair 1994: 2, 58–59), although similar arrangements have been identified at some of the wics (Morton 1992; Scull 2001; Stoodley 2002).

The rather unprepossessing group of burials I want to consider is frustrating to review because it is so few in number and yet is thought to represent the majority of the post-AD 700 population. To a certain extent such burials should be regarded as those that perhaps co-existed with, and succeeded, the 'final phase' cemeteries. They may also well fit in the 'archaic' category of cemeteries proposed by Lucy and Reynolds (Morris 1983: 49–62; Boddington 1990; Geake 1997; Lucy and Reynolds 2002: 20).

These burial grounds are known as 'open ground cemeteries', 'traditional lay cemeteries' or more often 'field cemeteries' (Blair 2005: 238, 243; Williams 2006: 23; Reynolds 2002, 185). They are thought to have been in use between the abandonment of furnished cemeteries and the start of churchyard burial, that is between the later seventh and the tenth centuries, or – to express the chronological range in terms of our evidence – between the abandonment of grave goods and the earliest documentary evidence for the church's growing interest in the process and location of burial. Ecclesiastical interest was shown, for example, through the imposition of soul-scot (to be paid at the open grave by Cnut's time: Loyn 1975: 256; Blair 2005: 432); the classification of churches, first attempted in Edgar's laws and subsequently developed in the eleventh century, which acknowledged the existence of thegns' churches with a graveyard and field chapels with no burial grounds (Loyn 1975: 249; Blair 2005: 422); and the rites for the consecration of cemeteries (Gittos 2002). While all of these developments were first recorded in the tenth century, there is little information about the speed with which these measures were adopted or implemented throughout the country.

How should these cemeteries be characterised? John Blair has provided the most recent and pertinent summary:

... burial in traditional lay cemeteries was not abandoned nor even necessarily marginalised, though after the early eighth century it becomes very hard to recognize. Apart from knives (over-whelmingly the commonest item in the late seventh century and still occasionally deposited beyond 800) they have no grave-goods, and they are always orientated [west–east] ... Typically they contain between five and thirty bodies, can be near settlements or away from them, and occasionally continue the old habit of reusing ancient sites ... Alongside the growing minster churchyards older and more diverse arrangements clearly persisted. (Blair 2005: 243–44)

John Blair's point that a traditional form of burial may have continued and remained influential beyond the eighth century, even though it becomes increasingly difficult to recognise after that date, is important. Equally significant is his view that such cemeteries co-existed with minster cemeteries, although he thinks 'from the tenth century ... that people at large were forced to bring their dead to the minsters and the scattered cemeteries were abandoned' (Blair 1994: 73).

There are perhaps less than fifty field cemeteries that have been identified for the whole of England, and Bromfield and Lewknor are the examples most often cited (e.g. Blair 2005: 238, 244; Williams 2006: 183–84). Bromfield, rescue-excavated in 1978–80, is notable because the cemetery is probably complete (of *c.* 35 graves) and it also existed within an Iron Age enclosure (Stanford 1995). The Bromfield cemetery is only loosely dated by the burial with an iron buckle (F40) to 650–750 (Stanford 1995: 136–39). Lewknor was excavated ahead of and during the construction of the M40. The 39 graves were originally interpreted as representing a late Roman cemetery based on the pottery found in some grave fills (Chambers 1973). Two skeletons were subsequently radiocarbon-dated (33 and 14) to 710–1020 and 710–1160 (Chambers 1976). The site raises the possibility that other cemeteries, originally interpreted as late Roman, might be of middle or later Saxon date. Lewknor also emphasises our reliance on radiocarbon dating to identify these cemeteries: none in the current sample of field cemeteries has high-precision dates, nor have the dates been subject to recent statistical analysis. Blair has identified some fifty burials and cemeteries from the Oxfordshire Sites and Monuments Record 'any or all of which could be Anglo-Saxon' (Blair 2005: 244 and also comments in Hadley 2007: 198, 201).

The following discussion attempts to review this slight cemetery information in the context of recent discussions concerning contemporary settlement sequences with the intention of gaining further insights into where the majority of the population was buried; and in the process we may discover more about medieval identities.

Table 12.1 lists the 17 field cemeteries I have found for the south and midlands. I have also included four from East Anglia for comparison, mainly because a clear relationship between a contemporary settlement and cemetery has been established. Cemeteries that may be related to minsters have been excluded (e.g. Dorchester: Blair 1994: 2, 58–59; Sedgeford: Cabot *et al.* 2004: 313–17, 319–21), as have single burials and cemeteries that are tentatively dated to the later Roman period. Table 12.1 includes very little information about the burials themselves or their pathology, partly because there is little such information and also because I have chosen to concentrate on burial numbers, date, topographic position and the relationship with potential contemporary settlements.

Most field cemeteries were unexpected discoveries in the course of redevelopment and were often very fragmentary because the graves were very shallow and disturbed, although the frequent references to disarticulated bones and empty graves would suggest that some of these cemeteries might be larger than they appear at first sight. Evidence for coffins or packings is rarely noted, and the most common finds, but always in a minority (usually two or three) of graves, are buckles and knives, from which it is assumed that the dead were buried in their clothing.

How should these cemeteries be interpreted? On the one hand they are regarded collectively, despite the small numbers, as the place where most of the rural population was buried; on the other, they are seen as individual cemeteries used by small communities or as family plots (even though little work has been done on non-metric traits). The emphasis is on small group identities (Blair 2005: 244; Williams 2006: 25–26, 218–19). This material is perplexing, and will remain so as long as it is treated as a separate category of evidence divorced from, for example, settlement data. Blair's most recent review sees these cemeteries in the context of the increasing power of the minsters over the religious lives of the local population, an essentially ecclesiastical interpretation that pays scant attention to settlement development, although it has also been recognized that later Anglo-Saxon cemeteries often have an ephemeral and changing character (Blair 2005: 228–45; Hadley 2007: 194).

On those few occasions where the living and the dead are brought together, such small-scale cemeteries are related to the shifting nature of settlements. The conclusion is therefore drawn that these field cemeteries came to an end in the ninth or tenth centuries, when stability was imposed on the landscape through the creation of villages, open fields and parish churches (e.g. Boddington 1990: 178, 194–97; Hadley 2007: 194–99).

Site	Location	Topography	Number	Date	Dates (2-sigma)	Reference
Brackmills	N'ants	Valley side of R. Nene. ? W limit established	23+	'Christian'	610–780	Chapman 1998
Milton Keynes	Bucks	180m from church	MNI 107; ?500	MS to C11+		Parkhouse et al. 1996: 199–221
Westbury	Bucks	W edge of DMV; in arable area;? W, N & S limits	c.7	late C7–early C8		Ivens et al. 1995: 71–74
Elstow	Beds	Under C11 Benedictine nunnery	270+	8/9 to 11		Baker 1969: 30
Kempston	Beds	Away from medieval settlement & church	8+	Mid to Late Saxon	820–940; 940–1040;	Dawson 1999: 30
Stratton	Beds	N edge of C10-12 settlement with MS material	'small group'	Mid-Saxon		Nenk et al. 1993: 247
Yarnton	Oxon	100m W of MS enclosed sett, early C8-9	6+	'C9'	770–890; 720–885	Hey 2004: 163, 261; Boyle 2004: 317–24
Chimney	Oxon	Cemetery established by Bampton minster	17; ?1,500	Late Saxon	890–1035; 900–1160;	Crawford 1989
Lewknor	Oxon	Promontory, removed from med settlement	39+	M-Late Saxon	710–1020; 710–1160	Chambers 1973; 1976
Bromfield	Shrops	Within IA enclosure	59+	mid 7–8		Stanford 1995
Stanmer	Sussex	Promontory, removed from med settlement	7+	Mid-Saxon		Gilks 1997: 113–25
Bedhampton	Hants	Bevis' Grave	MNI 88	C7–10		Geake 1997: 154; Cherryson 2007: 130
Ulwell	Dorset	Steep side of downland	57+	C7	610–890; 550–860; 420–690; 650–980	Cox 1988
Templecombe	Som	Next to earthworks of ?contemporary settlement and field system	11+	M-Late Saxon	681–974; 794–1026	Newman 1992
Eccles	Essex	Adjacent to Roman villa	200+	mid 7 +		Shaw 1994: 165–88
Saffron Walden	Essex	In area of ?Roman & later field system	200+	C9–12		Bassett 1982
Shepperton	Middx	300m SW of med sett; within ditched area, C6-12	20+	pre-1000		Canham 1979: 104–13
Whissonsett	Norfolk	Adjacent to MS enclosed sett; Later S ditches.	19+	'Mid-Saxon'		Gaimster and O'Connor 2006: 341
Ormesby	Norfolk	? S boundary	60, MNI 72	'Christian'		Nenk et al. 1997: 279
Bramford	Suffolk	Adjacent to MS sett in ditched enclosure	21+	'Mid-Saxon'		Nenk et al. 1996: 284–85
Carlton Colville	Suffolk	'Within' 6-early 8 sett.	24+	'Conversion'		Mortimer 2000b: 34–35

Villages and open fields are generally viewed as originating
and developing together – they are seen as inextricably linked. To
make open fields work – and to maintain or increase productivity
– cooperation between farmers was essential to the extent that it
helped generate a distinct social identity, usually called the village
community (Reynolds 1984: 110–11, 122–25, 150–53; Dyer 1985: 28–30;
Dyer 1994). We would expect a similar sense of identity to develop
wherever reasonably intensive farming was practised: it was therefore
not peculiar to village England. In the case of dispersed landscapes,
for example, cooperation (and the consequent social identity) would
be focused on the management of woodland and rough pastures (e.g.
Dyer 1994: 410).

OPPOSITE

Table 12.1: Later
Anglo-Saxon field
cemeteries from
southern England.

The scheme constructed to explain settlement change in
Northamptonshire – essentially from hamlet to village – has been
influential. During the eighth or early ninth century the dispersed
settlement pattern had been abandoned in favour of nucleated
settlements with their field systems which were well established by
the end of the ninth century. At some time in the tenth century a
'great replanning' took place that involved the reorganisation of both
villages and open fields, so that by the Norman Conquest the medieval
settlement pattern was formalised and complete (best summarised in
Brown and Foard 1998).

The tenth century is now seen as a formative period, associated with
the fragmentation of large estates and the subsequent development of
smaller manors and the emergence of a large group of minor aristocracy,
the thegns (Faith 1997: 153–77). It was also the time when the minsters'
authority weakened in the face of the creation of proprietary churches
(e.g. Blair 2005: 426–56). The combination of 'secular' and 'religious'
change thus triggered major alterations in the landscape. Increasing
state interest in political and economic control was facilitated by using,
and reinforcing, nascent forms of social organisation which became
part of the institutional structure – in particular the assemblies of the
vill and the hundred as the foundations of a system designed to make
the population accountable to the centre (Loyn 1984, 140–48; Reynolds
1999: 75–81).

To summarize current views about settlement change, between
perhaps 750 and 950 a new landscape dominated by village and open
fields had emerged. By the latter time the field cemeteries had been
abandoned because the local church with its graveyard was becoming
sufficiently well established to be the centre for local religious
activity and consequently also became a focal point for a community
identity.

The field cemetery data from the south and the midlands can support this scheme, but only partially. Some of the sample conforms to the settlement scheme, in the sense that some cemeteries are dated as 'Middle Saxon' and therefore probably went out of use with, or in the wake of, settlement change (e.g. Brackmills, Westbury, Stanmer, Yarnton, Bromfield, Whissonsett, Ormesby, Carlton Colville and Bramford). There are, however, others in the sample which differ in two main ways: firstly, some cemeteries have burials that are dated as late as the tenth and eleventh centuries (Elstow, Kempston, Milton Keynes, Chimney, Lewnor, Eccles, Saffron Walden, Shepperton, Bedhampton, Templecombe); and, secondly, some cemeteries were considerably larger than the 5 to 30 individuals given in the characterisation of the field cemetery above (Elstow, Milton Keynes, Chimney, Saffron Walden, Bedhampton, Ulwell and Ormesby).

The larger cemeteries deserve more attention. Reading the reports, you sense the excavators' frustration that their expectations have not been fulfilled. To have uncovered a large cemetery with later Saxon dates, often with intercutting graves suggesting intensive use, was somehow insufficient, because there was no sign of a church.

In 1876 the excavations of G.S. Gibson at Saffron Walden uncovered at least 200 burials to the west of the medieval town. In a reconsideration of the cemetery material is the following:

> There must have been a church in or very close to the cemetery, though not obviously within the area of Gibson's excavations. There are, however, areas shown on the two plans onto which graves do not impinge, which are sufficiently large to have contained a small timber church of one or two cells. A masonry structure, even an entirely robbed one, would hardly have been missed; but if the church had been entirely timber built, its presence on the site might well have escaped the excavator's notice. (Bassett 1982: 14).

This cemetery has entered the literature as 'some 200 known burials were found at a site which perhaps also included a sunken-featured building and a small wooden church': there was some structural evidence for the former (Freke and Thacker 1987–88: 33; Bassett 1982: 11).

Similarly at Elstow, the site of a post-Conquest, eleventh-century Benedictine nunnery, some 270 burials were excavated below the later monastery:

> A graveyard of this size must have been associated with a church built either in stone or timber, or with both materials. Excavation has not yet provided any signs of a church but burials have appeared in nearly all the trenches, and are thus likely to have been outside a church. The Abbey church may have been built on the

site of the earlier structure, but only Saxon burials were found in the trenches at the east end of the original nave; nor was there any indication of such a building under the main east end. There is no hint of a pre-Conquest monastic establishment. (Baker 1969: 30)

These and others (Kempston, Milton Keynes, Lewknor and Shepperton) are also noted as being at a considerable distance from the medieval parish church, providing another reason for postulating an earlier church. The excavators' discomfort surely betrays an awareness that the tenth-century documentation mentioned above almost required them to have a church or that they needed a church to validate their data. Existing hypotheses cannot apparently accommodate any possibility that an intensively used cemetery could exist and continue without a local church. A recent commentary on the radiocarbon dates of the Lewknor cemetery reflects a similar attitude. The dates were AD 710–1020 and AD 710–1160: 'It is highly unlikely that the burials fall into the more recent span of the two sigma date as by this time burial within churchyards would have been the norm with little exception' (Boyle 2004: 320). It is also important, however, to remember that seven of these larger cemeteries have middle Saxon dates (Elstow, Kempston, Milton Keynes, Lewknor, Bedhampton, Ulwell and Saffron Walden) and could have originated before the development of local churches with their own graveyards. This, of course, is not to deny that churches with cemeteries existed from the tenth century, for we have the recently excavated examples of Ketton, Cherry Hinton and Raunds (Meadows 1998: 46–47; Bradley and Gaimster 2000: 252; Boddington 1996).

By contrast, there is the case of Chimney, in Oxfordshire, where a cemetery of at least 1500 burials has been claimed but there is no disappointment at failing to find a church (Crawford 1989). Three burials radiocarbon dated to between the tenth and mid-eleventh centuries (890–1035; 900–1110; 900–1160) are regarded as sufficiently close to a grant of the 950s, when the Chimney estate was given to the nearby minster at Bampton, to date and characterize the cemetery (Crawford 1989: 54–56). It 'is therefore an unequivocal case of a minster controlling a dependent cemetery' (Blair 1994: 73). There was, however, an acknowledgement that a burial with a knife was not necessarily as late as the dated burials and could potentially extend the cemetery back to the later seventh or eighth century, thus leaving open the possibility that Chimney had originated as a field cemetery (Blair 1994: 73; Boyle 2004: 320).

The small field cemeteries, then, could be associated with a dispersed settlement pattern that was abandoned by the ninth century, and those cemeteries which were larger and have later dates could be interpreted either as churchyards which were also later abandoned, or under the control of minsters. To put it somewhat crudely, one part of the field cemetery sequence – the earlier, smaller examples – can thus be matched to our existing archaeological data for settlement, while another part – the larger examples with some post-ninth-century dates – can be accommodated within the documentary evidence for the development of local churches.

Is there a way of interpreting the field cemetery that is systematic and consistent for the entire time span over which the cemeteries remained in use? Is it possible, for example, to incorporate some of the recent fieldwork and environmental data which appear to offer alternative sequences of land use and settlement in the eighth to eleventh centuries?

We are familiar with the evidence for increasing intensification in land use and the exploitation of new environmental zones in the eighth century, the period by which we also see settlements becoming better defined with boundaries (summarised in Astill 1997: 196–204; Reynolds 2003: 104–15). At about the same time in some parts of the country large areas of land were reorganized and set out as fields. In the Bourn valley in Cambridgeshire fields appear to have been laid out over at least four (later) parishes in a distinctive way with wide furlong divisions that allowed easy access from one end of the valley to another. These furlongs have been interpreted as narrow commons to allow animal husbandry alongside cereal cultivation. This mode of land use continued from the eighth or ninth century for some 200 years, after which the land was divided into fields dependent on individual settlements (Oosthuizen 2005; Oosthuizen 2006: 91–113).

In Devon a similar major restructuring of land units over a large area has been proposed in the eighth century, based on palynological data derived from sites close to arable areas rather than the more usual upland blanket bogs. In central Devon and the southern edge of Exmoor a distinctive form of land use, based on an increase of cereal cultivation without a significant reduction in pasture or woodland – known as convertible husbandry – was introduced and remained in use throughout the Middle Ages. The formalization of this south-west landscape maintained long-range routes and fixed the dispersed settlement pattern (Rippon *et al.* 2006). In both the Cambridgeshire and Devon cases there was an economic necessity for cooperation which may have generated a social identity.

These two examples also demonstrate the importance that was attached to long-range movement through these rearranged landscapes. Increasingly we are becoming aware of how contemporary settlements, such as Catholme and Yarnton, appear to have been keyed into long-distance routeways and thus integrated into a larger landscape (Losco-Bradley and Kinsley 2002: 2; Hey 2004: 43–57; Reynolds 2003: 132).

Surveys in the south and east midlands, including most recently the Whittlewood Project, have produced a different scheme for the development of villages and open fields. Having established that the Northamptonshire model of abandonment of dispersed settlement followed by villages relied on data from places known to be royal properties in the ninth century, there was room for alternative sequences for non-royal areas of the country (Jones and Page 2006: 103).

In the eighth-century south/east midlands dispersed settlement was the norm, associated with large arable and wooded areas (Lewis *et al.* 1997: 97; Jones and Page 2006: 84–89; Croft and Mynard 1993: 15–18, 93, 134). However, while some of these settlements in Whittlewood were deserted later, the majority continued as small places, and others in the ninth and tenth centuries grew into larger, nucleated settlements (Jones and Page 2006: 85–92). The sequence of the selective growth of some dispersed settlements into villages has been confirmed by excavations and fieldwork at other places in the region (Croft and Mynard 1993: 15–18; Lewis *et al.* 1997: 92–98).

What is perhaps more relevant for this enquiry is that, while some settlements changed, the surrounding landscape with a plentiful mixture of woodland, pasture and arable resources meant that it was unnecessary to reorganize the fields – they continued in a largely unchanged form for at least a further 200 years (Jones and Page 2006: 92–99; Jones 2004).

There is thus an opportunity to separate the development of fields from that of settlement nucleation – phenomena until now always thought to go hand in hand. The Cambridgeshire, Devon and south/east midlands material prompts us to consider the proposition that the fields were the oldest part of the later Saxon landscape. The antiquity of the fields – and the probability that working the fields created a common identity – raises the prospect that they were the most appropriate place for the burial of those who cultivated them.

Field cemeteries, a term which might be more appropriate than we first realised, could then potentially reflect a longer period of settlement and land use than was previously thought. Many of the cemetery reports comment on the significant distance from later Saxon and medieval settlements and churches; the lack of domestic material in grave fills (implying distance from domestic activities) has also been noted (Brackmills, Kempston, Milton Keynes, Lewnor, Stanmer, and Shepperton; but see Hadley 2007: 194–99 for a proposed association between later Anglo-Saxon cemeteries and domestic occupation). In addition a significant number appear to be located in or close to fields or field-like enclosures (Stratton, Westbury, Yarnton, Saffron Walden, Shepperton, Templecombe, Whissonsett, Bramford).

If we apply the south/east midlands settlement sequence hypothesis, the small cemeteries might indeed reflect a segment of the population which lived in dispersed settlements, but settlements that were not necessarily abandoned by the ninth century. Similarly, the larger cemeteries might belong to those who lived in settlements that were growing, eventually to become villages.

It is important in this context to recognise the value of the recent fieldwork around Yarnton, Oxfordshire. The project identified three settlements with eighth-century occupation in the vicinity – Yarnton, Cresswell Field and Worton – two of which continued to be occupied well into the ninth century (Yarnton and Worton: Hey 2004: summary at 43–46). The settlement most extensively excavated, called Yarnton, was by the ninth century small, but within a substantial enclosure. It was surrounded by fields which were intensively cultivated (Hey 2004: summarised at 45–49). A small contemporary cemetery of six (definite) or seven individuals was excavated 100m west of the settlement. Two of the burials were radiocarbon dated to AD 780–890 and AD 720–885. (The report also records that the cemetery may have been associated with a sunken-featured building and two possible earthfast structures, but in an isolated area: Hey 2004: 163, 261). The area became either paddock or arable in the later ninth or tenth century, when the settlement shifted to the north-east and the former settlement area was converted into enclosures (Hey 2004: 46, 49–52). In East Anglia two similar sequences have been excavated – small middle Saxon settlements within enclosures with small cemeteries beyond. In both instances the cemeteries were abandoned and absorbed into later Saxon fields (Whissonsett, Norfolk, and Bramford, Suffolk). There is, then, a potential relationship between some of these field cemeteries and fields.

Yarnton has a further contribution to make to our study of the disposal of the dead. In the secondary fills of the middle Saxon ditches enclosing the settlement were found three skeletons contemporary with the small cemetery, two of which were subadults, the third an adolescent. One of the burials was prone and overlay other skull fragments from at least four subadults (Boyle 2004: 320–21). Such 'special deposits' have also been found at Catholme, where five burials were found in the secondary fills of the enclosures (Losco-Bradley and Kinsley 2002: 40–41). Similar occurrences have also been reported from Little Paxton, Cheddar, West Stow and Higham Ferrers (Addyman 1969: 64; Rahtz 1979: 96–97; West 1986: 58; Boyle 2004: 321). Could this represent a reaffirmation (or commemoration) of the antiquity of the fields by the burying of some of the dead in the most field-like elements of the settlements? The similarly placed burials of animals in settlements, recently noted by Helena Hamerow, may also be relevant in this context (2006). The case of the excavated settlements at Cottam, Yorkshire (one of which has produced an adult female skull in a pit next to a major boundary, whose fill also contained other human bone fragments), should make us aware that one of the reasons why we have failed to recognize Middle Saxon settlements is that they (or more often their crop-marks) have been misidentified as Iron Age, and there may also be a similarity in the disposal of the dead (Richards 1999: 36, 85–86, 92–93, 99; Wilson 1981: 146–51).

There was an ambiguous relationship between fields and settlements. A ninth-century bishop of Orléans levied a fine for burial *'in agris suis'*, normally translated as 'on the deceased's own land', but in this context we might take it more literally and suggest that it refers to fields as well (Fry 1999: 42). Similarly, there is an account in the Annals of Fulda, under the year 858, concerning a man who was possessed by evil spirits. While there were clear political implications in the way this incident was reported, it is the manner in which the fields are mentioned that concerns us here:

> The spirit 'stirred up everyone's (i.e. the inhabitants of Chamund) hatred against one man, as if it were for his sins that everyone had to suffer such things; and so that he might be the more hated, the evil spirit caused every house which the man entered to catch fire. As a result the man was forced to live outside the *villa* in the fields (*in agris*) with his wife and children, as all his kin feared to take him in. But he was not even allowed to remain there in safety, for when with all the others he had gathered in and stacked his crops, the evil spirit came unexpectedly and burnt them. To try to appease the feelings of the inhabitants, who wished to kill him, he took the ordeal of hot iron and proved himself innocent of the crimes which were alleged against him (Reuter 1992: 44).

The fields were thus sufficiently far away to be suitable for the villagers to make a clear statement of disapproval and ostracism, but on the other hand sufficiently close to recall the outcast because he was still expected to help in the harvest.

The late tenth- or early eleventh-century account of an English field remedy ritual, the *aecerbot* charm, describes a procedure for the improvement of land that had become infertile or had been cursed by a sorcerer or poisoner. It was an elaborate ceremony which involved digging up a sod from each side of the field, taking these into the church to have four masses said over them, and having wood crosses inserted in the places from where the turves had been taken. A plough also received a similarly elaborate treatment including placing new seed, incense, fennel and hallowed salt in its beam, followed by Christian blessings. The commentary on this text interprets it as evidence of the church appropriating earlier practices to itself, and could stand as an example of the same process whereby burial was eventually relocated from field to churchyard (Hill 1977; Jolly 1996: 6–12).

We also need to take into account that the dates of some cemeteries extend into the eleventh or twelfth centuries, and may relate to the length of use of the associated fields and settlements rather than the activities of the church (Elstow, Kempston, Milton Keynes, Chimney, Templecombe and Saffron Walden). Migration of burial to the churchyard might be a much longer process than is suggested by the earliest documentation to record the practice, which might be essentially complete by the tenth century. Indeed, an extended process of the coming together of burial place and the local church may be one explanation for the observed sequences of churches being built over burials, as if the church could be a late addition to an existing cemetery (e.g. an early discussion by Morris 1983, 49–58; a recent summary of northern evidence in Hadley 2002: 220–21): it is also important to remember the continued use of non-church cemeteries beyond the tenth century in Ireland (Fry 1999: 43).

Another reason for considering a late survival of some of these field cemeteries is that burial location only appears to become more centralised in the high Middle Ages. Christopher Daniell, for example, has traced the end of the practice of burying criminals in peripheral locations and the start of their incorporation into institutional or monastic graveyards in the post-Conquest eleventh and twelfth centuries (Daniell 2002: 243–47). Perhaps the radiocarbon dates for some of the field cemeteries indicate that the eleventh and twelfth centuries was when field cemeteries were finally abandoned and the development of churchyards was complete. This period is also characterized by the working through of the Gregorian reforms which show an increased concern for the welfare of local congregations (e.g. Robinson 2004: 305–34). It is also when we see the final phase of settlement and field reorganization.

An important related topic, alluded to already but too complex to be fully considered here, is when and how parish churches and graveyards were founded. Some mention, however, has to be made of the issue because it has a bearing on the argument presented here. The proprietary model, which puts the aristocracy, particularly the lower echelons of that class – the thegns – at the centre of the process of local church creation, is generally accepted, particularly as it coincides with tenurial change and the creation of smaller, manorial-type estates out of larger units from the tenth century (e.g. Blair 2005: 385–96; Faith 1997: 153–77). Such a model adds fuel to the debate about the identity of the prime movers or agents in initiating change in medieval society (Dyer 1985; Harvey 1989; Lewis *et al.* 1997: 204–13). The tenth and eleventh centuries have also produced evidence for an alternative view. It is noticeable, for example, that in East Anglia and the midlands the focus for later Saxon settlements is increasingly being identified as a 'green' – that is, an area of communal pasture at the heart of settlements. Its management would contribute to the development of a group identity, and also emphasize the importance of field-like resources in the process (Warner 1987; Oosthuizen 2002; Jones and Page 2006: 96–99: Mortimer 2000a: 18–21).

David Stocker and Paul Everson's work on the early Romanesque church towers in Lincolnshire has found that over a third had been added to later Saxon churches which had been built on communal resources; that is greens, which were at the centre of villages (Stocker and Evison 2006: summarized at 64–67). A similar pattern occurs in Cambridgeshire (Oosthuizen 2006: 51–59). This implies that the community at large had agreed that a church should be built on communal land and this was therefore its project, reflecting the group's identity – a reminder that we have yet fully to understand the agency behind the creation of local churches.

This review has not reduced the frustration of dealing with field cemeteries that was mentioned at the beginning: in one sense it has made the issue more frustrating. It has accepted that such burial grounds were for the majority of the population, but I have spread their small number over an even longer period, arguing that the cemeteries were related to the development of the fields and settlements and the growing communal identity of the resident population, rather than to the documented burgeoning of church power in the tenth century.

Chapter 13

Rethinking later medieval masculinity: the male body in death

Roberta Gilchrist

Abstract

This paper reviews transitions in medieval masculinity through the archaeological evidence for burial rites. I take as my starting point an article by Heinrich Härke published in *Past and Present* in 1990, 'Warrior graves? The background of the Anglo-Saxon burial rite'. Recent theoretical approaches to the study of masculinity have emphasized the use of metonymy in constructing hegemonic values of masculinity, for instance the use of weapons as grave goods to create a naturalized equation of maleness with power. A case study is presented of clergy burials, *c.*1050–1150, a critical period in the redefinition of masculinity, as a new celibate priesthood was created by the Gregorian Reform. I argue that during the Middle Ages the clergy developed a monopoly over the expression of masculine identity through burial rites, replacing the earlier metonymy of weapons with the symbolism of the priest's role in the sacraments. Staging of the priest's corpse, including the placement of the chalice and paten, constructed a mystical masculinity that was focused on the consecrated body of the priest.

Introduction

Although we work on different time-spans within medieval archaeology, I share with Heinrich Härke a particular interest in the expression of medieval gender identity through burial rites. Working with Heinrich Härke at the University of Reading has been a privilege and a source of inspiration to my own teaching and research in medieval archaeology. I particularly admire the veracity with which he interrogates empirical evidence and theoretical interpretation in combination. As a tribute to Heinrich Härke, I have taken one of his most influential articles as a starting point for the reconsideration of a later medieval male burial rite.

Masculinity and the Anglo-Saxon 'warrior'

In 1990, Heinrich Härke published an article in the journal *Past and Present* entitled: 'Warrior graves? The background of the Anglo-Saxon burial rite'. This article revolutionized the theoretical interpretation of early medieval cemeteries by demonstrating that grave goods were not merely *reflective* of status in life (Williams 2007c: 112). Rather than representing the tools, personal property or legal status of the deceased, weapons were active in the symbolic expression of male identities that changed over time. This analysis was also pivotal to the field of gender archaeology that was emerging in 1990. Previous studies of early medieval cemeteries sought simplistic material correlates for gender: sets of grave goods that identified males and females and reflected their roles and status in life. Although Heinrich Härke never employed the term 'masculinity' in this work, gender archaeologists have cited his article as one of the key publications to successfully address masculinity through archaeological evidence (Hadley and Moore 1999: 30; Gilchrist 1999: 67).

To summarize, the article reassessed the premise that all weapon burials represent the graves of warriors by asking 'who was accorded a weapon burial, and who was excluded from it?' (Härke 1990a: 25). It considered excavated evidence from 47 English cemeteries dating from the fifth to the eighth centuries, in which nearly half of all identifiable male adult inhumations were accompanied by a weapon (47%). Weapon burials peaked in the mid-sixth century and then declined steadily until disappearing in the eighth century. It seems that this rite was actually most prevalent at a period of *decreased* military activity, according to historical sources such as Gildas and *The Anglo-Saxon Chronicle*, leading Härke to conclude that the weapon burial rite had nothing to do with actual intensity of warfare (Härke 1990a: 31–32).

Weapons were found with males ranging in age from 12 months to 60 years, and were included in the graves of some with physical impairments, including severe osteoarthritis and broken long-bones that had healed poorly. Further, there was a lack of correlation between individuals interred with weapons and skeletal injuries that may have been the result of battle wounds (Härke 1990a: 36). Burial with a weapon was therefore not determined by physical ability to fight, or by actual participation in combat. Härke proposed an absolute correlation of weapon burials with male sex. He suggested that the 'few exceptions can be explained as cases of secondary use of weapon parts (for example, detached spearheads being used as knives or weaving swords)' (Härke 1990a: 36). More recently, Nick Stoodley has concluded that there is evidence for the burial of weapons with females at only one excavated Anglo-Saxon cemetery: four females were interred with weapons at Buckland, Dover (Kent). He raises the possibility that this particular community accorded some women a ritual male status in death (Stoodley 1999a: 29–30, 176).

Härke's study detected a positive correlation between the presence of weapons and male stature, indicating that genetic descent was significant in determining which men were buried with weapons. Weapon burials also demonstrated a higher degree of labour investment in grave constructions such as coffins or wooden chambers. He concluded that the Anglo-Saxon weapon burial rite was a symbolic act: it 'was not the reflection of a real warrior function, but the ritual expression of an ethnically, socially and perhaps ideologically-based "warrior status"' (Härke 1990a: 43). In other words, 'warrior' was a form of masculinity that some Anglo-Saxon males were accorded on the basis of their family status, evoked through burial with weapons.

This conclusion resonates with the basic premise of masculinity studies: that masculinity is culturally constructed and does not equate simply with male sex. The work of Robert (Raewyn) Connell has been particularly influential in this field, arguing that masculinity is culturally constructed by creating a hierarchy of males in relation to the values of the most powerful (Connell 1995). 'Hegemonic masculinity' is defined by what brings the most prestige to males in a given society, and might be based on elements of class, ethnicity, age, profession and sexuality. Men who do not possess the attributes of the most powerful masculinity are marginalized and subordinated; the further down the male hierarchy they fall, the closer they come to the characteristics of femininity. By definition, women lack the essential qualities of hegemonic masculinity: both females and lesser males are marginalized by their absence of the most valued male traits and rendered culturally effeminate. Hegemonic and subordinate masculinities co-exist in the same society and they are in constant opposition; this tension leads to conflict, periods of crisis and the redefinition of masculinities. Crucial to Connell's model is the acknowledgement that several different masculinities may characterize a single society and, by implication, that distinctive archaeological signatures may represent respective masculinities within that society.

Material culture plays an active role in constructing hegemonic masculinity, as images and instruments of power – such as weapons –

construct masculinity through a metonymy that can be acquired or lost (Cornwall and Lindisfarne 1994: 20). Masculinity is mystified through the construction of the warrior and his weapon burial, to present this category of man as aggressive, active and dominant (Treherne 1995). Grave goods and the weapon burial rite constructed a relationship between power and a certain group of Anglo-Saxon men, which appeared to be 'natural' – masculinity in its purest form. But with the cessation of furnished burials during the eighth century, how did Anglo-Saxon men define and express hegemonic masculinity? In what way did Christianity impact on the hierarchy of medieval masculinities? The period of the eighth to the eleventh centuries was critical in the reformulation of masculinities: priests vied with warriors in the battle for male hegemony, and the clergy usurped traditional burial rites in the process.

Masculinity in crisis? Warriors, monks and priests

The Anglo-Saxon weapon burial rite declined during the seventh and eighth centuries, when burial with a simple iron knife came to signify adult masculinity. In a separate study, Härke concluded that 'as the weapon burial rite became limited to an even smaller number of comparatively rich burials, large knives became an alternative means of expressing adult status in poorer graves' (Härke 1989b). But why did the weapon burial rite rapidly decline and disappear? Conversion to Christianity did not result in the immediate suppression of the use of grave goods in traditional inhumation rites. Rich female burials of the seventh to ninth centuries integrated Christianity with the furnished burial rite (Crawford 2003). Many included objects with explicit Christian symbolism – it was even acceptable for a furnished burial in a Christian churchyard at Harrietsham (Kent) to include a crystal-ball, a potent symbol of Anglo-Saxon female magic (Blair 2005: 237).

Recently archaeologists have interpreted the shift away from furnished burial as being linked to economic and political factors, rather than stemming from religious transformations (Crawford 2004: 92). But the weapon burial rite may prove an exception to this rule. With the shift to churchyard burial came the concept of the cemetery as a delineated, sacred space. Certainly by the tenth century, churchyards were sanctified by rites of consecration that established the space within their boundaries as holy (Zadoro-Rio 2003: 19). Anglo-Saxon rites are well recorded: the bishop and clergy processed around the churchyard, sprinkling holy water to purify the enclosure; a second procession involved the bishop praying in each corner of the cemetery, and in its centre; finally, a mass was celebrated in the churchyard (Gittos 2002: 195–96). Consecrated burial grounds were inviolable: any form of bloodshed was prohibited, along with the bearing or burial of arms. Spilling of blood within the consecrated space caused pollution of the cemetery and its church, and its purification could be regained only by a rite of re-consecration.

Christianity impacted on male burial rites even before churchyard burial had become the norm. There was a new emphasis on segregation of burial by sex, with the exclusive interment of males in monastic cemeteries, for example at Ripon (North Yorks), Hereford (Hereford and Worcester), Burrow Hill (Suffolk) and Beckery Chapel, Glastonbury (Somerset) (Hadley 2004: 311). High-ranking clergy adopted the furnished burial rite and were interred in ornate ecclesiastical vestments. When St Cuthbert, bishop of Lindisfarne, died in 687, he was buried in his full vestments and these became renowned as relics with miracle-working properties. According to Bede, 'the garments that had clothed Cuthbert's hallowed body both before and after his death continued to possess healing virtues' (Colgrave and Mynors 1969: 31). Here, we see the emergence of burial rites associated with a different sort of elite Anglo-Saxon masculinity: the mystical masculinity that was acquired by the consecrated body of the holy man.

The Viking raids and subsequent settlements stimulated some revival of warrior symbolism in Anglo-Saxon commemoration. Dawn Hadley has identified a return to the display of elite masculinity through weapon burials and on martial sculpture that depicted warriors and hunting scenes, such as the tenth-century sculptures from Sockburn (Durham) and Middleton (North Yorks). She postulates that this may have been a response to the Viking threat, noting that 'during moments of intense social stress notions of masculinity were commonly re-evaluated in the early middle ages' (Hadley 2004: 318, 323). Within the Danelaw, military equipment has been found with burials in churchyards, including swords at Repton (Derbys), Kildale and Wensley (North Yorks), Ormside, Rampside and West Seaton (Cumbria), and Heysham (Lancs) (Richards 2002: 156, 160–61).

It has been suggested that, throughout western Europe, the later ninth century witnessed a crisis of masculinity in which the warrior aristocracy struggled to transform itself into a Christian elite (Nelson 1999: 123). The clergy occupied an uneasy middle ground in medieval definitions of gender: they were not men who bore arms or provided for dependents, they did not impregnate women; nor were they women who could bear children (Swanson 1999: 160). The monastic reform of the tenth century introduced a new emphasis on purity and more disciplined rules for celibate men who lived communally in monasteries (Frassetto 1998). A century later saw the Gregorian Reform of the priesthood, imposing chastity on the secular priests who lived outside monastic communities. There were practical reasons for the formalization of clerical celibacy, such as the prevention of the development of a hereditary priesthood that could alienate church property. Priests enjoyed unimpeded access to secular women, and the clergy's latent sexuality was perceived as a potential threat to the secular aristocracy. This anxiety is vividly illustrated in a panel of the Bayeux Tapestry entitled 'where a cleric and Aelfgyva'. An unnamed cleric transgresses the architectural frame in which Aelfgyva is enclosed, while a marginal figure below, naked and displaying a phallus, gestures to the scene. The image implies that she was sexually assaulted, and as a result, the honour of her clan insulted (Camille 1998: 16). A chaste priesthood would protect the chattels of both the church and the aristocracy. Most importantly, a celibate priesthood brought ideological gains to the church, enhancing the purity of the sacraments.

Aristocratic men were redefined socially and sexually between the eighth to the eleventh centuries; what were the implications for hegemonic masculinity? Who was at the top of the male hierarchy by the end of the eleventh century: secular, married men, or ecclesiastical, celibate men? The historian Joanne McNamara has termed this conflict the 'Herrenfrage', a masculine identity crisis in which two groups of male elite competed for supremacy, while at the same time struggling to control women (McNamara 1994). The new centrality of the sacraments provided the priesthood with a powerful advantage over both women and secular men. Theoretically at least, the priest was uncontaminated by sexual contact with women or by bloodshed caused by the bearing of arms. Like the churchyard, the consecrated body of the celibate priest was a sacred space; only the male body of the priest could mediate with the divine.

Priests' burials: symbols of mystical masculinity

While scholarship on early medieval burial rites has grown increasingly theorized, the study of later medieval Christian burials has remained largely conservative. The standard grave goods of the priest are well known, but these are regarded as the symbolic tools of his profession, to be presented at Judgement Day as evidence of his religious status. To what extent were priests' burials also statements of their particular masculine identity in life? What can we learn by assessing them in terms similar to those that Härke used for the Anglo-Saxon weapon burial rite?

The clergy adopted distinctive burial rites from *c*.1000 onwards, while those of the laity displayed relative uniformity until *c*.1150–1200 (Gilchrist and Sloane 2005). Attention was drawn to the burial place by the use of cists and other forms of lining such as crushed chalk or mortar, planks of wood or head support stones. Lead plaques and crosses were placed in some ecclesiastical graves and wooden rods or wands were deposited as grave goods with men, women and children from the early eleventh century onwards. By *c*.1100, the burials of priests were routinely accompanied by chalices and patens, while those of abbots and bishops included croziers, the staff of higher ecclesiastical office. Monks were buried in the habit of their orders or in animal hides, and bishops in their clothing of ritual consecration. Mortuary symbolism for the clergy was elaborated and standardized at precisely the period in which the priesthood was reformed, *c*.1050–1150 (ibid: 215). It was also at this time that the clergy established their monopoly over intercession for the dead, and took responsibility for burial of the laity in monastic and parish churchyards (Postles 1996: 622). Control over burial rites played a crucial role in this renegotiation of medieval masculine identities.

The principal grave goods used to symbolize the priest were the chalice and paten: the chalice is the sacred vessel used to contain wine during the ritual of the mass, representing the blood of Christ; the paten is the small shallow plate or disc of precious metal on which the eucharist is offered to God during the mass, and on which the consecrated host is subsequently placed. The chalices found in medieval burials represent the sacrificial chalice that was used by priests and bishops in the mass. It is important to distinguish these from the ministerial chalices that were employed for communion of the laity at Easter: ministerial chalices were larger vessels and were often provided with two handles (Catholic Encyclopedia). The sacrificial chalice was selected as a grave good to represent the exclusive right of the priest to mediate with the divine, and to signal his sacerdotal agency in transforming the wine into the actual blood of Christ.

Considerable numbers of chalices have been recovered through antiquarian and modern excavations in England, including exceptional assemblages of chalices or chalice and paten sets from Winchester Cathedral and York Minster, numbering 19 and 24 respectively, and dating from the later thirteenth to sixteenth centuries (Kjølbye-Biddle 1992: 239–44). A recent study of medieval monastic burials reported on 30 chalices from archaeological contexts that could be dated stratigraphically, suggesting that the earliest date from *c*.1100, with a peak in numbers in the thirteenth and fourteenth centuries (Gilchrist and Sloane 2005: 161). Who was accorded a priest's burial, and who was excluded from it? Interment with a chalice was even more exclusive than the earlier rite of weapon burial: to date, archaeological excavation confirms that chalices were deposited only with adult males. A skeleton sexed as a 'possible female' was buried at Carlisle Dominican friary with a 'possible chalice', but it has been postulated that this fragment of a relatively thick lead base derived instead from a lamp (McCarthy 1990: 186). There is no archaeological evidence to suggest that comparable objects were routinely deposited with religious women to denote their status, although abbesses and prioresses were sometimes buried with a crozier to represent their high office (Gilcrist and Sloane 2005: 126).

In contrast with the Anglo-Saxon 'warriors' who spanned a broad range of ages and physical conditions, there was an insistence that the male body of the priest should be a perfect adult specimen. Men with physical disabilities were discouraged from ordination, and those who acquired impairments through age or accident required a papal dispensation from bodily perfection in order to officiate (Swanson 1999: 166). This principle was based on the Old Testament prescription that he who 'hath any blemish, let him not approach to offer the bread of his God' (Leviticus 21: 17–20; Metzler 2006: 40). One archaeological example suggests that priests who had suffered physical impairments retained the right to employ clerical symbolism in their burials. A grave excavated from within the chapel at the hospital of St Giles by Brompton Bridge (Brough, North Yorks) contained a disabled male who is likely to have walked with a crutch; his remains were accompanied by a chalice and paten of lead and tin alloy. This elderly male showed osseous changes typical of an untreated slipped proximal femoral epiphyses of the right leg (Knüsel *et al.* 1992). Based on modern comparisons, it is likely that the injury occurred in late adolescence; the right wrist and hand exhibited signs of load-bearing commensurate with the habitual use of a crutch, indicating long-term disability. The hospital of Brompton Bridge served a variety of functions between the thirteenth and fifteenth centuries, but acted principally as an almshouse for the elderly (Gilchrist and Sloane 2005: 206). Such an institution may have welcomed a priest with impaired mobility as a religious incumbent, or, alternatively, the hospital sheltered the former priest as an inmate in his old age. In the later Middle Ages almshouses were established with the specific purpose of caring for infirm priests: the elderly inmates of Clyst Gabriel, near Exeter, suffered most commonly from blindness (Orme 1988: 7–8).

A priest's status in the male religious hierarchy was signalled through the material of his funerary chalice: priests were interred with lead or pewter chalices and bishops with silver or gilt chalices. Other materials were used where metal could not be spared, with pottery chalices recorded from the Cluniac abbey of Much Wenlock (Shropshire) and from Winchester, and a beeswax chalice from the Cistercian abbey at Hulton (Staffordshire) (Gilchrist and Sloane 2005: 163). Chalices made of pewter or fashioned from perishable materials were skeumorphs made specifically for funerary purposes; only silver chalices were consecrated for use in the mass (Oman 1957). The priest's distinction from other men was also emphasized through the location of his burial. For example, the priests' graves excavated at the Paradise cemetery in Winchester, located to the north of the cathedral, were focused on St Swithun's chapel (Kjølbye-Biddle 1992: 241). These men were not buried with the monks of the cathedral but had their own prestigious burial space nevertheless. Priests in secular cathedrals such as Salisbury, York and Wells were interred in hierarchical zones that distinguished between the canons and lesser priests or vicars. A chapter act from Wells dated to 1243 specified that the canons were to be buried in the cloister, while the vicars' graves were to be placed to the east of the Lady chapel (Gilchrist and Sloane 2005: 61; 47). Within monastic and cathedral churches like Lichfield and Hulton, priests' burials often focused on the *pulpitum* screen that separated the choir from the nave, the location of chapels where priests would have officiated. In parish churches such as All Saints, Barton Bendish (Norfolk) (Rogerson *et al.* 1987: 28), it was common for priests to be buried in the chancel, the most sacred space in the church and one exclusive to the clergy.

How were clerical grave goods placed in relation to the body of the priest, and at what point in the funerary rite? Many appear to have been placed upright, suggesting that they were deposited at the graveside, after the corpse and its container had been transported. Some were placed on the chest or in the hand of the corpse, while others stood to the right or left of the head or arm. It was usual for the paten to be placed on top of the chalice, and some were also associated with the corporal, the square piece of linen on which the consecrated host is placed during the mass (Gilchrist and Sloane 2005: 164). Excavations in the nave of Lichfield Cathedral in 2003–4 provide the best detailed evidence for these practices (Rodwell 2003–5: 5–6). The graves of three priests were excavated: all were stone-lined cists with timber coffins placed inside, and all yielded chalices and patens made of pewter. The position of the grave goods was different in each case (Fig. 13.1). A grave abutting the shrine of St Chad to the west had the chalice and paten placed by the head, before the coffin was filled with a mixture of charcoal and loam. The chalice and paten in a priest's burial flanking the shrine on the north was placed outside the coffin, but within the cist. The third grave was made next to the nave arcade in the thirteenth

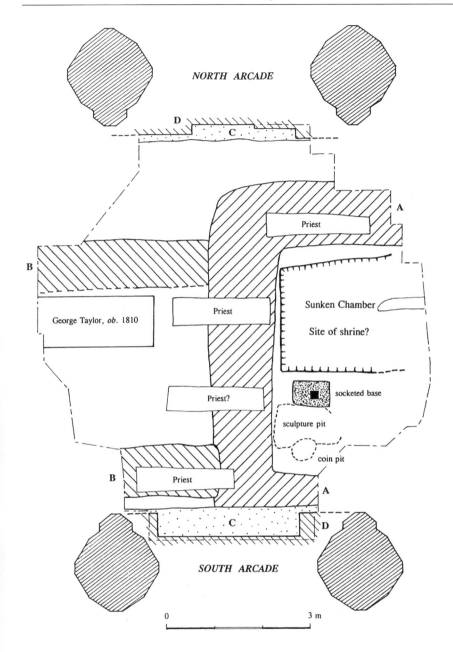

NORTH ARCADE

D

C

A

B

Priest

Priest

George Taylor, *ob.* 1810

Sunken Chamber

Site of shrine?

Priest?

socketed base

sculpture pit

coin pit

B

Priest

A

C

D

SOUTH ARCADE

0   3 m

Fig. 13.1: Plan of the excavations in the nave at Lichfield Cathedral in 2003–4, showing the graves of three priests which contained chalices and patens; a fourth possible priest's grave had been disturbed previously. Image reproduced with kind permission of Warwick Rodwell.

century and was remarkably well preserved (Fig. 13.2). The timber coffin was covered with a dark cloth on which was painted a red cross, and placed on this device was a little cross made of two twigs, each 5cm in length. Standing on top of the coffin lid next to the twig cross was a pewter chalice, with the paten resting on it. A folded linen cloth lay

Fig. 13.2: The well-preserved burial of a priest at Lichfield Cathedral, showing a timber coffin covered with a dark cloth on which a red cross was painted. On the cloth were placed a little cross made of two twigs, and a pewter chalice. A wand or rod was placed between the coffin and the surrounding cist. Image reproduced with kind permission of Warwick Rodwell.

on the paten, and between this textile and the paten were the remains of a eucharistic wafer (Fig. 13.3). Pitting in the interior of the pewter chalice is likely to have been caused by wine.

The Lichfield priest was accompanied not merely by symbols of his office, he was provided with the wafer and the wine, consecrated materials that had been transformed miraculously into the body of Christ. These materials represented the sacrifice of Christ's body for the salvation of humanity: they were crucial to the viaticum rite that would have been administered before the priest's death, and they served a powerful apotropaic purpose in accompanying his soul on its journey through purgatory. The element of display in the priest's burial also signalled his sacerdotal position as mediator in the transformative ritual of the mass.

What other forms of display, or social investment, accompanied the burial of priests? Härke's study of weapon burials confirmed that interments of the warrior group were marked out by greater investment in containers and grave constructions (1990a: 38). This observation applies equally well to medieval priests; of 30 recently excavated graves containing chalices, 10 were associated with surviving timber coffins, three were in stone coffins, two were marked by grave slabs, and two were interred in anthropomorphic grave cuts (Gilchrist and Sloane 2005: 161). Of the 19 priests' graves excavated at Winchester, only five were in stone cists and the remainder were in earth graves; however, the most elaborate grave in the Paradise cemetery was that of a priest, dated *c.*1320–60, who was holding a chalice covered with a paten. He was aged 35–45 years and was fully dressed for his burial, indicated by some gold threads on his right breast, a copper-alloy buckle between his thighs and a triangular hook or tag at his neck. An earlier priest's grave at the same site (*c.*1280–1320) had an iron trowel placed in the hands of the corpse, in addition to a chalice and paten standing to the left of the head (Kjølbye-Biddle 1992: 241; 239). The trowel had been wrapped in a linen cloth and was carefully placed with this elderly man, perhaps indicating his

Fig. 13.3: The pewter chalice that was placed on the coffin of the Lichfield priest, showing the small cross of twigs next to it, and the paten and folded linen cloth that were placed on top of the chalice. Image reproduced with kind permission of Warwick Rodwell.

status as a patron of church building (Biddle and Kjølbye-Biddle 1990: 791–92). Apotropaic objects were sometimes placed with the medieval dead, such as hazel or ash rods or wands, symbolic wayfaring sticks that may have served as charms to protect the dead on their journey through purgatory (Gilchrist and Sloane 2005: 171–75; Gilchrist 2008). The Lichfield priest had a wand placed between his coffin and the walls of the surrounding cist (Rodwell 2003–5: 6), while the grave from Hulton abbey that contained the beeswax chalice had six wooden wands placed around the body of the priest (Klemperer and Boothroyd 2004: 133).

The bodies of some clerics received further special treatment, as indicated by the well-preserved example of the Lichfield priest. His corpse was wrapped in cloth and tied in string like a parcel. His head was not covered or contained in the wrapping, but was left to rest on a leather pillow. The very poor survival of human bone, in contrast with the preserved hair of the corpse and the textile remains, may suggest that his body was treated with some form of embalming (Rodwell 2003–5). Medieval embalming techniques sometimes employed potentially corrosive lime or salt, in combination with beeswax and aromatic spices (Gilchrist and Sloane 2005: 108–9). The extraordinary survival of the Lichfield priest reveals that deliberate staging of the corpse took place after any such preparation was completed: the body was carefully wrapped to leave the face visible before it was placed in the coffin, suggesting that for some time the coffin was open for viewing. After the coffin was closed, it was covered with a special cloth and a cross of twigs was placed on the top; the priest's grave goods, together with the wafer and wine of the consecrated host, were carefully placed on top of the covered coffin; and finally a wand was deposited between the coffin and the surrounding stone cist. Clergy burials were staged to display the body of the priest with his symbols and materials of sacred office. These rites eased the passage of the priest's soul while at the same time consolidating his social and religious identity and his place in the masculine hierarchy. The early stages of the funerary rites would have been exclusive to the cathedral community, but the focus of the priests' burials around the *pulpitum* screen suggests that the laity had visual access to the final staging and interment of the corpse. These later medieval grave furnishings played a part in theatrical performances that were just as vital to male identity as had been those of their early medieval predecessors (Williams 2007c).

Conflicting secular and clerical masculinities: commemorating later medieval 'warriors'

Tensions between secular and clerical male elites continued throughout the later Middle Ages, with both groups subject to caricatures that marginalized their masculinity. Religious men were physically distinctive: their cleanly shaven faces, tonsure and clerical garb were feminizing, and they even rode side-saddle like women. The historian R.N. Swanson described priests as 'emasculine', quasi-transvestites who were victim to anti-clerical prejudice that was akin to misogyny (Swanson 1999: 167). Treatment of male head and body hair is linked with hegemonic masculinity in many cultures, with trans-gender or ritual specialists symbolized by characteristic visual languages of hair (Aldhouse-Green 2004). With development of the culture of chivalry, secular men of the aristocracy were also ridiculed for being effeminate. From the twelfth century onwards, men who shaved their beards, curled their hair and cultivated courtly manners were blamed for causing soldiers to be confused with priests or women (McNamara 1994: 9).

Secular men used clothing and material culture to reassert their active male sexuality, a visible contrast with the ambiguous gender of the celibate priest. Long-pointed shoes called *poulaines* became

fashionable in northern Europe as a result of the popular belief that the
size of the penis was linked to the length of the feet. Men stuffed the
tips of these phallic shoes as a public display of their virility (Murray
1996: 134). The later Middle Ages also witnessed the male fashion for
wearing knives and daggers with overtly penis-shaped hilts, known
by English contemporaries as the 'ballok-knyf' (Jones 2002: 258), and
de-sexualised in modern archaeological typologies as the 'kidney' type
(Hinton 2005: 250). An English priests' manual of *c.*1400 explicitly
warned the chaste cleric against taking up these notorious symbols of
the secular male:

> Hawking, hunting, and dancing
> Fashionable dagged clothes and pointed shoes,
> Will destroy your good reputation.
> I forbid you to go to markets and fairs
> You must wear respectable clothes,
> Do not wear a dagger or baldric
> (John Myrc, *Manuale Sacerdotis*,
> quoted in Cullum 1999: 185).

Myrc's injunctions repeat those that were in wide circulation from the
tenth century onwards, such as the Carolingian *Admonitio Synodalis*:

> Let no one go on the road with a stole; let no one of you wear lay
> clothes or diverse colours. Let none of you be drunken or litigious
> because the Lord's servant ought not to litigate. Let none of you
> bear arms in sedition, because our arms must be spiritual ones.
> Let no one indulge in the sport of birds or dogs. Do not drink in
> taverns. (Amiet 1964: 60–61)

Through distinctive burial rites and sacred grave goods, the priest
could signal his place in the male hierarchy. Within the limited range
of Christian funerary practice, what opportunity did the aristocratic
warrior have to represent his station? The burial of weapons was
excluded from consecrated ground, but elite men of warrior status
participated in new rites – or revived ancient ones – to express their
masculinity in death. Research by David Stocker and Paul Everson in
the Witham Valley (Lincolnshire) has suggested that monasteries may
have controlled the ritual disposal of weapons outside the consecrated
ground of cemeteries. In the medieval period, the Witham Valley was
densely settled by monasteries, which were linked by ten causeways
across the fenland. Artefacts recovered from the causeways confirm
that the ritual deposition of weapons had continued from the Bronze
Age to later medieval occupation. A total of 32 medieval weapons was
found, including 10 swords, five daggers/long knives, six axe heads and

six spearheads. Stocker and Everson (2003) surmise that the practice ceased in the late fourteenth century, when it became acceptable to display military equipment around the tomb in the church.

With the appropriation of masculine grave goods for exclusive use by the clergy, funerary commemoration provided a new vehicle for the display of warriorhood. Medieval cross slab grave covers were in use from the eleventh to the fourteenth century, but peaked in use in the twelfth and thirteenth centuries (Ryder 1985: 1). They were more common in regions with plentiful supplies of freestone suitable for carving, principally to the north of the Rivers Trent and Dee (Butler 1984: 247). The central cross was sometimes accompanied by secondary emblems that have been interpreted as representing the identity of the individual that the slab commemorated. The attributes have been classified into military, female, clerical and trade symbols. Military symbolism predominated and the sword was the most frequently represented emblem (Butler 1984: 251). In County Durham, for example, 29% of 550 known slabs depicted the sword (Ryder 1985: 18). Where swords occur in association with inscriptions or heraldic shields, it is clear that they commemorated males of military rank. The meaning is ambiguous, however, where the sword is used in conjunction with other

Fig. 13.4: Effigy of the Dorchester Knight, *c.1260*, in the south chancel aisle at Dorchester, Oxfordshire. The costume highlights the hips and legs of the knight's body, while the gesture emphasizes the physical movement of withdrawing the sword from the scabbard. Photograph by Roberta Gilchrist.

emblems, such as the chalice (a clerical symbol) or the shears (a female symbol) (Butler 1984: 250). Some permeability of gender boundaries may be suggested by this mixing of secondary emblems across categories of military, clerical, male and female.

The military effigies of the thirteenth and fourteenth centuries can also be reappraised in terms of masculine symbolism. The earliest effigies are ecclesiastic examples of the mid-twelfth century, but military effigies of knights developed an 'emphatic physicality' from the mid-thirteenth century. In common with the Anglo-Saxon 'warriors' who received weapon burials (Härke 1990a), men represented by military effigies had not necessarily seen active combat. Rachel Dressler described the writhing physicality of monuments such as the Dorchester Abbey knight (Oxfordshire), dated *c.*1260: 'The figure is husky and solidly built, with heavily muscled arms and legs. These brawny members twist and turn, thrusting themselves into the viewer's space and awareness' (Dressler 1999: 148). Dressler interprets this tomb genre as a social strategy on the part of local knights to compete with the nobility (Fig. 13.4). But these monuments may also have been engaged in the struggle between clerical and secular men for hegemonic masculinity. As Dressler acknowledges, the costumes worn by these knights emphasize the hips and legs of the male body, providing a greater degree of corporeal display than those of female or ecclesiastical tombs. Such displays constructed images of a virile sexuality for secular men, just as priests used burial rites to emphasize their sacred office and celibate body.

Conclusion: male mortuary rites and the redefinition of medieval masculinities

Burial rites were a powerful arsenal in the conflict between secular and clerical masculinities that emerged between the eighth to eleventh centuries, and continued right up to the Protestant Reformation. According to medieval models of masculinity, priests were less than male and not fully adult; they relied on patronage for their livings, and had not married or achieved the status of the head of a household (Cullum 1999: 194). Secular men were also less than ideal, reduced by the binaries of medieval gender to two primary activities: fighting and fornication. The emergence of chivalry tempered this brutalization of the secular male aristocracy. Its mythology drew on heroic traditions and one of its most enduring symbols harked back to the ritual disposal of weapons. In Thomas Malory's *Le Morte d'Arthur*, published in 1485, Arthur is crowned king after he removes a sword from a block of stone that is located in a churchyard, a space from which weapons were prohibited by the clergy. He later receives the sword Excalibur, which is salvaged from watery depths by the Lady of the Lake, and must be returned to its aqueous grave before Arthur dies. The practice of Christian burial in a consecrated churchyard was incompatible with the weapon burial rite, and yet the sword remained the key symbol of hegemonic masculinity in the collective memory of secular elite males. This nostalgia was expressed through the ritual deposition of weapons, their representation on grave slabs and effigies, and their celebration in chivalric literature. Evidently chivalric males were prone to a certain degree of 'chalice envy': the Arthurian tradition was equally obsessed with the legend of the holy grail, the sacred vessel that Christ used at the last supper to serve the first communion to the apostles, and which was allegedly brought to Glastonbury Abbey by Joseph of Arimathea.

If hegemonic masculinity was represented by the values of secular aristocratic men, priests were 'marginal' to medieval masculinity (after Connell 1995). Yet, their ambivalent position in the male hierarchy was challenged through the formalization of their office, emphasizing the sacerdotal power of the celibate body of the priest. Like ritual specialists in many cultures, the medieval priest was more liminal than marginal, the 'go-between', interceding between the earthly and divine, and poised equivocally between the genders of male and female. But can we classify the priest as an institutionalized 'third gender', an 'emasculine' gender category (after Swanson 1999)? His masculine gender is confirmed by insistence that the priest should possess a perfect male body. In medieval gender terms, the priest was both less and more than male: he could not bear arms or impregnate women, but the male body of the priest acquired a consecrated status. Staging of the male body in death was critical to this masculinity. Just as weapons had forged a metonymy of inherited military power for the Anglo-Saxon 'warrior', the grave goods of the chalice and paten created a metonymy of acquired sacred power for the medieval priest. These symbols adhered to the celibate male body and completed the mystical status of his masculinity.

Acknowledgements

I am grateful to Warwick Rodwell for kindly allowing reproduction of Figures 13.1–13.3. The data discussed for priests' burials result largely from a collaborative study with Barney Sloane on the archaeology of medieval monastic burials (2005); I gratefully acknowledge his contribution and AHRC funding of the original research. I would like to thank the two anonymous referees and the editors for their constructive comments on the draft text. The interpretation presented here remains the responsibility of the author.

Bibliography

Addyman, P. 1969. Late Saxon settlements in the St Neots area. II. The Little Paxton settlement and enclosures. *Proceedings of the Cambridge Antiquarian Society*, 62: 59–93.

Alcock, L. 1963. *Dinas Powys: An Iron Age, Dark Age and Early Medieval Settlement in Glamorgan*. Cardiff: Cardiff University Press.

Aldhouse-Green, M. 2004. Crowning glories: languages of hair in later Prehistoric Europe. *Proceedings of the Prehistoric Society*, 70: 299–325.

Aldworth, F. 1979. Droxford Anglo-Saxon cemetery, Soberton, Hampshire. *Proceedings of the Hampshire Field Club and Archaeological Society*, 35: 93–182.

Allen, W.L. and Richardson, J.B. 1971. The reconstruction of kinship from archaeological data: the concepts, the methods and the feasibility. *American Antiquity*, 36: 41–53.

Alt, K.W. and Vach, W. 1991. The reconstruction of 'genetic kinship' in prehistoric burial complexes: problems and statistics. In *Classification, Data Analysis, and Knowledge Organisation* (eds H.H. Bock and P. Ihm) New York: Springer, pp. 299–310.

Alt, K.W. and Vach, W. 1995. Odontological kinship analysis in skeletal remains: concept, methods, and results. *Forensic Science International*, 74: 99–113.

Ambrus, V. 2006. *Drawing on Archaeology: Bringing History to Life*. Stroud: Tempus.

Ambrus, V. and Aston, M. 2001. *Recreating the Past*. Stroud: Tempus.

Amiet, R. 1964. Une 'Admonitio synodalis' de l'époque carolingienne. Étude critique et édition. *Mediaeval Studies*, 26: 12–82.

Amos, W., Jow, H. and Burroughs, N. 2008. A combined Markov chain Monte Carlo and simulation based approach for inferring the colonisation history of the British Isles. In *Simulations, Genetics and Human Prehistory — a Focus on Islands* (eds S. Matsumura and P. Forster). Cambridge: McDonald Institute Monograph.

Anderson, S. and Birkett, D. 1993. The human skeletal remains from Burgh Castle. In *Caister-on-Sea: Excavations by Charles Green, 1951–1955* (eds M.J. Darling and D. Gurney). East Anglian Archaeological Reports 60. Norwich: Norfolk Archaeological Unit and Norfolk Museums Service, pp. 256–60.

Anke, B. 1998a. *Studien zur reiternomadischen Kultur des 4. bis 5. Jahrhunderts. Teil 1: Text and Karten*. Beiträge zur Ur- und Frühgeschichte Mitteleuropas 8. Weissbach: Beier and Beran.

Anke, B. 1998b. *Studien zur reiternomadischen Kultur des 4. bis 5. Jahrhunderts. Teil 2: Katalog and Tafeln*. Beiträge zur Ur- und Frühgeschichte Mitteleuropas 8). Weissbach: Beier and Beran.

Anke, B. 2007. Zur hunnischen Geschichte nach 375. In *Attila und die Hunnen* (ed. Historisches Museum der Pfalz Speyer). Stuttgart: Konrad Theiss Verlag, pp. 39–47.

Anon. 2000. *Understanding West Stow*. Bury St Edmunds: Suffolk County Council.

Anon. 2004. *Bede's World: Where History was Made*. Jarrow: Bede's Word and Jarrold.

Anthony, D.W. 1990. Migration in archaeology: the baby and the bathwater. *American Anthropologist*, 92: 895–914.

Arbman, H. 1943. *Birka. Untersuchungen und Studien. 1. Die Gräber*. Uppsala: Almqvist and Wiksell.

Arnold, C.J. 1980. Wealth and social structure: a matter of life and death. In *Anglo-Saxon Cemeteries 1979* (eds P. Rahtz, T. Dickinson, and L. Watts). British Archaeological Reports, British Series, Oxford: Archaeopress, pp. 81–142.

Arnold, C.J. 1997. *An Archaeology of the Early Anglo-Saxon Kingdoms*. Second Edition. London: Routledge.

Arrhenius, B. 1985. *Merovingian Garnet Jewellery*. Stockholm: Almqvist and Wiksell.

Artelius, T. 1996. *Långfärd och återkomst — skeppet i bronsålderns gravar*. Uppsats för licentiatexamen Göteborgs Universitet, Institutionen för arkeologi. Riksantikvarieämbetet Arkeologiska Undersökningar — Skrifter No 17. Kungsbacka: Riksantikvarieämbetet och Institutionen för Arkeologi, Göteborgs Universitet.

Artelius, T. 2000. *Bortglömda Föreställningar. Begravningsritual och Begravningsplats i Halländsk Yngre Järnålder*. Stockholm: Riksantikvarämbetet.

Astill, G. 1997. An archaeological approach to the development of agricultural technologies in medieval England. In *Medieval Farming and Technology. The Impact of Agricultural Change in Northwest Europe* (eds G. Astill and J. Langdon). Leiden: Brill, pp. 193–224.

Astill, G. and Wright, S. 1993. Perceiving patronage in the archaeological record: Bordesley Abbey. In *In Search of Cult* (ed. M. Carver). Woodbridge: Boydell, pp. 125–37.

Atkinson, D. 1916. *The Romano-British Site on Lowbury Hill in Berkshire*, Reading: University College Reading.

Back Danielsson, I.-M. 2007. *Masking Moments: The Transitions of Bodies and Beings in Late Iron Age Scandinavia*. Doctoral Dissertation, Department of Archaeology and Classical Studies, University of Stockholm.

Baker, D. 1969. Excavations at Elstow Abbey, Bedfordshire, 1966–68. Second interim report. *Bedfordshire Archaeological Journal*, 4: 27–41.

Bakker, L. 1993. Raetien unter Postumus — Das Siegesdenkmal einer

Juthungenschlacht im Jahre 260 n. Chr. aus Augsburg. *Germania*, 71: 369–86.

Barbujani, G. and Sokal, R. 1990. Zones of sharp genetic change in Europe are also linguistic boundaries. *Proceedings of the National Academy of Sciences*, 87: 1816–19.

Bärenfänger, R. 1988. *Siedlungs- und Bestattungsplätze des 8. bis 10. Jahrhunderts in Niedersachsen und Bremen*. 2 Volumes. British Archaeological Reports, International Series 398. Oxford: Archaeopress.

Barnes, M. 1994. *The Runic Inscriptions of Maeshowe, Orkney*. Uppsala: Institutionen för Nordiska Språk Uppsala Universitet.

Bartel, B. 1980. Collective burial and social organisation: A multivariate analysis of human population from Early Bronze Age Turkey. *Journal of Mediterranean Anthropology and Archaeology*, 1: 3–21.

Bassett, S. 1982. *Saffron Walden: Excavations and Research 1972–80*. London: Chelmsford Archaeological Trust and the Council for British Archaeology.

Bayliss, A. and Whittle, A. 2007. *Histories of the dead: building chronologies for five southern British long barrows*. Cambridge Archaeological Journal 17, Number 1 (Supplement). Cambridge: McDonald Institute for Archaeological Research.

Bazelmans, J. 1999. *By Weapons Made Worthy: Lords, Retainers and their Relationship in Beowulf*. Amsterdam: Amsterdam University Press.

Beattie, O. 1999. Sleep by the shores of those icy seas: death and resurrection in the last Franklin expedition. In *The Loved Body's Corruption: Archaeological Contributions to the Study of Human Mortality* (eds J. Downes and T. Pollard). Glasgow: Cruithne, pp. 52–68.

Becker, M. 2000a. Bekleidung — Schmuck — Ausrüstung. In Fröhlich 2000, pp. 127–47.

Becker, M. 2000b. Luxuriöser Haushalt für den Toten. In Fröhlich 2000, pp. 148–61.

Becker, M., Döhle, H.-J., Hellmund, M., Leineweber, R. and Schafberg, R. 2005. Nach dem großen Brand. Verbrennung auf dem Scheiterhaufen. Ein interdisziplinärer Ansatz. *Bericht der Römisch-Germanischen Kommission*, 86: 61–195.

Belinskij, A. and Härke, H. 1995. Cemetery excavation at Klin Yar, North Caucasus, 1993–94. *Newsletter of the Centre for the Archaeology of Central and Eastern Europe* 3 (March 1995). 4–5.

Belinskij, A. and Härke, H. 1996. British-Russian excavations at the cemetery of Klin Yar (North Caucasus): the 1995 season. *Newsletter of the Centre for the Archaeology of Central and Eastern Europe* 4. 11–14.

Belinskij, A. and Härke, H. forthcoming. *The Iron Age to early medieval cemetery of Klin Yar: excavations 1994–96 (with contributions by A. Buzhilova, S.L. Dudarev, I. Gavritukhin, T. Higham, D. Korobov, M.V. Koslovskaya, V.Yu. Malashev, M. Mednikova, S. Savenko, A.K. Shvyrva and R. Warren)*. Series: Forschungen in Eurasien. Berlin: Eurasia Institute of the Deutsches Archologisches Institut (DAI).

Bell, T. 2005. *The Religious Reuse of Roman structures in Early Medieval England*. British Archaeological Reports British Series 390. Oxford: Archaeopress.

Bengtsdotter, A. 1995. *Vikingatida Gravar vid Tuna och Valsgärde Gravfält.* Mitthögskolan — Östersund; Institutionen för kultur och humaniora. Unpubl. uppsats för Arkeologi C. Handledare: Britta Wennstedt Edvinger, Stig Welinder.

Bentley, R.A., Tayles, N., Higham, C., Macpherson, C. and Atkinson, T.C. 2007. Shifting gender relations at Khok Phanom Di, Thailand. *Current Anthropology*, 48: 310–14.

Besteman, J.C., Bos, J.M., Gerrets, D., Heidinga, H. and de Koning, J. 1999. *The Excavations at Wijnaldum. Vol 1.* Rotterdam: Balkema.

Biddle, M. and Kjølbye-Biddle, M. 1990. Chalices and patens. In *Object and Economy in Medieval Winchester: Artefacts from Medieval Winchester. Winchester Studies 7.2* (ed. M. Biddle). Oxford: Oxford University Press, pp. 789–99.

Bierbrauer, V. 1971. Zu den Vorkommen ostgotischer Bügelfibeln in Raetia II. *Bayerische Vorgeschichtsblätter*, 36(1): 131–65.

Bierbrauer, V. 2007. Ostgermanen im mittleren und unteren Donauraum. Die hunnische Herrschaft. In *Attila und die Hunnen* (ed. Historisches Museum der Pfalz Speyer). Stuttgart: Konrad Theiss Verlag, pp. 96–103.

Binchy, D. 1978. *Corpus iuris hibernici.* Dublin: Institiuìid Ard-Leìinn Bhaile Aìtha Cliath.

Binford, L. 1962a. Archaeology as anthropology. *American Antiquity*, 28: 217–25.

Binford, L. 1962b. *Archaeological investigations in the Carlyle Reservoir, Clinton Country, Illinois.* Southern Illinois University Museum Archaeological Salvage Report 17.

Binford, L. 1971. Mortuary practices: their study and their potential. In *Approaches to the Social Dimensions of Mortuary Practices* (ed. J. Brown) Society for American Archaeology, Memoir 25. Washington DC: Society for American Archaeology, pp. 6–29.

Binford, L. 1972. Galley Pond mound. In *An Archaeological Perspective* (ed. L. Bindford). New York: Seminar Press. pp. 390–420.

Birbeck, V. 2005. *The Origins of Mid-Saxon Southampton: Excavations at the Friends Provident St Mary's Stadium 1998–2000.* Salisbury: Wessex Archaeology.

Birkeli, E. 1943. *Fedrekult. Fra norsk folkeliv i hedens og kristentid.* Oslo: Dreyers Forlag.

Blair, J. 1994. *Anglo-Saxon Oxfordshire.* Stroud: Sutton.

Blair, J. 2005. *The Church in Anglo-Saxon England.* Oxford: Oxford University Press.

Bloch, M. 1971. *Placing the Dead. Tombs, Ancestral Villages and Kinship Organization in Madagascar.* New York: Seminar Press.

Blom, D. 2005. Embodying borders: human body modification and diversity in Tiwanaku society. *Journal of Anthropological Archaeology*, 24(1): 1–24.

Boddington, A. 1990. Models of burial, settlement and worship: the final phase reviewed. In *Anglo-Saxon Cemeteries. A Reappraisal* (ed. E. Southworth). Stroud: Sutton, pp. 177–99.

Boddington, A. 1996. *Raunds Furnells: the Anglo-Saxon Church and Churchyard.* London: English Heritage.

Bogaard, A. and Jones, G. 2007. Neolithic farming in Britain and central

Europe: contrast or continuity? In *Going Over. The Mesolithic-Neolithic Transition in North-West Europe* (eds A. Whittle and V. Cummings). Proceedings of the British Academy 144. Oxford: Oxford University Press, pp. 357–75.

Böhme, H.W. 1998. Beobachtungen zur germanischen Frauentracht im Gebiet zwischen Niederelbe und Loire am Ende der späten Kaiserzeit. In *Studien zur Archäologie des Ostseeraumes. Festschrift für Michael Müller-Wille* (ed. A. Wesse). Neumünster: Wachholtz, pp. 435–51.

Böhner, K. 1958. *Die fränkischen Altertümer des Trierer Landes.* Berlin: Germanische Denkmäler der Völkerwanderungszeit Serie B 1.

Bondioli, L. Corruccini, R.S. and Macchiarelli, R. 1986. Familial segregation in the Iron-Age community of Alfedena, Abruzzo, Italy, based on osteo-dental trait analysis. *American Journal of Physical Anthropology*, 71: 393–400.

Booth, P., Dodd, A., Robinson, M. and Smith, A. 2007. *The Thames through Time. The Archaeology of the Gravel Terraces of the Upper and Middle Thames. The early historical period: AD 1–1000.* Thames Valley Landscapes Monograph No. 27. Oxford: Oxford Archaeology.

Boyle, A. 2004. The Human Burials. In *Yarnton: Saxon and Medieval Settlement and Landscape. Result of Excavations 1990–96.* (G. Hey) Thames Valley Landscape Monograph 20. Oxford: Oxford Archaeology, pp. 317–24.

Boyle, A., Dodd, A., Miles, D. and Mudd, A. 1995. *Two Oxfordshire Anglo-Saxon Cemeteries: Berinsfield and Didcot.* Thames Valley Landscapes Monograph No. 8. Oxford: Oxford Archaeological Unit.

Boyle, A., Jennings, D., Miles, D. and Palmer, S. 1998. *The Anglo-Saxon Cemetery at Butler's Field, Lechlade, Gloucestershire.* Thames Valley Landscapes Monograph No. 10. Oxford: Oxford Archaeological Unit.

Boylston, A., Wiggins, R. and Roberts, C. 1998. Human skeletal remains. In *The Anglo-Saxon Cemetery at Castledyke South, Barton-on-Humber.* (G. Drinkall and M. Foreman). Sheffield Excavation Reports 6. Sheffield: Sheffield University Press, pp. 221–35.

Bradley, J. and Gaimster, M. 2000. Medieval Britain and Ireland, 1999. *Medieval Archaeology*, 44: 235–354.

Bradley, R. 1987. Time regained: the creation of continuity. *Journal of the British Archaeological Association*, 140: 1–17.

Bradley, R. 1988. Status, wealth and the chronological ordering of cemeteries. *Proceedings of the Prehistoric Society*, 54: 327–29.

Bradley, R. 1997. 'To see is to have seen': craft traditions in British field archaeology. In *The Cultural Life of Images: Visual Representation in Archaeology* (ed. B.L. Molyneaux). London: Routledge, pp. 62–72.

Bradley, R. 1998. *The Passage of Arms.* Second Edition. Oxford: Oxbow.

Bradley, R. 2007. *The Prehistory of Britain and Ireland.* Cambridge: Cambridge University Press.

Brassil, K.S., Owen, W.G. and Britnell, W.J. 1991. Prehistoric and early medieval cemeteries at Tandderwen, near Denbigh, Clwyd, *Archaeological Journal*, 148: 46–97.

Brather, S. 2000. Ethnische Identitäten als Konstrukte der frühgeschichtlichen Archäologie. *Germania*, 78: 139–77.

Broholm, H.C. 1937. Skibssætninger i Danmark. *Nationalmuseets Arbejdsmark*, 1937: 11–26.

Brookes, S. 2007a. Boat-rivets in graves in pre-Viking Kent: reassessing Anglo-Saxon boat-burial traditions. *Medieval Archaeology*, 51: 1–18.

Brookes, S. 2007b. Walking with Anglo-Saxons: landscapes of the dead in early Anglo-Saxon Kent. In *Early Medieval Mortuary Practices: New Perspectives* (eds S. Semple and H. Williams) *Anglo-Saxon Studies in Archaeology and History* 14. Oxford: Oxford University School of Archaeology, pp. 143–53.

Brothwell, D. 1959. The use of non-metric characteristics of the skull in different populations. In *Tagung Deutsh Gesellschat Anthropologie* Kiel: Göttingen Bericht 6, pp. 103–9.

Brothwell, D. 1981. *Digging Up Bones: The Excavation, Treatment and Study of Human Skeletal Remains*. Ithaca: Cornell University Press.

Brown, A. and Foard, G. 1998. The Saxon landscape: a regional perspective. In *The Archaeology of Landscape, Studies Presented to Christopher Taylor* (eds P. Everson and T. Williamson). Manchester: Manchester University Press, pp. 67–94.

Brown, J. 1971. *Approaches to the Social Dimensions of Mortuary Practices*. Memoir of the Society for American Archaeology 25. Washington DC: Society for American Archaeology.

Brown, J. 1995. On mortuary analysis — with special reference to the Saxe-Binford research program. In *Regional Approaches to Mortuary Analysis* (ed. L.A. Beck). New York: Plenum Press, pp. 3–26.

Brugmann, B. 2004. *Glass Beads from Early Anglo-Saxon Graves*. Oxford: Oxbow Books.

Buckberry, J. 2007. On sacred ground: social identity and churchyard burial in Lincolnshire and Yorkshire, c.700–1100 AD. In *Early Medieval Mortuary Practices* (eds S. Semple and H. Williams). *Anglo-Saxon Studies in Archaeology and History* 14. Oxford: Oxford University School of Archaeology, pp. 117–29.

Budd, P., Millard, A., Cherery, C., Lucy, S. and Roberts, C. 2004. Investigating population movement by stable isotope analysis: report from Britain, *Antiquity* 78: 127–40.

Buiksta, J.E. and Hoshower, L., 1994. Análisis de los restos humanos de la necropolis de Gatas. In *Proyecto Gatas: Sociedad y Economía en el Sureste de España c.2500–900 cal ANE* (edited by P.V. Castro et al.). Memoria de investigación presentada el la Consejería de Cultura de la Junta de Andalucía, pp. 339–98.

Buikstra, J.E., Castro, P.V., Chapman, R., González Marcén, P., Hoshower, L., Lull, V., Micó, R. Picazo, M., Risch, R., Ruíz, M. and Sanahuja, Ma.E. 1995. Approaches to class inequalities in the later prehistory of south-east Iberia: the Gatas project. In *The Origins of Complex Societies in Late Prehistoric Iberia* (ed. K. Lillios). Ann Arbor: International Monographs in Prehistory, pp. 153–86.

Bullough, D. 1983. Burial, community and belief in the early medieval West. In *Ideal and Reality in Frankish and Anglo-Saxon Society* (eds D. Bullough and R. Collins). Oxford: Blackwell, pp. 177–201.

Burgess, C. 1980. *The Age of Stonehenge*. London: Dent.

Burmeister, S. 2000. Archaeology and migration. *Current Anthropology*, 41(4): 539–67.

Butler, L. 1984. Symbols on medieval memorials. *The Archaeological Journal*, 144: 246–55.

Cabot, S., Davies, G. and Hoggett, R. 2004. Sedgeford: excavations of a rural settlement in Norfolk. In *Land, Sea and Home* (ed. J. Hines, A. Lane and M. Redknap). Leeds: Maney Publishing, pp. 313–23.

Camille, M. 1998. *The Medieval Art of Love. Objects and Subjects of Desire*. New York: Harry N. Abrams.

Campbell, E. 2001. Were the Scots Irish? *Antiquity*, 75: 285–92.

Campbell, E. and MacDonald, P. 1994. Excavations at Caerwent Vicarage Orchard Garden 1973: an extra-mural post-Roman cemetery. *Archaeologia Cambrensis*, 142: 74–98.

Campbell, J., John, E. and Wormald, P. (eds) 1982. *The Anglo-Saxons*. London: Penguin.

Canham, R. 1979. Excavations at Shepperton Green 1967 and 1973. *Transactions of the London and Middlesex Archaeological Society*, 30: 97–124.

Capelli, C., Redhead, N., Abernethy, J., Gratrix, F. and Wilson, J. 2003. A-Y chromosome census of the British Isles. *Current Biology*, 13: 979–84.

Carvajal-Carmona, L., Soto, I., Pineda, N. and Ortiz-Barrientos, D. 2000. Strong Amerind/White sex bias and a possible Sephardic contribution among the founders of a population in northwest Colombia. *American Journal of Human Genetics*, 67: 1287–95.

Carver, M. 1998. *Sutton Hoo: Burial Ground of Kings?* London: British Museum.

Carver, M. 1999. *Surviving in Symbols: A Visit to the Pictish Nation*. Edinburgh: Historic Scotland.

Carver, M. 2000. Burial as poetry: the context of treasure in Anglo-Saxon graves. In *Treasure in the Medieval West* (ed. E. Tyler). York: York Medieval Press, pp. 25–48.

Carver, M. 2002. Reflections on the meanings of monumental barrows in Anglo-Saxon England. In *Burial in Early Medieval England and Wales* (eds S. Lucy and A. Reynolds). Society for Medieval Archaeology Monograph 17. Leeds: Maney, pp. 132–43.

Carver, M. 2005. *Sutton Hoo: A seventh-century princely burial ground and its context*. Reports of the Research Committee of the Society of Antiquaries of London, No. 69. London: British Museum Press.

Castro, P.V., Chapman, R.W., Gili, S., Lull, V., Micó, R., Rihuete, C., Risch, R. and Sanahuja, Ma.E. 1993/4. Tiempos sociales de los contextos funerarios argáricos. *Anales de Prehistoria de la Universidad de Murcia*, 9–10: 77–107.

Castro, P.V., Chapman, R., Gili, S., Lull, V., Micó, R., Rihuete, C., Risch, R. and Sanahuja, Ma.E. 1999. Agricultural production and social change in the Bronze Age of southeast Spain: the Gatas Project. *Antiquity*, 73: 846–56.

Catholic Encyclopedia, Chalice. http://www.newadvent.org/cathen/03561a.htm Accessed 18th October, 2007.

Cavalli-Sforza, L., Menozzi, P. and Piazza, A., 1994. *The History and Geography of Human Genes*. Princeton: Princeton University Press.

Chambers, R. 1973. A cemetery site at Beacon Hill, near Lewknor. *Oxoniensia*, 38: 138–45.

Chambers, R. 1976. The cemetery site at Beacon Hill, near Lewknor, Oxon. 1972 (M40 Site 12): an inventory of the inhumations and a re-appraisal. *Oxoniensia*, 41: 77–85.

Chambers, R. 1987. The late and sub-Roman cemetery at Queenford Farm, Dorchester-on-Thames, Oxon. *Oxoniensia*, 52: 35–69.

Champion, T. 2004. The deposition of the boat. In *The Dover Bronze Age Boat* (ed. P. Clark). Swindon: English Heritage, pp. 276–81.

Chapman, A. 1998. Brackmills, Northampton. *Current Archaeology*, 159: 92–95.

Chapman, J. and Hamerow, H. 1997. Introduction: On the move again – migrations and invasions in archaeological explanation. *Migration and Invasion in Archaeological Explanation* (eds J. Chapman and H. Hamerow). British Archaeological Reports, International Series S664. Oxford: Archaeopress, pp. 1–9.

Chapman, R. 1990. *Emerging Complexity. The later prehistory of south-east Spain, Iberia and the west Mediterranean*. Cambridge: Cambridge University Press.

Chapman, R. 2003a. *Archaeologies of Complexity*. London: Routledge.

Chapman, R. 2003b. Other archaeologies and disciplines: mortuary analysis in the twenty-first century. In *Theory, Method and Practice in Modern Archaeology* (eds R.J. Jeske and D.K. Charles). Westport: Praeger, pp. 3–13.

Chapman, R. 2005. Mortuary Analysis. A matter of time? In *Interacting with the Dead. Perspectives on Mortuary Archaeology for the New Millennium* (eds G.F.M. Rakita, J.E. Buikstra, L.A. Beck and S.R. Williams). Gainesville: University of Florida Press, pp. 25–40.

Chapman, R.W., Kinnes, I. and Randsborg K. (eds) 1981. *The Archaeology of Death*. Cambridge: Cambridge University Press.

Charles-Edwards, T.M. 1972. Kinship, status and the origins of the hide. *Past and Present*, 56: 3–33.

Charles-Edwards, T.M. 1993. *Early Irish and Welsh Kinship*. Oxford: Oxford University Press.

Charles-Edwards, T.M. 1997. Anglo-Saxon Kinship Revisited. In *The Anglo-Saxons From the Migration Period to the Eighth Century: an Ethnographic Perspective* (ed. J. Hines). Studies in Archaeoethnology No. 2. Woodbridge: Boydell, pp. 171–204.

Charles-Edwards, T.M. 2000. *Early Christian Ireland*. Cambridge: Cambridge University Press.

Cherryson, A. 2007. Disturbing the dead: urbanisation, the church and the post-burial treatment of human remains in early medieval Wessex, c.600–1100 AD. In *Early Medieval Mortuary Practices* (eds S. Semple and H. Williams) *Anglo-Saxon Studies in Archaeology and History* 14. Oxford: Oxford University School of Archaeology, pp. 130–42.

Childe, V.C. 1945. Directional changes in funerary practices during 50,000 years. *Man*, 4: 13–9.

Church, A.J. and Brodribb, W.J. (trans.) 1952. *Cornelius Tacitus: The Annals and the Histories.* London: Encyclpaedia Britannica.

Clarke, D.V. 2007. Reading the multiple lives of Pictish symbol stones. *Medieval Archaeology*, 51: 19–39.

Clarke, M.D.E. (ed. and trans.) 1923. *The Hávamál with selections from other poems of the Edda, illustrating the wisdom of the north in heathen times.* Cambridge: Cambridge University Press.

Cochrane, A. and Russell, A. 2007. Visualizing archaeology: a manifesto. *Cambridge Archaeological Journal*, 17(1): 3–19.

Coles, B. 1993. Roos Carr and company. In *A Spirit of Enquiry. Essays for Ted Wright* (eds J. Coles, V. Fenwick and G. Hutchinson). Exeter: Wetland Archaeology Research Project, pp. 17–22.

Coles, B. 1998. Doggerland: a speculative survey, *Proceedings of the Prehistoric Society*, 64: 45–81.

Coles, J. and Taylor, J. 1971. The Wessex Culture — a minimal view. *Antiquity*, 45: 6–14.

Colgrave, B. and Mynors, R.A.B. (eds and trans.) 1969. *Bede: Historia Ecclesiastic Gentis Anglorum.* Oxford: Clarendon Press.

Connell, R.W. 1995. *Masculinities.* Cambridge: Polity Press.

Cook, A. and Dacre, M. 1985. *Excavations at Portway, Andover 1973–5.* Oxford University Committee for Archaeology Monograph No. 4. Oxford: Oxford University Committee for Archaeology.

Cornwall, A. and Lindisfarne, N. (eds) 1994. *Dislocating Masculinity. Comparative Ethnographies.* London: Routledge.

Corruccini, R.S. 1974. An examination of the meaning of cranial discrete traits for human skeletal biological studies. *American Journal of Physical Anthropology*, 40: 425–66.

Corruccini, R.S. Handler, R.J., Mutaw, R.J. and Lange, F.W. 1982. Osteology of a slave burial population from Barbados, West Indies. *American Journal of Physical Anthropology*, 59: 443–59.

Cox, P. 1988. A seventh-century inhumation cemetery at Shepherd's Farm, Ulwell near Swanage, Dorset. *Proceedings of the Dorset Natural History and Archaeological Society*, 110: 37–47.

Cramp, R. 1957. *Beowulf* and archaeology. *Medieval Archaeology*, 1: 57–77.

Crawford, S. 1989. The Anglo-Saxon cemetery at Chimney, Oxfordshire. *Oxoniensia*, 44: 45–56.

Crawford, S. 1999. *Childhood in Anglo-Saxon England.* Stroud: Sutton.

Crawford, S. 2000. Children, grave goods and social status in Early Anglo-Saxon England. In *Children and Material Culture* (ed. J. Sofaer Derevenski). London: Routledge, pp. 169–79.

Crawford, S. 2003. Anglo-Saxon women, furnished burial and the church. In *Women and Religion in Medieval England* (ed. D. Wood). Oxford: Oxbow Books, pp. 1–12.

Crawford, S. 2004. Votive deposition: religion and the Anglo-Saxon furnished burial. *World Archaeology*, 36.1: 87–102.

Cressey, M. and Sheridan, A. 2003. The excavation of a Bronze Age cemetery at Seafield West, near Inverness, Highland. *Proceedings of the Society of Antiquaries of Scotland*, 133: 47–84.

Crick, J. 2000. Women, wills and movable wealth in pre-conquest

England. In *Gender and Material Culture in Historical Perspective* (eds M. McDonald and L. Hurcombe) Basingstoke: Macmillan, pp. 17–37.

Crist, T.A.J. 2002. Empowerment, ecology, and evidence: the relevance of mortuary archaeology to the public, In *The Public Benefits of Archaeology* (ed. B.J. Little). Florida: University of Florida Press, pp. 101–17.

Croft, R. and Mynard, D. 1993. *The Changing Landscape of Milton Keynes*. Buckinghamshire Archaeological Society Monograph 5. Aylesbury: Buckinghamshire Archaeological Society.

Crossland, Z. 2000. Buried lives: forensic archaeology and the disappeared in Argentina. *Archaeological Dialogues*, 7(2): 146–59.

Crubézy, E. 1990. Merovingian skull deformations in the southeast of France. In *From the Baltic to the Black Sea: Studies in Medieval Archaeology* (eds D. Austin and L. Alcock). One World Archaeology 18. London: Unwyn Hyman, pp. 189–208.

Crumlin-Pedersen, O. and Thye, B. (eds) 1995. *The Ship as Symbol in Prehistoric and Medieval Scandinavia*. Copenhagen: National Museum.

Cullum, P.H. 1999. Clergy, masculinity and transgression in late medieval England. In *Masculinity in Medieval Europe* (ed. D.M. Hadley). London: Longman, pp. 178–96.

Cuppage, J. 1986. *Archaeological Survey of the Dingle Peninsula*. Ballyferriter: Oidhreacht Chorca Dhuibhne.

Curta, F. 2007. Some remarks on ethnicity in medieval archaeology, *Early Medieval Europe*, 15(2): 159–85.

Curtis, N.G.W. 2003. Human remains: the sacred, museums and archaeology. *Public Archaeology*, 3(1): 21–32.

Daniell, C. 1997. *Death and Burial in Medieval England*. London: Routledge.

Daniell, C. 2002. Conquest, crime and theology in the burial record: 1066–1200. In *Burial in Early Medieval England and Wales* (eds S. Lucy and A. Reynolds). Society for Medieval Archaeology Monograph, 17. London: Maney, pp. 241–54.

Dark, K.R. 1992. Epigraphic, art-historical and historical approaches to the chronology of Class I inscribed stones. In *The Early Church in Wales and the West: Recent Work in Early Christian Archaeology, History and Place-names* (eds N. Edwards and A. Lane). Oxford: Oxbow, pp. 51–61.

Dark, K.R. 1994a. *Civitas to Kingdom: British Political Continuity, 300–800*. Leicester: Leicester University Press.

Dark, K.R. 1994b. *Discovery by Design: the Identification of Secular Élite Settlements in Western Britain, AD 400–700*. British Archaeological Reports, British Series 237. Oxford: Archaeopress.

Dark, K.R. 2000. *Britain and the end of the Roman Empire*. Stroud: Tempus.

Dawson, M. 1999. A medieval cemetery at Brook Drive, Kempston. *Bedfordshire Archaeology*, 23: 111–17.

Deary, T. and Brown, M. 2001. *The Smashing Saxons and the Stormin' Normans*. London: Scholastic.

Deetz, J. 1960. *An Archaeological Approach to Kinship Change in Eighteenth-Century Arikara Culture*. Doctoral Dissertation, Harvard University.

Dennis, G.T. (ed.) 1984. *Maurice's Strategikon: Handbook of Byzantine Military Strategy*. Philadelphia: University of Pennsylvania Press.

Dick, S. 2004. Zu den Grundlagen des so genannten germanischen Königtums. In *Akkulturation. Probleme einer germanisch-romanischen Kultursynthese in Spätantike und frühem Mittelalter* (eds D. Hägermann, W. Haubrichs and J. Jarnut). Ergänzungsbände zum Reallexikon der Germanischen Altertumskunde, 41. Berlin and New York: de Gruyter, pp. 510–27.

Dickinson, T. 1976. *The Anglo-Saxon Burial Sites of the Upper Thames Region, and Their Bearing on the History of Wessex, circa AD 400–700*. Doctoral Dissertation, University of Oxford.

Dickinson, T. 1991. Material culture as social expression: the case of Saxon saucer brooches with running spiral decoration'. In *Studien zur Sachsenforchung 7* (ed. H.-J. Häßler), Hildesheim, Verlag August, pp. 39–70.

Dickinson, T. 2002. Review article: What's new in early medieval burial archaeology? *Early Medieval Europe*, 11(1): 71–87.

Dickinson, T. and Härke, H. 1992. *Early Anglo-Saxon Shields*. Archaeologia 110. London: Society of Antiquaries of London.

Dingwall, E.J. 1931. *Artificial Cranial Deformation*. London: Bale.

Dörges, H. 1960. *Die spätrömische Kaiserzeit und die Völkerwanderungszeit in Mecklenburg*. Leipzig: Unpublished PhD Thesis, Karl-Marx University.

Douglas, J. 1793. *Nenia Britannica*. London: Nichols.

Down, A. and Welch, M. 1990. *Chichester Excavations VII*. Chichester: Chichester District Council.

Dressler, R. 1999. Steel corpse: imaging the knight in death. In *Conflicted Identities and Multiple Masculinities. Men in the Medieval West* (ed. J. Murray). London: Garland, pp. 135–68.

Drew, K.F. 1988. *Law and Society in Early Medieval Europe: Studies in Legal History*. Aldershot: Variorum.

Duhig, C. 1998. The human skeletal material. In *The Anglo-Saxon Cemetery at Edix Hill, British Archaeological Reports (Barrington A), Cambridgeshire* (T. Malim and J. Hines). Council for British Archaeology, Research Report 112. York: Council for British Archaeology.

Dyer, C. 1985. Power and conflict in the English medieval village. In *Medieval Villages* (ed. D. Hooke). Oxford: Oxford University Committee for Archaeology, pp. 27–32.

Dyer, C. 1994. The English medieval village community and its decline. *The Journal of British Studies*, 33: 407–29.

Edwards, H.J. (trans.) 1917. *Julius Caesar: The Gallic War*. London: Heinemann.

Edwards, N. 2001. Early medieval inscribed stones and stone sculpture in Wales: context and function. *Medieval Archaeology*, 45: 15–39.

Edwards, N. 2007. *A Corpus of Early Medieval Inscribed Stones and Stone Sculpture in Wales Vol 2: South-West Wales*. Cardiff: University of Wales Press.

Effros, B. 2003. *Merovingian Mortuary Archaeology and the Making of the Early Middle Ages*. Berkeley: University of California Press.

Eisenschmidt, S. 1994. *Kammergräber der Wikingerzeit in Altdänemark.* Universitätsforschungen zur prähistorischen Archäologie 25. Bonn: Habelt.

Elgee, H. and Elgee, F. 1949. An Early Bronze Age burial in a boat-shaped wooden coffin from north-east Yorkshire. *Proceedings of the Prehistoric Society,* 14: 47–84.

Ellis, H.R. 1943. *The Road to Hel. A Study of the Conception of the Dead in Old Norse Literature.* Cambridge: Cambridge University Press.

Ellwood, T. (trans.) 1908. *The Book of the Settlement of Iceland by Ari Froði.* Kendal: T. Wilson.

Erdrich, M. 2001. *Rom und die Barbaren. Das Verhältnis zwischen dem Imperium Romanum und den germanischen Stämmen vor seiner Nordwestgrenze von der späten römischen Republik bis zum Gallischen Sonderreich.* Römisch-Germanische Forschungen 58. Mainz: Zabern.

Esmonde Cleary, S. 2001. The Roman to Medieval transition. In *Britons and Romans: Advancing an Archaeological Agenda* (eds S. James and M. Millett). Council for British Archaeology Research Report 125. London: Council for British Archaeology, pp. 90–97.

Evison, M. 1997. Lo the conquering hero comes (or not). *British Archaeology,* 23 April 19: 8–9.

Evison, M. 2000. All in the genes? Evaluating the biological evidence of contact and migration. In *Cultures in Contact* (eds D. Hadley and J. Richards). Turnhout: Brepols, pp. 277–90.

Evison, V. 1987. *Dover: Buckland Anglo-Saxon Cemetery.* Historic Buildings and Monuments Commission for England, Archaeological Report No. 3. London: English Heritage.

Faith, R. 1997. *The English Peasantry and the Growth of Lordship.* Leicester: Leicester University Press.

Falsetti, A.B. and Sokal R.R. 1993. Genetic structure of human populations in the British Isles, *Annals of Human Biology,* 20 (3): 215–29.

Faulkner, N. 2003. The debate about the end: a review of evidence and methods. *Archaeological Journal,* 159: 59–76.

Faulkner, N. 2004. The case for the Dark Ages. In *Debating late antiquity in Britain AD 300–700* (eds J. Gerrard and R. Collins). British Archaeological Reports, British Series 365. Oxford: Archaeopress, pp. 5–12.

Feustel, R. 1984. Das Adelsgrab von Nordhausen. *Alt-Thüringen,* 20: 140–206.

Filmer-Sankey, W. and Pestell, T. 2001. *Snape Anglo-Saxon Cemetery: Excavations and Surveys 1824–1992.* East Anglian Archaeology No. 95. Ipswich: Suffolk County Council.

Finch, J. 2000. *Church Monuments in Norfolk before 1850: An Archaeology of Commemoration,* British Archaeological Reports, British Series 317. Oxford: Archaeopress.

Fisher, P. and Ellis Davidson, H. (eds and trans.) 1979. *Saxo Grammaticus. The History of the Danes. Vol.* I. English Text. Cambridge: D.S. Brewer.

Floersch, J. and Longhoffer, J. 1997. The imagined death: looking to the past for relief from the present. *Omega,* 35 (3): 243–60.

Foreman, S., Hiller, J. and Petts, D. 2002. *Gathering the People, Settling the*

Land: The Archaeology of a Middle Thames Landscape: Anglo-Saxon to Post-Medieval. Oxford: Oxford Archaeological Unit.

Forster, P. 1995. Einwanderungsgeschichte Norddeutschlands. In *Friesche Studien II* (eds V. Flatings, A. Walker and O. Wilts). Odense: Odense University Press, pp. 129–40

Forster, P., Polzin T., and Rohl, A. 2006. Evolution of English basic vocabulary within the network of Germanic languages. In *Phylogenetic methods and the prehistory of languages* (eds P. Forster and C. Renfrew) Cambridge: Mcdonald Institute Monograph, pp. 131–37.

Forster, P., Romano, V., Cali F., Rohl, A. and Hurles, M. 2004. MtDNA markers for Celtic and Germanic language areas in the British Isles. In *Traces of Ancestry: studies in Honour of Colin Renfrew* (ed. M. Jones). Cambridge: McDonald Institute Monograph, pp. 99–111.

Forsyth, K. 2005. Hic memoria perpetua: the early inscribed stones of southern Scotland in context. In *Able Minds and Practised Hands: Scotland's Early Medieval Cculpture in the 21st century* (eds S. Foster and M. Cross). Society for Medieval Archaeology Monograph 23. Leeds: Maney pp. 113–34.

Fowler, C. 2004. *The Archaeology of Personhood*. London: Routledge.

Fowler, P. and Mills, S. 2004. Bede's World: A late-twentieth century creation of an early medieval landscape. In *The Reconstructed Past: Reconstructions in the Public Interpretation of Archaeology and History* (ed. J.H. Jameson) Walnut Creek: Altamira, pp. 109–26.

Fox, R. 1983. *Kinship and Marriage: an Anthropological Perspective*. Cambridge: Cambridge University Press.

Frassetto, M. (ed.) 1998. *Medieval Purity and Piety: Essays on Medieval Clerical Celibacy and Religious Reform*. New York: Garland.

Freke, D. and Thacker, A. 1987–88. The inhumation cemetery at Southworth Hall Farm, Winwick. *Journal of the Chester Archaeological Society*, 70: 31–80.

Friesinger, H. 1977. Die archäologischen Funde der ersten zwei Drittel des 5. Jh.s in Niederösterreich. In *Germanen, Awaren, Slawen* (ed. H. Windl). Katalog des Niederösterreichischen Landesmuseums. Neue Folge 75. Wien: Amt der Niederösterreichischen Landesregierung, pp. 62–72.

Fröhlich, S. (ed.) 2000. *Gold für die Ewigkeit — Das germanische Fürstengrab von Gommern*. Halle/Saale: Landesamt für Archäologie Sachsen-Anhalt / Landesmuseum für Vorgeschichte.

Fry, S.L. 1999. *Burial in Medieval Ireland 900–1500. A review of the written sources*. Dublin: Four Courts Press.

Frye, R. 2005. *Ibn Fadlan's journey to Russia. A tenth-century traveller from Baghdad to the Volga River*. Princeton: Markus Wiener Publishers.

Fulford, M., Handley, M. and Clark, A. 2000. An early date for Ogham: the Silchester Ogham stone rehabilitated. *Medieval Archaeology*, 44: 1–23.

Gaimster, M. and O'Connor, B. 2006. Medieval Britain and Ireland, 2005. *Medieval Archaeology*, 50: 271–400.

Gándara, M. 1982. La 'vieja' nueva arqueología. In *Teorías, Métodos y Técnicas en Arqueología*. Mexico: Reimpresiones del Boletín de Antropología Americana, pp. 59–159.

Geake, H. 1992. Burial practices in seventh- and eighth-century England. In *The Age of Sutton Hoo* (ed. M. Carver). Woodbridge: Boydell and Brewer, pp. 83–94.

Geake, H. 1997. *The Use of Grave-Goods in Conversion-Period England, c.600–c.850*. British Archaeological Reports, British Series 261. Oxford: Archaeopress.

Geake, H. 2002. Persistent problems in the study of conversion-period burials in England. In *Burial in Early Medieval England and Wales* (eds S. Lucy and A. Reynolds). Society for Medieval Archaeology Monograph, 17. London: Maney, pp. 144–55.

Geary, P. 1983. Ethnic identity as a situational construct in the early middle ages. *Mitteilungen der Anthropologischen Gesellschaft in Wien*, 113: 15–26.

Geary, P. 1988. *Before France and Germany. The creation and transformation of the Merovingian world*. Oxford: Oxford University Press.

Geary, P. 2002. *The Myth of Nations. The Medieval Origins of Europe*. Princeton: Princeton University Press.

Gebühr, M. 1996. Entry 'Fürstengräber', § 4. Römische Kaiserzeit. In *Hoops Reallexikon der Germanischen Altertumskunde*, 10. Berlin, New York: de Gruyter, pp. 185–95.

Gebühr, M. 1998. Angulus desertus? *Studien zur Sachsenforschung*, 11: 43–86.

Gebühr, M. 2001. Wege ins Jenseits. *Archäologische Informationen* 24(2): 191–8.

Geisler, H. 1990. Neue archäologische Quellen zur frühesten Geschichte der Baiern: Spätantike und frühmittelalterliche Gräberfelder aus Straubing. In *Typen der Ethnogenese unter besonderer Berücksichtigung der Bayern 2* (eds H. Friesinger and F. Daim). Veröffentlichungen der Kommission für Frühmittelalterforschung 13. Wien: Verlag der Österreichischen Akademie der Wissenschaften, pp. 89–100.

Geisler, H. 1998. *Das frühbairische Gräberfeld Straubing-Bajuwarenstrasse I*. Internationale Archäologie 30. Rahden: Marie Leidorf.

Geller, P.L. 2006. Altering identities: body modifications and the pre-Columbian Maya. In *Social Archaeology of Funerary Remains* (eds R. Gowland and C. Knüsel). Oxford: Oxbow, pp. 279–91.

Gerrard, J. and Collins, R. (eds) 2004. *Debating Late Antiquity in Britain AD 300–700*. British Archaeological Reports, British Series 365. Oxford: Archaeopress.

Giebel, M. (trans.) 1989. *Velleius Paterculus: Historia Romana*. Stuttgart: Reclam.

Gilchrist, R. 1999. *Gender and Archaeology. Contesting the Past*. London: Routledge.

Gilchrist, R. 2008. Magic for the dead?: The archaeology of magic in later medieval burials. *Medieval Archaeology*, 52: 119–59.

Gilchrist, R. and Sloane, B. 2005. *Requiem: the Medieval Monastic Cemetery in Britain*. London: Museum of London Archaeology Service.

Gilks, O.J. 1997. Excavations at Rocky Clump, Stanmer Park, Brighton, 1951–81. *Sussex Archaeological Collections*, 135: 113–25.

Gingell, C. 1978. The excavation of an early Anglo-Saxon cemetery at Collingbourne Ducis. *Wiltshire Archaeological Magazine*, 70/71: 61–98.

Gittos, H. 2002. Creating the sacred: Anglo-Saxon rites for consecrating cemeteries. In *Burial in Early Medieval England and Wales* (eds S. Lucy and A. Reynolds). Society for Medieval Archaeology Monograph 17. London: Maney, pp. 195–208.

Glasswell, S. 2002. *The Earliest English: Living and Dying in Early Anglo-Saxon England*. Stroud: Tempus.

Glob, P.V. 1971. *The Bog People*, London: Paladin.

Goffart, W. 1989. The theme of 'the Barbarian invasions' in late Antique and modern historiography. In *Das Reich und die Barbaren* (eds E. Chrysos and A. Schwartz). Vienna: Böhlau, pp. 87–107.

Goodacre, S., Helgason, A., Nicholson, J., Southam, L., Ferguson, L., Hickey, E., Vega, E., Stefansson, K., Ward, R. and Sykes, B. 2005. Genetic evidence for a family-based Scandinavian settlement of Shetland and Orkney during the Viking periods, *Heredity*, 95: 129–35.

Goody, J. 1973. *The Development of the Family and Marriage in Europe*. Cambridge: Cambridge University Press.

Gorecki, J. 2006. Ein Münzspektrum aus der Zeit des Kaiser Probus? In *Historisches Museum der Pfalz Speyer 2006*: 80–4.

Gowland, R. 2007. Beyond ethnicity: symbols of social identity from the fourth to sixth centuries in England. In *Early Medieval Mortuary Practices* (eds S. Semple and H. Williams). *Anglo-Saxon Studies in Archaeology and History* 14. Oxford: Oxford School of Archaeology, pp. 56–65.

Gräslund, A.-S. 1977. Bränning på platsen eller särskild bålplats? Några notiser om ett bränningsförsök. *Tor*, 17: 363–73.

Gräslund, A.-S. 1980. *Birka IV. The burial customs. A study of the graves on Björkö*. Uppsala: Almqvist and Wiksell.

Gräslund, A.-S. 2004. Dogs in graves — a question of symbolism? In *Pecus. Man and Animal in Antiquity* (ed. B. Santillo Frizell). Rome: The Swedish Institute, pp. 171–80.

Gräslund, B. 1987. *The Birth of Prehistoric Chronology. Dating Methods and Dating Systems in Nineteenth-century Scandinavian Archaeology*. Cambridge: Cambridge University Press.

Green, D.H. 1998. *Language and History in the Early Germanic World*. Cambridge: Cambridge University Press.

Griffiths, B. 1996. *Aspects of Anglo-Saxon Magic*. Hockwold-cum-Wilton, Norfolk: Anglo-Saxon Books.

Grimm, J. and Grimm, W. 1816/18. *Deutsche Sagen*. No. 23. Berlin: Nicolaische Buchhandlung.

Grøn, O., Hedeager Krag, A., Bennike, P. 1994. *Vikingetidsgravpladser på Langeland*. Middelelser fra Langelands Museum. Rudkøbing: Langelands Museum.

Guichard, P. and Cuvillier, J.-P. 1996. Barbarian Europe. In *A History of the Family* (eds A. Burguière, C. Klapisch-Zuber, M. Segalen and F. Zonabend). Oxford: Polity Press, pp. 318–78.

Hadley, D. 2001. *Death in Medieval England*. Stroud: Tempus.

Hadley, D. 2002. Burial practices in northern England in the later

Anglo-Saxon period. In *Burial in Early Medieval England and Wales* (eds S. Lucy and A. Reynolds). Society for Medieval Archaeology Monograph 17. London: Maney, pp. 209–28.

Hadley, D. 2004. Negotiating gender, family and status in Anglo-Saxon burial practices, c.600–950. In *Gender in the Early Medieval World. East and West, 300–900* (eds L. Brubaker and J.M.H. Smith). Cambridge: Cambridge University Press, pp. 301–23.

Hadley, D. 2007. The garden gives up its secrets: the developing relationship between rural settlements and cemeteries, c.750–1100. In *Early Medieval Mortuary Practices* (eds S. Semple and H. Williams). *Anglo-Saxon Studies in Archaeology and History* 14. Oxford: Oxford University School of Archaeology, pp. 194–203.

Hadley, D. and Moore, J.M. 1999. 'Death makes the man?' Burial rite and the construction of masculinities in the early middle ages. In *Masculinity in Medieval Europe* (ed. D. Hadley). London: Longman, pp. 21–38.

Hakenbeck, S. 2006. *Ethnic Identity in Early Medieval Cemeteries in Bavaria*. Unpublished PhD thesis. University of Cambridge.

Hakenbeck, S. 2008. Migration in archaeology: are we nearly there yet? *Archaeological Review from Cambridge* 23(2): 9–26.

Hall, R. 2007. *Exploring the World of the Vikings*. London: Thames and Hudson.

Hallam, E., Hockey, J. and Howarth, G. 1999. *Beyond the Body: Death and Social Identity*. London: Routledge.

Halliwell, M. 1997. Iron pseudomorphs of insect pupa cases from grave 39. In *The Anglo-Saxon Cemetery on Mill Hill, Deal, Kent* (K. Parfitt and B. Brugmann). The Society for Medieval Archaeology Monograph Series No. 14. London: Maney: p. 267.

Halsall, G. 1995a. *Early Medieval Cemeteries: An Introduction to Burial Archaeology in the Post-Roman West*. Glasgow: Cruithne.

Halsall, G. 1995b. *Settlement and social organisation: the Merovingian region of Metz*. Cambridge: Cambridge University Press.

Halsall, G. 2003. Burial writes: graves, texts and time in early Merovingian northern Gaul. In *Erinnerungskultur im Bestattungsritual* (eds J. Jarnut and M. Wemhoff). Munich: Wilhelm Fink, pp. 61–74.

Hamerow, H. 2006. 'Special deposits' in Anglo-Saxon settlements. *Medieval Archaeology*, 50: 1–30.

Handley, M. 1998. The early medieval inscriptions of Western Britain: function and sociology. In *The Community, the Family and the Saint: Patterns of Power in Early Medieval Europe* (eds J. Hill and M. Swan). Turnhout: Brepols, pp. 339–61.

Handley, M. 2001. The origins of Christian commemoration in late antique Britain. *Early Medieval Europe* 10.2: 177–99.

Harding. D. 2004. *The Iron Age in Northern Britain*. London: Routledge.

Hardt, M. 2004. *Gold und Herrschaft. Die Schätze europäischer Könige und Fürsten im ersten Jahrtausend*. Berlin: Akademie.

Härke, H. 1978. Probleme der optischen Emissionsspektralanalyse in der Urgeschichtsforschung: Technische Möglichkeiten und methodische Fragestellungen. *Praehistorische Zeitschrift* 53: 165–276.

Härke, H. 1979. *Settlement Types and Settlement Patterns in the West Hallstatt Province*. British Archaeological Reports International Series 57. Oxford: Archaeopress.

Härke, H. 1981. Anglo-Saxon laminated shields at Petersfinger – a myth. *Medieval Archaeology* 25: 141–4.

Härke, H. 1982. Early Iron Age hill settlement in west central Europe: patterns and developments. *Oxford Journal of Archaeology*, 1(2): 187–211.

Härke, H. 1983. Höhensiedlungen im Westhallstattkreis: ein Diskussionsbeitrag. *Archäologisches Korrespondenzblatt* 13. 461–77.

Härke, H. 1989a. Early Saxon weapon burials: frequencies, distributions and weapon combinations. In *Weapons and warfare in Anglo-Saxon England*. (ed. S.C. Hawkes) Oxford University Committee for Archaeology, 21. Oxford: Oxford University Press, pp. 49–61.

Härke, H. 1989b. Knives in early Saxon burials: blade length and age at death. *Medieval Archaeology* 33: 144–8.

Härke, H. 1989c. Transformation or collapse? Bronze Age to Iron Age settlement in West Central Europe (eds M.L.S. Sørensen and R. Thomas). *The Bronze Age – Iron Age transition in Europe*. British Archaeological Reports International Series 483. Oxford: Archaeopress, pp. 184–203.

Härke, H. 1989d. The Unkel Symposia: The beginnings of a debate in West German archaeology? *Current Anthropology* 30(3): 406–10.

Härke, H. 1990a. Warrior graves? The background of the Anglo-Saxon weapon burial rite. *Past and Present*, 126: 22–43.

Härke, H. 1990b. Comments on spears and shields. In The Anglo-Saxon cemetery at Wakerley, Northamptonshire: Excavations by Mr. D. Jackson, 1968–9 (B. Adams and D. Jackson). *Northamptonshire Archaeology* 22: 146–8

Härke, H. 1991. All quiet on the western front? Paradigms, methods and approaches in West German archaeology. In *Archaeological Theory in Europe* (ed. I. Hodder). London and New York: Routledge, pp. 187–222.

Härke, H. 1992a. *Angelsächsische Waffengräber des 5. bis 7. Jahrhunderts*. Zeitschrift für Archäologie des Mittelalters. Beiheft 6. Köln: Rheinland Verlag.

Härke, H. 1992b. Changing symbols in a changing society: the Anglo-Saxon weapon burial rite in the seventh century. In *The Age of Sutton Hoo* (ed. M. Carver). Woodbridge: Boydell, pp. 149–66.

Härke, H. 1994a. A context for the Saxon barrow. In Lowbury Hill, Oxon: A Reassessment of the Probable Romano-Celtic Temple and the Anglo-Saxon Barrow (M. Fulford and S. Rippon). *Archaeological Journal* 151: 158–211, pp. 202–6.

Härke, H. 1994b. Data types in burial analysis. In B. Sternqvist (ed.) *Prehistoric Graves as a Soruce of Information*, Konferenser 29. Stockholm: Almqvist and Wiksell International, pp. 31–40.

Härke, H. 1995a. Weapon burials and knives. In *Two Oxfordshire Anglo-Saxon Cemeteries* (A. Boyle, A. Dodd, D. Miles and A. Mudd). Thames Valley Landscapes Monograph 8. Oxford: Oxford Archaeological Unit, pp. 67–75.

Härke, H. 1995b. 'The Hun is a methodical chap': reflections on the German tradition of pre- and proto-history. In *Theory in Archaeology: a World Perspective* (ed. P.J. Ucko). London: Routledge, pp. 46–60.

Härke, H. 1996. Comments on the weaponry. In *The Anglo-Saxon cemetery at Empingham II, Rutland. Excavations carried out between 1974 and 1975* (J.R. Timby) Oxbow Monograph 70. Oxford: Oxbow, pp. 67–68.

Härke, H. 1997a. Early Anglo-Saxon social structure. In *The Anglo-Saxons From the Migration Period to the Eighth Century: an Ethnographic Perspective* (ed. J. Hines). Studies in Archaeoethnology 2. Woodbridge: Boydell, pp. 125–60.

Härke, H. 1997b. The nature of burial data. In *Burial and Society* (eds C.K. Jensen and K. Høilund Nielsen). Århus: Aarhus University Press, pp. 19–27.

Härke, H. 1997c. Final comments: ritual, symbolism and social inference. In *Burial and Society* (eds C.K. Jensen and K. Høilund Nielsen). Århus: Aarhus University Press, pp. 191–95.

Härke, H. 1997d. Material culture as myth: weapons in Anglo-Saxon graves. In *Burial and Society* (eds C.K. Jensen and K. Høilund Nielsen). Århus: Aarhus University Press, pp. 119–27.

Härke, H. 1998. Archaeologists and migration: a problem of attitude. *Current Anthropology*, 39: 19–45.

Härke, H. 1999. Collapse of empire and material-culture change: the case of the Soviet Union. *Medieval Archaeology*, 43: 183–85.

Härke, H. 2000a. Social analysis of mortuary evidence in German proto-historic archaeology. *Journal of Anthropological Archaeology*, 19 (4): 369–84.

Härke, H. 2000b. The circulation of weapons in Anglo-Saxon society. In *Rituals of Power from Late Antiquity to the Early Middle Ages* (eds F. Theuws and J.L. Nelson). Leiden: Brill, pp. 379–99.

Härke, H. 2000c. The German experience. In *Archaeology, Ideology, Society: The German Experience* (ed. H. Härke). Berlin: Peter Lang, pp. 12–39.

Härke, H. 2001. Cemeteries as places of power. In *Topographies of Power in the Early Middle Ages* (eds M. de Jong, F. Theuws and C. van Rhijn). The Transformation of the Roman World, 6. Leiden, Boston and Köln: Brill, pp. 9–30.

Härke, H. 2002. Kings and warriors. Population and landscape from Post-Roman to Norman Britain. In *The Peopling of Britain. The Shaping of a Human Landscape* (eds P. Slack and R. Ward). Oxford: Oxford University Press, pp. 145–75.

Härke, H. 2003a. Gender representation in early medieval burials: past reality or ritual display? In *Problemy vseobshchej istorii* (Problems of World History) 8 (ed. S.L. Dudarev). Armavir: AGPI, pp. 130–40.

Härke, H. 2003b. Beigabensitte und Erinnerung: Überlegungen zu einem Aspekt des frühmittelalterlichen Bestattungsrituals. In *Erinnerungskultur im Bestattungsritual* (eds J. Jarnut and M. Wemhoff). Munich: Wilhelm Fink, pp. 107–25.

Härke, H. 2004. The debate on migration and identity in Europe. *Antiquity*, 78: 453–6.

Härke, H. 2007a. Ethnicity, 'race' and migration in mortuary archaeology: an attempt at a short answer. In *Early Medieval Mortuary Practices* (eds S. Semple and H. Williams). *Anglo-Saxon Studies in Archaeology and History* 14. Oxford: Oxford University School of Archaeology, pp. 12–18.

Härke, H. 2007b. Invisible Britons, Gallo-Romans and Russians: perspectives on culture change. In *Britons in Anglo-Saxon England* (ed. N. Higham). Woodbridge: Boydell, pp. 57–67.

Härke, H. 2008. Trauer, Ahnenkult, Sozialstatus? Überlegungen zur Interpretation der Befunde im Gräberfeld von Klin-Yar (Nordkaukasus, Russland). In *Körperinszenierung – Objektsammlung – Monumentalisierung: Totenritual und Grabkult in frühen Gesellschaften* (eds C. Kümmel, B. Schweizer and U. Veit with M. Augstein). Tübinger Archäologische Taschenbücher 6. Münster, New York, München and Berlin: Waxmann, pp. 417–30.

Härke, H. forthcoming a. Weapons and weapon burials of the Anglo-Saxon cemetery of Blacknall Field, Pewsey. In *The Anglo-Saxon Cemetery of Blacknall Field, Pewsey* (eds K. Annable and B. Eagles). London: English Heritage.

Härke, H. forthcoming b. The weapon burials and knives of the Lechlade (Butler's Field) cemetery. In J. Timby. *The Anglo-Saxon cemetery of Butler's Field. Lechlade.* London: English Heritage.

Härke, H. and Belinskij B. 1999. The "Princess" of Ipatovo. *Archaeology* 52 (2): 20–1.

Härke, H. and Entwistle, R. 2002. An Anglo-Saxon quadruple weapon burial at Tidworth: a battle-site burial on Salisbury Plain? *Proceedings of the Hampshire Field Club and Archaeological Society*, 57: 38–52.

Härke, H. and Salter, C. 1984. A technical and metallurgical study of three Anglo-Saxon shield bosses. In *Anglo-Saxon Studies in Archaeology and History* 3 (eds S.C. Hawkes, J. Campbell and D. Brown). Oxford: Oxford University Committee for Archaeology, pp. 55–64.

Härke, H. and Williams, H. 1997. Angelsächsische Bestattungsplätze und ältere Denkmäler: Bemerkungen zur zeitlichen Entwicklung und Deutung des Phänomens. *Archäologische Informationen*, 20(1): 25–27.

Härke, H. and Wolfram, S. 1993. The power of the past, *Current Anthropology* 34(1): 182–84.

Härke, H. Belinskij, B., Kalmykov, A.A. and Korenevskij, S.N. 2000. The Ipatovo kurgan on the North Caucasian steppe (Russia). *Antiquity* 74 (286): 773–4.

Harris, A. 2003. *Byzantium Britain and the West: the Archaeology of Cultural Identity AD 400–650.* Stroud: Tempus.

Harvey, P. 1989. Initiative and authority in settlement change. In *The Rural Settlements of Medieval England* (eds M. Aston, D. Austin and C. Dyer). Oxford: Blackwell, pp. 31–44.

Haughton, C. and Powlesland, D. 1999. *West Heslerton: The Anglian Cemetery Volume II: Catalogue of the Anglian Graves and Associated Assemblages.* Yedingham: Landscape Research Centre/English Heritage.

Hawkes, J. 1999. Anglo-Saxon Sculpture: Questions of Context, in *Northumbria's Golden Age* (eds J. Hawkes and S. Mills) Stroud: Sutton, pp. 204–15.

Hawkes, S.C. 1977. Orientation at Finglesham: sunrise dating of death and burial in an Anglo-Saxon cemetery in east Kent. *Archaeologia Cantiana*, 92: 33–51.

Hawkes, S.C. 1981. Recent finds of inlaid iron buckles and belt-plates from seventh-century Kent. In *Anglo-Saxon Studies in Archaeology and History 2* (eds D. Brown, J. Campbell and S.C. Hawkes). British Archaeology Reports 92, Oxford: Archaeopress. pp. 49–70.

Hawkes, S.C. 1982. Finglesham: a cemetery in east Kent. In *The Anglo-Saxons* (eds J. Campbell, E. John and P. Wormald). London: Penguin, pp. 24–25.

Hawkes, S.C. and Grainger, G. 2006. *The Anglo-Saxon Cemetery at Finglesham, Kent*. Oxford University School of Archaeology Monograph No. 64. Oxford: Oxbow.

Hawkes, S.C. and Pollard, M. 1981. The gold bracteates from sixth-century Kent, in light of a new find from Finglesham. *Frühmittelalterliche Studien*, 15: 316–70.

Hawkes, S.C., Ellis Davidson, H.R. and Hawkes, C. 1965. The Finglesham Man. *Antiquity*, 39 (153): 17–32.

Heaney, S. (trans.) 1999. *Beowulf*. London: Faber and Faber.

Heather, P.J. 1995. The Huns and the end of the Roman Empire in western Europe. *English Historical Review*, 110 (435): 4–41.

Hedeager, L. 2001. Asgard reconstructed? Gudme — a 'central place' in the North. In *Topographies of Power in the Early Middle Ages* (eds M. de Jong, F. Theuws and C. van Rhijn). The Transformation of the Roman World, 6. Leiden, Boston and Köln: Brill, pp. 467–507.

Hedges, J.D. and Buckley, D.G. 1985. Anglo-Saxon Burials and Later Features Excavated at Orsett, Essex, 1975. *Medieval Archaeology*, 29: 1–24.

Heidinga, H.A. 1997. *Frisia in the First Millennium*. Utrecht: Matrijs.

Helms, M. 1988. *Ulysses' Sail. An Ethnographic Odyssey of Power, Knowledge, and Geographical Distance*. Princeton: Princeton University Press.

Helmuth, H. 1996. Anthropologische Untersuchungen zu den Skeletten von Altenerding. In *Das Reihengräberfeld von Altenerding in Oberbayern II* (eds H. Helmuth, D. Ankner and H.-J. Hundt). Germanische Denkmäler der Völkerwanderungszeit. Serie A 18. Mainz: Philipp von Zabern, pp. 1–143.

Herlihy, D. 1985. *Medieval Households*. Studies in Cultural History. Cambridge: Harvard University Press.

Herschend, F. 2001. *Journey of Civilization. The Late Iron Age View of the Human World*. Uppsala: Department of Archaeology and Ancient History.

Hey, G. 2004. *Yarnton: Saxon and Medieval Settlement and Landscape. Result of Excavations 1990–96*. Oxford: Oxford Archaeology.

Hey, G. and Barclay, A. 2007. The Thames Valley in the late fifth and early fourth millennium cal BC: the appearance of domestication and the evidence for change. In *Going Over. The Mesolithic-Neolithic Transition in North-West Europe* (eds A. Whittle and V. Cummings). Proceedings of the British Academy 144. Oxford: Oxford University Press, pp. 399–422.

Higham, N.J. 1992. *Rome, Britain and the Anglo-Saxons*. London: Seaby.

Hill, J.N. 1966. A prehistoric community in eastern Arizona. *Southwestern Journal of Anthropology*, 22: 9–30.

Hill, P. 1997. Whithorn and St Ninian: the Excavation of a Monastic Town, 1984–91. Stroud: Sutton.

Hill, T. 1977. The *aecerbot* charm and its Christian user. *Anglo-Saxon England*, 6: 213–21.

Hills, C. 1997. *Beowulf* and archaeology. In *A Beowulf Handbook* (eds R. Bjork and J. Niles) Exeter: University of Exeter Press, pp. 291–312.

Hills, C. 2003. *The Origins of the English*. London: Duckworth.

Hills, C. 2007. History and archaeology: the state of play in early medieval Europe. *Antiquity*, 81: 191–200.

Hills, C., Penn, K. and Rickett, R. 1984. *The Anglo-Saxon Cemetery at Spong Hill, North Elmham. Part III. Catalogue of Inhumations*. East Anglian Archaeology 21. Dereham: Norfolk Archaeological Unit and Norfolk Museums Service.

Hines, J. 1994. The becoming of the English: identity, material culture and language in early Anglo-Saxon England. In *Anglo-Saxon Studies in Archaeology and History 7* (ed. W. Filmer-Sankey). Oxford: Oxford University Committee for Archaeology, pp. 49–59.

Hines, J. 1997. *A New Corpus of Anglo-Saxon Great Square-Headed Brooches*. Woodbridge: Boydell.

Hines, J., Bayliss, A and Høilund Nielsen, K. forthcoming. *Anglo-Saxon England c.580–720: The Chronological Basis*.

Hinton, D. 2005. *Gold and Gilt, Pots and Pins. Possessions and People in Medieval Britain*. Oxford: Oxford University Press.

Hirst, S. 1985. *An Anglo-Saxon Inhumation Cemetery at Sewerby East Yorkshire*, York University Archaeological Publications 4. York: University of York.

Hirst, S. 2004. *The Prittlewell Prince: the Discovery of a Rich Anglo-Saxon Burial in Essex*. London: Museum of London.

Historisches Museum der Pfalz Speyer 2006 (ed.) *Der Barbarenschatz. Geraubt und im Rhein versunken*. Theiss: Stuttgart.

Hoare, F.R. (ed. and trans.) 2000. 'The Life of St Germanus of Auxerre'. In *Soldiers of Christ: Saints and Saint's Lives from Late Antiquity and the Early Middle Ages* (ed. T.F.X. Noble and T. Head). Pennsylvania: Pennsylvania State University Press, pp. 75–106.

Hodder, I. 1980. Social structure and cemeteries: a critical appraisal. In *Anglo-Saxon Cemeteries 1979. The Fourth Anglo-Saxon Symposium at Oxford* (eds P. Rahtz, T. Dickinson and L. Watts). British Archaeological Reports British Series 82. Oxford: Archaeopress, pp. 161–69.

Hodder, I. 1982. The identification and interpretation of ranking in prehistory: a contextual approach. In *Ranking, Resource and Exchange* (ed. C. Renfrew and S. Shennan). Cambridge: Cambridge University Press, pp. 150–54.

Hodder, I. 1990. *The Domestication of Europe: Structure and Contingency in Neolithic Societies*. Oxford: Blackwell.

Hodder, I. (ed.) 1991a. *Archaeological Theory in Europe*. London: Routledge.

Hodder, I. 1991b. Post-processual archaeology and the current debate. In *Processual and Post-processual Archaeologies: Multiple Ways of Knowing the Past* (ed. R.W. Preucel). Carbondale: Southern Illinois University, pp. 30–41.

Hodder, I. 1999. *The Archaeological Process*. Oxford: Blackwell.

Høilund Nielsen, K. 1994. Lindholm Høje Gravpladsen. In *Lindholm Høje. Gravplads og landsby* (eds E. Johansen and A.L. Trolle). Aalborg: Selskabet for Aalborgs Historie, pp. 27–38.

Høilund Nielsen, K. 1997. Die frühmittelalterlichen Perlen Skandinaviens. Chronologische Untersuchungen. In *Perlen. Archäologie, Techniken, Analysen* (eds U. von Freeden and A. Wieczorek). Bonn: Rudolf Habelt, pp. 187–96.

Høilund Nielsen, K. 1998. En gravplads fra Okholm — Fremmed eller lokal befolkning? *By, Marsk og Geest*, 10: 7–21.

Holbrook, N. 2000. The Anglo-Saxon cemetery at Lower Farm, Bishop's Cleeve: excavations directed by Kenneth Brown 1969. *Transactions of the Bristol and Gloucestershire Archaeological Society*, 118: 61–92.

Holbrook, N. and Thomas, N. 2005. An early medieval monastic cemetery at Llandough, Glamorgan: excavations in 1994. *Medieval Archaeology*, 49: 1–92.

Holtorf, C. 1998. The life-histories of megaliths in Mecklenburg-Vorpommern (Germany). *World Archaeology*, 30 (1): 23–38.

Holtorf, C. 2000–2007. *Monumental past. The Life-histories of Megalithic Monuments in Mecklenburg-Vorpommern (Germany)*. Electronic monograph. University of Toronto: Centre for Instructional Technology Development. http://hdl.handle.net/1807/245.

Hope, V. 2003. Remembering Rome. Memory, funerary monuments and the Roman soldier. In *Archaeologies of Remembrance: Death and Memory in Past Societies* (ed. H. Williams). New York: Kluwer Academic/Plenum Publishers, pp. 113–40.

Hope-Taylor, B. 1977. *Yeavering: An Anglo-British centre of early Northumbria*. London: HMSO.

Howarth, G. 2006. The rebirth of death: continuing relationships with the dead. In *Remember Me: Constructing Immortality* (ed. M. Mitchell). London: Routledge, pp. 19–34.

Howell, T.L. and Kintigh, K.W. 1996. Archaeological identification of kin groups using mortuary and biological data: an example from the American Southwest. *American Antiquity*, 61: 537–54.

Huck, T. 2007. Thüringer und Hunnen. In *Attila und die Hunnen* (ed. Historisches Museum der Pfalz Speyer). Stuttgart: Konrad Theiss Verlag, pp. 323–31

Hyslop, M. 1964. Two Anglo-Saxon cemeteries at Chamberlains Barn, Leighton Buzzard, Bedfordshire. *Archaeological Journal*, 120: 161–200.

Irving, E. 1997. Christian and pagan elements. In *A Beowulf Handbook* (eds R. Bjork and J. Niles) Exeter: University of Exeter Press, pp. 175–92.

Ivens, R., Busby, P. and Shephers, N. 1995. *Tattenhoe and Westbury: Two Deserted Settlements in Milton Keynes*. Buckinghamshire Archaeological Society Monograph 8. Aylesbury: Buckinghamshire Archaeological Society.

James, S. 1997. Drawing inferences: visual reconstructions in theory and practice. In *The Cultural Life of Images: Visual Representation in Archaeology* (ed B.L. Molyneaux). London: Routledge, pp. 22–48.

James, S. 1999. Imag(in)ing the past: The politics and practicalities of reconstructions in the museum gallery. In *Making Early Histories in Museums* (ed. N. Merriman). Leicester: Leicester University Press, pp. 117–35.

Jensen, C.K. 2005. *Kontekstuel kronologi. En revision af det kronologiske grundlag for førromersk jernalder i Sydskandinavien.* Højbjerg: Kulturlaget.

Jensen, C.K. and Høilund Nielsen, K. (eds) 1997a. *Burial and Society. The Chronological and Social Analysis of Burial Data.* Århus: Aarhus University Press,

Jensen, C.K. and Høilund Nielsen, K. 1997b. Burial Data and Correspondence Analysis. In *Burial and Society* (eds C.K. Jensen and K. Høilund Nielsen). Århus: Aarhus University Press, pp. 29–61.

Jettmar, K. 1953. Hunnen und Hsiung-nu — ein archäologisches Problem. *Archiv für Völkerkunde*, 6/7: 166–80.

Johansen, E., Knudsen, B. M. and Koch, J. 1992. *Fra Aalborgs fødsel til Grevens Fejde 1534. Aalborgs Historie 1.* Aalborg: Aalborg Kommune.

Jolly, K.L. 1996. *Popular Religion in Late Saxon England. Elf Charms in Context.* Chapel Hill: University of North Carolina.

Jones, M. 2002. *The Secret Middle Ages. Discovering the Real Medieval World.* Stroud: Sutton.

Jones, R. 1998. Early state formation in native medieval Wales. *Political Geography*, 17 (6): 667–82.

Jones, R. 2004. Signatures in the soil: the use of pottery in manure scatters in the identification of medieval arable farming regimes. *Archaeological Journal*, 161: 159–88.

Jones, R. and Page, M. 2006. *Medieval Villages in an English Landscape.* Macclesfield: Windgather.

Jones, S. 1997. *The Archaeology of Ethnicity.* London: Routledge.

Jones, W.H.S. (trans.) 1951. *Pliny: Natural History.* Cambridge, Mass.: Harvard University Press. 6 volumes.

Jørgensen, L. 1987. Family burial practices and inheritance systems: the development of an Iron Age society from 500 BC to AD 1000 on Bornholm, Denmark. *Acta Archaeologica*, 58: 17–54.

Jørgensen, L. 1991. Castel Trosino and Nocera Umbra: a chronological and social analysis of family burial practices in Lombard Italy, sixth to eighth century AD. *Acta Archaeologica*, 62: 1–58.

Jørgensen, L. and Nørgård Jørgensen, A. 1997. *Nørre Sandegård Vest: a cemetery from the 6th–8th centuries on Bornholm.* København: Det Kongelige Nordiske Oldskriftselskab.

Jørgensen, L., Alt, K.W. and Vach, W. 1997. Families at Kirchheim am Ries: analysis of Merovingian aristocratic and warrior families. In *Military aspects of Scandinavian society in a European perspective, AD 1–1300* (ed. L. Jørgensen). *Studies in Archaeology and History 2. Copenhagen: National Museum pp. 102–12.*

Joyce, R.A. 2005. Archaeology of the Body. *Annual Review of Anthropology*, 34: 139–58.

Jung, C.G. 1968. *The Archetypes and the Collective Unconscious.* Second Edition. (trans. R.F.C. Hull). London: Routledge and Kegan Paul.

Keiller, A. and Piggott, S. 1939. The chambered tomb in Beowulf. *Antiquity*, 13: 360–1.

Kellehear, A. 1996. *Experiences Near Death: Beyond Medicine and Religion.* Oxford: Oxford University Press

Kellehear, A. 2007. *A Social History of Dying.* Cambridge: Cambridge University Press.

Kirk, L. and Start, H. 1999. Death at the undertakers. In *The Loved Body's Corruption: Archaeological Contributions to the Study of Human Mortality* (eds J. Downes and T. Pollard). Glasgow: Cruithne, pp. 200–8.

Kiszely, I. 1978. *The Origins of Artificial Cranial Deformation in Eurasia from the Sixth Millennium B.C. to the Seventh Century A.D.* British Archaeological Reports, International Series 50. Oxford: Archaeopress.

Kjølbye-Biddle, B. 1992. Dispersal or concentration: the disposal of the Winchester dead over 2000 years. In *Death in Towns. Urban responses to the dying and the dead, 100–1600* (ed. S. Bassett). London: Leicester University Press, pp. 210–47.

Klemperer, W.D. and Boothroyd, N. 2004. *Excavations at Hulton abbey, Staffordshire 1987–1994.* Society for Medieval Archaeology Monograph 21. London: Maney.

Knight, J.K. 1992. The early Christian Latin inscriptions of Britain and Gaul: chronology and context. In *The Early Church in Wales and the West: Recent Work in early Christian Archaeology, History and Place-names* (eds N. Edwards and A. Lane). Oxford: Oxbow, pp. 45–50.

Knight, J.K. 1998. Late Roman and post-Roman Caerwent some evidence from metalwork. *Archaeologia Cambrensis*, 145: 34–66.

Knight, J.K. 1999. *The End of Antiquity: Archaeology, Society and Religion, AD 235–700.* Stroud: Tempus.

Knight, J.K. 2005. From villa to monastery: Llandough in context. *Medieval Archaeology*, 49: 93–107.

Knocker, G.M. 1956. Early burials and an Anglo-Saxon cemetery at Snell's Corner near Horndean, Hampshire. *Papers and Proceedings of the Hampshire Field Club and Archaeological Society*, 19(2): 117–70.

Knüsel, C.J., Chundun, Z.C, and Cardwell, P. 1992. Slipped proximal femoral epiphysis in a priest from the medieval period. *International Journal of Osteoarchaeology*, 2: 109–19.

Koch, A. 1998. Fremde Fibeln im Frankenreich. Ein Beitrag zur Frage nichtfränkischer germanischer Ethnien in Nordgallien. *Acta Praehistorica at Archaeologia*, 30: 69–89.

Koch, U. 1999. Nordeuropäisches Fundmaterial in Gräbern Süddeutschlands rechts des Rheins. In *Völker an Nord-und Ostsee und die Franken.* (eds U. von Freeden, U. Koch and A. Wieczorek). Bonn: Dr. Rudolf Habelt, pp. 175–94.

Kossack, G. 1974. Prunkgräber. Bemerkungen zu Eigenschaften und Aussagewert. In *Studien zur vor- und frühgeschichtlichen Archäologie. Festschrift für Joachim Werner zum 65. Geburtstag; Teil I.* Münchner Beiträge zur Vor- Und Frühgeschichte, Ergänzungsband 1 (eds G. Kossack and G. Ulbert). München: Beck, pp. 3–35.

Kuhn, A. and Schwartz, W. 1848. *Norddeutsche Sagen, Märchen und Gebräuche*. Leipzig: F.A. Brockhaus.

Künzl, E. 1993. *Die Alamannenbeute aus dem Rhein bei Neupotz. Plünderungsgut aus dem römischen Gallien*. RGZM Monographien 34. Bonn: Habelt.

Lai Sørensen, L. 1998. P. 335/98: Beretning over udgravningen på vikingetids gravpladsen Tollemosegård ved Græse, Museet Færgegården, 1998. MFG J.nr.113/97, 01.03.03, Tollemosegård, Græse sogn, Lynge-Kronborg herred, Frederiksborg amt. Unpubl. excavation report, Nationalmuseet København.

Laing, S. (trans.) and Beveridge, J. 1930a. *Heimskringla. The Norse King Sagas by Snorre Sturlason*. Everyman's Library 847, London, Toronto: J.M. Dent.

Laing, S. (trans.) and Beveridge, J. 1930b. *Heimskringla. The Olaf Sagas by Snorre Sturlason*. London: J.M. Dent.

Lancaster, L. 1958. Kinship in Anglo-Saxon society — II. *British Journal of Sociology*, 9 (4): 359–77.

Lane, A.R. and Sublett, A.J. 1972. Osteology of social organisation: residence pattern. *American Antiquity*, 37: 186–201.

Larson, L.M. 1935. *The Earliest Norwegian Laws Being the Gulathing Law and the Frostathing Law*. New York: Columbia University Press.

Leahy, K. 2007. *The Anglo-Saxon Kingdom of Lindsey*. Stroud: Tempus.

Lee, C. 2007. *Feasting the dead. Food and Drink in Anglo-Saxon Rituals*. Woodbridge: Boydell.

Leeds, E.T. 1936. *Early Anglo-Saxon Art and Archaeology*. Oxford: Clarendon.

Leeds, E.T. and Atkinson, R.J.C. 1944. An Anglo-Saxon cemetery at Nassington, Northants, *Antiquaries Journal*, 24: 100–28.

Lethbridge, T.C. 1931. *Recent Excavations in Anglo-Saxon Cemeteries in Cambridgeshire and Suffolk*. Cambridge Antiquarian Society Quarto Publications New Series No. III. Cambridge: Cambridge Antiquarian Society.

Lethbridge, T.C. 1936. *A Cemetery at Shudy Camps Cambridgeshire*. Cambridge Antiquarian Society Quarto Publications New Series No. V. Cambridge: Cambridge Antiquarian Society.

Levison, W. (ed.) 1910. Vita Vulframni episcopi Senonici auctore Pseudo-Iona. In *Monumenta Germaniae Historica. Script. rer. Mer. Tomus V, Passiones Vitaeque Sanctorum Aevi Merovingici* (ed. B. Krusch et W. Levison), Hannover: Hahn.

Lewis, C., Mitchell-Fox, P. and Dyer, C. 1997. *Village, Hamlet and Field. Changing Medieval Settlements in Central England*. Manchester: Manchester University Press.

Lippert, A. 1968. Ein Gräberfeld der Völkerwanderungszeit bei Grafenwörth, p.B. Tulln, NÖ. *Mitteilungen der Anthopologischen Gesellschaft in Wien*, 98: 35–46.

Llewellyn, N. 1991. *The Art of Death: Visual Culture in the English Death Ritual, c.1500–c.1800*. London: Reaktion.

Lloyd-Jones, J. 1997. Calculating bio-distance using dental morphology.

In *Computing and Statistics in Osteoarchaeology* (eds S. Anderson and K. Boyle). Oxford: Oxbow, pp. 23–30.

Long, J. and Long, J. 1999: *Near-Death Experience Research Foundation*. NDE Archives. Website: http://www.nderf.org.

Longacre, W.A. 1964. Archaeology as anthropology: a case study. *Science New Series*, 144: 1454–5.

Longacre, W.A. 1966. Changing patterns of social integration: a prehistoric example from the American Southwest. *American Anthropology, New Series*, 68: 94–102.

Lorentz, K. 2003. Cultures of physical modifications: Child bodies in ancient Cyprus. *Stanford Journal of Archaeology*, 2: 1–17.

Losco-Bradley, S. and Kinsley, G. 2002. *Catholme: an Anglo-Saxon Settlement on the Trent Gravels in Staffordshire*. Nottingham: University of Nottingham.

Losert, H. 2003. *Altenerding in Oberbayern*. Berlin, Bamberg and Ljubljana: Scrîpvaz/Založba ZRC.

Loyn, H. 1975. *Anglo-Saxon England and Norman England*. London: Longman.

Loyn, H. 1984. *The Governance of Anglo-Saxon England 500–1087*. London: Edward Arnold.

Lucy, S. 1997. 'Housewives, warriors and slaves?' Sex and gender in Anglo-Saxon burials. In *Invisible People and Processes: Writing Gender and Childhood into European Archaeology* (ed. J.S.E. Moore and S. Scott). Leicester: Leicester University Press, pp. 150–68.

Lucy, S. 1998. *The early Anglo-Saxon Cemeteries of East Yorkshire: an Analysis and Reinterpretation*. British Archaeological Reports, British Series 272. Oxford: Archaeopress.

Lucy, S. 2000. *The Anglo-Saxon Way of Death*. Stroud: Sutton.

Lucy, S. 2002. Burial practice in early medieval eastern Britain: Constructing local identities, deconstructing ethnicity. In *Burial in Early Medieval England and Wales* (eds S. Lucy and A. Reynolds). Society for Medieval Archaeology Monograph 17, London: Maney, pp. 72–87.

Lucy, S. and Herring, C. 1999. Viewing the 'Dark Ages': the portrayal of early Anglo-Saxon life and material culture in Museums. In *Making Early Histories in Museums* (ed. N. Merriman). Leicester: Leicester University Press, pp. 74–94.

Lucy, S. and Reynolds, A. 2002. Burial in early medieval England and Wales: past, present and future. In *Burial in Early Medieval England and Wales* (eds S. Lucy and A. Reynolds). Society for Medieval Archaeology Monograph 17. London: Maney, pp. 1–23.

Lull, V. 2000a. Death and society: a Marxist approach. *Antiquity*, 74: 576–80.

Lull, V. 2000b. Argaric society: death at home. *Antiquity*, 74: 581–90.

Lull, V. and Estévez, J. 1986. Propuesta metodológica para el estudio de las necrópolis argáricas. In *Homenaje a Luis Siret*. Seville: Junta de Andalucía, pp. 441–52.

Lull, V., Micó, R., Rihuete, C. and Risch, R. 2005. Property relations in the Bronze Age of southwestern Europe: an approach based on infant burials from El Argar (Almería, Spain). *Proceedings of the Prehistoric Society*, 71: 247–68.

Lund, A.A. 1988. *Germania*. Heidelberg: Winter.

Lyckner, K. 1854. *Deutsche Sagen und Sitten im hessischen Gauen*. Kassel: Oswald Bertram.

Lynch, F. and Musson, C. 2004. A prehistoric and early medieval complex at Llandegai, near Bangor, North Wales: excavations directed by C.H. Houlder 1966–67. *Archaeologia Cambrensis*, 150: 17–142.

Lyngstrøm, H. 1989. Lousgaard — éthundrede år efter J.A. Jørgensen og E. Vedel. *Aarbøger 1989*: 115–69.

Mack, A. 1998. *The association of Pictish symbol stones with ecclesiastical, burial, and 'memorial' areas*. Balgavies: Pinkfoot Press.

Madsen, C. 1995. No. 252. Møllegårdsmarken, 09.01.04 Gudme, Svendborg Amt. *Arkæologiske udgravninger i Danmark 1994*. København: Nationalmuseet. p. 152.

Madsen, O. 1994. Søndervang ved Bjerre. En østjysk gravplads fra yngre germansk jernalder og vikingetid. *Kuml*, 1991–92: 105–49.

Magie, D. (trans.) 1932. *Historia Augusta, Tyranni Triginta*. London: Heinemann. Vol. 3.

Malim, T. and Hines, J. 1998. *The Anglo-Saxon Cemetery at Edix Hill, British Archaeological Reports (Barrington A), Cambridgeshire*. Council for British Archaeology, Research Report 112. York: Council for British Archaeology.

Malory, T. 2004. *Morte D'Arthur*. London: Penguin.

Marschallek, K.H. 1964. Vor- und frühgeschichtliche Straßenforschung. Beispiele aus dem Nordseeküstenraum. In *Varia Archaeologica: Festschrift W. Unverzagt* (ed. P. Grimm). Berlin: Akademie-Verlag, pp. 410–27.

Marsden, B. 1999. *The Early Barrow Diggers*. Stroud: Tempus.

Marseen, O. 1971. *Vikingegravpladsen Lindholm Høje*. Aalborg: Aalborg Historiske Museum.

Martin, M. [1994] 2000. Späte Völkerwanderungszeit und Merowingerzeit auf dem Kontinent. In *Fibel und Fibeltracht* (eds H. Beck, H. Steuer, D. Timpe and R. Wenskus). Reallexikon der Germanischen Altertumskunde. Berlin: Walter de Gruyter, pp. 131–72.

Marx, K. and Engels, F. 1970. *The German Ideology*. (ed. C.J. Arthur). London: Lawrence and Wishart.

Marzinzik, S. 2003. *Early Anglo-Saxon Belt Buckles (Late 5th to Early 8th Centuries AD): Their Classification and Context*. British Archaeological Reports British Series 357. Oxford: Archaeopress.

Matsumura, S. and Forster, P. (eds) in press. *Simulations, Genetics and Human Prehistory — a Focus on Islands*. Cambridge: McDonald Institute Monograph.

McCarthy, M.R. (ed.) 1990. *A Roman, Anglian and medieval site at Blackfriars Street, Carlisle*. Carlisle: Cumberland and Westmorland Antiquarian and Archaeological Society Research Series 4.

McEvoy, B., Richards, M., Forster, P. and Bradley, D. 2004. The long durée of genetic ancestry: multiple genetic marker systems and Celtic origins on the Atlantic façade of Europe, *American Journal of Human Genetics*, 75: 693–702.

McGuire, R.H. 2002. *A Marxist Archaeology*. New York: Percheron Press.

McKinley, J. 2003. The Early Saxon cemetery at Park Lane, Croydon. *Surrey Archaeological Collections*, 90: 1–116.

McKinley, J. and Roberts, C. 1993. *Excavation and post-excavation treatment of cremated and inhumed human remains*. IFA Technical Paper Number 13. Birmingham: Institute of Field Archaeologists.

McMahon, A. and McMahon R. 2006. Why linguists don't do dates: evidence from Indo-European and Australian Languages. In *Phylogenetic methods and the prehistory of languages* (eds P. Forster and C. Renfrew). Cambridge: McDonald Institute Monograph, pp. 153–60.

McManus, D. 1991. *A Guide to Ogam*. Maynooth: An Sagart.

McNamara, J. 1994. The Herrenfrage: the restructuring of the gender system, 1050–1150. In *Medieval Masculinities. Regarding Men in the Middle Ages* (ed. C. Lees). Minneapolis: University of Minnesota Press, pp. 3–29.

Meadows, I. 1998. Ketton Quarry. In *Medieval Settlement Research Group Annual Report*, 13: 46–7.

Meaney, A.L. and Hawkes, S.C. 1970. *Two Anglo-Saxon cemeteries at Winnall, Winchester, Hampshire*. Society for Medieval Archaeology Monograph Series 4. London: Society for Medieval Archaeology.

Meier, J. 1950. *Ahnengrab und Rechtsstein*. Deutsche Akademie der Wissenschaften zu Berlin. Veröffentlichungen der Kommission für Volkskunde 1. Berlin: Akademie-Verlag.

Meillassoux, C. 1968. Ostentation, destruction, reproduction. *Economie et Société*, 1: 93–105.

Mellor, P.A. and Shilling, C. 1993. Modernity, self-Identity and the sequestration of death, *Sociology*, 27(3): 411–31.

Meskell, L. 1998. The irresistible body and the seduction of archaeology. In *Changing Bodies: Changing Meanings* (ed. D. Montserrat). London and New York: Routledge, pp. 139–61.

Metcalf, P. and Huntington, R. 1991. *Celebrations of Death: The Anthropology of Mortuary Ritual*. Second Edition. Cambridge: Cambridge University Press.

Metzler, I. 2006. *Disability in Medieval Europe. Thinking about physical impairment during the high Middle Ages, c.1100–1400*. London: Routledge.

Mitteis, H. and Lieberich, H. 1988. *Deutsche Rechtsgeschichte. Ein Studienbuch*. 18th ed. München: Beck.

Møbjerg, T. and Møller-Jensen, E. 2005. Birkgård. En lille familiegravplads fra yngre germansk jernalder. *Midtjyske fortællinger*, 2005: 29–38.

Molleson, T.I., Cox, M., Waldron, H.A. and Whittaker, D.K. 1993 *The Spitalfields project. York, Council for British Archaeology* (CBA Research report 86).

Montgomery, J., Evans, J.A., Powesland, D. and Roberts, C. 2005. Continuity or colonization in Anglo-Saxon England? Isotope evidence for mobility, subsistance practice and status at West Heslerton. *American Journal of Physical Anthropology*, 126: 123–38.

Moody, R.A. 1977. *Leben nach dem Tod* [original title: 'Life after life', 1975]. Reinbeck bei Hamburg: Rowohlt.

Morris, R. 1983. *The Church in British Archaeology*. Council for

British Archaeology Research Report 47. York: Council for British Archaeology.

Mortimer, C. 1990. *Some Aspects of Early Medieval Copper-Alloy Technology, as Illustrated by a Study of the Anglian Cruciform Brooch.* Doctoral Dissertation, University of Oxford.

Mortimer, R. 2000a. Village development and ceramic sequence: the middle to late Saxon village at Lordship Lane, Cottenham, Cambridgeshire. *Proceedings of the Cambridge Antiquarian Society*, 89: 5–33.

Mortimer, R. 2000b. Carlton Colville. *Medieval Settlement Research Group Annual Report*, 15: 34–5

Morton A.D. 1992. Burial in Middle Saxon Southampton. In *Death in Towns: Urban Responses to the Dying and the Dead, 100–1600.* Leicester: Leicester University Press, pp. 68–77.

Moser, S. 1998. *Ancestral Images, the Iconography of Human Origins,* Stroud: Sutton.

Moser, S. and Gamble, C. 1997. Revolutionary images: the iconic vocabulary for representing human antiquity. In *The Cultural Life of Images: Visual Representation in Archaeology* (ed. B.L. Molyneaux). London: Routledge, pp. 184–212.

Moser, S. and Smiles, S. 2005. Introduction: the image in question. In *Envisioning the Past: Archaeology and the Image*, (eds S. Smiles and S. Moser). Oxford: Blackwell, pp. 1–12.

Moshenska, G. 2006. The archaeological uncanny, *Public Archaeology*, 5(2): 91–9.

Mülle-Wille, M. 1987. *Das wikingerzeitliche Gräberfeld von Thumby Bienebek, Kr. Rendsburg-Eckernförde.* Teill II Offa-Bücher 62. Neumünster: Wacholtz.

Müller, R. 1987. Die spätrömische Festung Valcum am Plattensee. In *Germanen, Hunnen und Awaren* (eds W. Menghin, T. Springer and E. Wamers). Nürnberg: Germanisches Nationalmuseum, pp. 270–3.

Murphy, K. 1992. Plas Gogerddan, Dyfed: A multiperiod burial and ritual site. *Archeological Journal*, 149: 1–39.

Murray, A.C. 1983. *Germanic Kinship Structure: Studies in Law and Society in Antiquity and the Early Middle Ages.* Toronto: Pontifical Institute of Medieval Studies.

Murray, J. 1996. Hiding behind the universal man. Male sexuality in the Middle Ages. In *The Handbook of Medieval Sexuality* (eds V.L. Bullough and J.A. Brundage). New York: Garland, pp. 123–52.

Musty, J. 1969. The excavation of two barrows, one of Saxon date, at Ford, Laverstock, near Salisbury, Wiltshire. *Antiquaries Journal*, 49 (1): 98–117.

Myres, J.N.L. 1969. *Anglo-Saxon Pottery and the Settlement of England.* Oxford: Clarendon Press.

Myres, J.N.L. 1977. *A Corpus of Anglo-Saxon Pottery of the Pagan Period.* 2 Volumes. Cambridge: Cambridge University Press.

Næss, J.R. 1996. *Undersøkelser i jenalderens gravskikk på Voss.* (AmS-Rapport 7). Stavanger: Arkeologisk museum i Stavanger.

Nash-Williams, V. 1950. *The early Christian monuments of Wales.* Cardiff: University of Wales Press.

Neckel, G. and Niedner, F. 1942. Gylfi's Betörung. In: *Die jüngere Edda mit dem sogenannten ersten grammatischen Traktat.* Thule Altnordische Dichtung und Prosa. Zwickau/Sa: F. Allmann. Second Edition. Jena: Eugen Diederichs Verlag.

Nelson, J. 1999. Monks, secular men and masculinity, c.900. In *Masculinity in Medieval Europe* (ed. D. Hadley). London: Longman, pp. 121–42.

Nelson, J.L. 2004. Gendering courts in the early medieval west. In *Gender in the Early Medieval World* (eds L. Brubaker and J.M.H. Smith). Cambridge: Cambridge University Press, pp. 185–97.

Nenk, B., Haith, C. and Bradley, J. 1997. Medieval Britain and Ireland, 1996. *Medieval Archaeology*, 41: 241–328.

Nenk, B., Margeson, S. and Hurley, M. 1993. Medieval Britain and Ireland in 1991. *Medieval Archaeology*, 37: 240–313.

Nenk, B., Margeson, S. and Hurley, M. 1996. Medieval Britain and Ireland, 1995. *Medieval Archaeology*, 40: 234–318.

Newman, C. 1992. A late Saxon cemetery at Templecombe. *Somerset Archaeology and Natural History*, 136: 61–72.

Niles, J. 2007. *Beowulf and Lejre.* Tempe: Arizona Center for Medieval and Renaissance Studies.

Nordenborg Myhre, L. 2005. *Trialectic Archaeology. Monuments and Space in Southwestern Norway 1700–500 BC.* Stavanger: Arkeologisk museum i Stavanger.

Nordström, N. 2007. *De odöldliga. Förhistoriska individer i vetenskap och media,* Falun: Nordic Academic Press.

O'Shea, J. 1984. *Mortuary variability: an archaeological investigation.* Orlando: Academic Press.

O'Shea, J. 1995. Mortuary custom in the Bronze Age of southeastern Hungary: diachronic and synchronic perspectives. In *Regional Approaches to Mortuary Analysis* (ed. L.A. Beck). New York: Plenum Press, pp. 125–45.

Okasha, E. 1993. *Corpus of Early Christian Inscribed Stones of south-west Britain.* Leicester: Leicester University Press.

Olivier, L. 1999. The Hochdorf 'princely' grave and the question of the nature of archaeological funerary assemblages. In *Time and Archaeology* (ed. T. Murray). London: Routledge, pp. 109–38.

Oman, C. 1957. *English church plate 597–1830.* London: Oxford University Press.

Oosthuizen, S. 2002 Medieval greens and commons in the central province; evidence from the Bourn valley, Cambridgeshire. *Landscape History*, 24: 73–89.

Oosthuizen, S. 2005. New light on the origins of open-field farming? *Medieval Archaeology*, 49: 165–94.

Oosthuizen, S. 2006. *Landscapes Decoded. The Origins and Development of Cambridgeshire's Medieval Fields.* Hatfield: University of Hertfordshire.

Oppenheimer, S. 2006. *The Origins of the British,* London: Constable.

Orme, N. 1988. A medieval almshouse for the clergy: Clyst Gabriel Hospital near Exeter. *Journal of Ecclesiastical History*, 39.1: 1–15.

Ørsnes, M. 1966. *Form og stil i Sydskandinaviens yngre germanske jernalder.* København: Nationalmuseet.

Ortner, D.J. and Corruccini, R.S. 1976. The skeletal biology of the Virginia Indians. *American Journal of Physical Anthropology*, 45: 717–22.

Overing, G. and Osborn, M. 1994. *Landscape of Desire: Partial Stories of the Medieval Scandinavian World*. Minneapolis: University of Minnesota Press.

Owen-Crocker, G.R. 2000. *The Four Funerals in* Beowulf. Manchester: Manchester University Press.

Owen-Crocker, G.R. 2004. *Dress in Anglo-Saxon England*. Woodbridge: Boydell.

Pader, E.-J. 1980. Material symbolism and social relations in mortuary studies. In *Anglo-Saxon Cemeteries 1979* (eds. P. Rahtz, T. Dickinson and L. Watts) British Archaeological Reports, British Series 82, Oxford: Archaeopress, pp. 143–69.

Pader, E.-J. 1982. *Symbolism, Social Relations and the Interpretation of Mortury Remains*. British Archaeological Reports, International Series 130. Oxford: Archaeopress.

Parfitt, K. and Brugmann, B. 1997. *The Anglo-Saxon cemetery on Mill Hill, Deal, Kent*, The Society for Medieval Archaeology Monograph Series No. 14. Leeds: Maney.

Parker Pearson, M. 1982. Mortuary practices, society and ideology: an ethnoarchaeological study. In *Symbolic and Structural Archaeology* (ed. I. Hodder). Cambridge: Cambridge University Press, pp. 99–113.

Parker Pearson, M. 1999. *The Archaeology of Death and Burial*. Stroud: Sutton.

Parkhouse, J., Roseff, R. and Short, J. 1996. A late Saxon cemetery at Milton Keynes village. *Records of Buckinghamshire*, 38: 199–221.

Parnia, S. 2006. *What Happens When We Die. A Ground-Breaking Study into the Nature of Life and Death*. Second Edition. London: Hay House.

Penn, K. 2000. *Norwich Southern Bypass, Part II: Anglo-Saxon Cemetery at Harford Farm, Caistor St Edmund*. East Anglian Archaeology 92. Dereham: Norfolk Archaeological Unit and Norfolk Museums Service.

Penn, K. and Brugmann, B. 2007. *Aspects of Anglo-Saxon Inhumation Burials: Morning Thorpe, Spong Hill, Bergh Apton and Westgarth Gardens*. East Anglian Archaeology 119. Norwich, Norfolk Archaeological Unit and Norfolk Museums Service.

Petts, D. 2001. *Burial, Religion and Identity in sub-Roman and Early Medieval Britain: AD 400–800*. Doctoral Dissertation, University of Reading.

Petts, D. 2003. *Christianity in Roman Britain*. Stroud: Tempus.

Petts, D. 2004. Burial in western Britain AD 400–800: late antique or early medieval? In *Debating Late Antiquity in Britain AD 300–700* (eds J. Gerrard and R. Collins). British Archaeological Reports, British Series 365. Oxford: Archaeopress, pp. 77–87.

Phillips, C.W. 1940. The excavation of the Sutton Hoo ship-burial, *Antiquaries Journal*, 20: 149–202.

Phillpotts, B. 1913. *Kindred and Clan*. Cambridge, Cambridge University Press.

Philpott, R. 1991. *Burial practice in Roman Britain: A Survey of Grave*

Treatment and Furnishing. British Archaeological Reports, British Series 219. Oxford: Archaeopress.

Piggott, S. 1978. *Antiquity Depicted.* London: Thames and Hudson.

Plunkett, S. 2002. *Sutton Hoo.* London: The National Trust

Pohl, W. 1997. The role of the steppe peoples in eastern and central Europe in the first millennium A D. In *Origins of Central Europe* (ed. P. Urbańczyk) Warsaw: Scientific Society of Polish Archaeologists, pp. 65–78.

Pohl, W. (ed.) 2004. *Die Suche nach den Ursprüngen. Von der Bedeutung des frühen Mittelalters.* Forschungen zur Geschichte des Mittelalters 8. Wien: Österreichische Akademie der Wissenschaften.

Pohl, W. and Reimitz, H. (eds) 1998. *Strategies of distinction. The construction of ethnic communities, 300–800.* The Transformation of the Roman World, 2. Leiden: Brill.

Politis, G. and Alberti, B. (eds) 1999. *Archaeology in Latin America.* London, Routledge.

Porter, P. 1991. *Beowulf. Text and Translation.* Pinner: Anglo-Saxon Books.

Postles, D. 1996. Monastic burials of non-patronal lay benefactors. *Journal of Ecclesiastical History*, 47: 621–37.

Powlesland, D. 1997. Early Anglo-Saxon settlements, structures, form and layout. In *The Anglo-Saxons from the Migration Period to the Eighth Century. An Ethnographic Perspective* (ed. J. Hines). Woodbridge: Boydell, pp. 101–17.

Powlesland, D. 2003. *25 Years of Archaeological Reseach on the Sands and Gravels of Heslerton.* Yedingham: Landscape Research Centre.

Preidel, H. 1972. Das Markomannenreich König Marbods als Personalverband. *Časopis Moravského Musea*, 57: 115–22.

Preucel, R. 1995. The post-processual condition. *Journal of Archaeological Research*, 3: 147–75.

Price, N.S. 2002. *The Viking way. Religion and War in Late Iron Age Scandinavia.* Uppsala: Department of Archaeology and Ancient History, University of Uppsala.

Price, T.D., Knipper, C., Grupe, G. and Smrcka, V. 2004. Strontium isotopes and prehistoric human migration: the Bell Beaker period in central Europe. *European Journal of Archaeology*, 7: 9–40.

Price, T.D., Bentley, R.A., Lüning, J., Gronenborn, D. and Wahl, J. 2001. Prehistoric human migration in the Linearbandkeramik of Central Europe. *Antiquity*, 75: 595–603.

Price, T.D., Gruype, G. and Schröter, P. 1998. Migration in the Bell Beaker period of central Europe. *Antiquity*, 72: 405–11.

Pryor, F. 2004. *Britain AD: A Quest for Arthur, England and the Anglo-Saxons.* London: Harper-Collins.

Quensel-von-Kalben, L. 2000. Putting late Roman Burial Practice (from Britain) in context. In *Burial, Society and Context in the Roman World* (eds J. Pearce, M. Millett and M. Struck). Oxford: Oxbow, pp. 217–30.

Quitzmann, A. 1860. *Die heidnische Religion der Baiwaren. Erster faktischer Beweis für die Abstammung dieses Volkes.* Leipzig and Heidelberg: Winter'sche Verlagshandlung.

Rahtz, P. 1979. *The Saxon and Medieval Palaces at Cheddar*: British Archaeological Reports 65. Oxford: Archaeopress.

Rahtz, P., Dickinson, T. and Watts, L. (eds) 1980. *Anglo-Saxon Cemeteries 1979. The Fourth Anglo-Saxon Symposium at Oxford*. British Archaeological Reports, British Series 82. Oxford: Archaeopress.

Rahtz, P., Hirst, S. and Wright, S. 2000. *Cannington Cemetery*. Britannia Monograph Series 17. London: Society for the Promotion of Roman Studies.

Ramskou, T. 1953. Lindholm. Preliminary report of the 1952–1953 excavations of a Late Iron Age cemetery and an Early Medieval Settlement. *Acta Archaeologica*, 24: 186–96.

Ramskou, T. 1955. Lindholm Høje. Second preliminary report for the years 1954–55 on the excavation of a Late Iron Age cemetery and an Early Medieval settlement. *Acta Archaeologica*, 26: 177–85.

Ramskou, T. 1957. Lindholm Høje. Third preliminary report for the years 1956–1957 on the excavation of a Late Iron Age cemetery and an Early Medieval settlement. *Acta Archaeologica*, 28: 193–201.

Ramskou, T. 1976. *Lindholm Høje Gravpladsen*. København: Det kongelige nordiske Oldskriftselskab.

Randsborg, K. 1995. *Hjortspring: Warfare and Sacrifice in Early Europe*. Århus: Århus University Press.

Randsborg, K. and Christensen, K. 2006. *Bronze Age Oak-Coffin Graves*. Acta Archaeologica and Centre of World Archaeology. Copenhagen: Blackwell Munksgaard.

Ravn, M. 2003. *Death Ritual and Germanic Social Structure*. British Archaeological Reports International Series 1164. Oxford: Archaeopress.

Rawcliffe, C., and Wilson, R. (eds) 2004. *Norwich since 1550*. London and New York: Hambledon and London.

Redknap, M. 2002. *Re-Creations: Visualizing Our Past*. Cardiff: Cadw.

Redknap, M. and Lewis, J.M. 2007. *A Corpus of Early Medieval Inscribed Stones and Stone Sculpture in Wales Vol 1: South-East Wales and the English Border*. Cardiff: University of Wales Press.

Resi, H.G. 1989. *Gravplassen Hunn i Østfold*. Norske Oldfunn XII. Oslo: Universitetets Oldsaksamling.

Reuter, T. (ed.) 1992 *The Annals of Fulda*. Manchester: Manchester University Press.

Reynolds, A. 1999. *Later Anglo-Saxon England*. Stroud: Tempus.

Reynolds, A. 2002. Burials, boundaries and charters in Anglo-Saxon England: a reassessment. In *Burial in Early Medieval England and Wales* (eds S. Lucy and A. Reynolds). Society for Medieval Archaeology Monograph 17. London: Maney, pp. 171–89.

Reynolds, A. 2003. Boundaries and settlements in later sixth- to eleventh-century England. In *Anglo-Saxon Studies in Archaeology and History* 12 (eds D. Griffths, A. Reynolds and S. Semple). Oxford: Oxford University School of Archaeology, pp. 98–136.

Reynolds, A. 2009. *Anglo-Saxon Deviant Burial Customs*. Oxford: Oxford University Press

Reynolds, S. 1984. *Kingdoms and Communities in Western Europe, 900–1300*. Oxford: Oxford University Press.

Richards, J. 1999. *Meet the Ancestors*. London: BBC.

Richards, J.D. 1987. *The Significance of Form and Decoration of Anglo-Saxon Cremation Urns*. British Archaeological Reports British Series 166. Oxford: Archaeopress.

Richards, J.D. 1999. Cottam: an Anglo-Scandinavian settlement on the Yorkshire Wolds. *Archaeological Journal*, 156: 1–111.

Richards, J.D. 2002. The case of the missing Vikings: Scandinavian burial in the Danelaw. In *Burial in Early Medieval England and Wales* (eds S. Lucy and A. Reynolds). The Society for Medieval Archaeology Monograph, 17. London: Maney, pp. 156–70.

Richards, M., Forster, P., Tetzner, S., Hedges, R., and Sykes, B. 1994. Mitochondrial DNA and the Frisians, In *Friesische Studien II* (eds V. Faltings, A. Walker and O. Wilts). Odense: Odense University Press, pp. 141–63.

Richards, M., Smalley, K., Sykes, B. and Hedges, R. 1993. Archaeology and genetics: analysing DNA from skeletal remains, *World Archaeology*, 25 (1): 18–28.

Richards, M.B and Sykes, B.C, 1995. Authenticating DNA extracted from ancient skeletal remains, *Journal of Archaeological Science*, 22: 291–99.

Richardson, A. 2005. *The Anglo-Saxon Cemeteries of Kent*. British Archaeological Reports, British Series 391. Oxford: Archaeopress.

Rippon, S., Fyfe, M. and Brown, A. 2006. Beyond villages and open fields: the origins and development of an historic landscape characterised by dispersed settlement in south-west England. *Medieval Archaeology*, 50: 31–70.

Risch, R. 1998. Análisis paleoeconómico y medios de producción líticos: el caso de Fuente Alamo. In *Minerales y Metales en la Prehistoria Reciente. Algunos Testimonios de su Explotación y Laboreo en la Península Ibérica* (ed. G. Delibes de Castro). Valladolid: Universidad de Valladolid, pp. 105–54.

Risch, R. 2002. *Recursos naturales, medios de producción y explotación social. Un análisis económico de la industria lítica de Fuente Álamo (Almería), 2250–1400 antes de nuestra era*. Mainz am Rhein: Philipp von Zabern.

Rittner, V. 1973: *Kulturkontakte und soziales Lernen im Mittelalter. Kreuzzüge im Licht einer mittelalterlichen Biographie.* (Kollektive Einstellungen und sozialer Wandel im Mittelalter 1). Köln and Wien: Böhlau Verlag.

Rives, J.B. (ed. and trans.) 1999. *Tacitus: Germania*. Oxford: Oxford University Press.

Robinson, I.S. 2004. Reform and the Church 1073–1122. In *The New Cambridge Medieval History IV, c.1073–c.1195* (eds D. Luscombe and J. Riley-Smith). Camridge: Cambridge University Press, pp. 268–334.

Rodwell, W. 2003–5. Lichfield Cathedral: archaeology of the nave sanctuary. *Church Archaeology*, 7–9: 1–6.

Rodwell, W. 2007. St Peter's Church: its setting and community. In *St Peter's, Barton-upon-Humber, Lincolnshire. Volume 2: The Human Remains* (ed. T. Waldron). Oxford: Oxbow, pp. 1–14.

Roesdahl, E. 1977. *Fyrkat. En jysk vikingeborg II. Oldsagerne og gravpladsen.* Nordiske Fortidsminder Serie B, in quarto, 4. København: Det kgl. nordiske Oldskriftselskab.

Roesdahl, E. and Nordqvist, J. 1971. De døde fra Fyrkat. *Fra Nationalmuseets Arbejdsmark*, 1971: 15–32.

Rogerson, A., Ashley, S.J., Williams, P. and Harris, A. 1987. *Three Norman Churches in Norfolk*, East Anglian Archaeology Report 32. Norfolk: Norfolk Archaeological Unit and Norfolk Museums Service.

Rolfe, J.C. (trans.) 1952. *Ammianus Marcellinus: Rerum gestarum libri.* London: Heinemann. 3 volumes.

Rosser, Z., *et al.* 2000. Y-chromosomal diversity in Europe is clinal and influenced primarily by geography, rather than by language, *American Journal of Human Genetics*, 67: 1526–1543.

Rost, A. 2007. Characteristics of ancient battlefields: Battle of Varus (9 AD). In *Fields of Conflict. Battlefield Archaeology from the Roman Empire to the Korean War. Vol. 1, Searching for War in the Ancient and Early Modern World* (eds D. Scott, L. Babits and Ch. Haecker). Westport, Conn: Praeger Security International, pp. 50–7.

Rötting, I. 1985. *Siedlungen und Gräberfelder der Römischen Kaiserzeit.* Studien und Vorarbeiten zum Historischen Atlas Niedersachsens, 31. Heft. Hildesheim: Lax.

Rowe, J.H. 1962. Worsaae's law and the use of grave lots for archaeological dating. *American Antiquity*, 28: 129–37.

Rudebeck, E. 2001. Vägar, vägkorsningar och vadställen – liminala platser och arkeologi. In *Kommunikation i tid och rum* (ed. Lars Larsson). Report Series 82. Lund: Institute of Archaeology, University of Lund, pp. 93–112.

Rudebeck, E. 2002. Vägen som rituell arena. In Plats och Praxis. Studier av Nordisk Förkristen Ritual (eds K. Jennbert, A. Andrén and C. Raudvere) *Vägar till Midgård* 2. Lund: Nordic Academic Press, pp. 167–200.

Rudebeck, E. and Ödman, C. 2000. *Kristineberg. En gravplats under 4500 år.* Malmöfynd 7. Malmö: Stadsantikvariska Avdelningen Kultur Malmö.

Ryder, P.F. 1985. *The Medieval Cross Slab Grave Cover in County Durham.* Research Report 1. Durham: Architectural and Archaeological Society of Durham and Northumberland.

Sabom, M.B. 1982. *Erinnerungen an den Tod. Eine medizinische Untersuchung* [original title: 'Recollection of Death']. Berlin: Goldmann.

Sage, W., Hundt, H.-J. and Helmuth, H. 1973. Gräber der älteren Merowingerzeit aus Altenerding Ldkr. Erding (Oberbayern). *Berichte der Römisch-Germanischen Kommission*, 54: 213–317.

Salamon, Á. and Lengyel, I. 1980. Kinship interrelations in a fifth-century 'Pannonian' cemetery: an archaeological and palaeobiological sketch of the population fragment buried in the Mősz cemetery, Hungary. *World Archaeology*, 12 (1): 93–104.

Samson, A. 2006. Offshore finds from the Bronze Age in north-western Europe: the shipwreck scenario revisited. *Oxford Journal of Archaeology*, 25: 371–88.

Samson, R. 1987. Social structures from Reihengräber: mirror or mirage? *Scottish Archaeological Review* 4: 116–26.

Samuelsson, B.-Å. 2001. Kan gravar spegla vägars ålder och betydelse? In *Uppåkra. Centrum i analys och rapport* (ed. Lars Larsson). Uppåkrastudier 4. Acta Archaeologica Lundensia, Series in 8°, No. 36. Stockholm: Almqvist and Wiksell International, pp. 177–84.

Samuelsson, B.-Å. 2003. Ljungbacka – a Late Iron Age Cemetery in South-West Scania. *Lund Archaeological Review*, 2001 (7): 89–108.

Saunders, T. 2000. Class, space and 'Feudal' identities in Early Medieval England. In *Social Identity in Early Medieval Britain* (eds. W.O. Frazer and A. Tyrrell). Leicester: Leicester University Press, pp. 209–32.

Savory, H. 1980. *Guide Catalogue of the Bronze Age Collection*. Cardiff: National Museum of Wales.

Saxe, A.A. 1970. *Social Dimensions of Mortuary Practices*. Doctoral Dissertation, University of Michigan, Ann Arbor.

Sayer, D. 2007a. Drei südenglische Gräberfelder aus angelsächsischer Zeit und ihre Organisation. In *Innere Strukturen von Siedlungen und Gräberfeldern als Spiegel gesellschaftlicher Wirklichkeit? Akten des 57 Internationalen Sachsensymposiums* (eds C. Grünewald and T. Capelle). Münster (Westfalen): Veröffentlichungen der Altertumskommission für Westfalen, Vol. XVII, pp. 63–72.

Sayer, D. 2007b. *Community, Kinship and Household: An Analysis of Patterns in Early Anglo-Saxon Inhumation Cemeteries*. 2 Volumes. Doctoral Dissertation, University of Reading.

Schach-Dörges, H. 1997. 'Zusammengespülte und vermengte Menschen'— suebische Kriegerbünde werden sesshaft. In *Die Alamannen* (ed. Archäologisches Landesmuseum Baden-Württemberg). Stuttgart: Theiss, pp. 79–102.

Schildkrout, E. 2004. Inscribing the body. *Annual Review of Anthropology*, 33: 319–44

Schjødt, J.P. 2003. *Initiation, liminalitet og tilegnelse af numinøs viden. En undersøgelse af struktur og symbolik i førkristen nordisk religion*. Århus: Aarhus Universitet. Det Teologiske Fakultet.

Schlicht, E. n.d. Von alten Verkehrswegen. *Jahrbuch des Emsländischen Heimatvereins* 9 (Sonderdruck/Offprint).

Schliz, A. 1905. Künstlich deformierte Schädel in germanischen Reihengräbern. *Archiv für Anthropologie*, 3: 191–213.

Schlüter, W. 1970. Versuch einer sozialen Differenzierung der jungkaiserzeitlichen Körpergräbergruppe von Haßleben-Leuna anhand einer Analyse der Grabfunde. *Neue Ausgrabungen und Forschungen in Niedersachsen*, 6: 117–45.

Schmidt, B. 1987. Das Königreich der Thüringer und seine Provinzen. In *Germanen, Hunnen und Awaren* (eds W. Menghin, T. Springer and E. Wamers). Nürnberg: Germanisches Nationalmuseum, pp. 471–512.

Schnapp, A. 1996. *The Discovery of the Past*. London: British Museum Press.

Schrijver, P. 2007. What Britons spoke around 400 AD, In *Britons in Anglo-Saxon England* (ed. N. Higham). Woodbridge: Boydell, pp. 165–71.

Schröter, P. 1988. Zur beabsichtigten künstlichen Kopfumformung im völkerwanderungszeitlichen Mitteleuropa. In *Die Bajuwaren. Von*

Severin bis Tassilo 488–788 (eds H. Dannheimer and H. Dopsch).
Rosenheim and Mattsee: Prähistorische Staatssammlung München/
Landesregierung Salzburg, pp. 258–65.

Schubart, H., Pingel, V. and Arteaga, O. 2000. *Fuente Alamo. Las
Excavaciones Arqueológicas 1977–1991 en el Poblado de la Edad del
Bronce*. Sevilla: Junta de Andalucía, Consejería de Cultura.

Schülke, A. 1999. On christianization and grave-finds, *European Journal of
Archaeology*, 2(1): 77–106.

Schweissing, M.M. and Grupe, G. 2003. Stable strontium isotopes in human
teeth and bone: a key to migration events of the late Roman period in
Bavaria. *Journal of Archaeological Science*, 30 (11): 1373–1383.

Scull, C. 1993. Archaeology, early Anglo-Saxon society and the origins
of Anglo-Saxon kingdoms. In *Anglo-Saxon Studies in Archaeology
and History 6* (ed. W. Filmer-Sankey). Oxford: Oxford University
Committee for Archaeology, pp. 65–91.

Scull, C. 1997. Urban centres in Pre-Viking England? In *The Anglo-Saxons
from the Migration Period to the Eighth Century. An Ethnographic
Perspective* (ed. J. Hines). Woodbridge: Boydell, pp. 269–98.

Scull, C. 2000. How the dead live: some current approaches to the
mortuary archaeology of England in the fifth to eighth centuries AD.
Archaeological Journal, 157: 399–406.

Scull, C. 2001. Burials at Emporia in England. In *Wics. The Early
Mediaeval Trading Centres of Northern Europe* (eds D. Hill and
R. Cowie). Sheffield: Sheffield Academic Press, pp. 67–74.

Semple, S. 1998. A fear of the past: the place of the prehistoric burial
mound in the ideology of middle and later Anglo-Saxon England. *World
Archaeology* 30 (1): 109–26.

Semple, S. and Williams, H. (eds) 2007. *Early Medieval Mortuary Practices.
Anglo-Saxon Studies in Archaeology and History* 14, Oxford: Oxford
University Committee for Archaeology.

Shaw, R. 1994. The Anglo-Saxon cemetery at Eccles: a preliminary report.
Archaeologia Cantiana, 114: 165–88.

Shephard, J. 1979. The social identity of individuals in isolated barrows
and barrow cemeteries in Anglo-Saxon England. In *Space, Hierarchy
and Society: Interdisciplinary Studies in Social Area Analysis* (eds
B.C. Burnham and J. Kingsbury). British Archaeological Reports,
International Series 59. Oxford: Archaeopress. pp. 47–79.

Sherlock, S.J. and Welch, M.G. 1992. *An Anglo-Saxon Cemetery at Norton,
Cleveland*, Council for British Archaeology Research Report 82.
London: Council for British Archaeology.

Shilling, C. 1993. *The Body and Social Theory: Theory, Culture and Society*.
London: Sage.

Sigvallius, B. 1994. *Funeral Pyres. Iron Age Cremations in North Spånga*.
Stockholm: The Osteological Research Laboratory, Stockholm
University.

Sims-Williams, P. 2003. *The Celtic Inscriptions of Britain: Phonology and
Chronology, c.400–1200*. Oxford: Blackwell.

Sjösvärd, L. 1989. *HaukR – en rinker från Vallentuna*. Stockholm:
Riksantikvarieämbetet.

Skjølsvold, A. 1980. Refleksjoner omkring jernaldersgravene i sydnorske fjellstrøk. *Viking*, 43: 140–60.

Smiles, S. 2005. Thomas Guest and Paul Nash in Wiltshire: Two Episodes in the Artistic Approach to Brsmilesitish Antiquity. In *Envisioning the Past: Archaeology and the* Image (eds S. Smiles and S. Moser). Oxford: Blackwell, pp. 133–57.

Smith, C.R. 1856. Inventorium Sepulchrale, London: Privately Printed.

Smith, J.M.H. 2005. *Europe after Rome: A New Cultural History 500–1000.* Oxford: Oxford University Press.

Snyder, C. 1996. *Sub-Roman Britain (AD 400–600): A Gazetteer of Sites.* British Archaeological Reports, British Series 247. Oxford: Archaeopress.

Sofaer, J. 2006. *The Body as Material Culture*, Cambridge: Cambridge University Press.

Solberg, B. 2000. *Jernalderen i Norge. Ca. 500 f. Kr. – 1030 e. Kr.* Oslo: J.W. Cappelens Forlag.

Sopp, M. 1999. *Die Wiederaufnahme älterer Bestattungsplätze in den nachfolgenden vor- und frühgeschichtlichen Perioden in Norddeutschland.* Antiquitas Reihe 3, Abhandlungen zur Vor- und Frühgeschichte, zur klassischen und provinzial-römischen Archäologie und zur Geschichte des Altertums, Bd. 39. Bonn: Habelt.

Speake, G. 1989. *A Saxon Bed Burial on Swallowcliffe Down.* English Heritage Archaeological Report No. 10. London: English Heritage.

Spencer, A.J. 1982. *Death in Ancient Egypt.* London: Penguin.

Stanford, S. 1995. A Cornovian farm and Saxon cemetery at Bromfield, Shropshire. *Transactions of the Shropshire Archaeological and Historical Society*, 70: 95–141.

Sten, S. and Vretemark, M. 1992. Osteologische Analysen knochenreicher Brandgräber der jüngeren Eisenzeit in Schweden. *Zeitschrift für Archäologie*, 26: 87–103.

Steuer, H. 2003. Kriegerbanden und Heerkönige – Krieg als Auslöser der Entwicklung zum Stamm und Staat im ersten Jahrtausend n. Chr. in Mitteleuropa. Überlegungen zu einem theoretischen Modell. In *Runica – Germanica – Mediaevalia* (eds W. Heizmann and A. van Nahl). Ergänzungsbände zum Reallexikon der Germanischen Altertumskunde, 37. Berlin and New York: de Gruyter, pp. 824–53.

Stevenson, J. 1998. Saxon Bodies: A Great Melting Pot? In *London Bodies: The Changing Shape of Londoners from Prehistoric Times to the Present Day* (ed. A. Werner). London: Museum of London, pp. 50–59.

Stocker, D. and Everson, P. 2003. The straight and narrow way: fenland causeways and the conversion of the landscape in the Witham valley, Lincolnshire. In *The Cross goes North: Processes of conversion in northern Europe* (ed. M. Carver). Woodbridge: Boydell, pp. 271–88.

Stocker, D. and Evison, P. 2006. *Summoning St Michael. Early Romanesque Towers in Lincolnshire.* Oxford: Oxbow Books.

Stoodley, N. 1999a. *The Spindle and the Spear. A Critical Enquiry into the Construction and Meaning of Gender in the Early Anglo-Saxon Burial Rite.* British Archaeological Reports British Series 288. Oxford: Archaeopress.

Stoodley, N. 1999b. Burial rites, gender and the creation of kingdoms: the evidence from seventh-century Wessex. In *The Making of Kingdoms*. (eds T. Dickinson and D. Griffiths). *Anglo-Saxon Studies in Archaeology and History* 10. Oxford: Oxford University Committee for Archaeology, pp. 99–108.

Stoodley, N. 1999c. Post-migration age structures and age-related grave-goods in Anglo-Saxon cemeteries in England. *Studien zur Sachsenforschung*, 11: 187–97.

Stoodley, N. 2000. From the cradle to the grave: age organization and the early Anglo-Saxon burial rite, *World Archaeology*, 31(3): 456–72.

Stoodley, N. 2002. The origins of Hamwic and its central role in the seventh century as revealed by recent archaeological discoveries. In *Central Places in the Migration and Merovingian Periods: papers from the 52nd Sachsensymposium, Lund, August 2001* (eds B. Hardh and L. Larsson). (Acta Archaeologica Lundensia Series in 8? No 39). Stockholm: Almqvist and Wiksell, pp. 317–32.

Stringer, C. 2007. *Homo Britannicus*. London: Penguin.

Svanberg, F. 2003. *Death Rituals in South-east Scandinavia AD 800–1000*. Acta Archaeological Lundensia Series in 4° No 24. Stockholm: Almqvist and Wiksell International.

Swain, H. 2002. The ethics of displaying human remains from British archaeological sites, *Public Archaeology*, 2: 95–100.

Swain, H. 2007. *An Introduction to Museum Archaeology*. Cambridge: Cambridge University Press.

Swanson, R.N. 1999. Angels incarnate: clergy and masculinity from Gregorian Reform to Reformation. In *Masculinity in Medieval Europe* (ed. D.M. Hadley). London: Longman, pp. 160–77.

Swift, C. 2007. Welsh ogams from an Irish perspective. In *Ireland and Wales in the Middle Ages* (eds K. Jankulak and J. Wooding). Dublin, Four Courts Press, pp. 62–79.

Swift, E. 2000. *Regionality in Dress Accessories in the Late Roman West*. Monographies Instrumentum 11. Montagnac: Éditions Monique Mergoil.

Sykes, B. 2006. *Blood of the Isles*. London: Bantam Press.

Synnott, A. 1993. *The Body Social: Symbolism Self and Society*. London and New York: Routledge.

Tainter, J.R. 1975. Social inference and mortuary practices: an experiment in numerical classification. *World Archaeology*, 7: 1–15.

Tedeschi, C. 1995. Osservazioni sulla paleografia delle iscrizioni britanniche paleocristiane (V-VII sec.). Contributo allo studio dell'origine delle scritture insulari. *Scrittura e Civiltà*, 19: 67–121.

Tedeschi, C. 2001. Some observations on the palaeography of early Christian inscriptions in Britain'. In *Roman, Runes and Ogham: medieval inscriptions in the insular world and on the continent* (ed. J. Higgett). Donington: Shaun Tyas, pp. 16–25.

Tejral, J. 1974. Völkerwanderungszeitliches Gräberfeld bei Vyškov (Mähren). *Studie Archeologického ústavu Československé akademie věd v Brně*, 2(2): 1–60.

Tejral, J. 2007. Das Attilareich und die germanischen *gentes* im

Mitteldonauraum. In *Attila und die Hunnen* (ed. Historisches Museum der Pfalz Speyer). Stuttgart: Konrad Theiss Verlag, pp. 107–113.

Teschler-Nicola, M. and Mitteröcker, P. 2007. Von künstlicher Kopfformung. In *Attila und die Hunnen* (ed. Historisches Museum der Pfalz Speyer). Stuttgart: Konrad Theiss Verlag. pp. 270–79.

Thäte, E.S. 1993. Die Orientierung frühgeschichtlicher Bestattungen an älteren Denkmälern im sächsisch-angelsächsischen Raum. Unpublished MA dissertation. Westfälische Wilhelms-Universität Münster.

Thäte, E.S. 1996. Alte Denkmäler und frühgeschichtliche Bestattungen: Ein sächsisch-angelsächsischer Totenbrauch und seine Kontinuität. *Archäologische Informationen* 19 (1 and 2): 105–16.

Thäte, E.S. 2007a. *Monuments and minds. Monument reuse in Scandinavia in the second half of the first millennium AD*. Acta Archaeologica Lundensia Series prima in 4? 1 No. 27. Lund: Department of Archaeology and Ancient History.

Thäte, E.S. 2007b. A question of priority: houses and barrows as places for burials in late Iron Age Scandinavia. In *Early Medieval Mortuary Practices* (eds S. Semple and H. Williams) *Anglo-Saxon Studies in Archaeology and History* 14. Oxford: Oxford University School of Archaeology, pp. 183–93.

Thomas, C. 1971. *Britain and Ireland in early Christian times, AD 400–800*. London: Thames and Hudson.

Thomas, C. 1981. *Christianity in Roman Britain to AD 500*. London: Batsford.

Thomas, J. 2000. Introduction. The polarities of post-processual archaeology. In *Interpretive Archaeology. A Reader* (ed. J. Thomas). Leicester: Leicester University Press, pp. 1–18.

Thomas, J. 2008. *Monument, Memory and Myth. Use and Reuse of Three Bronze Age Round Barrows at Cossington, Leicestershire*, Leicester Archaeology Monograph 14. Leicester: University of Leicester Archaeological Services.

Thomas, M., Härke, H., German, G. and Stumpf, M. 2008. Limited social constraints on interethnic marriage: Unions, differential reproductive success and the spread of 'continental' Y chromosones in early Anglo-Saxon England. In S. Matsumura, P. Foster and C. Renfrew (eds) *Simulations, genetics and human prehistory*. McDonald Institute Monographs. Cambridge: McDonald Institute for Archaeological Research, pp. 61–70.

Thomas, M., Stumpf, M.P. and Härke, H. 2006. Evidence for an apartheid-like social structure in early Anglo-Saxon England. *Proceedings of the Royal Society B, Biological sciences*, 273: 2651–2657.

Thomas, M., Stumpf, M. and Härke, H. 2008. Integration verseus apartheid in post-Roman Britain: a response to Pattison. *Proceedings of the Royal Society*, 275: 2419–21.

Thompson, V. 2004. *Dying and Death in Later Anglo-Saxon England*. Woodbridge: Boydell.

Thorpe, L. (ed. and trans.) 1974. *Gregory of Tours. The History of the Franks*. London: Penguin.

Timpe, D. 1970. *Arminius-Studien*. Heidelberg: Winter.

Topf, A.L., Gilbert, M.T., Dumbacher, J.P., Hoelzel, A.R. 2006. Tracing the phylogeography of human populations in Britain based on 4th–11th century mtDNA genotypes. *Molecular Biology and Evolution*, 23: 152–61.

Torres-Rouff, C. 2002. Cranial vault modification and ethnicity in Middle Horizon San Pedro de Atacama, Chile. *Current Anthropology*, 43(1): 163–178.

Torres-Rouff, C. and Yablonsky, L.T. 2005. Cranial vault modification as a cultural artifact: a comparison of the Eurasian steppes and the Andes. *Homo*, 56: 1–16.

Toynbee, J.M.C. 1971. *Death and Burial in the Roman world*. London: Thames and Hudson.

Treherne, P. 1995. The warrior's beauty: the masculine body and self-identity in Bronze-Age Europe. *Journal of European Archaeology*, 3 (1): 105–44.

Trigger, B.G. 2006. *A History of Archaeological Thought*. Second Edition. Cambridge: Cambridge University Press.

Trolle, A.L. 1994. Udgravningen af Lindholm Høje. In *Lindholm Høje. Gravplads og landsby* (eds E. Johansen and A.L. Trolle). Aalborg: Selskabet for Aalborgs Historie, pp. 7–16.

Tyrell, A. 2000. *Corpus Saxonum*: Early medieval bodies and corporeal identity. In *Social Identity in Early Medieval Britain* (eds W.O. Frazer and A. Tyrell) Leicester: Leicester University Press, pp. 137–56.

Ucko, P.J. (ed.) 1995. *Theory in Archaeology. A World Perspective*. London: Routledge.

Ullrich, H. 1970. Anthropologische Untersuchung der 1967 aus dem Gräberfeld von Häven, Kreis Sternberg, geborgenen menschlichen Skelettreste. *Jahrbuch der Bodendenkmalpflege in Mecklenburg*, 1968: 283–306.

Valentin, J. 2004. Manor Farm, Portesham, Dorset: excavations on a multi-period religious and settlement site. *Proceedings of the Dorset Natural History and Archaeology Society*, 125: 23–69.

Vander Linden, M. 2007. What linked the Bell Beakers in third millennium BC Europe? *Antiquity*, 81: 343–52.

Vicent, J.M. 1991. Arqueología y filosofía: la teoría crítica. *Trabajos de Prehistoria*, 48: 29–76.

Voß, H.-U. 2005. Hagenow in Mecklenburg — ein frühkaiserzeitlicher Bestattungsplatz und Aspekte der römisch-germanischen Beziehungen. *Bericht der Römisch-Germanischen Kommission*, 86: 19–59.

Waas, M. 1965. *Germanen im römischen Dienst im 4. Jahrhundert n. Chr.* Bonn: Habelt.

Waldron, T. 2007. *St Peter's Barton-upon-Humber, Lincolnshire. Volume 2: The Human Remains*. Oxford: Oxbow.

Walter, T. 1995. Natural death and the noble savage. *Omega*, 30: 237–48.

Walter, T. 1999. *The Revival of Death*. London: Routledge.

Walton Rogers, P. 2007. *Cloth and Clothing in Early Anglo-Saxon England*. London: Council for British Archaeology.

Wareham, A. 2001. The transformation of kinship and the family in late Anglo-Saxon England. *Early Medieval Europe*, 10(3): 375–99.

Waring, E. (ed.) 1850. *Recollections and Anecdotes of Edward Williams.* London: Charles Gilpin.

Warner, P. 1987. *Greens, Commons and Clayland Colonisation: the origins and development of green-side settlement in east Suffolk.* Leicester: Leicester University Press.

Warner, R. 1982. The Broighter Hoard: a reappraisal, and the iconography of the collar. In *Studies on Early Ireland* (ed. B.G. Scott). Belfast: Association of Young Irish Archaeologists, pp. 29–38.

Watkins, T. 1982. The excavation of an Early Bronze Age cemetery at Barnes Farm, Dalgety, Fife. *Proceedings of the Society of Antiquaries of Scotland,* 112: 48–141.

Watson, A. 2004. Making space for monuments: notes on the representation of experience. In *Substance, Memory, Display: Archaeology and Art* (eds C. Renfrew, C. Gosden and E. DeMarrais). McDonald Institue Monographs. Cambridge: McDonald Institute for Archaeological Research, pp. 79–96.

Watts, D. 1991. *Christians and Pagans in Roman Britain.* London: Routledge.

Weale, M.E., Weiss, D.A., Jager, R.F., Bradman, N., Thomas, M. 2002. Y Chromosome Evidence for Anglo-Saxon mass migration, *Molecular Biology and Evolution,* 19: 1008–1021.

Webster, C. and Brunning, R. 2004. A seventh-century AD cemetery at Stoneage Barton Farm, Bishop's Lydeard, Somerset and square-ditched burials in Post-Roman Britain. *Archaeological Journal,* 161: 54–81.

Weddell, P.J. 2000. The excavation of a post-Roman cemetery near Kenn. *Devon Archaeological Journal,* 58: 93–126.

Welch, M. 1992. *Anglo-Saxon England.* London: Batsford.

Wenskus, R. 1961. *Stammesbildung und Verfassung. Das Werden der frühmittelalterlichen gentes.* Köln and Graz: Böhlau.

Wenskus, R. 1974. Probleme der germanisch-deutschen Verfassungs- und Sozialgeschichte im Lichte der Ethnosoziologie. In *Historische Forschungen für Walter Schlesinger* (ed. H. Beumann). Köln and Wien: Böhlau, pp. 19–46.

Werner, J. 1956. *Beiträge zur Archäologie des Attila-Reiches.* Bayerische Akademie der Wissenschaften. Abhandlungen. Neue Folge 38 A. München: Verlag der Bayerischen Akademie der Wissenschaften.

Werner, J. 1961. Fernhandel und Naturalwirtschaft im östlichen Merowingerreich nach archäologischen und numismatische Zeugnissen. *Bericht der Römisch-Germanischen Kommission,* 42: 307–46.

Werner, J. 1970. Zur Verbreitung frühgeschichtlicher Metallarbeiten. Werkstatt — Wanderhandwerk — Handel — Familienverbindung. *Antikvarisk Arkiv* 38: 65–81.

Werner, J. 1973. Bemerkungen zur mitteldeutschen Skelettgräbergruppe Haßleben-Leuna. Zur Herkunft der *ingentia auxilia Germanorum* des gallischen Sonderreiches in den Jahren 259–274 n. Chr. In *Festschrift für Walter Schlesinger* (ed. H. Beumann), 1. Köln and Wien: Böhlau, pp. 1–30.

Werner, J. 1989. Zu den römischen Mantelfibeln zweier Kriegergräber von Leuna. *Jahresschrift für mitteldeutsche Vorgeschichte* 72: 121–34.

West, S. 1986. *West Stow: the Anglo-Saxon Village*. Bury St Edmunds: Suffolk County Council. East Anglian Archaeology 24.

Whaley, J. (ed.) 1981. *Mirrors of Mortality. Studies in the Social History of Death*. London: Europa.

White, R.B. 1971–2. Excavations at Arfryn, Bodedern: long cist cemeteries and the origins of Christianity in Britain. *Transactions of the Anglesey Antiquarian Society and Field Club*: 1–51.

White, S.I. and Smith, G. 1999. A funerary and ceremonial centre at Capel Eithin, Gaerwen, Anglesey. Excavations of Neolithic, Bronze Age, Roman and Early Medieval features in 1980 and 1981. *Transactions of the Anglesey Antiquarian Society and Field Club*: 12–166.

Whitelock, D. 1955. *English Historical Documents c.500–1042. English Historical Documents I*. London: Methuen.

Whitelock, D. 1979. *English Historical Documents c.500–1042. English Historical Documents I*. Second Edition. London, Methuen.

Wickham, C. 2005. *Framing the Early Middle Ages. Europe and the Mediterranean, 400–800*. Oxford: Oxford University Press.

Wilbers-Rost, S. 2007. Total Roman Defeat at the Battle of Varus (9 AD). In *Fields of Conflict. Battlefield Archaeology from the Roman Empire to the Korean War. Vol. 1, Searching for War in the Ancient and Early Modern World* (eds D. Scott, L. Babits and Ch. Haecker). Westport, Conn.: Praeger Security International, pp. 121–32.

Wilbers-Rost, S., Uerpmann, H.-P., Uerpmann, M., Großkopf, B. and Tolksdorf-Lienemann, E. 2007. *Kalkriese 3. Interdisziplinäre Untersuchungen auf dem Oberesch in Kalkriese. Archäologische Befunde und naturwissenschaftliche Begleituntersuchungen*. Römisch-Germanische Forschungen 65. Mainz: Zabern.

Wilken, E. (ed.) 1912. Gylfaginning. In: *Die Prosaische Edda im Auszuge nebst Volsunga-saga und Nornagests-þáttr, Vol. I*. Bibliothek der ältesten deutschen Literatur-Denkmäler IX. Second Edition. Paderborn: Schöningh.

Willey, G.R. And Phillip, P. 1958. *Method and Theory in Archaeology*. Chicago: University of Chicago Press.

Williams, H. 1997. Ancient landscapes and the dead: the reuse of prehistoric and Roman monuments as early Anglo-Saxon burial sites. *Medieval Archaeology*, 41: 1–32.

Williams, H. 1998a. Monuments and the past in early Anglo-Saxon England. *World Archaeology* 30 (1): 90–108.

Williams, H. 1998b. The ancient monument in Romano-British ritual practices. In *TRAC 97: Proceedings of the Seventh Annual Theoretical Roman Archaeology Conference* (eds C. Forcey, J. Hawthorne and R. Witcher). Oxford: Oxbow, pp. 71–86.

Williams, H. 1999. Placing the dead: investigating the location of wealthy burials in seventh century England. In *Grave Matters. Eight Studies of First Millennium AD Burials in Crimea, England, and Southern Scandinavia. Papers from a session held at the European Association of Archaeologists Fourth Annual Meeting in Göteborg 1998* (ed. M. Rundkvist). British Archaeological Reports, International Series 781. Oxford: Archaeopress, pp. 57–81.

Williams, H. 2001. An ideology of transformation: cremation rites and animal sacrifice in early Anglo-Saxon England, In *The Archaeology of Shamanism* (ed. N. Price) London: Routledge, pp. 193–212.

Williams, H. 2002. Cemeteries as central places: landscape and identity in early Anglo-Saxon England. In *Central Places in the Migration and Merovingian Periods: Papers from the 52nd Sachsensymposium* (eds B. Hårdh and L. Larsson) Stockholm: Almqvist and Wiksell, pp. 341–62.

Williams, H. 2003. Remembering and forgetting the medieval dead. In *Archaeologies of Remembrance: Death and Memory in Past Societies* (ed. H. Williams). New York: Kluwer/Plenum, pp. 227–54.

Williams, H. 2005. Review article: rethinking early medieval mortuary archaeology. *Early Medieval Europe*, 13(2): 195–217.

Williams, H. 2006. *Death and Memory in Early Medieval Britain*, Cambridge: Cambridge University Press.

Williams, H. 2007a. Introduction: themes in the archaeology of early medieval death and burial. In *Early Medieval Mortuary Practices* (eds S. Semple and H. Williams) *Anglo-Saxon Studies in Archaeology and History* 14. Oxford: Oxford University Committee for Archaeology, pp. 1–11.

Williams, H. 2007b. Transforming body and soul: toilet implements in early Anglo-Saxon graves. In *Early Medieval Mortuary Practices* (eds S. Semple and H. Williams) *Anglo-Saxon Studies in Archaeology and History* 14. Oxford: Oxford University Committee for Archaeology, pp. 66–91.

Williams, H. 2007c. The Emotive Force of Early Medieval Mortuary Practices, *Archaeological Review from Cambridge*. 22(1): 107–23.

Williams, H. 2008. Anglo-Saxonism and Victorian archaeology: William Wylie's *Fairford Graves, Early Medieval Europe*, 16(1): 49–88.

Williams, H. and Williams, E.J.L. 2007. Digging for the dead: archaeological practice as mortuary commemoration. *Public Archaeology*, 6(1): 45–61.

Williams, P. and Newman, R. 2006. *Market Lavington, Wiltshire: An Anglo-Saxon cemetery and settlement*. Salisbury: Wessex Archaeology.

Williams, R.J. and Zeepvat, B. 1994. *Bancroft: A Late Bronze Age / Iron Age Settlement, Roman Villa and Temple Mausoleum: Volume 1: Excavations and Building Material*. Buckinghamshire Archaeological Society Monograph Series 7. Aylesbury: Buckinghamshire Archaeological Society.

Wilson, C.E. 1981. Burials within settlements in southern Britain during the Pre-Roman Iron Age. *Bulletin of the Institute of Archaeology*, 18: 127–70.

Wilson, J., Weiss, D., Richards, M., Thomas, M., Bradman, N. and Goldstein D. 2001. Genetic evidence for different male and female roles during cultural transitions in the British Isles, *Proceedings of the National Academy of Sciences of the USA*, 98: 5078–83.

Wiltschke-Schrotta, K. 2004/2005. Manipulierte Körper — Gedanken zur künstlichen Schädeldeformation. *Mitteilungen der Anthropologischen Gesellschaft in Wien*, 134/135: 11–27.

Winkler, E.-M. and Wicke, L. 1980. Hunnenzeitliche Skelettfunde mit künstlich deformierten Schädeln aus Gaweinstal in Niederösterreich. *Archaeologia Austriaca*, 64: 119–137.

Wolfram, H. 1983. *Geschichte der Goten. Von den Anfängen bis zur Mitte des sechsten Jahrhunderts*. München: Beck.

Woodward, A. 2002. Beads and beakers: heirlooms and relics in the British Early Bronze Age. *Antiquity*, 76: 1040–47.

Woodward, A., Hunter, J., Ixer, R., Maltby, M., Potts, P., Webb, P., Watson, J. and Jones, M. 2005. Ritual in some Early Bronze Age grave goods. *Archaeological Journal*, 162: 31–64.

Woolf, A. 2007. Apartheid and economics in Anglo-Saxon England. In *Britons in Anglo-Saxon England* (ed. N.J. Higham). Woodbridge: Boydell, pp. 115–29.

Youngs, S. 1989. *Work of the Angels*. London: British Museum Press.

Zadoro-Rio, E. 2003. The making of churchyards and parish territories in the early-medieval landscape of France and England in the 7th–12th centuries: a reconsideration. *Medieval Archaeology*, 42: 1–19.

Zaleski, C. 1987. *Otherworld Journeys: Accounts of Near-death Experiences in Medieval and Modern Times*. Oxford: Oxford University Press.

Zvelebil, M. and Jordan, P. 1999. Hunter fisher gatherer ritual landscape. In *Rock Art as Social Representation* (ed. J. Goldhahn). British Archaeological Reports, International Series 794. Oxford: Archaeopress, pp. 101–27.

Index

Contributors

Grenville Astill is Professor of Archaeology at the University of Reading. His research interests centre on medieval urban and rural issues, monasticism, technology, industry and landscape archaeology. He is associated with two long-term research projects. The Bordesley Abbey Project is one of the longest running research programmes on a European medieval monastery, based on a Cistercian foundation in Worcestershire. The results of the East Brittany Survey have recently been published and represent over twenty years archaeological, architectural and documentary research designed to investigate the development of the landscape of an extensive area over the last two thousand years. He recently contributed papers to the *Archaeological Journal* and to Davies, W., Halsall, G. and Reynolds, A. (eds), *People and Space in the Middle Ages 300–1300*.

Richard Bradley has held a personal chair in the Archaeology Department at Reading University since 1987. His fieldwork has centred on prehistoric settlements, landscapes and monuments in England, Scotland, Spain and Scandinavia. These include studies of Cranborne Chase, the Neolithic axe quarries of Great Langdale (Cumbria), the stone circles of north-east Scotland, the Clava Cairns of northern Scotland, the megalithic art of Orkney, the prehistoric land boundaries of Salisbury Plain, and the Copper Age cave sanctuary of El Pedroso (northern Spain). Recent books include *An Archaeology of Natural Places* (2000), *The Past in Prehistoric Societies* (2002), *Ritual and Domestic Life in Prehistoric Europe* (2005) and *The Prehistory of Britain and Ireland* (2007).

Stefan Burmeister is curator in the Museum und Park Kalkriese, Bramsche. He has curated exhibitions on the invention of early wagons (Landesmuseum für Natur und Mensch, Oldenburg) and currently has an exhibition on 2000 years of conflict in Germanic society. He has an MA and a PhD from Hamburg University where he studied gender, age and power in Late Hallstatt society. Between 1995 and 1997 Stefan was part of a research collaboration between Hamburg and Reading universities on Anglo-Saxon migration and methodology in archaeological investigations of migration. Stefan's recent publications have dealt with topics that include semiotics in archaeology in *Der Wert der Dinge – Güter im Prestigediskurs,* Hildebrandt, B. and Veit, C. (eds 2009), innovation in prehistoric societies in *Sozialarchäologische Perspektiven: Gesellschaftlicher Wandel 5000–1500 v. Chr. zwischen Atlantik und Kaukasus,* S. Hansen and J. Müller (eds), Germanic chiefly settlements in *Herrenhöfe und die Hierarchie der Macht im Raum südlich und östlich der Nordsee von der vorrömischen Eisenzeit bis zum frühen Mittelalter/ Wikingerzeit,* Scythian archaeology in *Das Altertum* and museum presentations in *European Journal of Archaeology* (forthcoming).

Robert Chapman is Professor of Archaeology at the University of Reading, where he has been employed since 1976. He has contributed to research on burial archaeology throughout his career, co-editing the influential *The Archaeology of Death* (1981), contributing papers on the subject (most recently in the journal *Mortality* and in Rakita, G., Buikstra, J., Beck, L. and Williams, S. (eds), *Interacting with the Dead*), working with burial data on the Gatas project in south-east Spain, and teaching (alongside Heinrich Härke) generations of students at Reading.

Roberta Gilchrist is Professor of Archaeology at the University of Reading and has recently been President of the Society for Medieval Archaeology. She has published extensively on gender, medieval archaeology and monasticism. Her most recent books include *Requiem. The Medieval Monastic Cemetery in Britain* (with B. Sloane, 2005; winner of the British Archaeological Award for Best Scholarly Publication, 2004–6) and *Norwich Cathedral: the Evolution of the English Cathedral Landscape* (2005; chosen by Choice USA as an Acclaimed Academic Title, 2007).

Susanne Hakenbeck is a junior research fellow at Newnham College, Cambridge and a fellow of the McDonald Institute for Archaeological Research. She completed her PhD on *Ethnic Identity in Early Medieval Cemeteries in Bavaria* in 2006 at the University of Cambridge. Her research focuses on migration and shifting identities on the European continent during the early medieval period. Her recent publications include papers in *Anglo-Saxon Studies in Archaeology and History* 14, and Grünewald, C. and Capelle, T. (eds), *Innere Strukturen von Siedlungen und Gräberfeldern als Spiegel gesellschaftlicher Wirklichkeit.*

Catherine Hills has been a lecturer in post-Roman archaeology in the Department of Archaeology, University of Cambridge since 1976. Her research interests focus on the early medieval period in Europe, especially the region around the North Sea. During the 1970s and 1980s she directed the excavation of the large Anglo-Saxon cemetery at Spong Hill, Norfolk which remains the only cemetery of its type in England to have been excavated and published in its entirety. It contained more than 2000 cremations and 57 inhumations, dating to the later fifth and sixth centuries AD. This was the basis for Catherine's

PhD and from it derived her interests in early Anglo-Saxon England and the early medieval period. Topics of interest to Catherine include the archaeology of burial, the identification of ethnicity, religious belief and migration in the archaeological record, and the relationship between history and archaeology. She also has an ongoing interest in the public presentation of archaeology. In the 1980s she presented two archaeological series on Channel 4, and in recent years has been much involved with the reconstructed Anglo-Saxon village at West Stow.

Karen Høilund Nielsen is Associate Professor in the Institute of History and Civilization at University of Southern Denmark. She has worked extensively across north-western Europe focussing on objects, people, death and society. Karen worked alongside John Hines and Alex Bayliss on the *Anglo-Saxon England c.570–720: the chronological basis* project, with English Heritage, Cardiff and Belfast University. She is also working on a project entitled: *Stavnsager to Constantinople: the adaptation of southern Scandinavia to a changing world, AD 450–600*. Her recent publications include papers in: Quast, D. (ed.), *Foreigners in Early Medieval Europe. Thirteen International Studies on early Medieval Mobility*; Brather, S. (ed.), *Zwischen Spätantike und Frühmittelalter. Archäologie des 4. bis 7 Jahrhunderts im Westen*; Bertašius, M. (ed.), *Transformatio Mundi. The Transition from the Late Migration Period to the Early Viking Age in the East Baltic*; and she co-authored a paper in: Castritus, H., Geuenich, D. and Werner M. (eds), *Die Frühzeit der Thüringer. Archäologie, Sprache, Geschichte*.

David Petts completed his PhD on early medieval burial in Wales and Western Britain under the supervision of Heinrich Härke in 2001. After spending five years working on a series of projects in the north-east of England, including the North-East Regional Research Framework and the Hadrian's Wall Research Framework, he was a lecturer in archaeology at the University of Chester before crossing the Pennines to Durham to take up a lectureship in the Department of Archaeology. His recent publications include *Christianity in Roman Britain* (2003) which won the 2006 Frend Prize for Early Christian Studies and *The Early Medieval Church in Western Britain* (2009).

Duncan Sayer is an associate lecturer in the Centre for Death and Society at University of Bath. He has a PhD in archaeology from the University of Reading where he studied with Heinrich Härke. He has been a visiting lecturer at the universities of Reading and Chester and has extensive fieldwork experience, having been a project officer for CAM ARC, Oxford Archaeology East, ASE and a senior archaeologist for PCA, London, and ARCUS. His research interests include ethics in burial archaeology, Anglo-Saxon cemeteries, kinship and the family as well as social change in medieval and post-medieval society. His recent publications include the medieval and early medieval chapters of *The Handbook of British Archaeology* and articles in *Antiquity* and *World Archaeology*. Duncan's books include *Ethics in Burial Archaeology*, which will be published in Duckworth's debates in archaeology series in 2010.

Eva S. Thäte is Visiting Research Associate at the University of Chester and is putting together a project to investigate boat graves in collaboration with the Arkeologisk museum in Stavanger, Norway. Eva has worked as a sessional lecturer at the University of Reading, and has excavated in south-west Norway. She completed her MA at the University of Münster in Germany, and her PhD with Heinrich Härke at the University of Reading. Before moving to England, Eva worked at various museums in north-west Germany, including the Ostfriesisches Landesmuseum in Emden, the Niedersächsisches Freilichtmuseum in Cloppenburg and the Landesmuseum für Kunst und Kulturgeschichte in Oldenburg. She also worked as an assistant manager at the Stiftung Kulturschatz Bauernhof (Rural Culture Heritage Trust) in Cloppenburg. Her recent publications include *Monuments and Minds; Monument Reuse in Scandinavia in the Second Half of the First Millennium AD* (2008). Eva has also contributed papers to *Anglo-Saxon Studies in Archaeology and History* 14, *Emder Jahrbuch* 79, *Archäologische Informationen* 19/1, and has a forthcoming paper in the Norwegian series *AmS-Varia* in cooperation with O.H. Hemdorff.

Howard Williams is Senior Lecturer in Archaeology at the University of Chester. He completed a PhD at the University of Reading supervised by Heinrich Härke addressing cremation in early Anglo-Saxon England. His research interests include the archaeology of historic periods, mortuary archaeology and the history of archaeology. His recent work has addressed mortuary practices and commemoration in the early Middle Ages and includes the book *Death and Memory in Early Medieval Britain* (2006) and articles in *Anglo-Saxon Studies in Archaeology and History* 14, *Cambridge Archaeological Journal* and *Medieval Archaeology*.